The
Supreme Court
Yearbook

1998–1999

The Justices of the Supreme Court. From left are Justices Sandra Day O'Connor, Anthony M. Kennedy, and Antonin Scalia; Chief Justice William H. Rehnquist; and Justices David H. Souter, Ruth Bader Ginsburg, Clarence Thomas, Stephen G. Breyer, and John Paul Stevens.

The

Supreme Court

Yearbook

1998–1999

CQ PRESS

A Division of Congressional Quarterly Inc.
Washington, D.C.

CQ Press
A Division of Congressional Quarterly Inc.
1414 22nd Street, N.W.
Washington, D.C. 20037

(202) 822-1475; (800) 638-1710

www.cqpress.com

Copyright © 2000 by Congressional Quarterly Inc.

Book design: Debra Naylor, Naylor Design Inc.

Cover: Chiquita Babb, Septima Design

Printed and bound in the United States of America

03 02 01 00 99   5 4 3 2 1

Photo credits: frontispiece, 323, 327, 337, Congressional Quarterly; 8, U.S. Senate, Reuters; 34, Dean Abramson, *ABA Journal;* 40, Robert Matthews; 49, courtesy Roy T. Englert Jr.; 52, 53, Bazelon Center for Mental Health Law; 57, AP/Wide World Photos; 62, William Spain; 68, Sirlin Photographers; 73, Kevin Kolczynski, *ABA Journal;* 77, U.S. Census Bureau; 153, 159, Reuters; 321, Joseph McCary; 325, Supreme Court; 329, 333, Collection, the Supreme Court Historical Society; 331, White House; 335, R. Michael Jenkins.

ISBN: 1-56802-468-1
ISBN: 1-56802-467-3
ISSN: 1054-2701

Contents

Preface

When the Supreme Court began its 1998–1999 term, legal experts were expecting an uneventful year. The justices had a meager calendar of less than gripping cases as they convened on the first Monday in October. By the time they finished their work in June, however, they had again made their mark on U.S. law and politics.

The Court handed down three major decisions limiting the federal government's power over the states. It gave employers a major victory in limiting the scope of the federal disability rights law. While those opinions cheered conservatives, other rulings heartened liberals. The Court ruled that school districts may be held liable for a student's sexual harassment of another student. It also overturned a controversial antiloitering law aimed at controlling youth gangs. And it struck down a state law limiting welfare benefits for new residents.

These decisions, along with the rest of the Court's work during the 1998–1999 term, are reported and analyzed in this, the tenth, edition of *The Supreme Court Yearbook*. Careful readers will notice some changes in appearance that we hope will make the book easier to use and read. The basic format, however, remains unchanged. The book includes an overview of the term (Chapter 1), accounts of some of the major cases (Chapter 2), capsule summaries of each of the Court's decisions (Chapter 3), a preview of the upcoming term (Chapter 4), and excerpts of the major decisions (Appendix). Our purpose also remains unchanged: to provide a comprehensive, accessible account of the Court's work in a convenient, annual series for those interested in what is often called the world's most powerful judicial body.

My thanks go to the many lawyers, reporters, and experts whose comments and coverage inform my understanding of the Court. I also want to thank the Court's new public information officer, Kathy Arberg, and her staff for their help. Kathy assumed the position this fall after the death of the Court's longtime public information officer, Toni House. She continues in Toni's tradition of providing diligent, professional service in helping inform the press and public about the Court's work. At CQ Press, thanks to Patricia Gallagher, Carolyn Goldinger, Christopher Karlsten, and Talia Greenberg for skillful and enthusiastic work in getting this year's book in print.

As always, I also want to thank my wife, Katie White, for her very special love and unstinting support, and our two exceptional children, Nicole and Andrew, for their patience and good cheer during the sometimes long hours of writing and editing.

Kenneth Jost
Washington, D.C.

Chapter 1

A "Consolidating" Term

The opinion of the Court in number 98-436, Alden against Maine, will be announced by Justice Kennedy." The Supreme Court of the United States was about to announce its last decisions for the 1998–1999 term, but Chief Justice William Rehnquist's matter-of-fact introduction conveyed no sense of anticipation or any hint of the sharp ideological conflict in the three rulings to come.

Anthony Kennedy, a mild-mannered former law professor, began. The case seemed far from consequential—a dispute about overtime pay between a group of probation officers and their employer, the state of Maine, involving the federal Fair Labor Standards Act, a New Deal–era wage and hour statute. But Kennedy's recitation quickly turned to the constitutional implications of the case.

The officers sued the state for back pay in federal court. But the Court's ruling three years earlier in *Seminole Tribe v. Florida* barred private citizens from suing states for money in federal court except for violations of constitutional rights. The officers then sued in Maine's state court system. But the state invoked a legal principle known as sovereign immunity to dismiss that suit as well. Maine's supreme court backed the state and threw the probation officers out of court.

"We now affirm," Kennedy said for the Court. "We hold that the powers delegated to Congress under Article I of the Constitution of the United States do not include the power to subject nonconsenting states to private suits for damages in state courts, and the state of Maine has not consented to the suit."

Kennedy's delivery quickened. The "founding generation" considered immunity from suit a "fundamental aspect of sovereignty," he said. The great architects of the Constitution—Hamilton, Madison, Marshall— assured the citizens of the new nation that the states would retain sovereign immunity under the new federal compact. Under the federal system,

Kennedy said, Congress cannot treat the states as "mere prefectures" or "corporations," but must accord them the "dignity" and "respect" befitting their status as dual sovereigns along with the national government.

Once Kennedy was finished, David Souter, a cerebral Yankee with a strong New England accent and a wry wit, spoke for the dissenters. The majority, he declared, "was clearly wrong" in its history, "clearly wrong again" in its legal theory. Congress had the power to enact wage and hour legislation for state employees. Sovereign immunity, he explained, "can only be a defense in a matter over which the state is sovereign." The Court's ruling created "a very peculiar state of affairs," Souter continued. State employees "have a right in theory, but they have no means to enforce that right."

The drama in the courtroom had become fully palpable. The audience sat hushed, spellbound. Two more decisions followed. They stemmed from another seemingly pedestrian dispute—a fight between a private New Jersey bank and a Florida state agency that marketed competing plans for families to save for college tuition. The Rehnquist Court's conservative majority had seized on them to continue rewriting the rules governing the power relationship between the federal government and the states.

No, Justice Antonin Scalia explained, College Savings Bank could not sue the Florida agency, the Florida Prepaid Postsecondary Education Expense Board, under a federal law prohibiting false advertising. Nor could the bank sue the agency for patent infringement under federal law either, Rehnquist announced in the final ruling. In each case, the five-member majority said that the federal government's power was blocked by sovereign immunity, a doctrine dating to the days of absolute monarchs and largely unknown to most Americans.

These rulings capped a three-year series of decisions by the Court's conservatives favoring the states in challenges to federal powers. The dissenters were the same in each of the federalism cases: four justices inconsistently liberal on some issues but united in a broad view of the national government's powers. Normally, dissenting opinions are not announced from the bench, but that day the outvoted justices took the opportunity afforded under an unwritten rule allowing each of them one chance each year to summarize a dissenting opinion in open court. Court watchers understood the message: these are important cases, and the disagreements are strongly felt.

Stephen Breyer, the avuncular former professor and one-time congressional aide, tried to lighten the proceedings as he followed Scalia's announcement. "I'm going to add a little bit about a certain amount of disagreement we have here," Breyer said, with a slight laugh. Still smiling, he allowed himself a pointed barb. Sovereign immunity, he said, was a philosophy "more akin to the thought of James I than of James Madison." John Paul Stevens, looking dapper in his bow tie and younger than his seventy-nine years, accused the conservatives of "setting loose a mindless dragon that chews gaping holes in the law."

After forty-five minutes, the session ended. The justices retreated behind the black curtains to straighten their desks before leaving Washington for the summer. The end of term had come uncommonly early—June 23—in part because of an uncommonly low number of decisions. The seventy-five signed opinions equaled a forty-five-year low also seen in the 1995–1996 term.

The reporters, lawyers, and experts who follow the Supreme Court closely had been prepared to give the year's output middling marks for drama or legal significance. With one day's rulings, however, the Court had given the country a stunning reminder of its power. In each of the three federalism cases, the Court was nullifying decisions by Congress that gave private citizens the right to sue state governments and collect money damages if the state government violated their rights under federal law. In each case, the outcome turned on a single vote among a group of nine unelected justices, who served for life and answered only to the law and their own consciences.

Rehnquist showed no emotion during the session, but the day's work must have been satisfying for the seventy-five-year-old chief justice. When he was appointed an associate justice in 1971, he was the most conservative member of a still somewhat liberal Court. Now, after thirteen terms as chief justice, he led a conservative Court that had turned his legal philosophy into the law of the land in areas such as states' rights, criminal law, and civil rights and civil liberties.

Federalism—the allocation of power between the national government and the states—had been a particular concern for Rehnquist. Two decades earlier, as an associate justice, he was the lone dissenter when the Court declared that criminal trials must normally be open to the press and the public. The Court had no business, Rehnquist said, deciding how justice was to be administered in each of the fifty states. Now, the Rehnquist Court was telling Congress—the elected representatives of the people— that it had no business telling a state that violated duly enacted federal laws to compensate citizens who were injured by such violations.

"It's a consolidation of Rehnquist Court themes," Thomas Baker, a law professor at Drake University, remarked later. "These are the things that

the Rehnquist Court will go down in history for: federalism and separation of powers."

The Court's other big story of the week also reflected a Rehnquist
theme: a narrow approach to interpreting laws passed by Congress. The
issue was how to interpret the Americans with Disabilities Act, the federal law that prohibits discrimination in employment against people with
mental or physical disabilities. Three cases raised the question whether
someone with a correctable condition like nearsightedness or high blood
pressure had a disability as defined by the law and thus qualified for protection under the act.

The Court said no—to the great relief of employers who had feared a
flood of disability rights claims from a ruling going the other way. To
answer the question, the Court applied Rehnquist's two-word philosophy
of statutory construction: "plain language." A statute meant exactly what
the words said—nothing more. Plaintiffs in the three cases all said that
Congress intended the disability rights law to have broad coverage for people with physical impairments. But for Rehnquist and his fellow conservatives, arguments about legislative intent were close to irrelevant. Since the
meaning of the law was clear, Justice Sandra Day O'Connor explained in
the main opinion, "we have no reason to consider the legislative history."

Despite the dismay among liberals over the federalism and disability
rights decisions, the Court's rulings were not uniformly conservative.
Liberals, in fact, could count some significant victories among the major
cases of the term. The Court struck down a Chicago ordinance aimed at
getting criminal gangs off the streets. It upset a popular cutback in welfare
benefits approved by Congress and enacted in eighteen states. It warned
states that they might be violating the disability rights law by keeping people with mental illnesses in hospitals rather than placing them in community treatment centers. And in a pair of somewhat mixed rulings, the Court
held that local schools could be forced to compensate students for sexual
harassment committed by fellow students and turned back an effort to set
a strict standard for awarding punitive damages under the federal law prohibiting racial and sexual discrimination in the workplace. (See Table 1-1.)

The variety in the rulings served as a useful reminder that the labels
"liberal" and "conservative" do not give a complete picture of the work of
the Court or the views of the individual justices. The conservative majority—Rehnquist, O'Connor, Scalia, Kennedy, and Clarence Thomas—
tended to favor states in federalism disputes, take a narrow approach
toward the rights of suspects and criminal defendants, and disfavor expansive interpretations of civil rights and civil liberties. The liberal-leaning

Table 1-1 CQ's Major Cases: U.S. Supreme Court, 1998–1999 Term

CQ each term selects the major cases for the Supreme Court's term. The selection is based on such factors as the rulings' practical impact; their significance as legal precedent; the degree of division on the Court; and the level of interest among interest groups, experts, and news media. Accounts of the major cases appear in Chapter 2; excerpts from the decisions can be found in the Appendix.

Name of Case	Vote	Holding
Alden v. Maine [pp. 33–39]	5–4	States protected from suits to enforce federal wage and hour law
Florida Prepaid Postsecondary Education Expense Board v. College Savings Bank [pp. 39–46]	5–4	No damage suits against states in federal court for false advertising
College Savings Bank v. Florida Prepaid Postsecondary Education Expense Board [pp. 39–46]	5–4	No damage suits against states in federal court for patent infringement
Sutton v. United Air Lines, Inc. [pp. 46–51]	7–2	Disability rights law limited for people with correctable impairments
Olmstead, Commissioner, Georgia Department of Human Resources v. L. C. [pp. 51–56]	6–3	Unnecessary segregation of mental patients may violate disability rights law
Davis v. Monroe County Board of Education [pp. 56–61]	5–4	Schools can be held liable for student-on-student sexual harassment
City of Chicago v. Morales [pp. 61–66]	6–3	Anti-gang loitering held unconstitutional for vagueness
Saenz, Director, California Department of Social Services v. Roe [pp. 66–71]	7–2	States cannot limit welfare benefits for new residents
Kolstad v. American Dental Association [pp. 72–76]	7–2, 5–4	Mixed ruling on punitive damages in job discrimination suits
Department of Commerce v. United States House of Representatives [pp. 76–81]	5–4	No statistical sampling in 2000 census for congressional apportionment

Here are some other especially noteworthy cases: *Ortiz v. Fibreboard Corp.*: restricts ability of businesses to craft mandatory settlements in mass liability cases without going into bankruptcy; *United States v. Sun-Diamond Growers*: limits use of federal law barring gifts to federal officials; *Wilson v. Layne*: permits damage suits against law enforcement for letting media accompany raids in private homes; *Reno v. Arab-American Anti-Discrimination Committee*: limits free speech rights of illegal immigrants.

justices—in order of seniority, Stevens, Souter, Ruth Bader Ginsburg, and Breyer—were more likely to uphold an expanded use of federal powers, be more scrupulous about protecting the rights of suspects and defendants, and take a broad view of individual rights in constitutional disputes. But exceptions to those general rules could readily be found in each justice's voting record in this term as in the past. *(See Table 1–2.)*

Indeed, conservative and liberal Court watchers alike often voiced disappointment that the justices they viewed as sharing their respective viewpoint were less than consistent in their votes and their opinions. "This is not a conservative activist Court," Daniel Troy, a conservative Washington lawyer and Court watcher, remarked after the end of the term. "This is a Court that by and large is tinkering at the edges." Burt Neuborne, a law professor at New York University and former legal director for the American Civil Liberties Union, similarly saw a lack of ideological commitment among the Court's left-of-center justices. "I call them the four centrists," Neuborne remarked. "There are no more liberals."

Still, the end-of-term federalism rulings spawned a rash of critical comments from liberal interest groups and experts. "This is the first time in more than sixty years where we see an aggressive, conservative activism," Louis Michael Seidman, a professor at Georgetown University Law Center, told the *Los Angeles Times.* Elliot Mincberg, legal director of People for the American Way, a liberal civil liberties group, agreed: "The notion of finding an unwritten principle of sovereign immunity in the Constitution, even though it's clearly not there, really does smack of judicial activism—that is, finding something that's not there in the text."

Conservatives, by contrast, applauded the rulings. "The Court once again reiterated that the states are serious players in our system of government," said John Roberts, a conservative Washington lawyer and one-time Rehnquist law clerk. At the same time, many conservatives minimized the practical significance of the decisions. "There are still very many remedies that are available against the states, and Congress can create still more without running afoul of these cases," said Eugene Volokh, a conservative constitutional law expert at UCLA Law School. The decisions, he said, "will not tremendously interfere with enforcement of federal law."

Whatever their long-term impact, the cases indicated self-confidence on the part of the Rehnquist Court majority. "This is a Court that doesn't defer to government at any level," Walter Dellinger, acting U.S. solicitor general for a year in President Clinton's administration, remarked to the *New York Times.* "The Court is confident it can come up with the right decisions, and it believes it is constitutionally charged with doing so."

Table 1-2 Justices' Alignment, 1998–1999 Term

This table shows the percentage of decisions in which each justice agreed with each of the other members of the Court. Of the seventy-five signed decisions for the 1998–1999 term, twenty-eight (or 37 percent) were unanimous.

The voting pattern showed two fairly regular groupings: a conservative bloc, consisting of Chief Justice Rehnquist and Justices O'Connor, Scalia, Kennedy, and Thomas; and a moderately liberal bloc, consisting of Justices Stevens, Souter, Ginsburg, and Breyer.

Each of the conservative justices voted with each of the other four in at least 80 percent of the cases. The closest alignments were between Rehnquist and Thomas (92 percent agreement) and Scalia and Thomas (the same). Each of the liberal justices voted with each of the other three at least 77 percent of the time. The closest alignment was between Souter and Ginsburg, who agreed in 88 percent of the cases.

Ginsburg and Breyer, President Clinton's two appointees, agreed somewhat less often than in previous years. They voted together more than 85 percent of the time in each of the previous two terms, but agreed only 80 percent of the time this term.

The widest gap was between Stevens on the left and Rehnquist and Thomas on the right. Stevens voted with each of them in only one-fifth of the nonunanimous decisions. Stevens voted with Scalia in one-fourth of the nonunanimous decisions.

	Rehnquist	Stevens	O'Connor	Scalia	Kennedy	Souter	Thomas	Ginsburg	Breyer
Rehnquist		19.1	76.1	83.0	74.5	42.6	87.2	31.9	41.3
		49.3	85.1	89.3	84.0	64.0	92.0	57.3	63.5
Stevens	19.1		32.6	27.7	34.0	63.8	19.1	70.2	67.4
	49.3		58.1	54.7	58.7	77.3	49.3	81.3	79.7
O'Connor	76.1	32.6		71.7	74.0	56.5	67.4	45.7	55.6
	85.1	58.1		82.4	83.8	73.0	79.7	66.2	72.6
Scalia	83.0	27.7	71.7		68.1	51.1	87.2	34.0	32.6
	89.3	54.7	82.4		80.0	69.3	92.0	58.7	58.1
Kennedy	74.5	34.0	74.0	68.1		59.6	68.1	51.1	47.8
	84.0	58.7	83.8	80.0		74.7	80.0	69.3	67.6
Souter	42.6	63.8	56.5	57.1	59.6		42.6	80.9	71.7
	64.0	77.3	73.0	69.3	74.7		64.0	88.0	82.4
Thomas	87.2	19.1	67.4	87.2	68.1	42.6		27.7	32.6
	92.0	49.3	79.7	92.0	80.0	64.0		54.7	58.1
Ginsburg	31.9	70.2	45.7	34.0	51.1	80.9	27.7		67.4
	57.3	81.3	66.2	58.7	69.3	88.0	54.7		79.7
Breyer	41.3	67.4	55.6	32.6	47.8	71.7	32.6	67.4	
	63.5	79.7	72.6	58.1	67.6	82.4	58.1	79.7	

Note: The first number in each cell represents the percented of agreement in divided decisions. The second number represents the percentage of agreement in all signed opinions.

Chief Justice William Rehnquist presides over the Senate's impeachment trial of President Bill Clinton. Rehnquist had limited duties as presiding officer, but he won praise from senators for carrying out his role in an evenhanded way. "I leave you now a wiser but not a sadder man," Rehnquist said following Clinton's acquittal on February 12.

Professor Baker agreed, likening today's Court to the liberal activist Court under Chief Justice Earl Warren. "The Rehnquist Court has a Warren Court view of itself," Baker said. "There's an underlying theme of judicial supremacy among these justices. They see the role of the Court as heroic, just as the Warren Court did."

The Conservative Majority

By the end of the term, the Court had gone an unusually long time— five years—without any change in membership. New issues arose each year, of course, but lawyers, experts, and observers had learned how to gauge the justices' likely alignments. "You don't have wild cards on this Court," David Vladeck, director of the Public Citizen Litigation Group,

Table 1-3 Justices in Dissent, 1998–1999 Term

Justice	8–1, 7–1	7–2	6–3, 5–3	5–4	Total	Percentage
			Division on Court			
Rehnquist	—	1	6	7	14	18.7%
Stevens	5	7	2	9	23	30.7
O'Connor	—	1	2	5	8	10.8
Scalia	—	2	4	6	12	16.0
Kennedy	—	2	2	5	9	12.0
Souter	—	1	3	9	13	17.3
Thomas	1	3	4	6	14	18.7
Ginsburg	1	3	6	10	20	26.7
Breyer	—	4	4	11	19	25.7

Note: Totals reflect cases where the justices dissented in whole or in part from the result or the major legal holding. There were seventy-five signed opinions during the 1998–1999 term. Because of recusals, Justices O'Connor and Breyer each participated in seventy-four cases.

remarked. "Each of the justices has been on the bench long enough, so you have a pretty good idea about what arguments they'll respond to."

The Court's five conservatives had been together even longer: for eight years since Thomas's tumultuous confirmation in October 1991. These justices continued to fall into two groups. Rehnquist, Scalia, and Thomas were the most consistent in taking conservative positions, while O'Connor and Kennedy had more mixed voting records. It was O'Connor and Kennedy who, on selected issues, voted with the Court's justices on the left to produce liberal rulings. In a way, they held the balance of power. The evidence could be seen in the statistics for the justices' dissents. O'Connor, with eight, and Kennedy, with nine, dissented in the smallest number of cases during the term; Scalia dissented in twelve cases, Rehnquist and Thomas in fourteen each. *(See Table 1–3.)*

Of the three core conservatives, Rehnquist showed the least ideological passion in his opinions. He preferred a lean writing style with few rhetorical flourishes, but his opinions still packed plenty of punch. His majority opinion in the patent infringement case, for example, made clear that the conservatives would closely scrutinize any laws passed by Congress subjecting states to private suits for claimed constitutional violations. Early in the term, he wrote a decision limiting the ability of someone temporarily inside another person's home for business purposes to challenge a police search of the premises. The opinion carefully tracked the specific facts of the case, but it also had the effect of cutting off any expansion of a 1990 decision that had allowed social guests to challenge a police search. Rehnquist had dissented from the earlier ruling.

Among the rest of Rehnquist's nine majority opinions for the term were two that somewhat expanded protections in search cases. Rehnquist wrote a unanimous decision striking down an Iowa law—unique among the states—that allowed police to search anyone stopped for a traffic violation. And in a closely watched dispute, Rehnquist again led all nine justices in concluding that police may be held liable in federal civil rights suits for inviting news reporters or photographers to accompany them on raids inside private homes. His opinion softened the blow for law enforcement, however, by effectively limiting the decision to future cases.

Rehnquist's dissenting opinions reflected his longstanding deference toward the states. He wrote the major dissent—for himself and Thomas—in the welfare case, defending the states' prerogatives to set lower benefits for newcomers as akin to minimum residency requirements in other contexts such as voting. In another states' rights case, he dissented from a ruling that struck down, on free speech grounds, parts of a Colorado law regulating petition circulators for ballot initiatives. And, in one significant concurring opinion, Rehnquist signaled a greater willingness than the rest of the justices to approve regulation of commercial speech—at least when the advertisement was for gambling.

Scalia, finishing his thirteenth term, had the reputation, in Professor Baker's words, as "the intellectual engine of the Rehnquist Court." Whether in the majority or in dissent, his opinions were marked by rigorous logic, unbending conservatism, and—often—stylistic flair. When he dissented in the Chicago loitering law case, Scalia mocked the decision by conjuring up the confrontation between the Jets street gang and Officer Krupke from the musical *West Side Story*. In his opinion in the College Savings Bank case, he carefully explained how a thirty-five-year-old precedent allowing private suits against states had been repeatedly weakened by subsequent decisions. "Today," Scalia continued, "we drop the other shoe: Whatever may remain of our decision . . . is expressly overruled."

Scalia's conservative views emerged in a number of areas during the term. He wrote an immigration law decision that broadly applied a new statute limiting judicial review of deportation cases and, for good measure, barred unlawful aliens from challenging deportation on free speech grounds. In an important, but little noted, civil procedure ruling, he led a narrow majority in limiting federal courts' power to block a defendant from disposing of assets until after the plaintiff has won a judgment. He wrote the 6–3 decision in a Wyoming case allowing police to search an automobile passenger's belongings after finding evidence of drug use by the driver. And he led the four dissenters from a decision that prohibited judges, on Fifth Amendment grounds, from using a defendant's refusal to testify at a sentencing hearing as a basis for increasing the sentence.

Rehnquist, Scalia, and Thomas remained closely aligned during the term. Scalia agreed with Rehnquist, for example, in 83 percent of the cases and with Thomas in 87 percent. But Scalia differed with the other two in some significant areas. He took a broader view of free speech claims, for example, and thus split with Rehnquist in voting to strike down the Colorado initiative law. Scalia's strict reading of criminal laws led him to side with defendants in some cases while Rehnquist voted with the government. And Scalia voted with the majority to strike down reduced welfare benefits for new residents, leaving Rehnquist and Thomas alone in dissent. Scalia's vote was surprising: he had appeared to favor upholding the law during argument, but he did not write a separate opinion to explain his vote.

Thomas continued to emerge during the term as an outspoken conservative, with the greatest willingness to rethink liberal decisions that had long since become established precedents. "He's the most maverick of the justices, the one that's most interesting to watch," Professor Volokh remarked. In a new book, *First Principles: The Jurisprudence of Clarence Thomas*, author Scott Gerber described Thomas as the Court's most conservative member over the past five years.

As the most junior of the conservatives, Thomas typically was not assigned to write majority opinions in the major cases. Of his seven majority opinions, perhaps the most important was a 5–4 decision that gave a pro-prosecution interpretation to the new federal death penalty law. The defendant, who had been sentenced to death after a somewhat long jury deliberation, argued on appeal that the jury should have been told that in case of a deadlock the judge would have been required to impose a life sentence without possibility of parole. Thomas rejected the argument, saying the requested instruction could undermine the government's "strong interest in having the jury express the conscience of the community on the ultimate question of life or death." In another criminal case, Thomas wrote a 7–2 decision allowing police to seize an automobile from a public place without a warrant after having observed it being used for drug trafficking.

Thomas gave a conservative cast to another decision—an ostensibly unanimous ruling requiring a lower federal court to reconsider a suit by white North Carolina voters challenging a congressional redistricting plan as racially motivated. All nine justices agreed that the lower court had not properly considered the state's defense in the case. But Thomas, writing for the five conservatives, said the evidence could have supported a finding of racial motivation. The liberal justices, concurring separately, indicated they disagreed.

It was in his separate concurring and dissenting opinions that Thomas's conservatism was most in evidence. In voting to uphold the Chicago anti-gang ordinance, Thomas, the Court's only African American, wrote emotionally about the terrorizing effects that street gangs have on law-abiding citizens in inner city neighborhoods. In the mental illness case, he sharply criticized the majority for intruding on the states' discretion in allocating mental health budgets. He also dissented in the welfare case, accusing the majority of misinterpreting the constitutional provision—the Privileges and Immunities Clause—that formed the basis for the decision. And in the self-incrimination case, Thomas went further than his fellow dissenter Scalia and called for overturning—not just narrowing—a forty-year-old precedent that the majority relied on for the decision.

O'Connor and Kennedy figuratively shared the Court's center positions, but differed in their judicial temperaments and approaches. O'Connor was pointed in her questions during oral argument, but cautious in her decisionmaking. She exemplified what University of Chicago law professor Cass Sunstein called the "minimalist" approach of deciding cases on the narrowest possible grounds, leaving bigger questions for another time. Kennedy was more deferential on the bench, and he too had a cautious, case-by-case approach at times. At other times, however, his opinions swept more broadly, and had a harder edge. The contrast could be seen in the two major decisions they wrote during the term: Kennedy's opinion in the Maine states' rights case and O'Connor's majority opinion in a politically charged ruling that barred the Clinton administration from using statistical sampling in the 2000 census for purposes of allocating congressional seats among the states.

Kennedy's opinion was a fifty-one page disquisition on legal history, political theory, and constitutional law. He stated his conclusions boldly: sovereign immunity was a "universal" concept when the Constitution was ratified; the Court had been "consistent" in upholding the states' immunity from suit since ratification of the Eleventh Amendment; the contrary evidence from the dissenters was "scanty and equivocal." There was no equivocation in the final result: Congress had "no power"—except under the Fourteenth Amendment—to subject states to private damage suits either in the state's own courts or in federal court.

O'Connor's opinion in the census case was more tentative in style as well as result. Opponents of sampling contended the plan violated the

Census Act as passed by Congress as well as the Constitution's requirement for an "actual enumeration" to be used in congressional apportionment. O'Connor dealt only with the first issue. She traced the history of
the Census Act and dissected the two statutory sections cited by each side
before concluding—with no rhetorical flourishes—that the opponents'
interpretation was correct. The four other conservatives joined
O'Connor's opinion, but they also joined a concurring opinion—written
by Scalia—that went further to say that sampling probably violated the
Constitution as well.

One of O'Connor's major opinions found her in sharp conflict with her
fellow centrist, Kennedy. The issue was a school system's liability for "student-on-student" sexual harassment under a federal law that prohibited
sex discrimination by schools that received federal financial assistance.
O'Connor wrote for a 5–4 majority holding that schools could be liable in
such cases. She carefully qualified the holding: liability could be imposed
only under fairly limited circumstances, and judges should throw out
insubstantial claims. Still, O'Connor showed some uncharacteristic emotion when she described the months-long sexual taunting endured by the
plaintiff in the case, a girl in the fifth grade at the time. Kennedy led the
four dissenters in a passionate rebuttal that warned of inevitable federal
intrusion into school discipline policies. "Federalism and our struggling
school system deserve better from this Court," he declared.

In their other noteworthy decisions, O'Connor and Kennedy for the
most part adopted traditional conservative positions. O'Connor led a 6–3
majority in imposing a new procedural hurdle for state prisoners challenging convictions through federal habeas corpus petitions. Kennedy led
a 5–4 Court to guarantee developers a jury trial in federal civil rights suits
challenging local zoning board restrictions as unconstitutional "takings"
of property. He also wrote a unanimous opinion barring refugee status for
immigrants who committed serious crimes in their home countries even
if they faced persecution if deported.

But both O'Connor and Kennedy also aligned with the Court's liberals from time to time. They both voted to strike down the Chicago loitering ordinance and lower state welfare payments for new residents.
They voted to limit states' ability to institutionalize mental patients who
qualified for community placement, although Kennedy took a narrower
stance than O'Connor. Kennedy wrote the 5–4 decision in the case
involving application of the Fifth Amendment at sentencing hearings;
O'Connor dissented. O'Connor wrote the 5–4 decision in an important
Indian rights case, allowing a Minnesota tribe to enforce hunting and fish-

ing limits in 13 million acres of public land in the center of the state; Kennedy dissented.

Many conservatives viewed O'Connor and Kennedy as disappointments. "I continue to be surprised by how unwilling the conservatives are to cut back on some of the expansive positions the Court has taken on social issues in the past," said Richard Samp, legal director of the conservative Washington Legal Foundation. But other Court watchers had more favorable views of the centrists, including some of those to the left of ideological center. "The center of the Court is a true conservative Court," Professor Neuborne observed. "It's committed to the application of existing doctrine in a principled way."

The Liberal Minority

The four liberal-leaning justices formed a less cohesive bloc than the conservative majority. The conservatives were all appointed by Republican presidents. The liberals included two justices appointed by Republican presidents—Stevens (named by Gerald Ford) and Souter (appointed by George Bush)—and two Democratic appointees: Ginsburg and Breyer, both named by President Clinton. The liberals had no single intellectual leader to match Scalia, and they lacked the votes for any of them to play the pivotal role that O'Connor and Kennedy had assumed. They differed among themselves in several areas—notably, criminal law and economic regulation, where Souter and Breyer often adopted more conservative positions than Stevens and Ginsburg. But they shared common views in areas such as civil rights, church-state issues, and state-federal relations.

As the justice with the most seniority after Rehnquist, Stevens had the power to assign the majority opinion if he was in the majority and the chief justice dissented. Stevens assigned himself two of the term's major cases: the rulings striking down the Chicago gang loitering ordinance and California's reduced welfare benefits for new residents. Both cases harked to controversial decisions from the Court's liberal era that embraced freedoms not explicitly recognized in the Constitution: a right to loiter and a right to travel. In the first case, Stevens endorsed what he called a "freedom to loiter for innocent purposes," but only two other justices—Souter and Ginsburg—joined that part of the opinion. He held a majority only for the more limited holding that the ordinance was unconstitutionally vague. In the welfare case, Stevens steered clear of the right to travel and instead said the law violated the provision in the Fourteenth Amendment prohibiting states from abridging the "privileges or immunities" of citizens. The opinion—joined by six other justices, all but Rehnquist and Thomas—stirred interest among liberals and conservatives alike for reviving a constitutional provision that had been all but ignored for more than a century.

Stevens's other opinions reflected his reputation as the most liberal justice on the Court. He wrote the opinion in an important 7–2 decision expanding local school systems' obligations under a federal law to pay for nursing services needed by students with disabilities. He wrote the main opinion in a criminal law case that appeared to limit prosecutors' ability to use an accomplice's confession against a defendant unless the accomplice testified at trial. He dissented from each of three decisions expanding police powers in search cases and wrote dissenting opinions in two of them, complaining that the majority had given more consideration to law enforcement than to the privacy rights of innocent citizens.

Overall, Stevens was the Court's most frequent dissenter. He dissented in twenty-three cases, including five where he was the lone justice in disagreement. He led the minority justices in several of the major cases, including the census dispute, the disability rights ruling, the punitive damage case, and the last of the states' rights decisions in the patent infringement dispute. Each was a forceful, pointed rejoinder to the conservative majority. In the disability rights case, for example, he accused the majority of "a crabbed vision" of the law's protections against discrimination. In the patent case, he said the ruling threatened to nullify the power granted to Congress under the Fourteenth Amendment to pass legislation to prevent states from violating due process or equal protection rights.

Souter, ending his ninth term, still had the reputation that developed early in his tenure as the slowest working of the justices. He wrote majority opinions in seven cases—along with Thomas, the lowest number for the term; the other justices wrote eight or nine each. Souter also had a relatively small number of separate concurring or dissenting opinions, and his total number of opinions—fourteen—was the lowest of all nine justices, according to an Associated Press tally.

Souter's most important opinions came on the final day of the term. He wrote the majority opinion in a significant 7–2 decision that overturned a $1.5 billion settlement in a big asbestos case and set tough conditions for companies to use class action rules as an alternative to bankruptcy in mass tort cases. The case was legally and factually complex; Souter's forty-seven page decision was detailed and intricate, carefully explaining why the agreement did not adequately protect the rights of all asbestos victims in the case. On the same day, Souter led the dissenters in the Maine states' rights case. The fifty-eight page opinion matched Kennedy's majority opinion in legal and historical detail and in rhetorical force. The ruling, Souter declared, amounted to "closing the courthouse door" to state employees.

Several of Souter's other majority opinions came in complex cases. He wrote a 5–4 criminal law decision that interpreted a new federal carjacking law to make it harder for prosecutors to seek enhanced penalties under the statute. He wrote a significant bankruptcy law decision backing creditors' rights in real estate reorganizations. And he wrote the Court's decision backing the Federal Trade Commission's authority to regulate nonprofit trade associations. The justices agreed unanimously on the FTC's powers, but they divided 5–4 on the specific issue: whether advertising guidelines adopted by the California Dental Association violated antitrust principles. Lower federal courts had ruled the guidelines a per se antitrust violation; Souter joined with four conservatives in sending the case back for reconsideration and suggesting the rules might have beneficial as well as negative effects on competition.

Ginsburg and Breyer, longtime federal appeals court judges before their appointments in 1993 and 1994, respectively, continued to get generally high marks for their legal abilities and relatively nonideological approaches. "They're highly competent, thoughtful, talented judges who apply existing doctrine fairly and with intellectual rigor," Neuborne observed. They were both active questioners on the bench, but, as the most junior justices, they did not get plum assignments, and many of their decisions were in relatively minor cases dealing with technical issues that only lawyers could fathom.

In her most important opinion for the term, Ginsburg led a fractured Court in holding that the Americans with Disabilities Act protected people with mental illnesses from "unnecessary segregation" in state mental hospitals instead of community treatment centers. The ruling was an important victory for disability rights advocates. Ginsburg softened the impact, however, by saying that even if a mental patient qualified for community placement, states could keep him or her on a waiting list if required by budget constraints.

The dissenting justices—Rehnquist, Scalia, and Thomas—said the ruling intruded on the states' prerogatives, but from the other side Stevens said Ginsburg gave too much deference to the states and separated him-self from part of her opinion.

Ginsburg's other major decision came in a case pitting a constitutional right—freedom of speech—against a state law regulating petition circula-tors for ballot initiatives. She wrote the decision striking provisions of a Colorado law that required petition circulators to wear badges, to be reg-istered voters, and to disclose any amounts they were paid for gathering signatures. Significantly, Ginsburg began by saying that she was "taking careful account" of precedents on regulating the initiative process; she then evaluated the state's attempts to justify the regulations before con-cluding that they did not pass constitutional muster.

Several other opinions reflected Ginsburg's seeming role as the Court's expert on tort law and civil procedure. She wrote one significant decision allowing the use of the federal antiracketeering law in insurance fraud cases, another lesser ruling limiting the use of state tort law against inter-national air carriers, and two highly technical decisions on arcane points of civil procedure. Her most important dissenting opinion also came on a civil procedure issue. The 5–4 ruling involved an effort by American investors who sued a Mexican holding company and asked for an injunc-tion to tie up the company's assets during the litigation. The Court said that lower federal courts had been wrong to issue the injunction. Ginsburg said the ruling was based on "an unjustifiably static conception" of federal courts' authority.

Breyer's majority opinions generated even less excitement. In the most important of his decisions, Breyer led a unanimous Court in extending federal judges' authority to exclude dubious testimony from "experts" not only in regard to scientific issues but in other areas as well. The ruling won warm praise from business interests that had long fought to keep what they called "junk science" out of personal injury lawsuits. In anoth er pro-business ruling, Breyer wrote the unanimous decision holding that a buyer does not violate antitrust laws simply by switching to a different supplier. And in one other unanimous decision, Breyer wrote the opinion striking down an Alabama tax law that imposed a higher levy on out-of-state corporations than on companies within the state.

In three other majority opinions, Breyer favored the interests of work-ers over their employers. He wrote the 5–4 decision allowing the Equal Employment Opportunity Commission to award damages in job dis-crimination complaints by federal workers. He wrote another 5–4 deci-sion allowing federal employee unions to raise new negotiating issues during the life of a collective bargaining contract. And he wrote a unanimous decision allowing disabled workers to sue their employers over alleged discrimination even if they are receiving Social Security disability benefits.

Breyer's most important dissent came on the final day of the term when he, Stevens, and Souter each read from the bench parts of their opinions challenging the three decisions protecting states from private suits to enforce federal laws. Each signaled at the end of his opinion that the liberal bloc was unwilling to accept the rulings as binding precedents. "I am not yet ready to adhere" to the limits on suits against states, Breyer said in his opinion. Stevens vowed to "continue to register my agreement" with the dissenting views in the cases. Even more bluntly, Souter predicted that the line of decisions was "unrealistic," "indefensible," and "probably . . . fleeting."

The unusual defiance of the importance of precedent—the doctrine known as "stare decisis"—underscored the close division on the Court on federalism and on some other issues. "We have a Court that is very closely balanced," Professor Douglas Kmiec remarked in an end-of-term wrap-up on the PBS "NewsHour with Jim Lehrer." Kathleen Sullivan, a liberal constitutional law expert and dean of Stanford Law School, agreed and went on to note that a Democratic president could shift the balance of power if one of the conservatives retired. For the moment, however, talk of possible vacancies was only that: talk. None of the justices showed imminent signs of retiring, and most observers expected that all of them would be loath to step down in a presidential election year.

Speculation about a potential vacancy arose briefly when it was announced that Ginsburg, age sixty-six, had undergone surgery for colon cancer on September 17. Talk of her possible retirement died down when the Court's public affairs office September 28 released details of Ginsburg's condition, and she went home from the hospital. The Court said that the Stage 2 cancer—the third most serious of four types described by physicians—had been detected and removed before it could spread to other parts of the body. Experts were quoted as saying that about 75 percent of Stage 2 colon cancer patients are cured. Ginsburg continued to work while recuperating and was on the bench when the Court began its 1999–2000 term on Monday, October 4.

Still, Court watchers thought it likely that any or all of the three oldest justices—Rehnquist, Stevens, and O'Connor—might consider stepping down during the next presidential term. (Both Stevens and O'Connor had been treated for cancer: Stevens for prostate cancer in 1992, and O'Connor for breast cancer in 1988.) The possibility of a vacancy raised the political stakes for the 2000 election for conservative and liberal interest groups alike. "We don't know who's going to retire," Professor Michael Gerhardt of William and Mary Law School remarked, "but it's safe to say, whoever gets replaced, that that replacement will have influence on the future of the Court's jurisprudence."

Chapter 2

The 1998–1999 Term

No one would ever accuse the Rehnquist Court of being in league with the American Civil Liberties Union. Since Rehnquist became chief justice in 1986, the Court has ratcheted down procedural protections in criminal cases, limited the use of affirmative action, and turned aside most pleas to recognize new constitutional rights—to the general consternation of the ACLU and other civil rights and civil liberties groups.

When the dust settled on the 1998–1999 term, however, the ACLU looked back on a fairly successful year. It won three of the four cases that it directly handled during the term, and the Court sided with ACLU positions in fourteen of the nineteen cases in which the organization had filed friend-of-the-court briefs.

"We did pretty well," said Stephen Shapiro, the ACLU's national legal director. But he had no illusions about an ideological shift on the Court. "There's no fundamental realignment, just a fortuitous mix of what cases came up to the Court in the term," Shapiro remarked. "I don't see this as evidence of a moderating trend."

Still, the ACLU's surprisingly positive results illustrated the difficulty of discerning any uniform trends in the year's decisions. States were the term's biggest winners, with three rulings limiting Congress's power to allow private citizens to bring damage suits against state governments for violating federal laws. But state and local governments also lost some significant cases. The Court allowed federal civil rights suits against local schools for sexual harassment committed by students. It restricted states' discretion to institutionalize people with mental illnesses. And it barred states from paying new residents lower welfare benefits than other recipients.

Business interests counted the term as generally successful. Employers were pleased with the rulings limiting the coverage of the federal disability rights law for people with correctable conditions. But employers got a mixed ruling on plaintiffs' ability to win punitive damages in federal job discrimination suits. And businesses facing mass tort suits—such as the litigation brought by victims of asbestos exposure—suffered a setback with a ruling making it extremely difficult to craft mandatory settlements of class actions.

Civil rights and civil liberties groups were wary of the Court's new federalism rulings, but had clear-cut victories in the ruling on state welfare benefits and in a decision striking down an anti-gang loitering law in Chicago that had been enforced primarily against minority youths. They counted the rulings on sexual harassment suits and punitive damages for job discrimination as victories despite some concerns that the Court set unnecessarily high standards for imposing liability. And they won several rulings in less publicized cases that yielded favorable interpretations of various federal civil rights laws.

In criminal cases, police and prosecutors continued to prevail most of the time. The Court broadened police powers in four of five search and seizure rulings and upheld death sentences in two closely watched cases despite acknowledged errors at trial. Criminal defense lawyers won a few victories, but they were fairly limited except for the loitering law decision. In the most noteworthy of the defense victories, the Court unanimously narrowed the scope of the federal law banning gifts to federal officials. The decision upset a conviction won by an independent counsel appointed to investigate allegations of influence-peddling by a Clinton administration cabinet member, one-time agriculture secretary Michael Espy.

Some observers said the varied patterns in the Court's decisions made it difficult to give it an ideological label. "This is not a Court that can be easily pigeonholed," William and Mary law professor Michael Gerhardt remarked on the PBS "NewsHour." Instead, Gerhardt said, the Court is "largely divided by pragmatic viewpoints."

Still, a look at the Court's most closely divided cases gave some evidence of an ideological fault line between the Court's conservatives and the more liberal justices. Of the seventeen cases decided by 5–4 votes, eight—nearly half—divided along the commonly recognized ideological lines, with Rehnquist, O'Connor, Scalia, Kennedy, and Thomas in the majority; and Stevens, Souter, Ginsburg, and Breyer in dissent. In six other cases, the liberal justices all voted together and formed a majority by picking up either Kennedy (four times) or O'Connor (twice). In the other three cases, at least three of the liberals stayed together; and four of the five conservatives voted together in two of those three. Those numbers suggested that even if the justices tried to make their decisions on a case-by-case basis, their individual legal philosophies guided their voting and gave Court watchers good clues on the likely results.

State and Local Governments

The Court gave state governments three new legal shields against being forced to pay damages to individuals or companies in lawsuits for violating federal laws. All three rulings came on 5–4 votes, with strongly written dissents from the liberal justices.

First, in a case involving a suit by Maine state employees, the Court held that Congress cannot "abrogate" or override states' sovereign immunity from suits under its power to regulate interstate commerce. The ruling threw out a suit by probation officers for back overtime pay, even though a federal court had ruled that they were entitled to it under the federal wage and hour statute.

Second, the Court ruled that states do not become subject to damage suits simply by engaging in commercial activities. That ruling—overturning a 1964 precedent—came in a false advertising suit between a private bank and a Florida state agency that both marketed college tuition savings plans.

Third, in a companion patent infringement suit between the bank and the Florida agency, the Court restricted Congress's power to provide for damage suits against state governments under a provision of the Fourteenth Amendment. That provision, section 5, authorizes Congress to pass legislation to enforce the due process and equal protection rights established in other sections of the amendment. In the specific case, the Court held that states could not be subjected to patent infringement suits because Congress had insufficient evidence of widespread patent violations by state governments.

The federalism rulings accounted for three of this term's five decisions striking down federal statutes on constitutional grounds, as well as the only time during the term that the Court explicitly reversed one of its prior decisions. *(See Tables 2–1 and 2–2.)*

Advocates for state governments praised the rulings. Richard Ruda, chief counsel for the State and Local Legal Center, called the rulings "a reaffirmation of the role of state governments in the federal system." But the decisions also created concerns among several other interest groups.

Mark Levy, a corporate lawyer in Washington, said the ruling in the false advertising suit "will raise problems in future cases where states are

Table 2-1 Laws Held Unconstitutional

The Supreme Court issued seven decisions during the 1998–1999 term that held unconstitutional federal laws or state laws or constitutional provisions.

Federal Laws	
Alden v. Maine [p. 145]	Fair Labor Standards Act (suits against states)
College Savings Bank v. Florida Prepaid Postsecondary Education Expense Board [p. 146]	Trademark Remedy Clarification Act
Florida Prepaid Postsecondary Education Expense Board v. College Savings Bank [p. 147]	Patent Remedy Act
Greater New Orleans Broadcasting Association, Inc. v. United States [p. 125]	Limits on broadcast advertising of casinos
Saenz v. Roe [p. 137]	Welfare reform law (authorizing different benefit levels for new state residents)

State Laws	
Buckley v. American Constitutional Law Foundation [p. 113]	Regulations for initiative petition circulators
Saenz v. Roe [p. 137]	Limit on welfare benefits for new state residents
South Central Bell Telephone Co. v. Alabama [p. 149]	Corporate franchise tax

acting as competitors with private businesses." Lawyers specializing in "intellectual property"—copyright and patent law—sharply criticized the decision barring the patent infringement suit. "Under this decision, a state can infringe a patent or copyright and no court in the country can do anything about it," Charles Sims, a New York lawyer for the Association of American Publishers and the Software and Information Industry Association, told the *Los Angeles Times*.

Public employee unions and organizations similarly complained that the ruling in the Maine case left state workers with no effective legal protections. "The Court said that the federal government itself could bring the suit, but that's not going to happen," Robert Scully, executive director of the National Association of Police Organizations, told the *New York Times*.

Table 2-2 Reversals of Earlier Rulings

The Supreme Court issued one decision during the 1998–1999 term that explicitly reversed a previous ruling by the Court. The ruling brought the number of such reversals during the Court's history to at least 216.

New Decision	Old Decision	New Holding
College Savings Bank v. Florida Prepaid Postsecondary Education Expense Board	Parden v. Terminal Railway Co. of Ala. Docks Dept.	State does not waive sovereign immunity by engaging in commercial activities

For his part, the ACLU's Shapiro called the rulings "troubling" for civil rights and civil liberties groups. "The principal question is how narrowly the Court will interpret Congress' section 5 authority under the Fourteenth Amendment," Shapiro explained. "The Court did seem to indicate a willingness to closely scrutinize Congress' judgment that particular legislation was necessary to enforce constitutional rights, and that causes me some worry."

Supporters of the rulings countered the criticisms by noting that the decisions left open several options for enforcing federal laws. Individuals or companies could still sue state officials to prevent future violations of federal law. Private damage suits were still permitted under civil rights laws that could be justified under the Fourteenth Amendment. And local governments do not enjoy protection against suits, the Court said; sovereign immunity belongs only to the states. "The rulings are not as radical as they were depicted," commented UCLA professor Eugene Volokh. "The cases will not tremendously interfere with the enforcement of federal law."

State and local governments lost on other issues during the term. The Court voted 7–2 to bar states from setting lower welfare payments for new residents. That ruling was based on a provision of the Fourteenth Amendment, the so-called Privileges and Immunities Clause, that had gone virtually unused since its ratification after the Civil War. The clause prohibits states from "abridging" the privileges and immunities of citizens, but provides no definition of what rights are included within the phrase. In a second ruling striking down a state law on constitutional grounds, the Court unanimously invalidated an Alabama tax scheme that favored in-state corporations over out-of-state companies. That decision was based on a well-established principle prohibiting laws that discriminate against interstate commerce.

The Court upheld state or local levies in two other, minor tax cases. In an Arizona case, it unanimously ruled that states can impose taxes on federal contractors for work performed on Indian reservations. The Court also upheld the imposition of a county "occupational tax" on federal judges; the case came from Jefferson County, Alabama, which includes Birmingham, seat of one of the state's federal courts.

Local governments suffered several setbacks during the term. The Court held, by a 5–4 vote, that local school boards may be held liable under a federal anti–sex discrimination law for one student's sexual harassment of another student. In his dissent, Kennedy complained of what he called the majority's "disregard for our federal balance" by permitting federal court suits in matters of school discipline. In another 5–4 decision, it ruled that landowners and developers can use the federal civil rights law to sue local governments for damages for so-called "regulatory takings" that improperly deny them valuable use of their land. Writing for the dissenters, Souter said the ruling might put federal court juries in the position of passing on the legitimacy of local zoning policies.

The Court also struck down as unconstitutionally vague a Chicago ordinance aimed at getting criminal gangs off the streets. Thomas, in dissent, said the decision nullified "the city's commonsense effort to combat gang loitering."

"You cannot say that this is just states rights carte blanche," Professor Gerhardt remarked. "The Court is being case-by-case, fact-by-fact, but it also has a clear preference for recognizing the structure of the Constitution as being one of a dual sovereignty."

Business, Labor, and Consumers

Business interests closed out the term with major victories in the three rulings placing limits on the application of the Americans with Disabilities Act to workers with correctable impairments and a partial victory in the ruling on punitive damages in job discrimination suits. "It was a very good term from our perspective," said Stephen Bokat, vice president and general counsel of the U.S. Chamber of Commerce, "although we weren't saying that until the end of the term."

Other business lawyers agreed. Corporate lawyer Mark Levy called the year "pretty favorable" for business. Charles Rothfeld, another corporate lawyer who follows the Court, said that out of nearly two dozen cases directly involving business interests, businesses won about thirteen, lost eight, and tied in two.

The disability rights rulings gave employers legal protections on three issues. First, employers were not required to make what the disability law called "reasonable accommodations" for the many people with impairments that did not rise to the level of a disability, such as correctable nearsightedness or high-blood pressure that was treatable with medication. Second, the rulings sanctioned the use of specified physical qualifications—such as height, weight, or eyesight—as job requirements. And one of the rulings also established that employers could use standards set by federal agencies—in the specific case, a vision standard for truck drivers—in setting their own requirements for employment.

The punitive damages ruling appeared at first to be a setback for employers. The Court rejected the argument by the defendant in the case, the American Dental Association, that punitive damages could be awarded in job discrimination cases under the federal civil rights law only after proof of "egregious" conduct. But the Court went on to rule, by a 5–4 vote, that an employer could avoid punitive damages by showing that it had made "good-faith efforts" to comply with the antidiscrimination law. Both Bokat and Levy said they expected few businesses to be required to pay punitive damages under that standard.

Business groups applauded a ruling giving federal judges more discretion to keep out expert testimony. The ruling, in a case against the Korean manufacturer Kumho Tire Company, extended to all types of expert witnesses restrictive guidelines laid down six years earlier in a case involving scientific testimony. "Generally, business litigants tend to put in better experts than their opponents do," Levy explained. "So they're generally trying to keep out what's been called junk science."

The Court took a narrow view of antitrust laws in two separate rulings—an approach generally favorable to big businesses, which are more likely to be defendants than plaintiffs in antitrust suits. In one case, the Court turned aside a claim that a regional telephone company violated antitrust laws by changing from one supplier to another. In the other, the Court required lower federal courts to reconsider a finding that advertising restrictions adopted by the California Dental Association restrained competition. "The Court was saying they needed a full trial to assess the economic realities and competitive effects in the particular case," Levy explained.

In one setback for businesses, the Court made it harder for companies facing big class action suits to craft so-called global settlements of claims.

The ruling upset a $1.5 billion accord negotiated by a former asbestos manufacturer, Fibreboard Corporation, with lawyers representing plaintiffs claiming that they or family members contracted various diseases from asbestos exposure. The settlement limited compensation for any future victims. The Court said those terms were unfair and set strict conditions, including separate legal representation for each class of potential plaintiffs, to approve any mandatory settlement.

David Vladeck, director of Public Citizen Litigation Group and a critic of such settlements, said few companies facing such litigation would be able to meet the criteria set by the Court. The result, he said, "may be that if you've got aggregated claims that are sufficient to put you into bankruptcy, then you have to go into bankruptcy."

Consumer groups claimed a victory in a case pitting the so-called Baby Bell regional telephone companies against long distance carriers on an issue of federal versus state regulation. The complex ruling generally upheld regulations adopted by the Federal Communications Commission governing the entry of long distance companies such as AT&T and MCI into local telephone markets effectively controlled by the Baby Bells, the companies that had been spun off from the old AT&T monopoly two decades earlier. Observers viewed the decision as likely to ease the way for competition in local telephone service.

In labor-related cases, the Court gave employers a major victory by ruling that companies are free to use pension fund surpluses as they see fit. Workers for Hughes Aircraft wanted the company to use a $1 billion surplus to increase benefits or reduce employee contributions, but the Court ruled unanimously that doing so was not required under the federal pension protection law known as ERISA—the Employee Retirement Income Security Act. Employers also applauded a decision upholding a Pennsylvania law aimed at controlling health care costs in workers' compensation claims. The justices unanimously rejected a due process challenge to the law, which required a so-called utilization review of medical claims before paying benefits.

Employers suffered a partial setback in another case testing a company's ability to use collective bargaining contracts to force workers to arbitrate claims under federal job discrimination laws. The justices said that workers cannot be required to give up their right to sue unless a mandatory arbitration clause explicitly covers civil rights claims. Civil rights groups argued discrimination claims could never be forced into arbitration, but the Court left open the question whether an explicit waiver could be enforced.

Federal workers prevailed in two decisions. In one, the Court backed the right of federal employee unions to negotiate about new issues during the life of a collective bargaining contract. In the other, it held that employees have a right to be accompanied by a union representative while being interviewed by representatives of an inspector general's office. Both rulings came on 5–4 votes; Kennedy joined with the Court's liberal bloc to form the majority in each. In a third case involving public employees, however, the Court ruled summarily that state universities can set workload standards for faculty members without including the issue in collective bargaining.

Individual Rights

The ACLU's three victories in the term included two of the year's major rulings: the decisions striking down Chicago's gang loitering law and California's lower welfare rates for new residents. Both rulings, Shapiro said, had significant implications for the future. Given the national concern about gang violence, Shapiro said it was "extremely important" for the Court to "reaffirm clearly that there are limits to be observed even in the name of law enforcement." And in the welfare case, he applauded the Court's revival of the Fourteenth Amendment's Privileges and Immunities Clause. The provision, Shapiro said, could become "another weapon in the arsenal" for protecting individual rights.

Conservatives bristled at the welfare ruling, but some saw the Privileges and Immunities Clause as a possible weapon against economic regulation. "That clause was specifically intended to protect economic liberties: the right to earn an honest living, the right to enter contracts, the right to acquire and use private property," said William Mellor, president of the libertarian Institute for Justice. Other conservatives had their doubts. "People who think it will have good effects are whistling in the dark," said Richard Samp of the conservative Washington Legal Foundation.

Disability rights advocates counted the ruling limiting the institutionalization of people with mental illnesses as a major victory. "This is the *Brown v. Board of Education* for the disabilities movement," said Ira Burnim, legal director of the Washington-based Bazelon Center for Mental Health Law, referring to the 1954 ruling that outlawed racial segregation in public schools. "This is the first time the Court has announced that needless institutionalization is discrimination." In similar vein, the Court's ruling in an Iowa case requiring local schools to pay for nursing services needed by a quadriplegic student in order to attend classes was seen as an important decision to help break down barriers for people with physical disabilities.

Those two victories were offset, however, by the losses for disability rights advocates in the three employment cases. "This radically restricts the number of people who come under the law's protection," said Chai Feldblum, a Georgetown law professor and longtime disability rights lawyer.

The Court ruled for minority groups in two voting rights cases. In one, the Court made it somewhat easier for states to defend congressional redistricting plans that create districts with high percentages of minority populations. The ruling, in a protracted dispute over North Carolina's congressional redistricting, held that judges cannot automatically assume that such plans are based on an impermissible racial motivation. In the other, the Court blocked a court consolidation plan in Monterey County, California. Latino groups opposed the plan, favoring instead multiple judicial districts to help elect minority candidates to the bench.

The Court also ruled, 5–4, that the federal Equal Employment Opportunity Commission (EEOC) can award compensatory or punitive damages in job discrimination claims brought by federal workers. The ruling came in a sex discrimination claim brought by a male worker. But it applied to other claims brought under the 1991 revision of Title VII, the federal law that also prohibits discrimination on the basis of race, national origin, or religion.

In three other cases, the Court expanded plaintiffs' rights in civil cases based on other federal statutes. In one, the Court allowed the use of the federal antiracketeering law in insurance fraud cases. It also permitted the use of a federal civil rights law in a wrongful discharge case brought by a worker who claimed he had been fired in retaliation for testifying against his company in a Medicare fraud investigation. And in a third case the Court made it easier for patients to sue hospitals under a recent federal law aimed at preventing the "dumping" of high-cost emergency patients to other facilities.

Immigrant rights advocates suffered two serious losses, one of them in a case handled by the ACLU. In that case, the Court turned aside a challenge to deportation orders issued against a group of eight aliens charged more than a decade earlier with supporting a terrorist organization. In addition to curtailing judicial review of deportation cases, the Court held that unlawful aliens have no First Amendment right to avoid deportation on grounds that they have been singled out because of their political views. In a second case, the Court barred refugee status for immigrants who had committed serious crimes in their home countries even if they faced political persecution if deported.

The Court's rulings in traditional First Amendment areas produced two victories for free speech claimants. The Court unanimously struck down a partial federal ban on broadcast advertising for casinos and divided 6–3 in invalidating parts of a Colorado law regulating people who circulate petitions for ballot initiatives. Both decisions largely applied existing doctrines protecting commercial and political speech and left parts of the challenged regulations on the books.

In a third case, the justices rejected a First Amendment challenge to a law banning the use of obscene e-mails to annoy or harass other people. The April 19 ruling in *ApolloMedia Corp. v. Reno* summarily affirmed a decision by a special three-judge federal court involving a provision of the 1996 Communications Decency Act that banned "obscene, lewd, lascivious, filthy or indecent" e-mails sent with the intent to "annoy, abuse, threaten, or harass another person." The three-judge court upheld the law, but narrowed it to apply only to messages meeting the stringent legal test for obscenity. The justices voted 8–1 to uphold the lower court ruling; Stevens said he would have scheduled the case for full argument.

In one other dispute with First Amendment implications, the Court ruled that law enforcement officers may be ordered to pay damages in federal civil rights suits for inviting news reporters or photographers to accompany them on raids inside private homes. The rulings in companion cases—one of them brought by ACLU lawyers—involved suits by private citizens against federal or local officers and did not deal with the separate question whether media organizations themselves could be liable for damages. But media law experts said the decisions would likely curtail the practice of "media ride-alongs."

Criminal Law

Law enforcement's setback in the Chicago gang loitering case was offset by victories in most other important criminal law rulings. "On the whole, the term was largely favorable from a law enforcement perspective," said Kent Scheidegger, legal director for the California-based

Criminal Justice Legal Foundation, which filed friend-of-the-court briefs in six cases during the term. "The defense won some cases," Scheidegger continued, "but pretty much they won the ones they should have won."

Scheidegger's group, in fact, decided not to file a brief in support of the gang loitering law. Afterward, he said the decision left cities and states free to craft more specific laws to deal with gang violence—as the justices in the majority said. Some other pro–law enforcement Court watchers disagreed. "I think it's pretty clear that they were saying that they weren't going to let cities enforce this kind of law," said Richard Samp of the Washington Legal Foundation.

Both Scheidegger and Lisa Kemler, head of the National Association of Criminal Defense Lawyers' amicus brief committee, identified two Court rulings in capital punishment cases as among the most significant decisions for the term. In one, the Court voted 5–4 to uphold a death sentence under the new federal death penalty law even though the trial judge gave the jury incorrect instructions on one issue. In the other case, the Court upheld a death sentence in a Virginia case even though the prosecution had withheld information from the defendant at trial. The Court voted 7–2 that the information would not have affected the outcome.

In both cases, Scheidegger praised the Court for upholding the death sentences, saying that the errors "were not something that would really have made a difference." Kemler, a defense attorney in Alexandria, Virginia, disagreed. The decision in the Virginia case, she said, "gives prosecutors official license to withhold exculpatory evidence." As for the federal case, Kemler called it "outrageous" for a capital sentence to be upheld when the jury had been misinstructed.

The Court did give defense lawyers a partial victory in the federal death penalty case. It interpreted the law, passed in 1994, as barring a death sentence in the event of a jury deadlock in the penalty phase; the maximum sentence a judge can impose, the Court said, is life imprisonment without possibility of parole. And the justices forced a retrial in another Virginia death penalty case after ruling unanimously that prosecutors should not have introduced a confession by an accomplice who refused to testify at the defendant's trial.

In search and seizure cases, the Court continued to give police more deference even than some state courts were prepared to allow under the Fourth Amendment. In four cases, the Court set aside decisions by state appellate courts that ruled police searches illegal. The Court ruled in a Wyoming case that police can search the belongings of passengers in a car after finding evidence of drug use by the driver. It held in a Florida case that police do not need a warrant under a state forfeiture law to seize a car that had been used in drug trafficking. In a Minnesota case, the Court held that someone in another person's home for business purposes has no standing to challenge a police search. And in an unsigned opinion in a Maryland case the Court said that police did not need to show special urgency before conducting a warrantless search of an automobile believed to be carrying illegal drugs.

Those pro–law enforcement rulings were offset by only one decision. In that case, the Court unanimously struck down an Iowa law allowing police to search an automobile driver stopped for traffic violations even if the driver is not placed under arrest. An end-of-term review of the Fourth Amendment decisions in the newspaper *Legal Times* carried this headline: "A Right That Keeps Shrinking."

The Court also issued one ruling that will make it somewhat more difficult for state prison inmates to use federal habeas corpus petitions to challenge their convictions or sentences. By a 6–3 vote, it ruled that a federal court normally cannot consider an issue unless the inmate has raised it before the state's highest court—even if the state court exercises only limited review over criminal cases.

The few defense victories included several that narrowly interpreted federal criminal laws—an apparent reflection of the Court's general aversion to broadly construing statutory language. In the most important, the Court unanimously narrowed the scope of the federal anti-gift statute by ruling that prosecutors must prove a connection between a gift to an official and a specific official act that the gift was intended to influence. The ruling barred the conviction won by an independent counsel's office of an agricultural trade association that had given thousands of dollars' worth of gifts to one-time agriculture secretary Michael Espy.

In other rulings on federal statutes, the Court voted 5–4 to limit somewhat the ability of prosecutors to win enhanced sentences against defendants under a new federal carjacking law. Another decision made it more difficult for prosecutors to use a law aimed at drug kingpins. The statute provided for a minimum twenty-year prison sentence for a defendant convicted of operating a "continuing criminal enterprise" on the basis of three or more separate drug offenses. By a 6–3 vote, the Court held that jurors must unanimously agree on each of the charged offenses in order to return a conviction under the law.

The only broad procedural victory for criminal defendants came on a Fifth Amendment issue. By a 5–4 vote, the Court said judges cannot use a defendant's refusal to testify at a sentencing hearing as a basis for increasing the penalty imposed. Kennedy wrote the opinion, forming the majority with the Court's four liberal justices.

Overall, the Court favored state or federal prosecutors in eleven out of eighteen signed opinions. Defense lawyer Kemler appeared resigned to the Court's pro–law enforcement stance. "It was more bad than good. It's always more bad than good," she said. "They're reading the constitutional rights that would apply to an accused very, very narrowly."

States

Court Again Curbs Private Suits to Enforce Federal Laws

Alden v. Maine, decided by a 5–4 vote, June 23, 1999; Kennedy wrote the opinion; Souter, Stevens, Ginsburg, and Breyer dissented. *(See excerpts, pp. 263–282.)*

State probation officers have to put in long hours, and work at unusual times, to monitor criminal offenders released under court supervision instead of being sent to prison. A group of Maine's probation officers claimed that the federal wage-and-hour law entitled them to time-and-a-half pay for overtime. A federal judge agreed.

The judge's ruling in 1994 settled the question for future years, but the officers said the state owed them back overtime pay as well. That part of the suit was proceeding when the Supreme Court issued a decision in 1996 sharply limiting the ability of private individuals to sue states for damages in federal courts.

The probation officers then filed the same suit in Maine's state courts, but the state invoked a centuries-old doctrine called sovereign immunity to block the claim there as well. In a major victory for states, the Supreme Court this term backed Maine's position. The 5–4 ruling cheered states' rights advocates, but left supporters of federal powers complaining that states could now violate many federal laws with relative impunity.

Background. The Supreme Court had fought two pitched battles many years earlier on the question whether the federal Fair Labor Standards Act could be applied to state and local government employees. Initially, the Court held, in a 5–4 decision in 1976, that Congress had infringed on the Tenth Amendment's protections for state sovereignty by extending the wage and hour law to state and local governments. Rehnquist, then an associate justice, wrote the majority opinion. Nine years later, the Court reversed itself,

Maine state probation officer John Alden, one of the plaintiffs in a suit seeking back overtime pay under the federal wage-and-hour law. The Supreme Court ruled the suit should be thrown out because of the state's sovereign immunity.

in a second 5–4 decision, and upheld Congress's power to set wage and hour standards for state and local workers. Rehnquist, this time in dissent, predicted that "in time" his side would again prevail.

A year later, President Ronald Reagan elevated Rehnquist to chief justice and named Scalia, a likeminded conservative on federalism issues, to Rehnquist's seat as associate justice. Over the next five years, Rehnquist gained two more allies—Kennedy and Thomas—on issues involving state versus federal powers. Along with O'Connor, the five justices formed a potential majority for reversing the deferential attitude the Court had shown toward federal powers since the New Deal.

The shift in the Court's jurisprudence emerged slowly. In 1992 it struck down a federal law aimed at forcing states to take responsibility for radioactive waste from private nuclear power plants. Three years later, it struck down a law making it a federal crime to possess a gun near a school. Two years after that, it ruled a second gun control law unconstitutional: the Brady Act's provisions requiring local law enforcement agencies to conduct background checks on prospective gun purchasers. In the same year, it threw out a popular law aimed at protecting religious practices from state and local laws. In each of the decisions, the conservative majority said that Congress had overstepped its powers and intruded on areas that the Constitution left to the states.

One other pro–states' rights decision came in 1996 on an obscure federal law aimed at resolving disputes between the states and Indian tribes over gambling on Indian reservations. One provision of the law gave tribes the right to sue a state in federal court if it refused to negotiate over gambling issues. By a 5–4 vote, the Court in *Seminole Tribe of Florida v. Florida* said that provision violated the Eleventh Amendment, which has been held to bar most private suits against states in federal court. Writing for the majority, Rehnquist said that Congress's power to regulate interstate commerce did not override the Eleventh Amendment's protection for states from federal court suits. In a dissent, Souter complained the ruling would prevent Congress from providing a federal forum for a broad range of actions against states for violations of federal laws. *(See* Supreme Court Yearbook, 1995–1996, *pp. 42–46.)*

The Case. Maine's probation officers' pay dispute began in the early years after the Court's 1985 decision requiring states to comply with the Fair Labor Standards Act. Because most state and local government jobs paid more than the minimum wage required by the law, overtime pay became the most frequent source of disagreement between states and their workers. The federal law required time-and-a-half pay for overtime and limited employers' ability to allow compensatory time off to avoid the premium pay. Salaried and "professional" workers, as defined by somewhat ambiguous Labor Department regulations, were exempted from the provisions.

The state employees' union negotiated a contract provision with the state for a 16 percent pay premium for the probation officers instead of overtime. In 1992, however, about 60 of the 100 probation officers filed suit in federal court demanding overtime under the federal law. The state argued that the probation officers were professionals and therefore not covered by the overtime provisions, but a federal judge in 1993 rejected the argument. In a second ruling, in 1994, the judge cleared the way for a trial on how much back pay the state owed.

The Supreme Court's *Seminole* decision stopped that suit in its tracks. The federal appeals court in Boston in July 1997 agreed with the state that the Court's decision barred the probation officers' effort to win back pay in federal court. The federal law, however, also authorized suits in state courts to enforce its provisions. So the probation officers turned to Maine courts. State's attorneys moved to dismiss the action on the ground of sovereign immunity, which bars suits against a government in its own courts without its consent. The doctrine originated in England, where a famous maxim held, "The King can do no wrong." The doctrine held sway in the United States through the 1800s, but it was weakened in the twentieth century by laws and court rulings allowing private claims against the federal or state governments under certain circumstances.

Still, the general rule in Maine and many other states barred suits for money against the government unless specifically authorized by law. Maine's attorneys argued that the state had no law allowing suits for overtime pay by state workers, so the probation officers' suit should be dismissed. The probation officers argued the Supreme Court's decision in *Seminole* left them no other legal remedy. But in August 1998, the Maine Supreme Court, in a 5–2 decision, ordered the suit dismissed. Upholding the state's sovereign immunity, the state high court said that the limits on congressional power recognized in *Seminole* "may not be circumvented simply by moving to a state court."

The probation officers, backed by the Clinton administration, asked the Supreme Court to review the decision. The justices, in November, agreed. Initially, the case attracted little attention. But one constitutional expert, Erwin Chemerinsky of the University of Southern California Law Center, called the case "the sleeper" for the Court's term.

Arguments. The justices' questions, during a spirited hour-long argument on March 31, made clear the Court's ideological divisions on the issue. They also gave strong indications that the conservative majority was prepared to give the states another victory.

Kennedy led the way for the conservatives. "I can't conceive of the Constitution being ratified if it were perceived that states could be sued in their own courts," he said. Liberal justices sharply disagreed. If Congress has passed valid legislation affecting the states, Souter said, "why doesn't it follow that Congress can decide where the laws can be enforced?"

Representing the probation officers, longtime labor attorney Laurence Gold told the justices the Maine decision was based on "a wholly extraordinary notion" of sovereign immunity. "We're dealing with a situation where Congress is sovereign," he said. Solicitor General Seth Waxman agreed. Upholding the decision, Waxman warned, would mean that Congress's power to regulate interstate commerce would be written "in disappearing ink."

Conservative justices were unmoved. The system of dual federal and state sovereignty itself was "an extraordinary notion," Scalia retorted to Gold, but also a fundamental principle of the Constitution. O'Connor noted that the workers still had other remedies. The federal government could sue to enforce the law on the workers' behalf, or they could ask a court to bar future violations of the law.

In his turn, Maine's state solicitor, Peter Brann, began with the history of the Constitution. "There is no evidence that the states gave up sovereign immunity" in ratifying the Constitution, he told the justices.

Liberal justices sharply challenged the state's attorney. Stevens forced Brann to acknowledge that the Constitution itself was silent on the issue. Souter followed by asking why the federal government could sue a state without specific constitutional authorization, but private citizens could not. Breyer ended by raising the possibility that the federal government could respond by simply setting up an administrative agency to enforce the law. "Why do you want the federal Big Brother breathing down your neck?" he asked.

At the hour's end, it appeared none of the justices' minds had been changed by the arguments. The next day, the *New York Times* headline ventured a prediction: "Justices Seem Ready to Tilt More Toward States in Federalism."

Decision. Kennedy spoke for the Court in giving the states a resounding victory on June 23, the last decision day of the term. Sovereign immunity, Kennedy declared, was "a fundamental aspect of the sovereignty which the States enjoyed before the ratification of the Constitution, and which they retain today." The vote was 5–4. Speaking for the dissenters, Souter was defiant and caustic. "The majority," he said, "could not be more fundamentally mistaken."

Kennedy began with the framing of the Constitution, which he said reserved to the states "a substantial portion" of sovereignty. At the time, Kennedy continued, governmental immunity from private suits was universally considered to be "central to sovereign dignity." The Tenth Amendment, part of the Bill of Rights, validated the states' sovereignty. So did the Eleventh Amendment, which overturned an early Supreme Court decision allowing a private suit in federal court against the state of Georgia.

The Constitution never would have been ratified if it had given Congress power to "abrogate" or override the states' immunity from suit,

Kennedy said. Nothing in the nation's subsequent history suggested that Congress had that power either. And as a practical matter, allowing Congress to authorize a private damage suit against a state could pose "a severe and notorious danger" to the state's budget and simultaneously shift political power from the state's elected officials to the courts. In short, Kennedy concluded, such a power "strikes at the heart of political accountability so essential to our liberty and republican form of government."

The ruling, Kennedy said in a final section, did not give states a right to disregard the Constitution or federal law. Many states had softened sovereign immunity on their own. In addition, Congress has the power under the Fourteenth Amendment to enact legislation protecting equal protection and due process rights against the states. Individual state officers could also be sued for violating federal law, and local governments enjoyed no immunity from suit at all. Subjecting states to private suits in their own courts without their consent, on the other hand, was simply "unnecessary to uphold the Constitution and valid federal statutes as the supreme law."

Kennedy's fifty-one-page opinion was joined by Rehnquist, O'Connor, Scalia, and Thomas. It was the same five-vote majority seen in the Court's last four pro–states' rights decisions, aligned against the same four dissenters: Stevens, Souter, Ginsburg, and Breyer.

Souter's fifty-eight-page dissent was densely laden in text and footnotes with history and legal theory, but his summary from the bench conveyed the force of the liberal justices' disagreement. Souter challenged Kennedy point by point. Sovereign immunity was not universal when the Constitution was ratified, it was not broadly confirmed by the Tenth Amendment or the Eleventh Amendment, and it was not—as Kennedy maintained—implicit in the structure of the Constitution itself.

"The State of Maine is not sovereign with respect to the national objective" of the federal labor law, Souter said. The Constitution's Supremacy Clause specifically requires state courts to enforce federal law. Blocking a suit against a state by a citizen "whose federal rights have been violated," Souter concluded, substitutes "politesse" toward the states "in place of respect for the law." Nor could the federal government be expected to enforce the rights of 4.7 million state employees nationwide. The idea, Souter said, was "pure whimsy."

Souter concluded by openly predicting the ruling would be short-lived, likening it to discredited Court decisions of the early twentieth century barring government regulation of business and industry. The immunity ruling, Souter said, "will prove the equal of its earlier experiment in laissez-faire, the one being as unrealistic as the other, as indefensible, and probably as fleeting."

Reaction. The ruling, along with the two other pro–states' rights decisions issued the same day, ignited the same kind of heated debate outside the courtroom as it did among the justices. "Supreme Mischief," the *New York Times* declared in a headline on an editorial. The *Wall Street Journal* described the rulings more approvingly: "The Federalism Revolution."

In Maine, probation officers were bitterly disappointed. "We know the state violated federal law," Ray Dzialo, a probation officer who was also president of the Maine State Employees Association, told the *Portland Press Herald.* "They clearly are using this to hide from their responsibilities."

But Deputy State Attorney General Paul Stern defended the ruling. "The states are very happy and relieved by this," Stern told the newspaper. "It ensures that Congress cannot create a laundry list of private actions against the state that could throw states into a fiscal crisis."

States

Rulings Bar Patent Claims, False Advertising Suits

College Savings Bank v. Florida Prepaid Postsecondary Education Expense Board, decided by a 5–4 vote, June 23, 1999; Scalia wrote the opinion; Breyer, Stevens, Souter, and Ginsburg dissented. *(See excerpts, pp. 283–296.)*

Florida Prepaid Postsecondary Education Expense Board v. College Savings Bank, decided by a 5–4 vote, June 23, 1999; Rehnquist wrote the opinion; Stevens, Souter, Ginsburg, and Breyer dissented. *(See excerpts, pp. 296–309.)*

A commercial dispute between a New Jersey bank and a Florida state agency that both marketed savings plans for college tuition costs became the vehicle for a pair of pro–states' rights decisions by the Supreme Court.

College Savings Bank claimed that the state agency, the Florida Prepaid Postsecondary Education Expense Board, infringed its patented methodology for calculating the cost of the product. The bank, based in Princeton, New Jersey, also charged the Florida agency with misleading advertising about its own savings plan. The bank sued, taking advantage of two federal laws passed in 1992 allowing for private suits against states for patent infringement and for trademark violations or false advertising.

Peter Roberts, president of College Savings Bank. The Supreme Court blocked the bank's efforts to sue a Florida state agency for patent infringement and false advertising.

The Florida agency countered with a motion to dismiss both suits on the ground that the laws violated the Eleventh Amendment's protection against federal court suits against states. In a pair of 5–4 decisions, the Supreme Court this term agreed. The ruling cheered states, but left businesses that compete with commercial activities of state governments with nowhere to turn but the state's own courts in the event of a legal dispute.

Background. Two largely unrelated trends converged to form the backdrop for College Savings Bank's suits against the Florida agency. First, states had engaged in an increasing number of commercial ventures in the second half of the twentieth century. In particular, state university systems became important players in intellectual property fields—acquiring valuable patents, copyrights, and trademarks through applications of scientific research. Meanwhile, the Supreme Court, with a conservative majority coalescing from the mid-1980s, was adopting stricter rules for Congress to follow before it could subject states to federal court suits for their business-like activities.

The Court in 1964 had held, in a case involving a state-owned railway, that states engaging in commercial activities "constructively waived" or gave up their immunity from private federal court suits under the Eleventh Amendment. The vote in the case, *Parden v. Terminal Railway of the Alabama State Docks Department*, was 5–4; the dissenting justices objected to the "constructive waiver" theory, but agreed that Congress could have passed a law specifically authorizing private suits against the state railroad.

Two decades later, the Court tightened the rules for Congress in a little noticed case, *Atascadero State Hospital v. Scanlon* (1985). The justices said that Congress could "abrogate" or override states' immunity from suit only by "unambiguously" providing for private enforcement actions. The Court applied the rule strictly in cases over the next few years. Meanwhile, lower federal courts, following the Court's lead, were ruling in some cases that states could not be sued in federal court for copyright, patent, or trademark violations.

Congress responded by passing laws specifically providing for private suits against states for copyright infringement in 1991 and then, in 1992, for patent infringement and for violations of the federal Lanham Act, which protects trademarks and also prohibits false or misleading advertising. The two 1992 laws—the Patent and Plant Variety Protection Remedy Clarification Act and the Trademark Remedy Clarification Act—were both enacted with little controversy and no organized opposition from state governments. Sponsors said the laws were needed to close enforcement gaps, but acknowledged there was no evidence of massive patent infringement or trademark violations by state governments.

The Case. Robert Green had no inkling of these legal issues when he founded College Savings Bank. At a time when college tuition costs were rising an average of nearly 9 percent per year, Green saw a need for families to have an assured way of saving for their children's higher education. His answer was the College Sure CD—a certificate of deposit aimed at providing a sufficient return to pay for college tuition costs years in the future. Green patented his method for pricing the CD and began marketing it in 1987.

States were coming up with similar plans for their own public universities. Michigan, in 1986, was the first state to establish an "educational trust" that allowed families to pay current prices for tuition into a state-run fund in exchange for a guarantee to cover future tuition costs, no matter how high. Florida followed suit in 1987, using a more cumbersome title for the board established to administer the fund. By the mid-1990s, more than twenty states had some form of prepaid tuition programs, and almost all the rest were considering such plans. Florida's plan was going well. By 1996 it had sold more than 375,000 tuition or dormitory contracts, and 18,000 students had used its benefits. And the plan had amassed a $184 million surplus.

Green viewed the states as unfair competitors. The bank sued Florida Prepaid in federal court in New Jersey in 1994, claiming that the state agency had copied parts of his patented methodology in operating its plan. A year later, the bank added a false advertising count. The new complaint charged the state agency gave misleading descriptions of its tuition plan—for example, by claiming that the fund's investments were backed by the "full faith and credit" of the federal government.

The two-part suit was pending when the Supreme Court issued in 1996 a major ruling, *Seminole Tribe of Florida v. Florida*. In a 5–4 decision, the Court held that Congress had no authority under its power over interstate commerce to permit private suits against states in federal court. Florida promptly cited the ruling as grounds for dismissing College Savings Bank's case. The bank responded by claiming that Congress had passed the patent and trademark remedy acts under its power to enforce the provisions of the Fourteenth Amendment. The trial judge ruled for Florida on both counts and dismissed the suit. The appeals of the patent and false advertising counts went to different courts.

The federal appeals court for the Third Circuit sided with the state, issuing a ruling in December 1997 that the revised trademark law was unconstitutional under *Seminole*. It also rejected the bank's argument that Florida had consented to the suit under the *Parden* constructive waiver theory. The court suggested that *Seminole* might have overruled the thirty-year-old case, but in any event said that education was a "core function" of state government rather than a commercial activity that could be subject to suit. Six months later, however, the U.S. Court of Appeals for the Federal Circuit, which has exclusive jurisdiction over patent cases, ruled for the bank on the patent issue. It held that Congress had power under the Fourteenth Amendment to protect property rights of private patent-holders against infringement by state governments.

The bank appealed the Third Circuit's ruling, and the state appealed the Federal Circuit's decision on the patent issue. In the meantime, the Court in June 1998 had issued one other decision that was to affect the outcome: *City of Boerne v. Flores*. In striking down a religious freedom law passed by Congress, the Court said that any legislation aimed at enforcing Fourteenth Amendment rights against the states must be "proportional" to the constitutional violation being targeted. Against the background of that additional pro–states' rights ruling, the Supreme Court agreed in January to hear both the bank's and Florida's appeals and scheduled the cases to be heard together in its final week of arguments for the term.

Arguments. The justices appeared divided along their established ideological lines when the two cases were argued on April 20. Conservative justices favored the states' claimed immunity from suits. "The government has no power to revoke the sovereign immunity of the states," Scalia declared. Liberal justices countered by saying that states should be subject to suit when they engage in commercial ventures. "It acts like a duck, treat it like a duck," Breyer said. "It acts like a business, treat it like a business."

In both cases, much of the argument centered on Congress's power to protect private rights under the Fourteenth Amendment. In the trademark dispute—the first of the cases argued—conservative justices voiced doubt that a business had a protectable property right to be free from a competitor's misleading advertising about its own product. "It certainly is not like any traditional property right," O'Connor said.

"It's not constitutionally permissible to parse property rights between those that are protectable under the Fourteenth Amendment and those that aren't," the bank's attorney, David Todd, responded. The bank's entire business was "threatened" by the Florida agency's false advertising, Todd added.

The Clinton administration disagreed with the bank's property right argument, but still said the claim should be allowed on the ground that Florida had consented to the suit by engaging in a commercial business. "The state has a free and voluntary choice," Solicitor General Waxman said. Rehnquist and other conservatives appeared skeptical.

The state's lawyer, William Mallin, a private attorney from Pittsburgh, played to the justices' doubts on both points. "There is nothing to suggest that Congress was addressing a due process problem with regard to advertising by the states," Mallin said. As for a "constructive waiver" to be sued, Mallin called outright for overruling *Parden*, the case that first recognized the theory.

In the patent case, Jonathan Glogau, an assistant state attorney general, followed a similar tack in questioning the basis for subjecting the state to a federal court suit. "The mere infringement of a patent is not a constitutional wrong," he said. In any event, Glogau said, the bank could have sued in state court for a "taking" of its property or for a business tort.

Liberal justices challenged Glogau by asking about the need for a uniform federal law to protect patents and other forms of intellectual property. "People need security that their intellectual property rights are not going to be infringed," Breyer said. But Glogau said states had to be free to provide legal remedies for any patent violations "unless and until those remedies are shown to be inadequate."

In his turn, the bank's attorney, Kevin Culligan, said it was up to Congress to decide what remedy was appropriate. Waxman agreed. Congress decided, he said, that there was a "unique" problem in protecting patents and that "whatever available remedies there were in the states were inadequate."

Decision. The rulings in the two cases—handed down on June 23, the last decision day of the term—gave the states bigger legal victories than anticipated even by pro–states' rights observers. The patent act was invalid, Rehnquist said, because Congress had identified no "pattern of constitutional violations" to justify invoking its Fourteenth Amendment powers. The trademark act's provision for false advertising suits against the states, Scalia said, was unconstitutional because the law did not protect the kind of property right covered by the Fourteenth Amendment. Finally, the Court overruled the 1964 *Parden* decision, thus freeing states from the threat of federal court suits whenever they engaged in commercial activities.

Announcing the decisions in reverse order of seniority, Scalia began with the trademark law. The bank said the law protected a right to be free from misleading advertising or a more general right to be "secure" in its business interests. "Neither of these qualifies as a property right protected by the Due Process Clause," Scalia said flatly. As for the "constructive waiver" theory, Scalia said that *Parden* was inconsistent with other cases requiring an "unequivocal" waiver of a state's sovereign immunity. After noting that the Court had already narrowed the 1964 ruling in several decisions, he declared: "Today, we drop the other shoe: Whatever may remain of our decision in *Parden* is expressly overruled."

In the second case, Rehnquist acknowledged that a patent was a property right covered by the Fourteenth Amendment. But, he continued, "the legislative record still provides little support for the proposition that

Congress sought to remedy a violation" in enacting the patent remedy law. Congress had "scant" evidence of patent infringements by the states. The law was also objectionable, Rehnquist said, because of its "indiscriminate scope." Congress had not tried to limit patent suits to states that refused to provide other legal remedies or to specific types of claims, such as "nonnegligent infringement or infringements authorized pursuant to state policy."

The Court's conservative bloc formed the majority in each case: Rehnquist, O'Connor, Scalia, Kennedy, and Thomas. The four more liberal justices dissented in each: Stevens, Souter, Ginsburg, and Breyer. In both cases, the dissenters declared that they were not ready to accept the limits on suits against states established by the *Seminole* decision in 1996 and thought the patent and trademark remedies were justified in any event under the Court's other precedents.

Speaking for the dissenters in the trademark case, Breyer began by defending the *Parden* decision. "When a state engages in commercial activity, sovereign immunity has no significant role to play," he said. As for *Seminole*, he said the ruling's limit on Congress's power to override the states' immunity "threatens the Nation's ability to enact economic legislation needed for the future." Stevens added a separate dissent, briefly questioning whether the Florida board was correctly treated as an arm of the state government in the first place.

Stevens spoke for all four dissenters in the patent case, emphasizing the need for uniformity in patent law as well as Congress's prerogatives to enact "prophylactic" legislation to deter patent infringements by the states. The law was justified, Stevens said, because of evidence before Congress that state remedies for patent violations "would likely be insufficient to compensate inventors whose patents had been infringed" and that infringements by the states were "likely to increase." And he too closed by attacking the *Seminole* decision, calling it "a dramatic expansion of the judge-made doctrine of sovereign immunity" and promising to continue to dissent from its use in future cases.

Reaction. States' rights advocates could hardly have expected more from the Court's rulings in the two cases along with the decision the same day in a third case, *Alden v. Maine*, barring Congress from authorizing suits in state court to enforce federal law. *(See pp. 33–39.)* "I jumped up and down for joy," Glogau, the Florida state's attorney, recalled a few weeks later. More seriously, he said the rulings "vindicated our position that there was no constitutional problem out there that Congress needed to remedy."

Todd, the bank's attorney, called the rulings "most disappointing." "Obviously, the bank feels that having to compete in a situation where you can't get someone into court is an enormous injustice." As of mid-summer, he said the bank had no plans to pursue any legal remedies against the state in Florida courts.

Glogau, however, repeated that the bank did have legal options in Florida courts: a so-called inverse condemnation case for the "taking" of the patent or a business tort suit. "He may not like the remedy he's got, but that's too bad," Glogau said. "That's one of the inherent difficulties of a dual sovereignty system of government. In the rare situations where the states are accused of infringing on a patent, you're going to have to forgo your federal infringement action and pursue a remedy in state court."

Disability Rights

Job Protections Limited for "Correctable" Impairments

Sutton v. United Air Lines, Inc., decided by a 7–2 vote, June 22, 1999; O'Connor wrote the opinion; Stevens and Breyer dissented. *(See excerpts, pp. 242-254.)*

Twin sisters Karen Sutton and Kimberly Hinton long had the ambition to become pilots for a major commercial airline. They had both flown for regional carriers and were certified by the Federal Aviation Administration. They met airlines' basic requirements for age, education, and experience.

When they got interviews with United Air Lines in 1992, however, the company turned them down. The reason: Sutton and Hinton were both nearsighted. Even though they had 20/20 vision with contact lenses, United said they did not meet the company's standard qualification for pilots: 20/100 or better uncorrected vision in both eyes.

Sutton and Hinton went to court. They contended that the company had discriminated against them on the basis of a disability in violation of the federal Americans with Disabilities Act or ADA. Two lower federal courts rejected their claim, and this term the Supreme Court followed suit. Employers said the decision fulfilled Congress's intent and established a common sense guide for businesses to follow in interpreting the law. But disability rights advocates said the ruling was a setback that had the perverse effect of penalizing people for taking steps to correct or control physical impairments.

Background. Congress passed the ADA in 1990. The act prohibited discrimination on the basis of disability in employment, public services, and public accommodations. The goal of opening up employment opportunities for people with physical or mental disabilities seemed deceptively simple. But the law was actually quite complex, filled with ambiguous terms that invited litigation and defied easy answers from the courts.

The threshold question of who was disabled for purposes of invoking the law's protections became one of the major issues. The law gave a three-prong definition of disability: "a physical or mental impairment that substantially limits one or more of the major life activities of such individual," "a record of such an impairment," or "being regarded as having such an impairment." Wheelchair-users obviously fit the definition. But many of the more than 100,000 claims filed with the Equal Employment Opportunity Commission between 1992 and 1998 came from people with less obvious handicaps: back problems, emotional conditions, neurological disorders, and so forth. A relatively small number—about 2.5 percent of the total—came from people with vision problems.

Employers believed that the law was, as management attorney Peter Petesch put it, "beginning to run amok" and hampering their ability to set physical qualifications for jobs. Disability rights advocates, however, noted that employers won more than 90 percent of the complaints that went to court. They argued that in many instances employers were setting physical standards beyond those really needed to perform specific jobs.

The Case. With their experience as pilots for regional carriers, Sutton and Hinton had no doubt about their qualifications for a pilot's job at United. The Denver-based airline, however, said its uncorrected vision standard was essential for safety—a precaution, for example, against the possibility of losing or misplacing glasses or contact lenses during flight.

In their federal court suit, Sutton and Hinton contended that they were disabled under the ADA because their uncorrected vision "substantially limited" such normal daily activities as shopping, driving, or watching television. But they also contended that with corrective lenses they were "qualified" for the job—and therefore that United's refusal to hire them amounted to discrimination on the basis of their disability. The airline countered that the women were not disabled because, with corrective lenses, they were not limited at all in their daily activities. That argument conflicted with an EEOC regulation that called for a person's disability to be determined without regard to any corrective or mitigating measures. The airline argued that the agency had misinterpreted the law.

A federal judge in Denver dismissed the suit, and in December 1997 the appeals court for the Tenth Circuit agreed. The three-judge panel agreed with the airline that the EEOC regulation was "in direct conflict" with the ADA. The issue, the court said, was "whether the impairment affects the individual in fact, not whether it would hypothetically affect the individual without the use of corrective measures." On that basis, the court agreed that Sutton and Hinton were not disabled and ordered their claim dismissed.

Sutton and Hinton asked the Supreme Court to review the decision, pointing out that most other federal appeals courts had agreed with the EEOC that disability claims should be considered without regard to corrective measures. The justices in January 1999 agreed to review their case, along with two other cases with similar issues. In *Murphy v. United Parcel Service, Inc.*, the Tenth Circuit had followed its ruling in *Sutton* and barred a disability discrimination claim by a Kansas truck driver, Vaughn Murphy, who was fired because of high blood pressure even though he controlled the condition with medication. In the other case, *Albertsons, Inc. v. Kirkingburg*, the Ninth Circuit had reinstated a discrimination claim by an Oregon truck driver who was fired because he had monocular vision— in effect, was blind in one eye; the driver, Hallie Kirkingburg, compensated for the deficiency and had an impeccable safety record driving for a large grocery chain. All three cases were scheduled for argument in late April, during the final two days of argument for the term.

Arguments. Justices across the ideological spectrum appeared skeptical of the broad definition of disability advanced by lawyers for the plaintiffs in the three cases. Murphy's case was argued first, on April 27, and O'Connor and Scalia challenged the arguments from the truck driver's attorney from the start of his allotted half hour. The next day, April 28, the lawyer for Sutton and Hinton, Van Aaron Hughes, got the same treatment.

Scalia began by noting that the law's preamble put the number of people with disabilities at 43 million. "There are more than that many people who wear glasses," he declared. Souter followed by personalizing the issue. "I have difficulty reading restaurant checks in dim light," he said. "That's clearly a limitation, but not a substantial one," Hughes responded. "Why not?" Souter quipped. "The waiter thinks so."

For his part, Kennedy questioned how a broad definition of disability fit with Congress's declared goal in the law of protecting a "discrete and insular minority" from social prejudice. "That whole concept seems to drop out under your reading of the statute," he said.

Hughes clung to his position. "The inability to perform a major substantial life activity without correction is itself a disability," he said. Both he and Edwin Kneedler, a deputy solicitor general supporting the broad reading of the law, left the justices unsatisfied about how to avoid making it overly broad. Souter confessed at one point that he was "at sea" on how to interpret the law.

In his turn, the airline's attorney, Roy Englert, argued the law was intended to cover "a very specific class" of people. "This statute is absolutely not designed to require every employer to ignore every physical qualification," he said. He noted that the Navy required a stricter standard for its pilots—20/30 uncorrected vision—than United did.

Roy Englert, winning attorney for employer in disability rights case

Breyer, however, appeared dissatisfied. Englert's argument, he suggested, would allow employers to circumvent the law by saying, "That person is just not good enough to work here, but good enough to work somewhere else."

Arguments in the third case—the Oregon truck driver, Kirkingburg, with monocular vision—ran a parallel course, complicated by an experimental Transportation Department program that lowered the vision standard for federally certified drivers. Again, the opposing lawyers clashed on whether the grocery chain had a justified concern for safety in setting job qualifications. But Edwin Dumont, an assistant solicitor general supporting the driver's case, contended the company was adopting a "fundamentally illogical" position by insisting that Kirkingburg was not disabled but refusing to employ him as a driver because he could not see well enough to drive. Scalia was unmoved: "I don't see that as inconsistent at all."

Decision. The Court rejected Sutton's and Hinton's disability claims along with Murphy's by 7–2 votes in parallel decisions on June 22. "Congress did not intend to bring under the statute's protections all those whose uncorrected conditions amount to disabilities," O'Connor wrote for the majority in *Sutton*. She then dispensed with Murphy's case in a shorter opinion relying on the earlier decision. The dissenting justices—Stevens and Breyer—complained that the majority had given the law a "miserly" construction that would leave employers free to use "irrational stereotypes" to exclude many people with physical impairments from the workplace.

O'Connor cited three reasons for concluding that the ADA did not include uncorrected physical impairments within the definition of disability. First, the law defined a disability as an impairment that "substantially limits" a major life activity "presently—not potentially or hypothetically," she said.

Second, the law required an "individualized" assessment of potential disabilities, but considering a physical impairment in its uncorrected state would require use of "general information" about its effects. Finally— "and critically"—O'Connor pointed to the 43 million figure in the statute. That number, she said, "reflects an understanding that those whose impairments are largely corrected by medication or other devices are not 'disabled' within the meaning of the ADA."

Nor could Sutton and Hinton sustain a claim that they had been "regarded as" disabled when United refused to hire them, O'Connor said. Because global airline pilot is only "a single job," O'Connor said, the allegation was insufficient to show that United regarded them as disabled. "Indeed, there are a number of other positions utilizing petitioners' skills, such as regional pilot and pilot instructor to name a few, that are available to them," O'Connor wrote.

Six justices—Rehnquist, Scalia, Kennedy, Souter, Thomas, and Ginsburg—joined O'Connor's opinion. Ginsburg wrote a brief concurrence. Congress intended, she said, "to restrict the ADA's coverage to a confined, and historically disadvantaged, class."

Stevens challenged O'Connor's reading of the statute point by point. The three-part definition, he said, was intended to cover any individuals "who now have, or ever had, a substantially limiting impairment." The majority's definition, he said, would leave out many people that Congress clearly intended to protect: people with artificial limbs, for example, or diabetics. As for employers' right to set job qualifications, Stevens said it was "eminently within the purpose" of the ADA to require businesses to explain, for example, why 20/100 uncorrected vision was a valid requirement for a specific position. Breyer joined Stevens's opinion and added a brief dissent of his own.

In the third case —actually announced first, by Souter, in reverse order of seniority—the Court also rejected Kirkingburg's disability claim. The ruling gave businesses one more bit of legal leeway: Employers were free to rely on federally established job qualification standards—like the Transportation Department's vision standard for truck drivers—without justifying them in each individual case brought under the disability law. The vote on that legal principle was unanimous; Stevens and Breyer refused to join the rest of Souter's opinion, which cited *Sutton* in judging Kirkingburg's disability claim on the basis of his corrected rather than uncorrected vision.

Reaction. Business groups had high praise for the Court's rulings, while disability rights advocates voiced alarm. The ruling had no immediate effect on Sutton and Hinton: Sutton was flying for a regional airline, and Hinton had taken time out of her career to raise a family. But their lawyer, Hughes, said he was worried about the ruling's long-term impact. "I am concerned about whether the act, as the Court has interpreted it, can perform the functions that Congress intended to perform," he said.

But Englert, United's attorney, dismissed what he called the predictions of "cataclysm" from the disability rights community. "The justices were sensitive to the need to protect the people that Congress intended to protect, and they wrote the opinion with that sensitivity in mind," he said. "The predictions that people with prostheses won't be considered disabled are quite overblown."

Disability Rights

"Unnecessary Segregation" of Mentally Ill Curbed

Olmstead, Commissioner, Georgia Department of Human Resources v. L. C., decided by a 6–3 vote, June 22, 1999; Ginsburg wrote the main opinion; Thomas, Rehnquist, and Scalia dissented. *(See excerpts, pp. 230-242.)*

Lois Curtis spent most of her life after age fourteen in and out of mental hospitals in her home state of Georgia. Elaine Wilson was admitted to one of the state's mental hospitals more than thirty times for treatment over a long period of homelessness. Both women were diagnosed as mildly retarded; Curtis also suffered from schizophrenia, and Wilson from what doctors termed a "personality disorder."

Doctors for both women, however, said they could live in a community-based facility such as a group home rather than in a mental hospital. But the state's mental health department turned down Curtis's and

Lois Curtis

Wilson's requests for a community placement, alternately saying that the women's problems still required hospitalization or that the community facilities were all full.

Curtis and Wilson turned to the courts for help. They claimed that the federal Americans with Disabilities Act (ADA) required states to place people with mental illnesses in "the least restrictive" appropriate facility. And this term the Supreme Court, at least in part, agreed. Unnecessary institutionalization may constitute discrimination under the disability rights law, the Court held in a significant victory for mental health advocacy groups. But the Court also said that states can take budget limitations into account in equitably providing treatment for people with mental disabilities.

Background. Mental hospitals were viewed as a progressive reform when they were first established in the United States in the mid-nineteenth century. By the mid-twentieth century, however, mental hospitals were widely viewed as warehouses where people with mental disabilities were confined in often wretched conditions and given little to nothing by way of treatment or habilitation.

Congress cited the unnecessary "institutionalization" of people with mental illnesses as one form of discrimination when it passed the Americans with Disabilities Act in 1990. The law became best known for provisions that barred employers and public accommodations from discriminating against employees or customers because of mental or physical disabilities. A lesser-known provision—Title II—applied to public services. It provided that "no qualified individual" could be "excluded from participation" or "denied the benefits" of a public program, service, or activity, or "be subjected to discrimination," on account of a disability.

Many states had already begun shifting people with mental illnesses out of hospitals and into community-based facilities. By 1999 only 68,000 people were in state mental institutions nationwide—compared to more than 500,000 during the 1950s. Mental health advocates generally applauded the trend, which they said provided better care often at less expense. Some officials and advocates, however, worried that too many people with mental illness were being moved, not into community treatment facilities, but into the streets, where they contributed to a growing homelessness problem.

Georgia lagged in the move toward deinstitutionalization, according to mental health advocates. State officials disputed the accusation, but they also contended that community facilities added to the necessary expense of maintaining hospitals for

Elaine Wilson

people who needed institutionalization. With a limited mental health budget, the state insisted, some people who could live in community-based settings simply had to wait until slots opened up.

The Case. Curtis had been admitted to Georgia Regional Hospital in Atlanta, one of the state's seven mental institutions, on an emergency basis in May 1992 after she threatened a community job supervisor with a knife. She claimed that her condition had stabilized within a year, but that the state made no efforts over a three-year period to find her another community placement. In May 1995 she filed suit in federal court in Atlanta, claiming that the state's failure to place her in a community-based residential program violated Title II of the ADA and implementing regulations issued by the Justice Department. Wilson intervened in the suit in 1996, after having been kept in a locked ward at the hospital for more than a year.

At trial, state officials said they had no funds to provide a community placement for Curtis and Wilson. Judge Marvin Shoob rejected the defense. The state had programs to provide community-based services that actually cost less than hospitalization, the judge said in his March 1997 ruling. In any event, Shoob said, "unnecessary segregation" of peo-

ple with mental disabilities amounted to per se discrimination according
to the disability rights law, whatever the cost. Shoob issued a preliminary
injunction requiring community placement for Curtis—who in fact had
been placed in a group home while the case proceeded—and for Wilson.

On appeal, the Eleventh U.S. Circuit Court of Appeals was more
receptive to the state's defense. The appeals court said that the ADA
required states to provide community treatment if recommended by an
individual's doctors *unless* such a placement would require "a fundamental alteration" in the state's treatment program—using a phrase from the
Justice Department regulations. To consider that issue, the appeals court
sent the case back to Judge Shoob to decide whether community placement would cost more and, if so, whether the additional cost was "unreasonable" in light of the state's mental health budget. The appeals court
ruling left the preliminary injunction in place, however. So the state
appealed to the Supreme Court, which agreed in November 1998 to hear
the case.

Arguments. The justices appeared both divided and uncertain during the
hour-long arguments of the case on April 21. Liberal justices appeared
receptive to arguments that the ADA required community-based treatment for people who could live outside a mental hospital. "If there's no
justification for the disparate treatment," Stevens asked, "why doesn't the
statute apply?"

Conservative justices, on the other hand, indicated sympathy with
Georgia's position that states should be largely free to decide what services to provide, and where to provide them. "This is not isolation and segregation," Scalia said. "This is the state offering services and saying,
'These are the services we have.'"

Arguing the state's position, Patricia Downing, a senior assistant state
attorney general, insisted that hospitalization could not amount to discrimination under the law. "The mere fact that a person could be treated
would not make hospital treatment discriminatory," she told the justices.
But Michael Gottesman, a professor at Georgetown University law school
representing Curtis and Wilson, disagreed. Once a state decides to provide services for people with mental illnesses, Gottesman said, "you have
to provide them in the most integrated environment possible."

Significantly, several justices voiced concerns about injecting the courts
into the process of determining appropriate treatment for people with
mental disabilities. And Breyer pointedly raised the fear that a decision
requiring community treatment could backfire. "I would like reassur-

ance," Breyer said, that "people won't be pushed out" of hospitals and onto the streets. "That's the real world," he said.

Decision. The Court's decision June 22 took a tentative approach. "Unjustified isolation" of people with mental illnesses "is properly regarded as discrimination based on disability," Ginsburg wrote for a narrow five-justice majority. But, she continued, states also must maintain "a range of facilities" for people "with diverse mental disabilities" and administer services "with an even hand." On that basis, she said, courts considering a state's "fundamental alteration" defense must consider "not only the cost of providing community-based care to the litigants, but also the range of services the State provides others with mental disabilities, and the State's obligation to mete out those services equitably."

Since the appeals court had adopted an "unduly restrictive" standard, the case had to be sent back for reevaluation, Ginsburg said. Four justices—Stevens, O'Connor, Souter, and Breyer—joined most of Ginsburg's opinion. In a final section, Ginsburg made the state's "leeway" more explicit. A state could satisfy the ADA's "reasonable modifications" requirement by showing that it had "a comprehensive, effective working plan for placing qualified persons with mental disabilities in less restrictive settings" and "a waiting list that moved at a reasonable pace." Stevens separated himself from that section. Instead, in a brief opinion, he said he would have simply affirmed the appeals court's decision, but joined the bulk of Ginsburg's opinion in order to create a majority decision.

Kennedy provided a sixth vote for sending the case back for further proceedings, but his concurring opinion read like a partial dissent. He agreed that unnecessary segregation could amount to a violation of the ADA, but set a stricter standard than Ginsburg's and voiced doubts that Curtis's and Wilson's complaint had made a case. And in an opening passage he worried that states might be "pressured" into "placing marginal patients" into community settings without needed services and attention. Breyer joined that part of the opinion, but not the rest.

In a twelve-page dissent, Thomas, joined by Rehnquist and Scalia, challenged the basic premise that unnecessary segregation could amount to discrimination under the ADA. The ruling, Thomas said, "creates a new species of discrimination" by looking at an individual "in isolation" rather than "comparing him to otherwise similarly situated persons." The ruling also infringed on principles of federalism, he said, by inviting courts to impose "a standard of care" despite the states' "historical role as the dominant authority in providing services to individuals with disabilities."

And it ignored fiscal realities. Continuing institutional treatment while waiting for community placement slots to open, Thomas said, does not establish discrimination. "Rather," he concluded, "it establishes no more than the fact that [states] have limited resources."

Reaction. Mental health advocates were enthusiastic about the ruling. "This is one big win for people with disabilities," Curt Decker, executive director of the National Association of Protection and Advocacy Systems, told reporters. The reaction from state officials was muted. Most states were ostensibly committed to deinstitutionalization in any event.

In Georgia, Sue Jamieson, the Atlanta legal aid attorney who had started the suit, called the ruling "a tremendous victory." But lawyers working on the case also acknowledged the Court left the state with some discretion in complying with the ruling. Indeed, Tommy Olmstead, the human resources commissioner named as defendant in the suit, called the ruling "very positive." "The Court gave the state flexibility to administer services with an even hand," he said.

Wilson said the decision made her feel "real good." "The hospital life can be bad," she told the Associated Press in an interview from a community center in Jonesboro, Georgia. "So in the long run, I hope this helps a lot of other handicapped people get placement in the real world."

Sexual Harassment

Schools Can Be Liable for Students' Misconduct

Davis v. Monroe County Board of Education, decided by a 5–4 vote, May 24, 1999; O'Connor wrote the opinion; Kennedy, Rehnquist, Scalia, and Thomas dissented. *(See excerpts, pp. 197–214.)*

LaShonda Davis was only ten years old when she suffered through five months of crude sexual taunts and advances in the 1992–1993 school year. Her tormentor, a fellow fifth-grader at Hubbard Elementary School in Forsyth, Georgia, repeatedly tried to fondle her. He told her he wanted to get in bed with her. Once, he suggestively put a doorstop in his pants to act out his intentions toward her.

Both LaShonda and her mother, Aurelia Davis, complained about the behavior to teachers and to the principal, but nothing seemed to happen. Only after Mrs. Davis complained to the local sheriff did she get the help

she wanted. The boy—identified
only as G. F.—was charged with sexual battery and pleaded guilty to the
charge.

Still frustrated with the school's
inaction, Mrs. Davis filed a federal
court suit the next year seeking damages from the Monroe County
Board of Education and from the
school superintendent and school
principal. In one count of the complaint, she charged the school board
with violating a federal law—known
as Title IX—that prohibited sexual
discrimination by any school that
receives federal funds. The school
board responded by contending that
it could not be liable for "student-
on-student" sexual harassment.

**Aurelia Davis, mother of LaShonda
Davis, with media**

In a closely divided decision, the
federal appeals court in Atlanta
agreed and dismissed Davis's Title IX suit. But this term the Supreme
Court reinstated the suit. By a 5–4 vote, the Court held that schools can
be held liable for one student's sexual harassment of another—but only if
the behavior is serious and school officials know of the behavior and are
"deliberately indifferent" to complaints about it.

Background. The term *sexual harassment* was not coined until the 1970s, but
over succeeding decades it became common parlance in workplaces, in
schools, and in the courts. Feminist groups, supported by civil rights and
civil liberties organizations, spearheaded the effort to protect women from
unwelcome sexual behavior ranging from coercive propositions and come-
ons to crude banter and "locker-room" jokes. By the 1990s, most employers as well as most schools, colleges, and universities had some sort of policy aimed at preventing sexual harassment.

The Supreme Court played an important part in the development. In
1986 the Court first ruled that "severe or pervasive" sexual harassment in
the workplace could amount to sex discrimination under the federal job
bias law, Title VII of the Civil Rights Act of 1964. Six years later, the
Court held that sexual harassment was also covered by a later law, Title IX

of the Education Amendments of 1972. That law provided that no one could be "excluded from participation in," "denied the benefits of," or "subjected to discrimination" on the basis of sex in "any education program or activity receiving Federal financial assistance." Ruling unanimously in *Franklin v. Gwinnett County Public Schools*, the Court in 1992 held that the law contained an "implied right of action" for victims of sexual harassment to recover money damages from school systems.

The ruling spurred complaints and lawsuits dealing with sexual misconduct not only by teachers, but also by students. The effort to define correct behavior between boys and girls proved to be controversial—as when a first-grade boy in North Carolina was suspended in 1996 for kissing a classmate on the cheek. Meanwhile, the Court in 1998 moved to limit school systems' exposure to damage awards in sexual harassment suits involving teachers. In a 5–4 decision, *Gebser v. Lago Vista Independent School District*, the Court held that school boards could be forced to pay damages for misconduct by teachers only if ranking officials knew of the behavior and failed to take steps to prevent it.

The Case. LaShonda's lawsuit, filed in federal court in Atlanta in May 1994, painted a vivid picture of the misconduct by her classmate and its effect on her. LaShonda and her mother reported G. F.'s advances to her teacher shortly after they began, in December 1992. Over the next five months, LaShonda grew more and more desperate. By May 1993, she told her mother she "didn't know how much longer she could keep [G. F.] off her." Her grades suffered; at one point she wrote a suicide note.

The complaint also painted a vivid picture of seeming indifference on the school's part. LaShonda's teacher assured her mother that the principal had been informed of the problem, but turned aside her request to meet with him. The teacher also denied LaShonda's request to move to another desk away from G. F. When Davis finally met with the principal, he allegedly told her that he would "have to threaten" G. F. "a little harder," but also asked why LaShonda was the only girl complaining.

Without answering the allegations, the school board moved to dismiss the complaint on the ground that schools were not responsible for student-on-student sexual harassment. Judge Wilbur Owens agreed. He ruled that G. F.'s behavior was "not part of an education program or activity" for purposes of Title IX. A three-judge panel of the Eleventh U.S. Circuit Court of Appeals, ruling two years later, disagreed and reinstated Davis's suit. But the full court decided to rehear the case and, in August 1997, voted 6–5 to dismiss the complaint. In reaching that conclusion, the appeals court majority said that Title IX had given school systems no notice that they might be liable for preventing one student from sexually harassing another.

Other federal appeals courts had recognized such suits. Davis's lawyers, backed by the Clinton administration and civil rights groups, urged the Court to hear the case to resolve the issue. The justices agreed, accepting the case for review at the opening of the 1998–1999 term.

Arguments. A majority of the justices appeared decidedly skeptical of Davis's suit when the case was argued on January 12. "Little boys tease little girls," O'Connor said at the start of the hour-long session. "Is every one of those incidents going to lead to a lawsuit?" In similar vein, Scalia asked, "Why does [a school district] have an obligation to act when little kids tease each other?"

Verna Williams, an attorney with the National Women's Law Center in Washington representing Davis, insisted, however, that Title IX required school districts to take some steps to prevent sexual harassment between students. If the school district knows about the behavior, Williams said, "it must take reasonable steps to address and remedy." But Williams sought to allay the justices' concerns about a cascade of lawsuits. "We don't think every teasing would be sexual harassment," she said.

The concession hardly slowed the critical questions. Kennedy pressed both Williams and the Clinton administration's lawyer, Deputy Solicitor General Barbara Underwood, about the danger of federal judicial oversight of school discipline issues. Allowing such suits, Kennedy said, would result in "a federal code of conduct for every classroom in the country."

Liberal justices—expected to be more receptive to Davis's arguments—were muted during the argument. Souter and Breyer echoed the conservative justices' concerns about bringing classroom issues into the courts. Only Stevens and Ginsburg seemed strongly inclined to rule in Davis's favor.

For his part, the school board's attorney, Warren Plowden, played to the justices' fears. "The potential for litigation here is enormous," he said. Stevens raised a hypothetical question: Could school officials be held responsible for sitting by while boys repeatedly prevented girls from using the school's athletic field? Plowden, sticking to his position, said no.

Decision. The Court's decision May 24 defied the tone of the arguments. O'Connor, speaking for a five-justice majority, said school districts could be held liable for sexual harassment between students. She spent much of her twenty-three page opinion, however, setting strict standards for such suits. Even so, the ruling provoked a bitter dissent—written by Kennedy—that warned the decision would result in "an avalanche of litigation" and make federal courts "the final arbiters of school policy."

O'Connor began by acknowledging that a school board could be held liable under Title IX only for its own misconduct. But Davis's suit, she continued, was aimed at the school's "*own* decision to remain idle in the face of known student-on-student harassment." Echoing her own opinion for the Court a year earlier in the teacher harassment case, *Gebser*, O'Connor said that "deliberate indifference to known acts of harassment" by a student as well as a teacher could amount to a violation of Title IX "in certain limited circumstances." She added, however, that the behavior must be "so severe, pervasive, and objectively offensive that it can be said to deprive the victims of access to the educational opportunities or benefits of the school." As one example, O'Connor invoked Stevens's hypothetical: denying girls physical access to an athletic field or computer lab.

Throughout, O'Connor tried to soften the impact of the decision. "Damages are not available for simple acts of teasing and name-calling," she wrote. School administrators could be held responsible only for a "clearly unreasonable" response—or lack of response—to student harassment. Courts could throw out suits without trial if plaintiffs failed to make their case. Davis's allegations, however, met that test; so the case was sent back for trial. Stevens, Souter, Ginsburg, and Breyer concurred in the opinion.

Kennedy's dissent was longer by half than O'Connor's opinion, and he emphasized his disagreement by reading major portions from the bench. Title IX gave school districts no warning that they might be liable for students' misbehavior. The majority's "fence" to limit the "staggering" number of potential lawsuits was "made of little sticks." Most importantly, he wrote, the ruling "clears the way for the federal government to claim center stage in America's classrooms." Rehnquist, Scalia, and Thomas joined his opinion.

The courtroom presentation featured an unusual exchange between O'Connor and Kennedy, centrists who occupied adjacent seats on the bench. Kennedy concluded his dissent by saying the ruling would "teach little Johnny a perverse lesson in Federalism." O'Connor anticipated the point in her earlier summary of the decision. The ruling, she said, "assures that little Mary may attend class."

Reaction. Nationally, civil rights and women's rights advocates generally praised the ruling, although some trial lawyers said the ruling set a difficult standard for plaintiffs to meet. Lawyers for the National Association of School Boards also predicted the ruling would not lead to a rash of verdicts against local schools. "We can live with it," said Lisa Brown, a Houston lawyer who wrote a brief for the organization.

In Georgia, Warren Plowden, the lawyer who represented the Monroe County School Board before the Court, predicted in similar vein that Davis was unlikely to prevail in the eventual trial. "It's going to be tough for any plaintiff to win any of these cases," he told the *Washington Post*.

Davis herself acknowledged that she and her daughter had only won one round in the legal battle. "We've still got to get with our lawyers to figure out where we go from here," she told the Associated Press. Still, Davis took pride in the ruling. "That's what makes me proud, is that we were able to make a difference," she said.

Criminal Law

Chicago's Anti-Gang Loitering Ordinance Struck Down

City of Chicago v. Morales, decided by a 6–3 vote, June 10, 1999; Stevens wrote the main opinion; O'Connor, Kennedy, and Breyer wrote concurring opinions; Thomas, Rehnquist, and Scalia dissented. *(See excerpts, pp. 214-230.)*

A parade of witnesses came before the Chicago City Council in 1992 to complain about the terrorizing effects that criminal gangs were having in their neighborhoods. The witnesses, many of them elderly African American women, said the gangs created a pervasive sense of fear, menacingly eyeing law-abiding citizens as they went about their daily activities on the city's streets.

Chicago lawmakers responded by enacting a novel ordinance aimed at getting the gangs off the streets. The ordinance gave police the power to order anyone found "loitering" on the streets with supposed gang members to disperse. Anyone who refused could be arrested. Over the next three years, police made more than 40,000 arrests under the law.

Criminal defense lawyers and civil liberties groups argued the law violated the federal and Illinois constitutions by letting police order people off the streets with no evidence that they were doing anything wrong. Illinois courts agreed and blocked enforcement of the law. This term the Supreme Court also found the law unconstitutional. The dissenting justices said the 6–3 ruling eliminated a powerful weapon for policing Chicago's gang-infested neighborhoods. But civil liberties advocates said the ordinance proved to have little effect in reducing crime and the city could now focus its efforts on more productive law enforcement tactics.

Luis Guiterrez was not a gang member, but he was one of thousands of Chicago youths arrested under an anti-loitering law aimed at youth gangs. The Supreme Court this term ruled the local ordinance unconstitutional.

Background. Laws against loitering and vagrancy had been on the books in America since colonial times and went largely unchallenged before the 1960s. The civil rights revolution and the Supreme Court's rulings guaranteeing legal representation for the poor in criminal cases combined, however, to encourage challenges to many such local ordinances. In several cases the Court found loitering laws unconstitutional—most notably in a 1972 decision, *Papachristou v. City of Jacksonville*. In that ruling, the Court voided a broadly worded Jacksonville, Florida, ordinance as unconstitutionally vague.

In the same year, however, the Court, in a Kentucky case, had upheld a criminal conviction under a state disorderly conduct statute for refusing to obey a police officer's order to move on. Even though the facts were different—the defendant had been arrested while police were investigating a traffic violation—lawyers from the Chicago corporation counsel's office and from other state and local government groups hoped the decision would give the Court some precedent for upholding the Chicago ordinance.

In addition, they thought the conservative Court of the 1990s was likely to give a more favorable reception to the ordinance than the Court had given to the Jacksonville measure a quarter-century earlier, especially given the heightened concern in big cities across the nation about street gangs. The Justice Department in 1993 estimated there were more than 16,000 youth gangs with more than half a million members around the country.

The lawyers from the Illinois chapter of the American Civil Liberties Union who challenged the ordinance, however, felt confident that the Court would find the measure constitutionally defective. They pointed to two aspects of the law in particular. First, the law defined "loitering" to mean being on the public streets "with no apparent purpose." Second, the law allowed police to issue a dispersal order to anyone found in the presence of someone "reasonably suspected" of being a gang member. Both provisions, the ACLU attorneys contended, gave police too much leeway in enforcing the law and gave law-abiding citizens too little notice about exactly what conduct the ordinance was making illegal.

The Case. People arrested under the ordinance—virtually all of them black or Hispanic—began challenging the measure as their cases came to court. Trial judges in some cases held the laws unconstitutional, but others upheld the ordinance. Two sets of appeals—one case handled by the Illinois ACLU, the other by the state public defender's office in Chicago—reached the state's intermediate-level appellate court in 1995. The appeals court agreed the measure was unconstitutional and issued a preliminary injunction barring the city from enforcing it.

As the legal challenge moved toward the Illinois Supreme Court, supporters and opponents of the ordinance also debated its effect on crime in the city. City officials said major gang-related crimes such as drive-by shootings and homicides all decreased dramatically in 1995, while gang-related homicides went up again in 1996—the year after enforcement of the ordinance was blocked. Harvey Grossman, the state ACLU's legal director, countered that gang-related homicides were falling again in 1997. In any event, he said the statistics paralleled broad national trends on crime and had little to do with the antiloitering ordinance.

The state high court issued its ruling in November 1997. Unanimously, the justices held the law unconstitutional. The court agreed with the ACLU's two major points that the law gave "absolute discretion" to police to determine what constituted loitering and "complete discretion" to determine whether someone was a gang member.

The city, backed by the Clinton administration, anticrime groups, and state and local government organizations, asked the U.S. Supreme Court to review the decision. After the justices agreed, the ACLU lawyers picked up support from civil rights groups, including the NAACP and the Mexican American Legal Defense and Educational Fund, as well as the National Association of Criminal Defense Lawyers.

Arguments. Chicago's ordinance got a decidedly skeptical reception from justices from the center of the court's ideological spectrum to the left during oral arguments on December 9. "How does a person who is not a gang member know that he is doing something wrong?" Kennedy asked. Souter said the law allowed police to decide who could use public streets. "Some people like to walk or sit or stand and watch the cars go by," he said. "This ordinance is making a silent assumption that some purposes are worthy, and some are not."

Defending the ordinance, the city's deputy corporation counsel Lawrence Rosenthal tried to stress the gangs' menacing effects on law-abiding citizens. But justices constantly returned to the issue of arbitrary enforcement. O'Connor asked whether the ordinance could be tightened by permitting police to order someone to disperse only if he was doing something "illicit." Rosenthal demurred. "One should not underestimate the difficulty of enforcing an ordinance like that," he said.

In his turn, Grossman argued the law "requires police officers to engage in a surreal exercise" of determining a person's purpose for being on public streets. Scalia interrupted to compare the ordinance to drunken-driver roadblocks. "Is the constitutional right to move any greater than the constitutional right to stand still?" he asked. Later, Rehnquist challenged him on the vagueness issue. "There's nothing vague about a person telling a person to move on," he said.

Rosenthal got the last word, using four minutes of rebuttal to return to the theme of public safety. "Law-abiding citizens are afraid to use these public places," he said. "The Constitution," he said in closing, "does not protect the right to stand next to a gang member."

Decision. The Court's 6–3 decision June 10 to invalidate the ordinance was less decisive than the vote suggested. In the main opinion, Stevens concluded that the law "affords too much discretion to the police and too little notice to citizens who wish to use the public streets." But only two justices—Souter and Ginsburg—joined his opinion in full. O'Connor and Breyer in one opinion and Kennedy in another agreed the ruling gave police too much discretion, but distanced themselves from Stevens's endorsement of a constitutional "freedom to loiter."

The dissenting justices were uncommonly sharp in criticizing the decision. The ruling, Thomas wrote, "has denied our most vulnerable citizens the very thing that Justice Stevens elevates above all else—the 'freedom of movement.' And that is a shame." Scalia wrote a separate dissent and emphasized his disagreement by reading portions from the bench. In an extemporaneous line that did not appear in his written opinion, he declared that if he lived in a gang-infested neighborhood, "I would trade my right to loiter in the vicinity of a gang member for the liberation of my neighborhood in an instant."

Stevens spoke for all six justices in the majority in only one substantive section of his opinion: a four-page passage saying the ordinance violated the requirement that a legislature "establish minimal guidelines to govern law enforcement." He went further in two earlier sections. "The freedom to loiter for innocent purposes is part of the 'liberty' protected by the Due Process Clause," he declared, citing the 1972 *Papachristou* decision. Because the law "infringes on constitutionally protected rights," he continued, the Court could strike it down in its entirety because of the vagueness in the definition of loitering. "It is difficult to imagine," Stevens wrote, "how any citizen of the city of Chicago standing in a public place could know if he or she had an 'apparent purpose.' "

O'Connor, joined by Breyer, said that even though the ordinance was "unconstitutionally vague," the city could rewrite the measure—and pointed to suggestions in Stevens's opinion for laws specifically targeting gang members or specific areas of the city or prohibiting loitering with "a harmful purpose." Kennedy, in a briefer concurrence, said he agreed that a citizen engaged in "innocent conduct" had no way to know why a police officer was telling him to disperse.

Scalia's twenty-eight-page dissent—which neither of the other dissenters joined—criticized both the substance and methodology of the various opinions from the majority. He said there was "not the slightest evidence for the existence of a constitutional right to loiter." The law did not apply to innocent conduct, but only to "a willful failure to obey a police order." Nor, he said, was it unconstitutionally vague, because an order to disperse gave "adequate notice of the prohibited conduct."

Writing for all three dissenters, Thomas cited the long history of loitering and vagrancy laws to rebut Stevens's suggestion of a constitutional right to loiter. He cited history as well to justify the discretion to officers under the ordinance. Police "have long had the authority and the duty to order groups of individuals who threaten the public peace to disperse," he wrote. Nor, he said, was the ordinance defective because of inadequate notice to the public. "There is nothing 'vague' about an order to disperse," he wrote.

Thomas's most emotional passages came in describing what he called the "inestimable . . . human costs" of criminal street gangs. He quoted witnesses from the Chicago City Council hearings at length about their fears of walking the streets. "By invalidating Chicago's ordinance," Thomas wrote, "I fear that the Court has unnecessarily sentenced law-abiding citizens to lives of terror and misery."

Reaction. Chicago officials tried to put the ruling in the best light by vowing to rewrite the ordinance along the lines suggested by the majority justices. "The road map they have provided gives state and local governments, for the first time, a legal avenue to address the terrible problems that communities face when gangs take over the public ways," corporation counsel Brian Crowe said in a statement.

Grossman, the ACLU lawyer, called the ruling "an important reaffirmation of the need to reduce discretion in police street enforcement." But he also voiced regret that the Court did not deal more explicitly with the freedom of movement issue. "The Court will be faced with those same questions again," he said.

In Chicago, Grossman discounted the likelihood that the loitering ordinance would be rewritten, but said the city had adopted some law enforcement tactics that had been proposed as alternatives to the measure. "The state's attorney has introduced a program of street-corner surveillance to actually go after the hot street corners," Grossman said. "Before, police were simply trying to scatter these people. Now they're actually going after the bad guys."

Welfare

States Barred From Cutting Benefits for Newcomers

Saenz, Director, California Department of Social Services v. Roe, decided by a 7–2 vote, May 17, 1999; Stevens wrote the opinion; Rehnquist and Thomas dissented. *(See excerpts, pp. 185-196.)*

"Brenda Roe" moved with her husband to California from Oklahoma in 1997 after her husband lost his job and while she was pregnant with the couple's first child. Roe—a pseudonym used in later litigation—had never received public assistance in Oklahoma, but she applied for welfare in

California after medical complications forced her husband to stay home with her rather than look for work.

Concerned that the state's relatively high welfare benefits were encouraging people to move to the state, California lawmakers had approved a measure in 1992 limiting new residents to the level of welfare benefits in their former states. The measure was blocked by litigation, but was finally put into effect after Congress in 1996 authorized states to set lower rates for new residents in a broad welfare reform measure.

For Roe, the law meant that she was to receive $307 per month —Oklahoma's stipend for a family of three—rather than the level set in California: $565 a month. She challenged the restriction as a violation of her constitutional rights—specifically, a supposed "right of travel" from state to state. This term, the Supreme Court agreed that the measure was unconstitutional. The 7–2 decision closed the door on one popular idea for trimming welfare costs and breathed life into a long-ignored constitutional provision that prohibits the states from "abridging" the "privileges or immunities" of citizens of the United States or any state.

Background. Congress established the first national program for providing aid to needy families with children at President Franklin D. Roosevelt's urging in the midst of the Great Depression in 1936. The program—which came to be known as Aid to Families with Dependent Children or AFDC—was jointly financed by the federal government and the states, with benefit levels determined by each individual state.

By the 1960s the "welfare system" had become politically unpopular. Many Americans viewed AFDC as a costly program that discouraged work and encouraged illegitimacy, especially among minority groups. The critique—strongly disputed by welfare advocates—had sufficient strength to lead lawmakers in many states to enact supposed reforms aimed at cutting back benefits or tightening the eligibility requirements. Among the changes were laws passed in two states and the District of Columbia to deny AFDC payments to new residents for a one-year waiting period.

The Supreme Court in 1969 ruled those laws unconstitutional in a controversial 6–3 decision, *Shapiro v. Thompson*. Without specifying its basis, the Court recognized a constitutional "right to travel," called it a "fundamental right," and said neither the states nor the federal government could "penalize" the exercise of that right except to further a "compelling governmental interest." Saving money did not qualify, the Court added. The Court reaffirmed the ruling five years later in a decision that ruled a one-year waiting period for nonemergency medical care for the poor violated

Eloise Anderson, California director of social services when the state enacted a law lowering welfare benefits for new residents

the Equal Protection Clause. But the Court also issued a number of rulings that appeared to uphold waiting periods in other contexts—notably, eligibility for in-state tuition rates at public colleges and universities.

California returned to the idea of limiting benefits for new residents in 1992. Instead of prohibiting AFDC payments altogether, the law simply provided that new residents were limited for one year to the levels they would have received in their prior states. California's welfare chief, Eloise Anderson, later said the law was aimed at "discouraging people from coming to California just for higher benefits." California, in fact, had the sixth highest AFDC payments in the country, but its cost of living was also among the highest.

Under federal law, California had to obtain approval from the secretary of the Health and Human Services Department to implement the rate differential. But Congress eliminated that requirement in 1996 as part of a broad welfare overhaul, the Personal Responsibility and Work Opportunity Reconciliation Act. The act specifically authorized states to establish differential rates for new residents for a twelve-month period. The law also changed the name of the AFDC program to Temporary Assistance for Needy Families—although the new name was slow to move into common usage.

The Case. California's 1992 law was quickly challenged by welfare recipients once the state had received the needed waiver from the federal government to put it into effect. Citing *Shapiro*, federal Judge David Levi issued a preliminary injunction against implementing the measure, later upheld by the federal appeals court for California. The state appealed to the Supreme Court. By the time the case reached the Court, the waiver had been invalidated on administrative law grounds. The justices heard arguments in the case, but then ruled that it was moot—legally over.

With the passage of the federal welfare overhaul, California moved to reinstate the benefits limit. Again, the law was quickly challenged. Lawyers from the American Civil Liberties Union Foundation of Southern California filed a constitutional attack on the law on behalf of Roe and a second welfare recipient called Anna Doe, who had moved to the state from Washington, D.C., to look for work but quit a job because it was too stressful. As a single mother of one child, her stipend was fixed at $330 per month—Washington's benefits—rather than California's $456 per month.

Judge Levi again enjoined the state from putting the limit into effect. In his opinion, he noted that the state could achieve the same cost saving—estimated at $22.8 million—by a modest overall reduction in benefits. The federal appeals court again upheld the injunction, and the state again asked the Court to review the ruling. The Court agreed to review the case as it prepared to open the new term in September 1998. A number of states filed briefs supporting California's position, while welfare rights groups joined the ACLU in opposing the limit on benefits. For its part, the Clinton administration—which had previously opposed the rate differential for new residents—filed a brief defending the constitutionality of the congressional enactment and calling for the case to be sent back to lower courts to reexamine California's purpose in making the change.

Arguments. California's defense of the benefits limit went badly from the opening of the state's attorney's argument before the Court on January 13. A clear majority of the justices—liberals as well as the centrist conservatives O'Connor and Kennedy—voiced strong doubts about the law, while only Rehnquist and Scalia were openly supportive.

Theodore Garelis, a deputy state attorney general, opened by linking the limit to what he called "a congressionally enacted program of welfare reform." O'Connor quickly turned to the right to travel issue. "Our statute does not impact either a right to travel or any fundamental right," Garelis said. O'Connor was unpersuaded. "You'd have a hard time telling a family that is forced to live on welfare that instead of getting California's say $600 a month that it has to live on $300 a month for a year, that that's not a penalty," she said. "This has grave consequences for the family."

Ginsburg jumped in, lifting a passage almost verbatim from the ACLU lawyers' brief. The genius of the United States, she said, is that "people can pick their states, but the states can't pick their people." Garelis tried to explain the benefits limit as a budget move, but Kennedy forced him back. "I thought the whole purpose was to discourage migration," he said.

Garelis said the state was merely "removing an incentive to migrate." Kennedy pounced: "So there is an impact on the right to travel."

Scalia tried to help out: "You're saying that removing an incentive is not the same as a deterrent." Breyer noted that *Shapiro* rejected cost-savings as a defense to barring benefits for newcomers altogether. "Why is it constitutional if you're only saving a little bit less money?" he asked.

Solicitor General Seth Waxman also faced sharp questions from justices as he tried to defend the federal law. "Congress is not fencing anybody out," Waxman said. Justices were dubious. "I don't see how the federal government can do it any more than the states," O'Connor said.

In his turn, the ACLU's Mark Rosenbaum faced openly critical questions from Scalia, who asked why it was constitutional for a state to charge higher hunting license fees for nonresidents. "I would like to be able to get a Louisiana hunting license at Louisiana resident rates," Scalia said. Rosenbaum insisted the difference was residency: "When an individual becomes a resident, that person becomes the state's own."

Decision. The Court's decision on May 17 to invalidate the California law, on a lopsided 7–2 vote, came with what the *New York Times* called "a ringing endorsement of the right of equal citizenship" for all persons. "Citizens of the United States, whether rich or poor, have the right to choose to be citizens of the state wherein they reside," Stevens wrote for the majority. "The states, however, do not have any right to select their citizens."

Significantly, Stevens based the decision squarely on the Fourteenth Amendment's so-called Privileges and Immunities Clause: "No state shall make or enforce any law which shall abridge the privileges or immunities of citizens of the United States." Dissenting justices both defended the California law as a legitimate residency requirement and criticized the revival of what they called "the previously dormant" constitutional provision.

Stevens acknowledged that the Court in *Shapiro* had not explained the basis for recognizing a right to travel even though it was "firmly embedded in our jurisprudence." He explained that the right included three components: the right to cross state borders freely, the right to be treated "as a welcome visitor" when temporarily present in a state, and—for permanent residents—"the right of the newly arrived citizen to the same privileges and immunities by other citizens of the same State."

A law treating newly arrived citizens differently, Stevens said, is subject to a "strict" standard of review. California's law did not pass muster. The evidence introduced in the lower court indicated that the number of persons who travel to California to obtain higher benefits was "quite small—surely not large enough to justify a burden on those who had no such motive." In any event, the state had expressly disavowed that purpose. And, Stevens concluded, "such a purpose would be unequivocally impermissible."

The federal law authorizing the states to set welfare differentials made no difference, Stevens added. "Congress may not authorize the states to violate the Fourteenth Amendment," he wrote. Six justices joined the opinion: O'Connor, Scalia, Kennedy, Souter, Ginsburg, and Breyer. Scalia provided no explanation for his apparent change of view after argument.

In the main dissent, Rehnquist said the ruling "ignores a State's need to assure that only persons who establish a bona fide residence receive the benefits provided to current residents of the State." He noted that the Court had upheld one-year residency provisions for receiving in-state tuition rates at public colleges, getting a divorce, or voting in party primary elections. "States may surely do the same for welfare benefits," he said.

Thomas joined Rehnquist's opinion and added a dissent of his own criticizing the use of the Privileges and Immunities Clause. The majority's use of the clause to strike down a government benefit, Thomas said, "was likely unintended" when the amendment was ratified. Rehnquist joined his opinion.

Reaction. The decision appeared to invalidate laws enacted in some fifteen states—although most had gone unenforced, like California's, because of legal challenges. Rosenbaum, the winning ACLU lawyer, hailed the decision. The ruling, he said, "means California has to knock down the 'keep out' signs at its border."

The state's Democratic governor, Gray Davis, issued a mildly worded statement saying he was "disappointed" with the decision. Anderson, who served as welfare chief when the law was enacted under a Republican governor, also voiced disappointment. But she said the issue had become less important because of changes aimed at requiring welfare recipients to work or lose benefits after specified time periods.

Among legal experts, the ruling's greater interest was its revival of the Privileges and Immunities Clause. Liberal scholars such as Harvard's Laurence Tribe were enthusiastic. He said the decision could provide the basis for "a jurisprudence of fundamental personal rights." But there was interest as well among conservatives. Writing in the *Wall Street Journal*, John Yoo, a law professor at the University of California at Berkeley, said the decision might "provide more momentum to the continuing effort to restore the constitutional protections of individual economic rights."

Civil Rights

Mixed Ruling on Punitive Damages in Job Discrimination Suits

Kolstad v. American Dental Association, decided by 7–2 and 5–4 votes, June 22, 1999; O'Connor wrote the opinion; Rehnquist and Thomas dissented from one part of the decision; Stevens, Souter, Ginsburg, and Breyer dissented from another part. *(See excerpts, pp. 254–263.)*

After working for the American Dental Association for four years, Carole Kolstad thought she was the best qualified candidate when the group's top lobbying job in Washington opened up in 1992. But the position went instead to Tom Spangler, who had worked in another job in the office for only two years.

Believing that she had been passed over because of her sex, Kolstad sued the association under the federal law against discrimination in employment: Title VII of the Civil Rights Act of 1964. She brought the suit under a recent revision of the law, the Civil Rights Act of 1991, which for the first time allowed plaintiffs in job bias suits to receive compensatory and punitive damages in addition to the previously recognized remedies: back pay and reinstatement.

A federal jury agreed with Kolstad's complaint and awarded her $52,718 in back pay. But the trial judge and the federal appeals court in Washington both ruled that Kolstad had not proved the association guilty of sufficiently bad conduct to warrant an award of punitive damages.

Kolstad took the issue to the Supreme Court, which this term agreed with her that the lower courts had set too strict a standard for imposing punitive damages. But the Court also said that employers could avoid penalties in an individual case if they had made "good-faith efforts" to comply with the civil rights law.

Background. After more than three decades, the 1964 civil rights act was credited with bringing about pervasive changes in U.S. workplaces. Blatant racial and sexual discrimination had been largely eliminated, and employers had instituted a host of procedures to try to assure equal employment opportunities for women and for racial and ethnic minorities. Still, civil rights advocates said less visible discrimination persisted, especially in promotions for women and minorities. And civil rights lawyers said that plaintiffs faced difficult obstacles in bringing suits under Title VII and that the law did not provide the most powerful deterrent against discriminatory conduct by employers: punitive damages.

Congress gave civil rights lawyers much of what they wanted in a broad revision of Title VII in 1991. Lawmakers acted after the Court had issued a number of rulings in 1989 raising procedural hurdles for plaintiffs in job bias suits. After two years of vigorous lobbying, Congress passed a bill aimed at overturning some of the Court's decisions. In addition, the law allowed plaintiffs to collect compensatory and punitive damages from employers in cases of "intentional discrimination."

Compensatory damages were permitted for future financial losses as well as emotional pain and suffering and other intangible injuries.

Carole Kolstad

Punitive damages were allowed only against private employers and only if the plaintiff showed that the employer had engaged in a discriminatory practice "with malice or with reckless indifference to the federally protected rights of an aggrieved individual." The law limited the total amount of compensatory and punitive damages in any individual case: the caps ranged from $50,000 to $300,000 depending on the employer's size.

The Case. Kolstad, an attorney, had been the dental association's director of federal agency relations for four years when she learned in September 1992 that the group's longtime lobbyist planned to retire. She immediately tried to apply for the position. According to her later testimony, however, the director of the Washington office rebuffed her efforts to meet with him. And Kolstad's secretary told her that Spangler, who held the title of legislative counsel, was being groomed for the job.

During a week-long trial in October 1994, Kolstad's lawyer, Joseph Yablonski, argued that Spangler had been "secretly pre-selected" for the lobbying job even though Kolstad was better qualified. She had ten years' relevant experience, counting her time with the association and her previous work for the Defense Department as a lawyer and lobbyist on Capitol Hill. Spangler had been with the association for two years and had only four previous years' experience in legislative affairs. Kolstad also testified that the office director had a habit of making derogatory references to women and telling off-color jokes.

The association's lawyers argued that Spangler was in fact the better-qualified applicant for the job, but the jury was unpersuaded. Judge Thomas Penfield Jackson viewed the evidence differently. He refused to let the jury consider awarding punitive damages and allowed the verdict and back-pay award to stand only after stating from the bench that he disagreed with it.

Both sides appealed to the U.S. Court of Appeals for the District of Columbia. A three-judge panel backed Kolstad's argument that the punitive damages issue should have gone to the jury. But the full court, dividing 6–5, disagreed. It held in May 1998 that punitive damages could be awarded only in cases of "egregious" misconduct by an employer. That ruling conflicted with decisions by other federal courts, and the Supreme Court decided in November to take up Kolstad's case to resolve the issue.

Arguments. Kolstad's position drew an outpouring of supporting briefs from civil rights groups as well as the Clinton administration, while business groups lined up to urge the Court to back the appeals court's reading of the 1991 law. The case presented a seeming difficulty for conservative justices, who were often skeptical of punitive damage awards but also committed to sticking to the "plain language" of a statute in interpreting its meaning.

Representing Kolstad in the arguments before the Court on March 1, Eric Schnapper, a University of Washington law professor and veteran civil rights litigator, insisted that the appeals court had added its own prerequisite for punitive damages and thereby undermined one of Congress's central purposes in passing the law. Solicitor General Seth Waxman, representing the administration, agreed. "Congress has made that determination," Waxman said.

Both lawyers faced critical questions from conservative justices, who suggested their interpretation would allow punitive damages in virtually all intentional discrimination cases. "Do you think Congress intended to make it harder to get punitive damages than compensatory damages?" O'Connor asked.

In his turn, the dental association's lawyer, Raymond Fay, contended that Congress had intended to restrict punitive damages by adopting the strict standard—"egregious behavior"—recognized at common law. But liberal justices challenged his reading. "Even though [the law] means that punitive damages can be imposed pretty regularly," Breyer said, "that's what it seems to say."

Decision. The Court's June 22 decision vindicated Kolstad's straightforward reading of the 1991 law. By a 7–2 vote, the Court rejected the appeals court's requirement of egregious misconduct to allow punitive damages. Egregious misconduct may be evidence of "malice" or "reckless indifference," O'Connor wrote, but the law "does not limit plaintiffs to this form of evidence" to satisfy those conditions.

O'Connor stressed, however, that punitive damages would not be permitted in many cases of intentional discrimination. In some cases, she said, an employer might be "unaware of the relevant federal prohibition." In others, an employer might discriminate "with the distinct belief that its discrimination is lawful"—for example, in the case of a "novel" theory of discrimination or a mistaken belief in the legitimacy of a stated job qualification.

Having disposed of that issue, O'Connor in the second half of her opinion raised and answered a second question: when to hold an employer liable for punitive damages for discriminatory conduct by individual managers. The common law limits so-called vicarious liability for punitive damages, O'Connor said, and for good reason. "Holding employers liable for punitive damages when they engage in good faith efforts to comply with Title VII," she wrote, would be unfair. It also would "reduce the incentive for employers to implement antidiscrimination programs."

On that basis, O'Connor said the case needed to be returned to lower courts to give Kolstad a chance to show "malice" or "reckless indifference" on the dental association's part and to give the association itself a chance to show whether it "had been making good faith efforts to enforce an antidiscrimination policy."

The limit on vicarious liability caught Court observers by surprise. The dental association had not argued the point; in fact, the issue had been raised only in a friend-of-the-court brief filed by the U.S. Chamber of Commerce. The Court's other four conservatives, Rehnquist, Kennedy, Scalia, and Thomas, joined that part of O'Connor's opinion. In a partial dissent, Rehnquist said he agreed with the appeals court's egregiousness requirement, but joined the other part of O'Connor's opinion, which he said would place "a complete bar" to punitive damages "in many foreseeable cases." Thomas joined Rehnquist's opinion.

From the other side, liberal justices agreed with O'Connor's conclusion about the standard for punitive damages, but complained about the limit on employers' liability. Stevens called the discussion "gratuitous" and "ill advised" because none of the parties had raised or argued the question. The issue was not even relevant, Stevens said, because the promotion decision that Kolstad challenged had been made by top officials—the head of the Washington office and the association's executive director in Chicago—not by midlevel managers. Souter, Ginsburg, and Breyer joined Stevens's opinion.

Reaction. The Court's ruling defied simple assessments. The *Washington Post* and *Los Angeles Times* both described the ruling in headlines as helping workers in discrimination suits, while the *New York Times* said the ruling raised "hurdles" to punitive damage awards.

Kolstad had no public reaction. She had stayed out of sight throughout the litigation; Yablonski refused even to say where she had worked since leaving the dental association in 1995. For his part, the lawyer said he was "delighted" with the Court's main ruling, but said he "wished that the Court had not reached out" to rule on the liability issue. Still, Yablonski insisted that the limitation on liability would have "no impact" on the outcome of the case on remand.

Peter Sifkas, the dental association's general counsel, disagreed. He praised the Court for setting "a very narrow path" for punitive damage claims to go to the jury and for providing "a safe harbor for employers" with good-faith policies to prevent discrimination. Sifkas also predicted that the association would still avoid punitive damages in any further proceedings. "It's our view that the trial judge will not send this issue to the jury," he said.

Census

Court Bars Sampling in Count for House Seats

Department of Commerce v. United States House of Representatives, decided by a 5–4 vote, January 25, 1999; O'Connor wrote the opinion; Stevens, Souter, Ginsburg, and Breyer dissented. *(See excerpts, pp. 171–184.)*

The Supreme Court found itself thrust this term into an overtly partisan fight between a Democratic administration and a Republican-controlled House of Representatives over how to conduct the census, the constitutionally required count of the nation's population used to apportion seats in the House among the states.

Census enumerators prepare to conduct the population count required under the Constitution every ten years to apportion seats in the House of Representatives among the states. The Supreme Court blocked a Clinton administration plan to use statistical sampling techniques in the census to reduce the undercount of minority groups.

The administration wanted to use statistical sampling as a supplement to an actual headcount to reduce what many experts said was an inevitable undercount using traditional mail and door-to-door techniques. But Republicans disputed the need for sampling and warned that the administration might manipulate the figures for partisan purposes.

Lower federal courts barred the use of sampling in a pair of lawsuits challenging the administration's plan: one by the House itself, another by private plaintiffs. Despite concerns about stepping into a dispute between Congress and the executive, the Court this term agreed. The 5–4 decision—based on a reading of the Census Act—forced the Census Bureau back to the drawing boards and left Congress and the administration still arguing about the best way to try to get a universal population count.

Background. The Constitution requires an "actual enumeration" every ten years—the so-called decennial census—to decide how many seats each state has in the House of Representatives. Initially, federal marshals conducted the headcount from written lists collected town by town. By the twentieth century, Congress established the Census Bureau as part of the Commerce Department to carry out the count.

Despite the increasing cost and sophistication, Census Bureau officials and other population experts believed by the 1940s that the headcount was missing many Americans—particularly poor, predominantly minority populations in big cities. In the 1960s, civil rights groups became sufficiently concerned about the undercount to initiate a campaign aimed at getting a better response among African Americans for the 1970 census.

A decade later, concern about the undercount had spread to local officials and members of Congress. As the 1980 figures were being tallied, New York City filed a federal court suit to try to force the Census Bureau to make a statistical adjustment to correct for the undercount. The litigation lasted seven years before a federal judge finally ruled the adjustment was not "technically feasible or warranted."

For the 1990 census, the Census Bureau itself recommended a statistical adjustment, only to be vetoed by the secretary of commerce, Robert A. Mosbacher, a one-time Republican party fundraiser serving in a GOP administration. New York City again led a legal challenge. By a unanimous vote, the Supreme Court in 1996 refused to interfere with what Rehnquist called Mosbacher's "entirely reasonable" decision (*Wisconsin v. City of New York*).

By the time of the ruling, however, a Democratic administration was moving ahead with plans to use statistical sampling techniques in the 2000 census. It noted that the 1990 census was believed to have missed about 2 percent of the population—more than 4 million people—and that the undercount was greater than it had been in the 1980 census.

The Case. The Census Bureau promised intensified use of traditional techniques to count at least 90 percent of the population before turning to sampling. Under its so-called integrated coverage management plan, census enumerators would then do an even more intensive, door-by-door canvass of selected areas to get a statistical estimate of the people that had been missed. That would then be used to make population projections, census tract by census tract, to get the final tallies.

The administration said the plan was scientifically valid, but opponents said it was legally defective. They argued that sampling violated the constitutional command for an "actual enumeration" as well as a provision of the Census Act, section 195, that provided that sampling could be used "except for purposes of apportionment." The administration countered that another part of the statute, section 141, gave the Census Bureau broad discretion in conducting the headcount. It also insisted that the use of sampling would satisfy the constitutional definition.

Opponents filed two suits after Congress in late 1997 forced through an appropriations rider providing for legal challenges to be heard by special, three-judge courts with direct appeal to the Supreme Court. The House of Representatives itself filed one suit in Washington, naming the Department of Commerce as defendant. A second suit—*Glavin v. Clinton*—was filed in federal court in Alexandria, Virginia, by a group of plaintiffs headed by Michael Glavin, president of the conservative Southeastern Legal Foundation.

Both courts ruled in favor of the opponents on statutory grounds without reaching the constitutional issue. The court in Washington ruled on August 24, 1998. The government immediately appealed, and the Court announced on September 9 that it would take up the case. The court in Virginia ruled on September 24, and the justices consolidated the two cases for argument early in the term—soon enough to allow a decision before spring.

Arguments. Conservative justices struggled during the arguments November 30 to reconcile apparent doubts about the use of statistical sampling with concerns about entertaining the House suit to block the administration's plan. Liberal justices echoed the reluctance to get involved in the dispute, but indicated support for the use of sampling to try to reduce the undercount.

With the expanded time for argument, the justices allowed Solicitor General Seth Waxman to give a detailed explanation of the administration's plan. Waxman stressed that enumerators would use mailings and physical visits to reach a 90 percent count before using sampling—"integrated coverage management," in the Census Bureau's jargon—as "a quality check" on the enumeration.

Rehnquist interrupted: "You use this to change the results." Waxman insisted the techniques were "highly reliable." Rehnquist persisted: "How do you know in advance that there will be inaccuracies?" Waxman noted the history of undercounts, dating to 1790. But O'Connor joined in voicing doubts. "Most people think that 'actual enumeration' means this count," she said. "How do you get around that?"

Souter and Breyer ventured more supportive questions before Souter finally turned to the question of standing. The way for Congress to control the way the census is conducted, Waxman responded, is "legislation, not litigation." As for the private plaintiffs, "it seems to us they're seeking an advisory opinion," he said. Rehnquist and Scalia demurred. How could the census be challenged after the fact? Scalia asked.

In her turn, Maureen Mahoney, a private lawyer representing the House, was immediately challenged on the standing issue. Mahoney, a one-time Rehnquist law clerk, said the Court needed to intervene "to resolve this legal dispute that has created an impasse between the two branches," Congress and the executive. Souter was skeptical: "Are we opening up a very large door?" A few minutes later, Scalia was more emphatic. "I don't like injecting us in a battle between the two branches," he said. "They would survive. I'm not sure we would."

Mahoney also faced sharp questions from Stevens and Breyer on her opposition to sampling. What should census enumerators do, Stevens asked, if no one answered the doors at a big apartment building: put down zero? "That's right," Mahoney said. "It's an objective standard." Breyer was incredulous: "You mean, even if the lights go on and off in the evening?"

For the private plaintiffs, attorney Michael Carvin defended their standing to bring the suit on the ground that several states—including Indiana—were in danger of losing a seat in the House in the post-2000 apportionment. The tainted figures would also likely be used, he said, to apportion state legislative seats and to allocate federal moneys to states and local governments. As for sampling, he reiterated that under the Constitution as well as the statute sampling could not be used—"regardless of its relative accuracy."

Decision. The Court's decision came with unusual speed on January 25 and satisfied the conservative justices' doubts about sampling as well as their misgivings about entertaining the House suit. By a 5–4 vote, the Court held that sampling violated the Census Act; four of the five also said sampling might violate the Constitution's requirement for an actual enumeration. But the ruling technically came in the suit filed by the private plaintiffs. The Court then simply dismissed the appeal of the House's suit, without deciding whether it had been properly brought.

In a carefully constructed opinion, O'Connor first said that one of the private plaintiffs—an Indianan—"undoubtedly" satisfied the requirement for legal standing because of his allegation that his state would lose one representative in the House under a statistically adjusted count. Turning to the merits, O'Connor traced the history of the two Census Act provisions and concluded that the "broad grant of authority" to use sampling contained in section 141 was limited by the "narrower and more specific" section 195. "There is only one plausible reading of the amended section 195," she wrote. "It prohibits the use of sampling in calculating the population for purposes of apportionment."

Significantly, however, O'Connor also said the law "requires" the use of sampling in deriving population counts for other purposes—a qualification that tempered victory claims by Republicans afterwards. Four justices—Rehnquist, Scalia, Kennedy, and Thomas—joined O'Connor's opinion. Scalia wrote a long concurrence—joined by the other three but not O'Connor—saying that it was "unquestionably doubtful" that sampling satisfied the constitutional requirement for an actual enumeration for use in congressional apportionment.

In the main dissent, Stevens concluded that sampling was consistent with both the Census Act and the Constitution. The act, he said, "unambiguously authorizes the Secretary of Commerce to use sampling procedures when taking the decennial census. That this authorization is constitutional is equally clear." Souter and Ginsburg joined most of Stevens's opinion, but disagreed with his view that the House had standing to bring its suit. Breyer agreed with Stevens on that issue, joined part of the opinion, and wrote a separate dissent to stress that the administration planned to use sampling only as "a supplement" of a traditional count.

Reaction. Newspaper headlines cast the ruling in partisan terms: "Democrats Are Set Back," the *Wall Street Journal* proclaimed. The Republicans' newly installed House Speaker, Dennis Hastert of Illinois, immediately urged the administration to "abandon its illegal and risky polling scheme and start preparing for a true head count."

Instead, administration officials said that the ruling appeared to pave the way for a "two-number census"—one count based on traditional enumeration techniques to be used for congressional apportionment and a second tally for other purposes derived in part from statistical sampling. Republicans called that idea confusing and unnecessarily expensive. The sparring continued into spring and summer as the GOP-controlled Congress resisted the administration's pleas that more money was needed for the census because of the restriction.

Chapter 3

Case Summaries

For two months at the start of 1999, Chief Justice Rehnquist took on another job in addition to his normal duties at the Supreme Court. He presided over the Senate's impeachment trial of William Jefferson Clinton, president of the United States. The impeachment trial, stemming from Clinton's efforts to conceal a sexual liaison with a former White House intern, Monica Lewinsky, marked only the second time in U.S. history that the Senate had considered removing the president for what the Constitution ambiguously calls "high crimes and misdemeanors." Impeachment trials of other federal officials are presided over by the vice president, who serves as president of the Senate. But the Constitution specifies that the chief justice preside over a Senate trial of the president.

The trial ended on February 12, with Clinton's acquittal on both of the articles of impeachment that had been approved by the House of Representatives. Rehnquist won high marks for his handling of the trial. His duties were limited. The Senate itself determined the procedures to be followed. Rehnquist's job was to read questions the senators wanted to put to the opposing lawyers in the trial, to rule on the relatively infrequent objections raised by senators to remarks during the debates, and to maintain order and decorum.

Senators in both parties appeared satisfied that Rehnquist had discharged his duties in an evenhanded manner. He also allowed himself an occasional witticism that lightened the otherwise stone-serious proceedings. "The parliamentarian tells me this is all out of order," Rehnquist remarked at one point—with a small grin rarely seen when he presides over the Supreme Court.

At the end of the trial, Rehnquist acknowledged the "culture shock" of moving from "the structured environment of the Supreme Court to what

I shall call, for want of a better phrase, the more free-form environment of the Senate." "I leave you now," Rehnquist continued, "a wiser but not a sadder man." He said he had been impressed by the Senate leaders' ability to agree on procedural rules and by the quality of debate in the Senate's closed sessions on the impeachment articles. The senators returned the praise. They gave Rehnquist a standing ovation as he left the chamber to cross the street to the Supreme Court building and resume his normal schedule.

The smooth conclusion of the impeachment trial belied the concerns widely voiced beforehand that Rehnquist's duties might adversely affect the Court's operations. Democratic lawmakers used the issue during the House debate over approving the impeachment articles; they warned that a Senate trial could result in a months-long shutdown of Supreme Court business. Some legal experts with no evident partisan purpose also voiced concerns that Rehnquist could not keep the Court going at its regular pace if he was preoccupied with an impeachment trial.

Those fears proved to be misplaced. At Rehnquist's insistence, the Senate scheduled the impeachment proceedings so as not to interfere with the Court's arguments in January and February. And far from falling behind in its work, the Court actually issued its final decision of the term on June 23—the earliest closing date since 1969.

"It was a significant accomplishment, the way he was able to discharge his unusual duties, presiding over the impeachment trial, to universal acclaim, without the Court missing a beat," said Washington attorney John Roberts, a former Rehnquist clerk. "It certainly made for some long days for him, and yet there wasn't a missed beat in the Supreme Court proceedings at all."

Suzanna Sherry, a University of Minnesota law professor who had been among those warning of possible delays in the Court's work, gave Rehnquist partial credit for the accomplishment. "Rehnquist did a lot to forestall problems," Sherry remarked, "but the fact that the impeachment trial was mercifully short helped. If he'd had to do that for three months, it might have affected the Court."

One other factor also helped—the Court's unusually light caseload. The Court issued signed decisions in only seventy-five cases. That number represented a 20 percent drop from the ninety signed opinions in the previous term. And along with an equally low output in the 1995–1996 term, it represented the smallest number of decisions since the 1953–1954 term, when the Court issued sixty-five signed decisions. *(See Figure 3–1.)*

Figure 3-1 Supreme Court Caseload, 1960–1998 Term

Total cases on docket

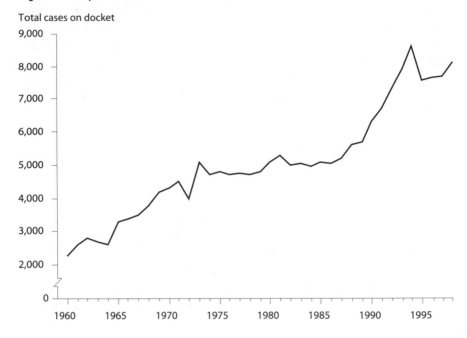

Number of signed opinions of the Court

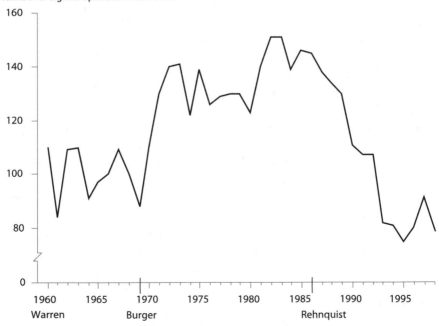

Output had been declining during much of Rehnquist's thirteen-year tenure as chief justice, but the trend still left Court watchers at a loss for a satisfactory explanation. "People have dozens of reasons why it's happening," Roberts remarked. "I don't think it's deliberate in that the justices are saying they only want to take on so many cases. But it's obviously a product of the way they're looking at each individual petition these days, and it must be different from twenty years ago when they took twice as many cases."

As always, the Court passed up any number of interesting, and important, legal issues. The Court never gives an official explanation why it declines to hear a case—or, in Court parlance, "denies certiorari." The only clues are occasional dissenting or separate statements from justices who favored granting review. In one case this term, for example, the Court refused to consider a California inmate's plea that a long prison term—twenty-five years to life—imposed under the state's "three-strikes" law after his conviction for shoplifting a $20 bottle of vitamin pills amounted to "cruel and unusual punishment" under the Eighth Amendment. The four liberal justices signed a statement saying the case raised a "substantial question," but three of them said it was better to wait for other lower court rulings before taking up the issue. Only Breyer said he voted to grant review in the California case itself.

Early in the term, the Court "denied cert" in two cases that observers had widely expected the justices to hear. In October the justices declined to take up a case challenging a Cincinnati ordinance that barred the enactment of laws to prohibit discrimination against homosexuals. A federal appeals court decision upholding the ordinance seemed to contradict the Court's 1996 ruling striking down a similar Colorado law. But three justices—Stevens, Souter, and Ginsburg—joined in a statement minimizing the significance of the Court's refusal to hear the case. They said the actual meaning of the Cincinnati ordinance was sufficiently ambiguous to make the case a poor candidate for Supreme Court review.

One month later the Court declined to review a decision by the Wisconsin Supreme Court upholding a state program allowing the use of taxpayer-funded vouchers for poor children to attend religious schools. School vouchers had become a major battleground among opposing sides in the church-state debates, and lawyers on both sides of the Wisconsin case had urged the Court to grant review. Only Breyer voted to hear the case. Supporters of so-called school choice programs took the Court's action as a positive sign. Opponents cautioned against reading too much into the action, but also acknowledged privately that the Court's recent rulings were trending toward a relaxation of restrictions on government aid to parochial schools.

The Court created confusion with some of its other "cert denials." In October, on the opening day of the term, the Court left standing a policy adopted by a local school board in Indiana requiring random drug testing for high school students participating in any extracurricular activity. In March, however, the Court refused to consider reviving a policy adopted by a different Indiana school board that required any student suspended from school to undergo drug testing before returning to classes. A federal appeals court ruled the program unconstitutional, and the Court declined to hear the school board's plea to review the decision.

The decline in the number of decisions came despite a near-record number of cases sent to the Court for possible review. The Court's total docket included 8,083 cases—a 5 percent increase over the previous term and just shy of the record 8,100 cases in the 1994–1995 term. The increase, however, was entirely due to indigent cases, most of them from criminal defendants and prisoners. These are called *in forma pauperis* cases or IFPs, and the petitioners are not required to pay the normal $300 cost for docketing a case. The number of "paid cases" actually declined slightly, from 2,432 cases in the 1997–1998 term to 2,387 in the current term.

In addition to its signed decisions, the Court also issued six unsigned or *per curiam* opinions. Typically, the Court uses this procedure to reverse lower court decisions that clearly misinterpret Supreme Court precedents or statutory or constitutional provisions. The opinions are usually relatively brief and are often unanimous. The Court also issues a *per curiam* opinion if—after a recusal by one of the justices—the remaining justices are evenly divided. That happened once this year, in an important business law case involving shareholder suits over fraud or other misconduct by corporate officers or directors. The issue was whether shareholders who were not involved in the original suit can intervene on appeal to try to undo a settlement that they believe is unfavorable for the company. A federal appeals court barred the shareholders' appeal. O'Connor recused herself, and the other justices split 4–4 on the case—leaving the appeals court decision on the books but setting no precedent on the issue.

Overall, the Court was somewhat more divided in its decisions than in recent years. The justices were unanimous in slightly more than one-third of their signed opinions (twenty-eight of seventy-five). In the 1997–1998 term, nearly half of the decisions were unanimous. The justices divided five-to-four in seventeen cases—nearly one-fourth of the total. In the previous term, 5–4 decisions accounted for about one-sixth of he total. Of the

Figure 3-2 Vote Divisions on Cases Decided in 1998–1999 Supreme Court Term

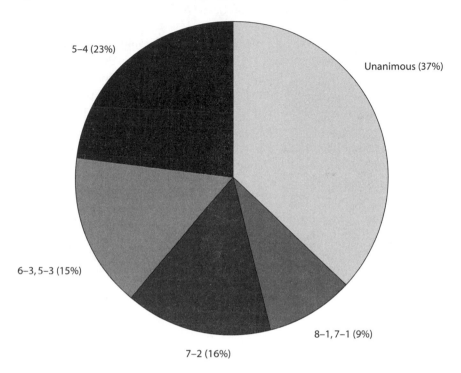

5–4 (23%)

Unanimous (37%)

6–3, 5–3 (15%)

8–1, 7–1 (9%)

7–2 (16%)

remaining decisions for the current term, there were seven with one dissenting vote, twelve with two dissenting votes, and eleven with three dissenting votes. *(See Figure 3–2.)*

Following are summaries of the seventy-five signed opinions and six *per curiam* opinions issued by the Court during the 1998–1999 term. They are organized by subject matter: business law, courts and procedure, criminal law and procedure, election law, federal government, First Amendment, immigration law, individual rights, labor law, property law, states, and torts.

Business Law

Antitrust

Nynex Corp. v. Discon, Inc., decided by a 9–0 vote, December 14, 1998; Breyer wrote the opinion.

The automatic antitrust rule against group boycotts does not apply to an individual buyer's decision to purchase goods or services from one seller instead of from another.

The ruling narrowed an antitrust complaint brought by a New York telephone-equipment removal company, Discon, Inc., that charged the local telephone company, Nynex Corp., with improperly terminating a contract for its services. Discon claimed that Nynex shifted its business to another company to stifle price competition in the equipment-removal market and pass the costs on to consumers. A federal district court dismissed the complaint, but the Second U.S. Circuit Court of Appeals reinstated the suit and said Discon might be able to recover under the per se antitrust rule against group boycotts.

In a unanimous decision, the Court said Discon could not use the per se rule against group boycotts and could recover damages only if it proved that Nynex's action had an anticompetitive effect. Applying the per se rule, Breyer said, would transform cases involving "improper business" behavior into treble-damages antitrust cases and "discourage firms from changing suppliers—even where the competitive process itself does not suffer harm."

Bankruptcy

Bank of America National Trust and Savings Association v. 203 North LaSalle Street Partnership, decided by an 8–1 vote, May 3, 1999; Souter wrote the opinion; Stevens dissented.

Partners or stockholders in a business in a bankruptcy proceeding cannot acquire an equity interest in the reorganized concern by investing new money without safeguards to ensure the fairness of the transaction.

The ruling bolstered creditors' rights, but failed to completely resolve a recurrent question in bankruptcy cases: whether the so-called old equity holders can emerge as owners after reorganization by contributing money or labor. Generally, bankruptcy law gives creditors "absolute priority" to any assets of the business. But some federal courts recognized a so-called "new value" corollary that allowed stockholders to own all or part of the company by making additional investments. The Court itself had recognized a new value corollary in a 1939 decision, but the enactment of a new bankruptcy code in 1978 left the status of the ruling uncertain.

The issue reached the Court in a dispute between a real estate partnership that owned fifteen stories in a high-rise Chicago office building and the bank that financed the venture. The partnership filed for bankruptcy after defaulting on the mortgage and proposed a reorganization plan that called for an infusion of $6 million in capital with the partnership to retain ownership. The bank, which was to be paid about one-sixth of its unsecured claim of $38 million, objected. But the plan was approved by the bankruptcy court, a federal district court judge, and the Seventh U.S. Circuit Court of Appeals.

In a nearly unanimous decision, the Court said the reorganization plan should not have been approved. Writing for six justices, Souter said that the partnership could not acquire equity in the reorganized business because no one else had been able to "compete for that equity" or "propose a competing reorganization plan." Even if a new value corollary was recognized, Souter said, the bankruptcy code prohibited reorganization plans that gave stockholders "exclusive opportunities free from competition and without benefit of market valuation."

In a separate concurrence, Thomas, joined by Scalia, said the bankruptcy code imposed a flat prohibition on allowing stockholders to acquire equity in the reorganized business. The majority opinion, Thomas said, "thickens the fog" around the issue.

In a lone dissent, Stevens said he would have explicitly recognized a new value corollary. "In some cases old equity may be the most likely source of new capital," Stevens wrote. He also criticized the majority's decision for adding new procedural requirements to the statute.

International Trade

United States v. Haggar Apparel Co., decided by 9–0 and 7–2 votes, April 21, 1999; Kennedy wrote the opinion; Stevens and Ginsburg dissented in part.

The government won a partial and possibly determinative victory in its effort to deny a major clothing manufacturer a tariff exemption on pants that are permapressed in Mexico.

The dispute involved a tariff provision that allows an exemption from duties for products made from components manufactured in the United States but assembled abroad. The exemption applied if the foreign operations included assembly or "operations incidental to the assembly process." Haggar Apparel sought an exemption for pants assembled and permapressed in Mexico, claiming that the permapressing was "incidental" to the assembly. The Customs Service—in line with a regulation issued in 1975—ruled the permapressing was not incidental to assembly and denied the exemption. The Court of International Trade disregarded the regulation, agreed with Haggar, and ruled the company was entitled to a refund.

Unanimously, the Court held that the trade tribunal did not give the required deference to the Customs Service regulation. "Like other courts, the Court of International Trade must, when appropriate, give regulations *Chevron* deference," Kennedy wrote, referring to an important administrative law precedent, *Chevron v. Natural Resources Defense Council, Inc.* (1984).

The ruling sent the case back to the trade tribunal for reconsideration. Stevens, joined by Ginsburg, agreed on the legal ruling, but said he would have gone further to uphold the regulation and deny the refund.

Patents

Dickinson, Acting Commissioner of Patents and Trademarks v. Zurko, decided by a 6–3 vote, June 10, 1999; Breyer wrote the opinion; Rehnquist, Kennedy, and Ginsburg dissented.

The federal appeals court that hears patent cases was told to give greater deference to rulings by the Patent and Trademark Office.

The ruling, in an otherwise routine patent case, changed a long-established policy of somewhat stricter judicial review of decisions by the patent office. The issue arose after the U.S. Court of Appeals for the Federal Circuit—which has exclusive jurisdiction over appeals in patent cases—overturned as "clearly erroneous" the patent office's decision to reject an inventor's application for a patent on a method for increasing computer security. The patent office argued that the federal Administrative Procedure Act (APA) required the court to exercise more deferential review and uphold a decision unless it was "arbitrary, capricious [or] an abuse of discretion" or "unsupported by substantial evidence." The appeals court disagreed, citing what it called an established practice of stricter judicial review of patent office decisions prior to passage of the APA in 1946.

By a 6–3 vote, the Court ruled that the appeals court was bound by the more deferential standard of review established by the APA. Breyer said that the appeals court had not explained "why direct review of the [patent office's] patent denials demands a stricter fact-related review standard than is applicable to other agencies."

Writing for the dissenters, Rehnquist agreed with the appeals court that the stricter review standard was established before passage of the APA. He also said the result conflicted with the APA's purpose of "raising the minimum standards of review and not by lowering those standards which existed at the time."

Pfaff v. Wells Electronics, Inc., decided by a 9–0 vote, November 10, 1998; Stevens wrote the opinion.

The statutory prohibition against patenting an invention that has been on sale for more than a year applies even if the inventor did not complete a working prototype before offering the device for sale.

The decision blocked a patent infringement suit by the inventor of a computer chip socket, Wayne Pfaff, against Wells Electronics, Inc., for manufacturing a competing device. Pfaff completed a contract to sell 30,000 of the sockets to Texas Instruments, Inc., on April 8, 1981, based on a sketch of the device. He applied for a patent on the device more than one year later, on April 19, 1982. The Patent Act provides that no one is entitled to patent an "invention" that has been "on sale" more than one year before filing a patent application. The U.S. Appeals Court for the Federal Circuit cited that section in ordering the dismissal of Pfaff's suit.

In a unanimous opinion, the Court agreed. The Patent Act's "on-sale bar" applies, Stevens wrote, if the product "is the subject of a commercial offer for sale" and is "ready for patenting" more than one year before the application for a patent is filed.

Shareholder Suits

California Public Employees' Retirement System v. Felzen, affirmed by an equally divided Court, January 20, 1999; *per curiam* (unsigned) opinion; O'Connor did not participate.

The Court upheld, on a tie vote, a lower court decision that limited legal challenges to settlements of shareholder suits against officers or directors of corporations for financial misconduct.

The deadlock left unresolved an important procedural issue involving so-called derivative suits—actions by shareholders seeking to recover, on behalf of a corporation, moneys lost because of financial misconduct by officers or directors of the company. The often lucrative litigation goes by the name derivative suits because the shareholders' rights are said to "derive" from the corporation's.

The dispute before the Court stemmed from a suit brought by shareholders of the Archer Daniels Midland Co. seeking to recover $190 million that the agricultural processing company paid in 1996 in a major price-fixing case. The shareholders agreed to settle the suit for about

$8 million in legal fees and certain limited corporate governance reforms. Two large institutional shareholders—the state employees' pension funds in California and Florida—sought to appeal the settlement as inadequate, but the Seventh U.S. Circuit Court of Appeals said the Federal Rules of Civil Procedure only allowed appeals by parties to the original suit. The two pension funds disagreed and argued that appeals by other shareholders would help prevent collusive settlements between the original plaintiffs and the company involved in the suit.

O'Connor did not participate because of a financial conflict of interest. The remaining justices divided 4–4. The Court does not announce individual votes in tie cases. But questioning during the argument indicated the justices were divided along expected ideological lines, with conservatives inclined to bar the appeal and more liberal justices inclined to permit it.

Courts and Procedure

Attorney Fees

Martin, Director, Michigan Department of Corrections v. Hadix, decided by a 7–2 vote, June 21, 1999; O'Connor wrote the opinion; Ginsburg and Stevens dissented in part.

Limits on attorney's fees in prison condition lawsuits in federal courts imposed by Congress in 1996 apply to any work by lawyers performed in pending cases after the date of enactment.

The ruling split the difference between opposing views of provisions of the Prison Litigation Reform Act of 1995, signed into law on April 26, 1996. The law set a maximum rate for court-awarded attorney's fees in prison conditions suits of 150 percent of the rate allowed to court-appointed lawyers in criminal cases. As of 1999 that resulted in a cap of $112.50 per hour. Lawyers in two Michigan prison cases, who had been receiving $150 per hour for work in monitoring implementation of court decrees, argued the caps did not apply to pending cases. State officials, on the other hand, said the limits applied to pending cases, including work performed before enactment of the law. The Sixth U.S. Circuit Court of Appeals agreed with the lawyers in barring any retroactive application of the law.

By a 7–2 vote, the Court said the caps could be applied to work done after the law was signed. O'Connor said that applying the law to work done prior to enactment would have "a retroactive effect" inconsistent with the normal rule that statutes operate prospectively only. But, she continued, there was "no retroactive effect" with respect to work performed after the effective date.

In a partial dissent, Ginsburg, joined by Stevens, said the law should not apply to any work in cases pending when the law was signed. "Applying [the law] to pending matters significantly alters the consequences of the representation on which the lawyer has embarked," she wrote.

Attorneys

Conn v. Gabbert, decided by a 9–0 vote, April 5, 1999; Rehnquist wrote the opinion.

Law enforcement officers did not violate a criminal defense lawyer's civil rights when they searched him in a manner that interfered with his consultation with a client testifying before a grand jury.

The ruling rejected a civil rights suit brought by a Los Angeles lawyer, Paul Gabbert, against two Los Angeles prosecutors in a high-profile murder case, David Conn and Carol Najera. The prosecutors obtained a warrant to search Gabbert's briefcase to look for a letter supposedly written by his client that would contradict testimony that she had given as a defense witness. Gabbert was searched in the courthouse at the same time his client was testifying before a grand jury. He claimed in his suit that the search violated his right to practice his profession. The claim was rejected by a lower court, but reinstated by the Ninth U.S. Circuit Court of Appeals.

Unanimously, the Court held that the search did not violate any Fourteenth Amendment right. "The Fourteenth Amendment right to practice one's calling is not violated by the execution of a search warrant," Rehnquist wrote, "whether calculated to annoy or even to prevent consultation with a grand jury witness."

All justices but Stevens joined Rehnquist's opinion. Stevens wrote a separate concurrence, describing the search as "shabby" and suggesting Gabbert might have a claim for a violation of his Fourth Amendment protection against unreasonable searches.

Cunningham v. Hamilton County, Ohio, decided by a 9–0 vote, June 14, 1999; Thomas wrote the opinion.

An attorney ordinarily cannot appeal a judge's decision to impose sanctions for misconduct during a lawsuit while the case is still going on.

The ruling rejected an effort by an Ohio lawyer, Teresa Cunningham, to get an early appeal of a federal judge's ruling imposing a $1,494 penalty for discovery abuse during a civil rights suit against Hamilton County. The Sixth U.S. Circuit Court of Appeals ruled that the issue did not fall within any of the exceptions to the general rule against so-called inter-locutory appeals—appeals before the end of trial.

Unanimously, the Court agreed. Allowing an interlocutory appeal of a sanction for discovery abuse, Thomas said, "would undermine" the pur-pose of the rule allowing such penalties—"to protect courts and opposing parties from delaying or harassing tactics." Thomas acknowledged that the inability to get an early appeal could impose "a hardship" on a lawyer and noted that a judge could delay enforcing any sanction until the end of trial. In a concurring opinion, Kennedy said a lawyer might be able to use a special procedure—a so-called writ of mandamus—to contest a penalty in case of "an exceptional hardship."

Class Actions

Ortiz v. Fibreboard Corp., decided by a 7–2 vote, June 23, 1999; Souter wrote the opinion; Breyer and Stevens dissented.

Federal courts cannot approve mandatory class settlements in mass tort cases unless the money available for compensation is definitely fixed and potential conflicts of interest between classes of claimants are addressed.

The ruling set aside a $1.5 billion global settlement of claims against the asbestos manufacturer Fibreboard Corp. negotiated by lawyers represent-ing the company, two of its insurers, and a group of plaintiffs. A federal court judge in Texas and the Fifth U.S. Circuit Court of Appeals both approved the mandatory settlement, over the objections of other asbestos victims who argued that the accord was unfair to future claimants. In upholding the fairness of the settlement, the appeals court agreed with the lawyers who negotiated the agreement that the value of Fibreboard's insur-ance policies plus the contribution made by the company amounted to a "limited fund" available to pay claimants. The Supreme Court ordered the appeals court to reconsider the case following its decision in another asbestos case, *Amchem Products v. Windsor* (1997), which limited courts' dis-cretion to approve some types of class settlements in mass tort cases under Rule 23 of the Federal Rules of Civil Procedure. On remand, the appeals court again approved the settlement by a 2–1 vote. The dissenting judge argued that the use of the "limited fund" rationale was improper because the only limit on money for compensation stemmed from the settlement itself.

By a 7–2 vote, the Court set strict requirements for approval of con-tested class action settlements. Writing for the majority, Souter first said that the limited fund rationale can be used only when the fund is "shown to be limited independently of the agreement of the parties to the action." In addition, any settlement must ensure an "equitable pro rata distribution," Souter wrote, with conflicts between different groups of claimants addressed by "independently represented subclasses."

In a concurring opinion, Rehnquist, joined by Scalia and Kennedy, agreed that the settlement could not be approved under the terms of Rule 23. But he also praised the judge's handling of the case, warned of the costs of further litigation, and urged Congress to craft a legislative solution.

Writing for the dissenters, Breyer said the settlement substantially met the conditions set out in the Court's opinion and chided the majority for second-guessing the lower courts' handling of the case. "Judges can and should search aggressively for ways, within the existing framework of the law, to avoid delay and expense so great as to bring about a massive denial of justice," Breyer wrote.

Expert Testimony

Kumho Tire Co., Ltd. v. Carmichael, decided by 9–0 and 8–1 votes, March 23, 1999; Breyer wrote the opinion; Stevens dissented in part.

Trial judges have broad discretion to apply a test developed for determining the admissibility of scientific testimony to any expert evidence based on technical or other specialized knowledge.

The ruling—a victory for business and insurance groups—stemmed from an effort by plaintiffs in a Georgia automobile accident case to introduce testimony by evidence from a supposed tire expert blaming the mishap on a defective tire. The trial judge ruled the testimony inadmissible, citing standards for reliability established by the Court's 1993 decision, *Daubert v. Merrell Dow Pharmaceuticals, Inc.* That ruling required judges to exercise a "gatekeeping" function regarding scientific testimony and listed four criteria to consider in determining reliability: the testability of a scientific method, peer review, potential rate of error, and general rate of acceptance within the scientific community. On appeal, however, the Eleventh U.S. Circuit Court of Appeals held that the *Daubert* tests applied only to scientific testimony, not to engineering or other kinds of expert evidence.

Unanimously, the Court held that the appeals court decision was wrong and went on to rule, by an 8–1 vote, that the trial judge was correct in barring the tire expert's testimony. "Some of *Daubert's* questions can help to evaluate the reliability even of experience-based testimony,"

Breyer wrote. But he stressed that judges "must have considerable leeway" in deciding how to determine the reliability of testimony and were not required to apply any or all of *Daubert*'s criteria in a particular case. Appellate courts should review those decisions on a relaxed "abuse of discretion" standard, Breyer concluded.

In a concurring opinion, Scalia, joined by O'Connor and Thomas, suggested that a judge's failure to apply one or more of the *Daubert* criteria could amount to an abuse of discretion in a particular case. Stevens, dissenting in part, said he agreed with the legal holding, but would have sent the case back to the Eleventh Circuit to decide whether the testimony should have been excluded.

Injunctions

Grupo Mexicano de Desarrollo, S. A. v. Alliance Bond Fund, Inc., decided by a 5–4 vote, June 17, 1999; Scalia wrote the opinion; Ginsburg, Stevens, Souter, and Breyer dissented.

Federal courts have no power in a suit for money damages to block the defendant from transferring assets before a judgment. The sharply divided ruling represented a setback for creditors.

The ruling nullified a preliminary injunction issued by a lower federal court in a dispute between a Mexican holding company that had issued bonds for construction of a toll road and some U.S. investors in the bonds. Because of financial difficulties, the holding company, Grupo Mexicano de Desarrollo (GMD), missed scheduled interest payments in August 1997. Four months later, Alliance Bond Fund, representing some of the bondholders, filed suit for the amount due. The fund also asked the court to bar GMD from transferring any assets pending the outcome of the suit. It claimed that GMD was already transferring assets and favoring Mexican creditors over U.S. investors. The court issued the preliminary injunction, and the Second U.S. Circuit Court of Appeals upheld it.

By a 5–4 vote, however, the Court held that the lower courts had exceeded their powers. Federal courts, Scalia wrote, have no power to "interfere with the debtor's disposition of his property at the instance of a nonjudgment creditor." He said that such a remedy was "historically unavailable" in English courts at the time of the creation of the federal court system and would "radically alter the balance between debtor's and creditor's rights."

Writing for the dissenters, Ginsburg said the decision was based on "an unjustifiably static conception" of federal courts' powers. The ruling, she said, "holds federal courts powerless to prevent a defendant from dissipating assets, to the destruction of a plaintiff's claim, during the course of judicial proceedings."

Removal

El Paso Natural Gas Co. v. Neztsosie, decided by a 9–0 vote, May 3, 1999; Souter wrote the opinion.

Two energy companies won a procedural victory in their effort to avoid a trial in Indian courts in a suit by Indian plaintiffs for alleged radiation-exposure injuries from uranium mining.

The ruling said that a lower federal court, rather than a Navajo tribal court, should decide where the suit by three members of the Navajo tribe was to be tried. The plaintiffs alleged injuries from environmental exposure to radioactive and other hazardous materials. The companies removed the cases to federal court under the broad preemption provisions of a 1988 amendment to the Price-Anderson Act, which generally limits liability of nuclear power companies resulting from "a nuclear incident." The federal district court and the Ninth U.S. Circuit Court of Appeals ruled that the tribal court should have the first opportunity to rule on the application of the law.

Unanimously, the Court held that the law required federal courts rather than tribal courts to rule on its application to the suits. The 1988 law, Souter said, "expressed an unmistakable preference for a federal forum, at the behest of the defending party, both for litigating a Price-Anderson claim on the merits and for determining whether a claim falls under Price-Anderson when removal is contested."

Murphy Brothers, Inc. v. Michetti Pipe Stringing, Inc., decided by a 6–3 vote, April 5, 1999; Ginsburg wrote the opinion; Rehnquist, Scalia, and Thomas dissented.

The thirty-day time period for a defendant to file a motion to move a case from state to federal court starts only after official service of the complaint or summons, not after informal notice of the suit.

The ruling involved a provision of federal law stating that a defendant in a state court suit has "thirty days after the receipt . . . through service or otherwise, of a copy of" a complaint to file a motion to "remove" the case to federal court. The issue arose in a routine commercial dispute where the plaintiff faxed a copy of the complaint to the defendant shortly after filing. The defendant filed the removal notice thirty days after being served, but forty-four days after receiving the faxed copy. The Eleventh U.S. Circuit Court of Appeals said the time period began to run when the defendant received the facsimile copy.

The Court disagreed. The time period starts, Ginsburg wrote, only after official notice of the suit, "not by mere receipt of a complaint unattended by any formal service." Writing for the three dissenters, Rehnquist said that under the "plain language" of the statute "the receipt of [the] facsimile triggered the 30-day removal period."

Ruhrgas AG v. Marathon Oil Company, decided by a 9–0 vote, May 17, 1999; Ginsburg wrote the opinion.

Federal courts considering cases removed from state courts have leeway in deciding which of two jurisdictional issues—jurisdiction over the defendant or over the subject of the lawsuit—to rule on first.

The ruling stemmed from a legally complex suit originally brought in Texas state court by Marathon Oil Company against the German natural gas company Ruhrgas AG over marketing of gas being produced from a North Sea field by a Marathon subsidiary. Ruhrgas removed the case to federal court and then sought to dismiss the suit on the ground that its contacts with Texas were insufficient to establish personal jurisdiction. Marathon argued that the case was improperly removed because federal courts had no jurisdiction over the subject matter of the lawsuit. The federal court agreed with Ruhrgas on the personal jurisdiction issue. But the Fifth U.S. Circuit Court of Appeals—interpreting a 1998 Supreme Court precedent—held that the subject matter jurisdictional issue had to be considered first.

Unanimously, the Court said the appeals court had misread the prior ruling. The lower court, Ginsburg wrote, had acted properly in deciding the "straightforward personal jurisdiction issue" raised by Ruhrgas rather than the "difficult and novel question" presented in Marathon's subject-matter challenge. "It is hardly novel," Ginsburg wrote, "for a federal court to choose among threshold grounds for denying audience to a case on the merits."

Criminal Law and Procedure

Capital Punishment

Jones v. United States, decided by a 5–4 vote, June 21, 1999; Thomas wrote the opinion; Ginsburg, Stevens, Souter, and Breyer dissented.

Juries in federal death penalty cases need not be told that in the event of a deadlock the judge will sentence the defendant either to death or to life imprisonment without possibility of parole.

The ruling—in the Court's first case involving the comprehensive Federal Death Penalty Act of 1994—upheld the conviction and death sentence of a former Army officer, Louis Jones Jr., for the kidnap-murder of a female private in 1995. After convicting Jones of the offense, the jury deliberated for a day-and-a-half before sentencing him to death. On appeal, Jones argued that the jury should have been told that under the law a deadlock would mean that the judge would impose sentence and that his choices would be limited to death or to life imprisonment without parole. Jones also contended that the judge's instructions misled jurors into thinking that he could impose a lesser sentence and that two "aggravating factors" given to jurors for consideration—the victim's age and background and the effect of the crime on the victim's family—were improper. The Fifth U.S. Circuit Court of Appeals upheld the conviction and sentence after rejecting most of the arguments. It did agree that the two aggravating factors were improper, but said that the error did not affect the jury's decision.

By a 5–4 vote, the Court upheld the sentence. Writing for the majority, Thomas said that Jones's requested instruction about the judge's sentencing options "has no bearing on the jury's role in the sentencing process" and might undermine the "strong governmental interest" in having the jury express "the conscience of the community" in capital cases. He also said that the judge's instructions did not mislead the jury. On the aggravating factors, Thomas said they were not errors and, in any event, were harmless.

Writing for the four dissenters, Ginsburg criticized what she called "the flawed trial proceedings, and this Court's tolerance of the flaws." "I would reverse and remand so that the life or death decision may be made by an accurately informed trier," she wrote.

Confrontation

Lilly v. Virginia, decided by a 9–0 vote, June 10, 1999; Stevens wrote the main opinion; Scalia and Thomas wrote partial concurring opinions; Rehnquist wrote an opinion concurring in the judgment.

A Virginia death row inmate won a round in his effort to overturn his murder conviction because of the use of a statement by an accomplice who refused to testify at trial.

Benjamin Lilly, his brother Mark, and a third man were charged in the abduction-killing of a Virginia Technical University student in a drunken robbery spree in 1995. Mark Lilly gave police a statement admitting his role in the robberies but claiming that Benjamin masterminded the crimes and killed the victim. Benjamin Lilly was tried separately. Mark Lilly refused to testify, but prosecutors introduced his statement over Benjamin's attorney's objections. In appealing his conviction and death sentence, Benjamin Lilly claimed that the introduction of Mark's statements violated his right under the Sixth Amendment's Confrontation Clause to cross-examine witnesses against him. The Virginia Supreme Court rejected the argument, saying that Mark's statement fell within a recognized exception that allows the use of a self-incriminating statement by an unavailable witness despite the normal rule against hearsay evidence.

The justices unanimously agreed that the use of the brother's statement was wrong and that the case should go back to the Virginia Supreme Court to determine whether the mistake required a new trial or was a "harmless error" that did not affect the verdict. In the main opinion, Stevens concluded that the use of Mark's statement violated Benjamin's Confrontation Clause rights. "Accomplices' confessions that inculpate a criminal defendant are not within a firmly rooted exception to the hearsay rule as that concept has been defined in our Confrontation Clause jurisprudence," Stevens wrote.

Three justices—Souter, Ginsburg, and Breyer—joined all of Stevens's opinion. Scalia did not join the main parts of the opinion and instead wrote a brief concurrence calling the use of Mark's statement a "paradigmatic Confrontation Clause violation."

In an opinion concurring in the judgment, Rehnquist said Stevens's opinion went too far by imposing "a complete ban on the government's use of accomplice confessions . . . that inculpate a codefendant." O'Connor and Kennedy joined the opinion. Thomas, in a separate concurrence, also said that a blanket ban on accomplice confessions was unjustified.

Criminal Offenses

Holloway v. United States, decided by a 7–2 vote, March 2, 1999; Stevens wrote the opinion; Scalia and Thomas dissented.

The Court made it easier to obtain convictions under a newly enacted federal carjacking law by softening the requirement for proving an intent to kill or injure the victim.

The ruling interpreted a 1994 amendment to the anti-carjacking law passed two years earlier that defined the offense to be taking a motor vehicle "by force or intimidation . . . with the intent to cause death or serious bodily harm." A New York man, François Holloway, challenged his conviction by claiming that in several carjackings he and his accomplice had never planned to harm the victims unless they resisted. A lower federal court and the Second U.S. Circuit Court of Appeals both upheld the conviction.

By a 7–2 vote, the Court agreed that "conditional intent" to kill or harm the victim satisfies the requirement for a conviction under the law. "Congress intended to criminalize the more typical carjacking carried out by means of a deliberate threat of violence," Stevens wrote, "rather than just the rare case in which the defendant has an unconditional intent to use violence regardless of how the driver responds to his threat."

In separate dissenting opinions, Scalia and Thomas argued that the law did not cover cases of "conditional intent." "The carjacker who intends to kill if he is met with resistance . . . has an 'intent to kill if resisted,' " Scalia wrote. "He does not have an 'intent to kill.' "

Jones v. United States, decided by a 5–4 vote, March 24, 1999; Souter wrote the opinion; Kennedy, Rehnquist, O'Connor, and Breyer dissented.

The Court made it harder to impose long prison sentences under a recently enacted federal carjacking law in a closely divided decision that could affect penalty enhancements under other criminal statutes.

The ruling came in an appeal by a California man, Nathaniel Jones, convicted of a 1992 carjacking and given a twenty-five year prison sentence. The federal carjacking law, first enacted in 1992 and amended in 1994, provided in one section for a fifteen-year prison sentence and established more severe sentences in two subsequent sections: twenty-five years' imprisonment if "serious bodily injury" results and up to life imprisonment if a death results. Jones was indicted only under the first section, but evidence at trial showed that one of the victims suffered some permanent hearing loss from a blow to his head during the crime.

After a jury convicted Jones, the judge, citing the "serious bodily injury" provision, imposed a twenty-five-year prison term. Jones argued that the injury amounted to an "element" of the offense that prosecutors were required to include in the indictment and prove beyond a reasonable doubt at trial. The judge and the Ninth U.S. Circuit Court of Appeals both rejected the argument. The Court agreed to hear Jones's appeal on March 30, 1998, just one week after a ruling in a somewhat similar case, *Almendarez-Torres v. United States.* In that case, the Court held, by a 5–4 vote, that an immigration law provision establishing longer prison terms based on an alien's prior convictions amounted to a sentencing factor rather than a separate offense.

In Jones's case, however, the Court ruled that the serious bodily injury provision did amount to a separate offense. Writing for the majority, Souter concluded that Congress "probably intended serious bodily injury to be an element defining an aggravated form of the crime." A different interpretation, he added, would create "constitutional doubt" under the Sixth Amendment's jury trial provision by "removing [the jury's] control over facts determining a statutory sentencing range."

Writing for the dissenters, Kennedy called the ruling a "strained reading" of the statute and a departure from previous rulings, including the *Almendarez-Torres* decision. "Our precedents admit of no real doubt regarding the power of Congress to establish serious bodily injury and death as sentencing factors rather than offense elements," he wrote.

Stevens and Scalia wrote short concurring opinions, both stating flatly that it was—in Scalia's words—"unconstitutional to remove from the jury the assessment of facts that alter the congressionally prescribed range of penalties to which a criminal defendant is exposed." Thomas, who had voted with the majority in the *Almendarez-Torres* decision, switched sides in Jones's case but did not write separately to explain his reasoning.

United States v. Sun-Diamond Growers of California, decided by a 9–0 vote, April 27, 1999; Scalia wrote the opinion.

A conviction under the federal illegal gratuity statute requires the prosecution to prove a connection between a gift to a federal official and a specific act motivating the gift.

The ruling set aside the 1996 conviction of Sun-Diamond Growers of California for giving Agriculture Secretary Michael Espy about $5,900 in gifts, including tickets to tennis matches, luggage, and other presents. An independent counsel prosecuted the trade association under a federal law that makes it illegal to give a federal official, or for the official to receive, "anything of value . . . for or because of any official act performed or to be performed by such public official. . . ." The prosecution argued that the gifts violated the statute because Espy had regulatory issues before him affecting the association and its members. Sun-Diamond argued successfully to the federal appeals court in Washington that the statute required the prosecution to show a link between the gift and a specific official action.

Unanimously, the Court upheld the appeals court's decision overturning the conviction. The independent counsel's interpretation of the law,

Scalia said, "does not fit comfortably with the statutory text" and would lead to "peculiar results"—for example, criminalizing token gifts to the president or other federal officials. In addition, Scalia said that a narrow reading was "more compatible" with the "intricate web of regulations, both administrative and criminal," governing acceptance of gifts by officials.

Espy was also prosecuted under the statute, but was acquitted by a federal jury in Washington in December 1998.

Discovery

Strickler v. Greene, Warden, decided by a 7–2 vote, June 17, 1999; Stevens wrote the opinion; Souter and Kennedy dissented.

A Virginia death row inmate failed to set aside his murder conviction or death sentence despite the prosecution's failure to turn over potentially useful evidence for his defense.

The ruling left standing Tommy David Strickler's capital murder conviction for the 1990 robbery-murder of a university student in Harrisonburg, Virginia. Strickler was sentenced to death, and an accomplice was convicted of first-degree murder and given a life sentence. A federal district court judge, ruling on Strickler's habeas corpus petition, set aside the conviction. The judge ruled that the prosecution had violated the so-called Brady rule—named for the Supreme Court decision, *Brady v. Maryland* (1963)—by failing to turn over notes of the police interview with an eyewitness to the abduction. The witness had testified at Strickler's trial and depicted him as the instigator of the crime; the notes cast doubt on her memory and her account. On appeal, the Fourth U.S. Circuit Court of Appeals said Strickler's *Brady* claim was "procedurally defaulted" because he could have raised it in state courts. The appeals court also rejected the claim on the merits, saying the materials would have provided "little or no help" to Strickler's defense in the trial or sentencing phase.

The Court held, with only Thomas dissenting, that Strickler could raise the *Brady* issue, but agreed with the appeals court in rejecting the claim on the merits. Writing for the majority, Stevens said Strickler could raise the issue because prosecutors had misled his lawyer into believing that all materials from police files had been turned over. But Stevens also said the failure to turn over the notes of the witness's interview had not prejudiced him. "[Strickler] has not convinced us that there is a reasonable probability that the jury would have returned a different verdict if [the witness's] testimony had been either severely impeached or excluded entirely," Stevens wrote.

In a dissent, Souter, joined by Kennedy, said that Strickler might not have been sentenced to death if he had been able to challenge what Souter called the witness's "gripping" account of the abduction.

Thomas joined parts of Stevens's opinion, but dissented to consider the *Brady* claim. He did not write separately to explain his views.

Drug Offenses

Richardson v. United States, decided by a 6–3 vote, June 1, 1999; Breyer wrote the opinion; Kennedy, O'Connor, and Ginsburg dissented.

The Court made it harder to convict a federal defendant under a "drug kingpin" statute by requiring jurors to agree unanimously on each of three offenses needed to trigger the law.

The ruling set aside the conviction of a reputed Chicago gang leader, Eddie Richardson, under the federal "continuing criminal enterprise" law. The statute provided a minimum twenty-year prison sentence for anyone convicted of a drug offense that was part of "a continuing series of violations." A jury convicted Richardson after the trial judge refused to instruct the panel that it had to agree unanimously on which offenses constituted the three violations required under the law. The Seventh U.S. Circuit Court of Appeals upheld the conviction.

By a 6–3 vote, the Court reversed the conviction, saying a jury must unanimously agree on which specific violations make up the series of offenses under the law. Failing to impose a unanimity requirement, Breyer said, "will cover-up wide disagreement among the jurors about just what the defendant did, or did not, do."

Writing for the dissenters, Kennedy said the ruling "rewards those drug kingpins whose operations are so vast that the individual violations cannot be recalled or charged with specificity."

Habeas Corpus

Calderon, Warden v. Coleman, decided by a 5–4 vote, December 14, 1998; *per curiam* (unsigned) opinion; Stevens, Souter, Ginsburg, and Breyer dissented.

The Court overturned a decision requiring resentencing in an old murder case because the federal appeals court did not properly consider the effect of a constitutional defect at trial.

The unsigned ruling—issued without hearing oral argument—ordered a new hearing in a federal habeas corpus case brought by a California death row inmate, Russell Coleman. He sought to overturn his 1981 death sentence because of a jury instruction, held improper under state law, regarding the governor's power to commute prison sentences. A federal district court agreed, and the Ninth U.S. Circuit Court of Appeals upheld the decision.

By a 5–4 vote, the Court said the appeals court had not properly applied its most recent precedent limiting habeas corpus relief in cases of so-called harmless error. Before granting a new trial or sentence, the Court said, a lower federal court "must find that the error . . . had a substantial and injurious effect or influence on the jury's verdict."

Writing for the dissenters, Stevens said the appeals court decision was "unquestionably correct" even if it contained "a slight flaw" in its explanation why the invalid instruction was not harmless error.

O'Sullivan v. Boerckel, decided by a 6–3 vote, June 7, 1999; O'Connor wrote the opinion; Stevens, Ginsburg, and Breyer dissented.

State inmates ordinarily cannot raise a claim in a federal habeas corpus petition unless the issue has been presented to the state's highest court—even if the tribunal exercises limited review in criminal appeals.

The ruling, tightening the so-called exhaustion requirement in habeas corpus cases, came in an effort by an Illinois inmate, Darren Boerckel, to overturn a 1977 rape conviction. Boerckel raised a number of issues in his appeal to the intermediate state appeals court, but omitted some of them in his petition for leave to appeal to the Illinois Supreme Court. Years later, he raised those claims in a federal habeas corpus petition. A lower federal court dismissed the petition, but the Seventh U.S. Circuit Court of Appeals reinstated it, ruling that Boerckel had not been required to present all the claims to the state high court.

The Court disagreed. Inmates must invoke "one complete round of the State's established appellate review process" before raising a claim in a habeas corpus petition, O'Connor said.

In a dissenting opinion, Stevens, joined by Ginsburg and Breyer, said the ruling would "impose unnecessary burdens on habeas petitioners" and "thwart the interests of state supreme courts that administer discretionary dockets."

Peguero v. United States, decided by a 9–0 vote, March 2, 1999; Kennedy wrote the opinion.

A federal judge's failure to inform a defendant of the right to appeal a sentence is no basis for setting aside the sentence if the defendant knows of his right anyway.

The ruling rejected an effort by a Pennsylvania man, Manuel DeJesus Peguero, to set aside a 274-month prison sentence imposed in 1992 for federal drug charges. Peguero filed a habeas corpus petition because of the judge's failure to tell him he could appeal the sentence. But evidence showed Peguero had immediately told his lawyer to appeal the sentence. A lower court and the Third U.S. Circuit Court of Appeals both rejected Peguero's petition.

Unanimously, the Court agreed. "A district court's failure to advise the defendant of his right to appeal does not entitle him to habeas relief if he knew of his right and hence suffered no prejudice from the omission," Kennedy wrote.

Harmless Error

Neder v. United States, decided by a 6–3 vote, June 10, 1999; Rehnquist wrote the opinion; Scalia, Souter, and Ginsburg dissented.

A Florida man failed to overturn a real estate fraud conviction because the judge failed to instruct the jury about one element of the offense: the "materiality" of false statements used to carry out the scheme.

The ruling turned aside a plea by Ellis E. Neder Jr. to overturn convictions for federal mail, wire, and bank fraud and filing a false income tax return in connection with a multimillion-dollar series of real estate schemes in the 1980s. A fraud conviction requires proof of a "material" false statement, but the judge told the jury that the issue was for the court rather than the panel to decide. After Neder's conviction, the Supreme Court in 1995 held that materiality was a jury issue. The Eleventh U.S. Circuit Court of Appeals upheld Neder's conviction anyway. It ruled that the faulty jury instruction was harmless error because Neder had not contested the issue of materiality.

The Court unanimously held that materiality is an element of federal fraud offenses but voted 6–3 that a harmless error analysis could be applied to uphold the conviction. Writing for the majority, Rehnquist said that the error "did not render Neder's trial 'fundamentally unfair,' as that term is used in our cases."

The decision sent the ruling back to the appeals court to apply the harmless error test again. Four justices—O'Connor, Kennedy, Thomas, and Breyer—joined all of Rehnquist's opinion. Stevens concurred on a separate ground.

In a dissent, Scalia, joined by Souter and Ginsburg, said the ruling infringed Neder's right to a jury trial. "Depriving a criminal defendant to have the jury determine his guilt of the crime charged . . . can never be harmless," Scalia wrote. In his opinion, Stevens said he agreed with much of Scalia's reasoning.

Loitering

City of Chicago v. Morales, decided by a 6–3 vote, June 10, 1999; Stevens wrote the main opinion; O'Connor, Kennedy, and Breyer wrote concurring opinions; Thomas, Rehnquist, and Scalia dissented.

A local ordinance aimed at preventing loitering by gang members was struck down because it gave police too much discretion to arrest people for disobeying an order to get off the public streets.

The splintered ruling invalidated a 1992 Chicago criminal ordinance that authorized police to tell someone loitering on the streets with someone suspected of being a criminal gang member to disperse and to arrest anyone who refused. The Illinois Supreme Court, ruling in a challenge brought by more than sixty people arrested under the ordinance, held the law unconstitutional on grounds it was "impermissibly vague" and "an arbitrary restriction on personal liberties."

The Court voted 6–3 to strike the law down, but the justices in the majority wrote four separate opinions to say why. In a part of the opinion joined by all six, Stevens concluded that the law gave "too much discretion to the police and too little notice to citizens who wish to use the public streets." But only two justices—Souter and Ginsburg—joined another section in which Stevens said that what he called "the freedom to loiter for innocent purposes" was protected by the Due Process Clause of the Fourteenth Amendment.

In a partial concurring opinion, O'Connor, joined by Breyer, agreed that the law was "unconstitutionally vague," but said a more narrowly written ordinance could be upheld. In a separate partial concurrence, Kennedy said the ordinance did not give adequate notice of what police would consider to be prohibited conduct. Breyer also wrote a separate concurrence.

In a sharply written dissent, Thomas, joined by Rehnquist, disagreed that the law was unconstitutionally vague or that people have a fundamental right to loiter. "The ordinance does nothing more than confirm the well-established principle that the police have the duty and the power to maintain the public peace, and, when necessary, to disperse groups of individuals who threaten it," Thomas wrote. Scalia wrote a separate dissent—both longer and sharper—that Rehnquist and Thomas did not join. He said the "minor limitation" imposed by the ordinance was "a small price to pay for liberation of [the] streets." *(See story, pp. 61–66; excerpts, pp. 214–230.)*

Search and Seizure

City of West Covina v. Perkins, decided by a 9–0 vote, January 13, 1999; Kennedy wrote the opinion.

Police are not constitutionally required to tell someone whose property has been seized during a search what procedures to use to try to reclaim the items.

The ruling came in a suit brought by Lawrence Perkins seeking to recover property, including $2,629 in cash, taken in a search of his home by police in West Covina, California, while looking for a former boarder wanted in a murder investigation. The Ninth U.S. Circuit Court of Appeals allowed the suit to go forward. It said that due process required police to tell Perkins of "the procedure for contesting the seizure or retention of the property taken" along with other particulars about the search.

In a unanimous decision, the Court overturned what it called the appeals court's "far-reaching notice requirement." Due process, Kennedy wrote, requires police "to take reasonable steps" to notify an owner that property has been seized, but not to provide notice of the laws governing return of the property. "Once the property owner is informed that his property has been seized, he can turn to these public sources to learn about the remedial procedures available to him," Kennedy said.

Six justices joined Kennedy's opinion. In a separate concurrence, Thomas, joined by Scalia, suggested that any requirement to notify an owner of the seizure of property should be based on common law rather than the Due Process Clause.

Florida v. White, decided by a 7–2 vote, May 17, 1999; Thomas wrote the opinion; Stevens and Ginsburg dissented.

Police do not need a search warrant to seize an automobile that is subject to forfeiture because it has been used in illegal activity such as drug trafficking.

The ruling upheld the cocaine possession conviction of a Florida man, Tyvessel Tyvorus White, who claimed police acted improperly in seizing his car while arresting him on other charges. Police had observed White using his car to deliver cocaine on three previous occasions, but did not get a warrant to seize the car. After arresting White and seizing the car, police found two pieces of crack cocaine in the ashtray. White sought to suppress the evidence, arguing that police were required to obtain a warrant to seize the car. The Florida Supreme Court, in a divided decision, agreed.

By a 7–2 vote, the Court ruled that the Fourth Amendment does not require police to obtain a warrant "before seizing an automobile from a public place when they have probable cause to believe that it is forfeitable contraband." Thomas said the decision was justified by "the need to seize readily movable contraband" and the "greater latitude" given to police "in exercising their duties in public places."

In a brief concurrence, Souter, joined by Breyer, said the opinion did not constitute an endorsement of warrantless seizure of contraband not found in public.

Writing for the dissenters, Stevens said police had "weak support" for the warrantless seizure when the previous drug dealing occurred more than two months earlier. "One must assume that the officers . . . simply preferred to avoid the hassle of seeking approval from a judicial officer," Stevens wrote.

Knowles v. Iowa, decided by a 9–0 vote, December 8, 1998; Rehnquist wrote the opinion.

Police officers cannot automatically conduct a full search of an automobile after stopping the driver for a traffic citation.

The ruling reversed the marijuana conviction of an Iowa man, Patrick Knowles, stemming from a search of his car after he was stopped for speeding. An Iowa law—unique among the states—gave police authority to search a car after making a traffic stop even if the driver was not placed under arrest. The Iowa Supreme Court, by a 5–4 vote, rejected Knowles's effort to suppress the small quantity of marijuana and a "pot pipe" found during the search and upheld the conviction.

In a brief unanimous opinion, the Court ruled that the search violated the Fourth Amendment's prohibition against unreasonable searches. Rehnquist said the reasons permitting police to search an automobile after a custodial arrest—the need to protect officers' safety and to preserve evidence—do not apply when a driver is not arrested. The threat to officer safety "is a good deal less" in an ordinary traffic stop, Rehnquist said, and the officers had "all the evidence necessary to prosecute" the speeding offense without a search.

Maryland v. Dyson, decided by a 9–0 vote, June 21, 1999; *per curiam* (unsigned) opinion.

Police do not need to show special urgency before searching an automobile as long as they have probable cause to believe that the car contains contraband, such as illegal drugs.

The ruling reinstated the conviction of a Maryland man, Kevin Dyson, for possession of twenty-three grams of crack cocaine that was found in a duffel bag in the trunk of his car. Police had stopped Dyson based on an informant's tip that he would be returning to Maryland from New York with drugs in the car. The Maryland Court of Special Appeals threw out the conviction, saying there was "no exigency" for the police to search the car without first obtaining a warrant.

In a brief opinion, issued without hearing argument, the Court reversed the state court's decision. The state court's holding was "squarely contrary" to the Court's prior rulings, the unsigned opinion stated.

Minnesota v. Carter, decided by 6–3 and 5–4 votes, December 1, 1998; Rehnquist wrote the opinion; Breyer concurred in the judgment but disagreed with the legal holding; Ginsburg, Stevens, and Souter dissented.

Someone in a private premises for business purposes on a short-term basis has no standing to object to a police search of the location.

The ruling upheld the cocaine conspiracy convictions of two men, Wayne Thomas Carter and Melvin Johns, arrested after a police officer in a Minneapolis suburb saw them bagging cocaine while inside a third person's apartment. Carter and Johns, who were in the apartment for about two and a half hours, had agreed to give a small quantity of cocaine to the tenant in return for permission to use the apartment. The two men moved to suppress the evidence on grounds that the officer had conducted an illegal search by observing them from outside the apartment on the basis of an anonymous tip. A trial court and an intermediate appeals court ruled they had no standing to contest the search, but the Minnesota Supreme Court disagreed, found the search illegal, and overturned the convictions.

In a divided opinion, the Court said that Carter and Johns could not contest the search because they had "no legitimate expectation of privacy" while inside the apartment. The ruling narrowed a prior decision, *Minnesota v. Olson* (1980), that allowed an overnight house guest to contest a search. Rehnquist said Carter and Johns's case was different because of "the purely commercial nature of the transaction," "the relatively short period of time on the premises," and "the lack of any previous connection . . . [with] the householder." The Court did not rule on the legality of the search.

Four justices joined Rehnquist's opinion. In an opinion concurring in the judgment, Breyer said the two men did have standing to contest the search, but concluded the officer did nothing illegal by "observing the apartment from a public vantage point."

In a dissenting opinion, Ginsburg argued that anyone who is invited into a home "to share in a common endeavor" should "share his host's shelter against unreasonable searches and seizures." Stevens and Souter joined the opinion.

Wyoming v. Houghton, decided by a 6–3 vote, April 5, 1999; Scalia wrote the opinion; Stevens, Souter, and Ginsburg dissented.

Police who have probable cause to believe a driver is carrying illegal drugs or other contraband can search a passenger's belongings even if the passenger is not suspected of wrongdoing.

The ruling—significantly expanding police discretion in automobile searches—reinstated the drug conviction of a Wyoming woman, Sandra Houghton, found to be carrying a syringe with methamphetamine in her purse during a search of a car in which she was a passenger. Police stopped the car for a routine traffic violation, saw a syringe in the driver's pocket, and began searching the car after the driver said he had formerly used illegal drugs. They found the drugs in Houghton's purse, which had been lying next to her in the back seat. Reversing her conviction, the Wyoming Supreme Court held that a passenger's personal effects are "beyond the scope" of a search unless the passenger has the opportunity to conceal what the police are looking for.

In a divided ruling, the Court held that police in such cases may "inspect" a passenger's belongings that are "capable of concealing the object of the search." Scalia said that the search was reasonable under historical practice and the Court's prior rulings. In addition, he said that the search was justified under a balancing of the passenger's interests and those of the government. Passengers "possess a reduced expectation of privacy, with regard to the property that they transport in cars," Scalia wrote, while the governmental interests are "substantial."

In a concurring opinion, Breyer said the search might not have been justified if the purse had been "attached" to Houghton's clothing.

Writing for the three dissenters, Stevens said the decision contradict-ed prior Court rulings and reduced passengers' privacy. "The State's legit-imate interest in law enforcement does not outweigh the privacy concerns at issue," he wrote.

Self-Incrimination

Mitchell v. United States, decided by a 5–4 vote, April 5, 1999; Kennedy wrote the opinion; Scalia, Rehnquist, O'Connor, and Thomas dissented.

A judge may not use a defendant's refusal to testify at a sentencing hearing to draw conclusions about the facts of the offense.

The ruling required a new sentencing for a Pennsylvania woman, Amanda Mitchell, who was given a ten-year prison term after pleading guilty to selling cocaine as part of a large drug trafficking conspiracy. Mitchell faced a mandatory ten-year sentence if she had sold more than five kilograms of cocaine, but she did not acknowledge a specific quantity in her guilty plea and declined to testify in her sentencing hearing. The judge ruled that Mitchell had waived her Fifth Amendment privilege against self-incrimination by pleading guilty and that he "held it against" her that she declined to testify. On that basis, the judge ruled Mitchell had sold more than the amount needed to trigger the ten-year sentence. The Third U.S. Circuit Court of Appeals upheld the sentence.

In a narrowly divided decision, the Court ruled that the judge's action violated Mitchell's privilege against self-incrimination. "Treating a guilty plea as a waiver of the privilege at sentencing would be a grave encroach-ment on the rights of defendants," Kennedy wrote for the majority. He went on to say that a judge may not draw an "adverse inference" against a defendant regarding the facts of the crime from a defendant's refusal to testify at sentencing. "The Government retains the burden of proving facts relevant to the crime at the sentencing phase and cannot enlist the defendant in the process at the expense of the self-incrimination privi-lege," Kennedy wrote.

Writing for the four dissenters, Scalia said the ruling was an unjustified "extension" of the Court's prior rulings that a defendant's failure to testi-fy cannot be used against her at trial. "There is no reason why [the privi-lege against self-incrimination] must also shield her from the natural and appropriate consequences of her uncooperativeness at the sentencing stage," Scalia wrote. In a brief additional dissent, Thomas called for reconsidering the earlier decisions preventing prosecutors from using a defendant's failure to testify at trial.

Venue

United States v. Rodriguez-Moreno, decided by a 7–2 vote, March 30, 1999; Thomas wrote the opinion; Scalia and Stevens dissented.

Someone who uses a gun while committing a violent crime across state lines can be prosecuted for a federal firearms provision in any state where the crime occurred even if he did not use the gun in that state.

The ruling upheld the conviction and mandatory consecutive five-year prison term of a Texas man, Jacinto Rodriguez-Moreno, for using a gun during a kidnaping that began in Texas and continued into New Jersey, New York, and Maryland. Rodriguez-Moreno had been hired to find a drug dealer suspected of stealing a large quantity of cocaine and took the middleman in the transaction captive to help find the dealer. He threatened the captive's life with a .357 magnum revolver at the end of the crime in Maryland. After he was prosecuted and convicted in federal court in New Jersey, Rodriguez-Moreno argued that Maryland was the only place to bring the firearms charge. The Third U.S. Circuit Court of Appeals agreed.

By a 7–2 vote, the Court held that venue for the firearms charge was appropriate in any place where the underlying offense occurred. "A kidnaping . . . does not end until the victim is free," Thomas wrote. "It does not make sense, then, to speak of it in discrete geographic fragments."

In a dissent, Scalia, joined by Stevens, said it was "unmistakably clear" that the law allowed the prosecution only in a place where both the underlying offense and the use of the firearm occurred. This defendant, Scalia wrote, "has been prosecuted for using a gun during a kidnaping in a State and district where all agree he did not use a gun during a kidnaping."

Election Law

Initiatives

Buckley, Secretary of State of Colorado v. American Constitutional Law Foundation, Inc., decided by 9–0 and 6–3 votes, January 12, 1999; Ginsburg wrote the opinion; O'Connor and Breyer dissented in part; Rehnquist dissented.

The Court struck down major provisions of a Colorado law imposing requirements on people who circulate petitions for ballot initiatives, saying they imposed unjustifiable restrictions on constitutionally protected political speech.

The invalidated provisions required petition circulators to be registered voters, to wear identification badges while gathering signatures, and to disclose any amounts they were paid. The Tenth U.S. Circuit Court of Appeals, ruling in a challenge brought by a pro-initiative group and several individuals involved in the initiative process, said the requirements violated the First Amendment. The state appealed, saying the provisions helped combat fraud and gave voters valuable information about initiative proponents.

The justices voted 6–3 to strike down the registered voter and financial disclosure provisions and unanimously agreed that the registered voter requirement was unconstitutional.

Writing for five justices, Ginsburg said that the provisions "unjustifiably inhibit the circulation of ballot-initiative petitions." The registered voter requirement "drastically reduces . . . the pool of petition circulators," Ginsburg said, "without impelling cause." Similarly, she said the badge requirement "discourages participation in the petition circulation process . . . without sufficient cause." As for the financial disclosure provisions for individual petition circulators, Ginsburg said it was "no more than tenuously related" to the state's interests given other provisions requiring pro-initiative groups to disclose total contributions and expenditures.

Concurring separately, Thomas agreed that the provisions were invalid but said Ginsburg had relaxed the standard for judging election law provisions limiting political speech. He said all the provisions should be evaluated on the basis of "strict scrutiny," the most stringent constitutional standard.

In a partial dissent, O'Connor, joined by Breyer, said she would uphold the registration requirement and financial disclosure provisions. She described the registration requirement as "a neutral qualification for participation in the petitioning process" and said the financial disclosure provision "effectively combats fraud and provides valuable information to the public."

The ruling left in place some other initiative regulations, including a provision that petition circulators be at least eighteen years old and that they attach to each petition at the time of filing an affidavit containing the circulator's name and address. But in a separate dissent, Rehnquist said the ruling cast doubt on many election law provisions regulating both the initiative and candidate nomination process, including laws in many states requiring people circulating initiative or candidate petitions to be residents of that state.

Reapportionment and Redistricting

Hunt, Governor of North Carolina v. Cromartie, decided by a 9–0 vote, May 17, 1999; Thomas wrote the opinion; Stevens, Souter, Ginsburg, and Breyer concurred separately.

A federal court must hold a trial in a suit challenging a redistricting plan as a racial gerrymander when the state's motivation for the plan is in dispute.

The ruling—the Court's third in the dispute—sent back to a three-judge federal court a challenge to a North Carolina congressional redistricting plan adopted in 1997. The plan replaced a scheme that the Court threw out because one of the districts—the Twelfth—was improperly drawn to include a majority black population. The new Twelfth District was about 47 percent black and was more compact than the previous district. White voters nonetheless brought a challenge to the new plan. The three-judge court ruled the plan unconstitutional on a motion for summary judgment, before a full trial. The panel said the "uncontroverted material facts" showed that the Twelfth District was drawn on the basis of "racial identification" rather than for the political purpose of producing a majority Democratic district, as the state contended.

Unanimously, the Court said the lower court should have held a full trial because of the dispute over the motivation for the plan. "Reasonable inferences from the undisputed facts can be drawn in favor of a racial motivation finding or in favor of a political motivation finding," Thomas wrote for five of the justices.

In a separate concurring opinion, four justices led by Stevens questioned whether the evidence showed any racial motivation at all. All four had dissented from the Court's previous ruling in 1996 that invalidated the first plan. In its first ruling in the dispute, the Court in 1993 had established the precedent that white voters could bring an equal protection challenge to racially drawn districting plans.

Voting Rights

Lopez v. Monterey County, decided by an 8–1 vote, January 20, 1999; O'Connor wrote the opinion; Thomas dissented.

A county subject to the Voting Rights Act's preclearance requirement must obtain advance approval for a change in election procedures even if it results from a state law that does not have to be precleared.

The ruling reinstated a Voting Rights Act suit by Hispanic voters in Monterey County, California, contesting a change required by state law to consolidate the county's municipal courts. The county—but not the state—was covered by the 1965 law's requirement to obtain advance approval from either the Justice Department or a federal court in Washington for changes in election procedures. A three-judge federal district court ruled the preclearance requirement did not apply because California was not covered and the county had no discretion to disregard the state law.

By an 8–1 vote, the Court disagreed. Writing for six justices, O'Connor said the situation fell within the law's language requiring preclearance "whenever [a covered jurisdiction] shall enact or seek to administer" any voting change. The law, she wrote, "provides no indication that Congress intended to limit preclearance obligations to covered jurisdictions' discretionary actions." She also rejected arguments that applying the law to the county infringed on state sovereignty.

Concurring separately, Kennedy, joined by Rehnquist, said the preclearance requirement applied because the county had urged the state legislature to enact the law requiring the court consolidation.

In a lone dissent, Thomas said the preclearance requirement should apply only to "those voting changes that are the direct product of a covered jurisdiction's policy choices." Applying the law to require advance approval of the changes mandated by state law, he said, raised "grave constitutional concerns."

The decision was the Court's second ruling in the case. Earlier, the Court in 1996 had overturned the district court's decision to put into effect a judicial districting plan that had not been submitted for preclearance.

Federal Government

Census

Department of Commerce v. United States House of Representatives, decided by a 5–4 vote, January 25, 1999; O'Connor wrote the opinion; Stevens, Souter, Ginsburg, and Breyer dissented.

The Census Bureau may not use statistical sampling to determine population counts to be used in apportioning seats in the House of Representatives among the states. However, the ruling allowed the use of adjusted population figures for other purposes, including legislative and congressional redistricting and allocation of federal aid to state and local governments.

The politically charged ruling represented a victory for Republican opponents of the Clinton administration's plan to use statistical sampling techniques in an effort to achieve a more accurate count in the 2000 census. The Census Bureau, part of the Commerce Department, developed the plans to try to reduce the acknowledged undercount of minorities and others in previous censuses. Republicans opposed the plan. They contended that the statistical techniques were unnecessary and were susceptible to political manipulation.

Two suits were filed challenging the Census Bureau's plans as a violation of the Census Act and of the constitutional provision requiring an "actual enumeration" of the population every ten years to allocate House seats among the states. The Republican-controlled House filed suit in federal district court in the District of Columbia, while individuals in several states filed a second suit, *Glavin v. Clinton*, in federal district court in Alexandria, Virginia, outside Washington. Three-judge courts agreed with the challengers in both cases on statutory grounds without ruling on the constitutional issue. In appealing the decision, the Commerce Department challenged the legal standing of the House and the individual plaintiffs to bring the suits.

In a closely divided ruling, the Court upheld the ruling in the *Glavin* case and then dismissed the government's appeal of the suit filed by the House. On standing, O'Connor said an Indiana resident qualified to bring the suit because of his claim that his state would lose a seat under an adjusted population count and residents of other states qualified because of the claimed effects on intrastate legislative redistricting. On the merits, O'Connor based the decision on a 1976 amendment of part of the Census Act—section 195—that allowed the use of sampling "except for the determination of population for apportionment purposes." She rejected the government's argument that other provisions of the law gave the Census Bureau discretion to use sampling even for apportionment. The "only plausible" reading of the 1976 amendment, O'Connor said, was that it "prohibits the use of sampling in calculating the population for purposes of apportionment."

In a concurring opinion, Scalia—joined by Rehnquist, Kennedy, and Thomas—indicated he was inclined to agree as well with the constitutional argument raised by opponents of sampling. "It is in my view unquestionably doubtful whether the constitutional requirement of an 'actual enumeration' is satisfied by statistical sampling," Scalia wrote.

In the major dissenting opinion, Stevens said that the 1976 amendment did not override what he called "the unlimited grant of authority" to use statistical sampling contained in a separate section of the Census Act, section 141. He also rejected the constitutional challenge, saying that sampling was "a legitimate means of making the 'actual enumeration' that the Constitution commands." Souter and Ginsburg joined the major parts of Stevens's opinion, but disagreed with his finding that all of the plaintiffs had standing to bring the suits. Breyer agreed with most of Stevens's opinion, but analyzed the statutory issue slightly differently. He said sampling was justified because it was being used "to supplement" actual enumeration methods, not "as a substitute" for them. *(See story, pp. 76–81; excerpts, pp. 171–184.)*

Federal Regulation

AT&T Corp. v. Iowa Utilities Board, decided by votes of 8–0, 7–1, and 5–3, January 25, 1999; Scalia wrote the opinion; Souter dissented from one part of the ruling; Thomas, Rehnquist, and Breyer dissented from another, broader part; O'Connor did not participate.

The Federal Communications Commission has authority under the Telecommunications Act of 1996 to regulate the price and other conditions for new telephone companies to gain access to local telephone networks.

The decision went on to uphold all but one of the local-competition rules governing pricing and interconnection requirements that had been challenged by the so-called Baby Bells, the local telephone companies created in the breakup of the former AT&T monopoly in the 1980s. But the Court struck down as overbroad a provision aimed at assuring new telephone companies access to most of the "elements" of the local telephone networks.

The ruling—a setback for state regulators as well as the Baby Bells—came in consolidated legal challenges to FCC rules issued under the landmark 1996 law aimed at opening up local telephone markets to competition. The state regulators, through the National Association of Regulatory Utility Commissioners and individual state agencies, contended that the FCC rules infringed on their traditional powers to regulate intrastate telephone service and went beyond the original 1934 Communications Act. The local telephone companies—known in the industry as local exchange carriers or LECs—challenged specific provisions that imposed somewhat favorable terms for long-distance companies like AT&T to connect to their local networks and compete in providing local telephone service.

The challenges to the FCC rules were combined in a proceeding before the Eighth U.S. Circuit Court of Appeals in St. Louis. The appeals court struck down several of the FCC regulations on grounds that they either exceeded the agency's rulemaking authority or went beyond the specific provisions of the 1996 law. It upheld some of the challenged provisions, however. The FCC and the long-distance carriers asked the Court to review the decision, and the state regulators and the local telephone companies filed cross-petitions for review.

The Court upheld the FCC's general authority by a 5–3 vote and reinstated or upheld all but one of the challenged rules by unanimous votes. The justices voted 7–1 to strike down the network elements rule. The voting crossed ideological lines. Scalia wrote the Court's opinion, while fellow conservative Thomas wrote the main dissent. Rehnquist and Breyer joined Thomas's dissent; Souter was the lone dissenter on the network elements rule.

On the rulemaking issue, Scalia noted that the Communications Act, as amended in 1938, included broad authority for the FCC to "prescribe such rules and regulations as may be necessary and in the public interest to carry out" its provisions. "Since Congress expressly directed that the 1996 Act, along with its local-competition provisions, be inserted into the Communications Act of 1934," Scalia wrote, "the Commission's rulemaking authority would seem to extend to implementation of the local-competition provisions."

The network elements issues stemmed from the FCC's broad definition of the phrase to include directory assistance and vertical switching functions such as caller I.D., call forwarding, and call waiting. It adopted a broad rule generally guaranteeing new entrants blanket access to all of those services. The FCC also adopted an "unbundling rule" that prohibited the local carrier from separating elements that had previously been combined. A separate "pick and choose" rule allowed a new telephone carrier to demand access to any individual network element covered by the requirement without taking—and paying the cost of—all others. Finally, the FCC's "all elements" rule allowed a new company to gain access to local networks without building any of its own facilities.

Scalia said the FCC had reasonably interpreted what he termed an ambiguous statute in promulgating each of the specific provisions. But he said the blanket access rule went beyond the statute, which required the FCC to issue rules for determining when access was "necessary" or when denial of access would "impair" a new company's service. The law, Scalia wrote, "requires the Commission to determine *which* network elements must be made available, taking into account the objectives of the Act and giving some substance to the 'necessary' and 'impair' requirements."

In a partial dissent, Souter said he would uphold the access rules because he believed the FCC had "reasonably interpreted" the necessity and impairment requirements.

In the main dissent, Thomas said the ruling gave the FCC "unbounded authority to regulate a matter of state concern," in violation of a provision of the original Communications Act that barred the FCC from exercising jurisdiction over intrastate telephone service. He said he joined the ruling upholding the unbundling and pick-and-choose rules because they were not challenged on jurisdictional grounds. Rehnquist and Breyer joined his opinion. Breyer wrote a separate dissent, detailing economic arguments against the ratesetting formulas that the FCC adopted for interconnections.

O'Connor did not participate in the case because of a financial conflict.

California Dental Association v. Federal Trade Commission, decided by 9–0 and 5–4 votes, May 24, 1999; Souter wrote the opinion; Breyer, Stevens, Kennedy, and Ginsburg dissented in part.

The Court upheld the Federal Trade Commission's jurisdiction over nonprofit professional associations, but said a federal appeals court acted too quickly in sustaining the FTC's challenge to advertising restrictions adopted by a state dental association.

The ruling sent back for further consideration the FTC's challenge to ethics rules and policies adopted by the California Dental Association that required detailed disclosures regarding any advertised price discounts or claims as to quality of services. The dentists' group claimed the FTC had no jurisdiction because it was a nonprofit association that provided only minimal economic benefits to its members. After rejecting the jurisdictional challenge, the FTC ruled that the price restrictions were illegal per se because they restrained price competition. Alternatively, the commission ruled that both the price and nonprice restrictions were illegal under a so-called abbreviated rule of reason analysis—one that compares a policy's pro- and anticompetitive effects to determine its legality. The Ninth U.S. Circuit Court of Appeals upheld the FTC's jurisdiction, faulted it for using a per se analysis regarding the price restrictions, but upheld its conclusions under the rule of reason analysis.

The Court unanimously upheld the FTC's jurisdiction, but divided 5–4 on whether the agency or the appeals court had adequately considered the advertising guidelines' net effects on competition. On the jurisdictional issue, Souter noted that the Federal Trade Commission Act gave the FTC authority over any entity that carries on business for the profit "of its members." The dental association, he went on to say, provided a number of benefits to members—including financing arrangements, lobbying, litigation, marketing, and public relations. The activities, Souter said, "plainly fall within the object of enhancing its members 'profits.' "

In assessing the advertising policies, however, Souter said the FTC should have weighed "any costs to competition associated with the elimination of across-the-board advertising" against "gains to consumer information (and hence competition) created by discount advertising that is exact, accurate, and easily verifiable." Similarly, Souter said that "restricting difficult-to-verify claims" as to quality of service could be viewed as "a procompetitive ban on puffery."

In a partial dissent, Breyer, joined by Stevens, Kennedy, and Ginsburg, said that both the FTC and the appeals court were correct to conclude that the price and quality advertising restrictions had "obvious" adverse effects on competition. "I do not think it possible," Breyer wrote, "to deny the anticompetitive tendencies."

Roberts v. Galen of Virginia, Inc., decided by a 9–0 vote, January 13, 1999; *per curiam* (unsigned) opinion.

The Court eased the burden for recovering damages from hospitals for violating a federal law restricting the transfer of emergency patients to other facilities.

In a brief and unanimous opinion, the Court said that plaintiffs suing under the 1985 law do not need to show a hospital acted for an improper motive in transferring an emergency patient. The law, aimed at preventing the "dumping" of patients with potentially high medical costs and limited or no insurance, requires hospitals to provide "such treatment as may be required to stabilize" an emergency medical condition before transferring the patient.

The ruling stemmed from a suit by the guardian for a Kentucky woman, Wanda Johnson, who was admitted to the Humana Hospital–University of Louisville after being seriously injured in a traffic accident in 1992. After six weeks, the hospital transferred Johnson to a health facility in Indiana, but her condition deteriorated significantly afterward.

Two lower federal courts dismissed Johnson's suit, saying she had not proved the hospital had an improper motive for the transfer. The Court's unsigned opinion said the law contained no such requirement. The ruling left open other issues the hospital had raised in defending against the suit.

Your Home Visiting Nurse Services, Inc. v. Shalala, Secretary of Health and Human Services, decided by a 9–0 vote, February 23, 1999; Scalia wrote the opinion.

The Court limited the ability of health care providers to contest an insurance company's refusal to reconsider the amount of money the provider receives as reimbursement under the Medicare program.

The case involved a Medicare regulation that gave health care providers three years to ask an insurance company to reconsider a reimbursement decision. A nursing home company sought to challenge an insurer's refusal to reopen a reimbursement request before the Provider Reimbursement Review Board, but two lower federal courts said the regulation did not allow such an appeal.

Unanimously, the Court agreed. Scalia noted that the Medicare law gave providers only 180 days to appeal directly to the review board. "The statutory purpose of imposing an 180-day limit . . . would be frustrated by permitting requests to reopen to be reviewed indefinitely," he wrote.

Government Contracts

Department of the Army v. Blue Fox, Inc., decided by a 9–0 vote, January 20, 1999; Rehnquist wrote the opinion.

The Court refused to soften a longstanding rule that creditors cannot enforce liens on property of the federal government.

The ruling rejected an effort by a construction company, Blue Fox, Inc., to collect about $46,500 it was owed for its work as a subcontractor on a project to install a new telephone system at an Army base in Oregon. When the prime contractor, Verdan Technology, Inc., became insolvent, Blue Fox sought to place a so-called equitable lien—a noncontractual claim—on the money that the government owed to Verdan. It argued the suit was authorized by a provision of the Administrative Procedure Act permitting actions against federal agencies for "relief other than money damages." The suit was dismissed by a lower federal court, but reinstated by the Ninth U.S. Circuit Court of Appeals.

Unanimously, the Court held the suit amounted to an action for money damages that was barred by principles of sovereign immunity. "Liens, whether equitable or legal, are merely a means to the end of satisfying a claim for the recovery of money," Rehnquist wrote.

Military Affairs

Clinton, President of the United States v. Goldsmith, decided by a 9–0 vote, May 17, 1999; Souter wrote the opinion.

The Court limited the authority of the Court of Appeals for the Armed Forces while sidestepping a constitutional challenge to a law giving the president power to dismiss a service member following a court-martial conviction.

The ruling rejected an effort by an Air Force major, James Goldsmith, to block an order dismissing him from the service after his conviction on various charges for failing to practice safe sex or inform his sexual partners that he was HIV-infected. Goldsmith was given a six-year confinement and ordered to forfeit $2,500 of his monthly salary for six years, but the court-martial did not order his dismissal from the service. After his conviction became final, however, the president ordered Goldsmith dismissed under a 1996 law that allows the president to remove a service member after any court-martial conviction with a sentence of at least six-months' confinement. Goldsmith sought to block the order as a violation of due process and an impermissible retroactive punishment. The Court of Appeals for the Armed Forces, the highest military court, granted his plea, justifying its decision under the All Writs Act. That law gives federal courts authority to issue "all writs necessary or appropriate in aid of their respective jurisdictions."

Unanimously, the Court ruled that the military appeals court had exceeded its jurisdiction. The court "is not given authority, by the All Writs Act or otherwise, to oversee all matters arguably related to military justice," Souter wrote. Souter noted, however, that Goldsmith had other ways to challenge the dismissal order through military administrative procedures or afterwards in the courts.

Native Americans

Amoco Production Co. v. Southern Ute Indian Tribe, decided by a 7–1 vote, June 7, 1999; Kennedy wrote the opinion; Ginsburg dissented; Breyer did not participate.

Federal laws reserving ownership of coal on formerly public lands for the government did not apply to methane gas buried within coalbeds. Instead, the now valuable energy source belongs to private owners, the Court ruled.

The ruling favored a number of energy companies in a dispute over mineral rights on about 200,000 acres of land owned by the Southern Ute

Indian Tribe. Federal coal acts passed in 1909 and 1910 kept for the government the rights to coal on public lands being opened to homesteading. But the laws made no explicit mention of "coal gas," which was then considered a dangerous waste product of coal mining. The Ute tribe, which gained title to the land in 1938, sued in 1991 to establish rights both to the coal and to the methane gas. A lower federal court rejected the tribe's claim to the gas, and the Tenth U.S. Circuit Court of Appeals—voting 8–3—held that the government's reserved mineral rights included the methane gas.

By a nearly unanimous vote, the Court disagreed, citing what it called the "common understanding" of the definition of coal when Congress passed the laws. "Congress viewed [coalbed methane gas] not as part of the solid fuel resource it was attempting to conserve and manage, but as a dangerous waste product," Kennedy wrote.

Lawyers said the ruling could affect mineral rights on as many as 16 million acres of lands, mostly in the western United States. Ginsburg was the lone dissenter. "Congress would have assumed that the coal owner had dominion over" the coalbed gas, she wrote.

Minnesota v. Mille Lacs Band of Chippewa Indians, decided by a 5–4 vote, March 24, 1999; O'Connor wrote the opinion; Rehnquist, Scalia, Kennedy, and Thomas dissented.

The Court upheld the right of Chippewa Indians to hunt and fish free of state game regulation on 13 million acres of public land in central Minnesota.

The ruling came in a closely watched case that pitted eight Chippewa bands, supported by the federal government, against the state of Minnesota and a number of local governments and private property owners. The Chippewas claimed in a 1990 federal court suit that they had hunting and fishing rights on the lands under an 1837 treaty with the United States. The state and other parties argued those rights were terminated by an 1850 presidential order removing the Chippewas from parts of the Minnesota territory or by an 1855 treaty. Alternatively, they argued Minnesota's admission as a state automatically ended the Indians' hunting and fishing rights. A lower court and the Eighth U.S. Circuit Court of Appeals ruled in favor of the Chippewas.

By a 5–4 vote, the Court agreed. In an exhaustive historical reconstruction, O'Connor concluded that President Zachary Taylor had no authority under the 1837 treaty to issue the removal order and that the revocation of hunting and fishing rights in the order was also void. She went on to say that neither the 1855 treaty nor the act of Congress admitting Minnesota expressly terminated the Chippewas' hunting and fishing rights. "We conclude that the Chippewa retain the . . . rights guaranteed to them under the 1837 treaty," O'Connor wrote.

Writing for the four dissenters, Rehnquist disagreed on each of the three points. The presidential order contained an "ironclad revocation" of the Chippewas' hunting and fishing rights, Rehnquist said, and there was "simply no principled reason to invalidate" it. He called O'Connor's reading of the 1855 treaty "strained" and charged the decision effectively overturned an 1896 decision, *Ward v. Race Horse*, that upheld the sovereignty of newly admitted states over Indian hunting and fishing rights.

First Amendment

Commercial Speech

Greater New Orleans Broadcasting Association, Inc. v. United States, decided by a 9–0 vote, June 14, 1999; Stevens wrote the opinion.

The Court struck down a federal ban on broadcast advertising of casino gambling, saying the law was not well tailored to promote the interests advanced by the government to justify the restriction.

The ruling invalidated a law that, as originally enacted in 1934, prohibited radio or television stations from broadcasting any advertisements for lotteries or other games of chance. The law was amended in the 1970s and 1980s, however, to permit—under certain conditions—broadcast advertising of state-run lotteries, charitable lotteries, and Indian casinos. Broadcasters in Louisiana challenged the ban, but the Fifth U.S. Circuit Court of Appeals upheld the law twice, first in 1995 and again in 1998. Each time, the appeals court said the law was justified by the government's interest in stemming the social costs of gambling and in supporting the policies of states that prohibit casino gaming.

Unanimously, the Court said the ban could not survive under its recent approach to commercial speech. Stevens described the federal policy of discouraging gambling as "decidedly equivocal" and the ban on casino advertising as "pierced by exemptions and inconsistencies." He also noted that the government could try to alleviate the social costs of gambling through other, nonspeech-related regulations—such as limiting betting amounts, prohibiting the use of credit, or restricting the location of gambling facilities.

Seven justices joined Stevens's opinion. Rehnquist added a brief concurrence suggesting that some restrictions on gambling advertising might be upheld if they were part of a more comprehensive regulatory scheme. In a separate concurrence, Thomas said he would go further and invalidate any commercial speech regulation intended to "manipulate" consumer choices of a legal product or service.

Immigration Law

Deportations

Reno, Attorney General v. American-Arab Anti-Discrimination Committee, decided by 8–1 and 6–3 votes, February 24, 1999; Scalia wrote the opinion; Breyer and Ginsburg did not join part of the ruling; Souter dissented.

Illegal aliens cannot challenge the government's effort to deport them on grounds that they are being singled out because of their political views. The ruling also allowed retroactive application of a new law restricting judicial review of deportation cases.

The ruling came in the government's effort dating from 1987 to deport eight aliens—seven Palestinians and one Kenyan, dubbed the "L.A. Eight"—for activities in support of an alleged terrorist organization, the Popular Front for the Liberation of Palestine. The government charged the six temporary residents in the group with violating visa restrictions; the other two, who had resident alien status, were charged under an antiterrorist provision permitting deportation of an alien who belonged to an organization advocating the killing of government officers or unlawful destruction of property. In defending against the deportation, all eight claimed they had been unlawfully singled out on the basis of their political views, in violation of the First Amendment.

A lower federal court tentatively sustained their claim, and the Ninth U.S. Circuit Court of Appeals in 1995 upheld a preliminary injunction barring the deportations. While the case was pending, Congress passed a law—the Illegal Immigration Reform and Immigrant Responsibility Act of 1996—aimed at limiting judicial review of deportation cases. One provision, section 1252(g), stated that no court would have jurisdiction to hear any claim from a decision to "commence proceedings, adjudicate cases, or execute removal orders" in any deportation case "except as provided in this section." The Court agreed to review the case to determine whether the provision allowed any interim challenges before a final deportation order and, if not, whether the restriction applied retroactively.

The Court voted 8–1 that the jurisdiction limitation provision allowed aliens to challenge deportations only after the issuance of a final order and that the provision applied retroactively. In the main opinion, Scalia went further to say that illegal aliens have no constitutional right to claim selective enforcement as a defense against deportation. "When an alien's continuing presence in this country is in violation of the immigration laws," Scalia wrote, "the Government does not offend the Constitution by deporting him for the additional reason that it believes him to be a member of an organization that supports terrorist activity."

Six justices joined Scalia's analysis of the statutory issue, and Stevens concurred for slightly different reasons. But Ginsburg, joined by Breyer, said it was not necessary to decide the constitutional issue; she noted that the Court had specifically declined to include the question in granting review of the case.

In a lone dissent, Souter criticized what he called Scalia's "creative interpretation" of the jurisdiction-limiting provision. He also said the Court should not have decided the constitutional issue.

Immigration and Naturalization Service v. Aguirre-Aguirre, decided by a 9–0 vote, May 3, 1999; Kennedy wrote the opinion.

The Court strengthened immigration authorities' discretion to deport an alien who committed serious nonpolitical crimes outside the United States even if he faces persecution if returned to his native country.

The ruling overturned a federal appeals court decision favoring Juan Anibal Aguirre-Aguirre in his effort to avoid deportation to his native Guatemala. Aguirre had committed a variety of offenses, including burning buses, in Guatemala to protest increased bus fares. He sought to avoid being sent back to Guatemala under an immigration law provision that requires the attorney general to withhold deportation if an alien would face political persecution in his native country. The Immigration and Naturalization Service invoked an exception that permits deportation despite the risk of persecution if "there are serious reasons for considering that the alien has committed a serious nonpolitical crime." The Board of Immigration Appeals agreed with the INS, but the Ninth U.S. Circuit Court of Appeals said the BIA did not adequately consider the dangers Aguirre would face in Guatemala or the relation of his offenses to his political aims.

Unanimously, the Court said the appeals court should have given greater deference to the immigration board's interpretation of the law. "The BIA's determination that [the serious nonpolitical crime exception] requires no additional balancing of the risk of persecution rests on a fair and permissible reading of the statute," Kennedy wrote. He also said the immigration board had properly determined that "the violence and destructiveness" of Aguirre's crimes were "disproportionate" to his political objectives.

Individual Rights

Damage Suits

Davis v. Monroe County Board of Education, decided by a 5–4 vote, May 24, 1999; O'Connor wrote the opinion; Kennedy, Rehnquist, Scalia, and Thomas dissented.

A school district that receives federal aid may be required to pay damages to a student for severe sexual harassment by another student. The school district may be held liable if it knows of the sexual harassment and is deliberately indifferent to preventing it and if the behavior deprives the victim of access to educational opportunities or benefits provided by the school.

The ruling reinstated a suit by the mother of a Georgia girl, LaShonda Davis, brought under Title IX of the Education Amendments of 1972, which prohibits discrimination on account of sex by school districts receiving federal financial assistance. Davis claimed that a fellow fifth-grader subjected her to sexual taunting and advances over a five-month period and that the school's teachers and principal did nothing to prevent it or discipline the other student. The Fifth U.S. Circuit Court of Appeals upheld a lower court's dismissal of the suit, ruling that school districts cannot be held liable for student-on-student sexual harassment.

In a closely divided decision, the Court ruled that school districts could be held responsible for student-on-student sexual harassment but set conditions that the majority said would not lead to "sweeping" liability. O'Connor said that liability could be imposed for "deliberate indifference to known acts of harassment" by a student but only if the behavior is "severe, pervasive, and objectively offensive" and "undermines and detracts from the victims' educational experience."

Writing for the four dissenters, Kennedy said the ruling improperly expanded Title IX to apply to peer harassment suits and injected the federal government into a traditional area of state concerns. "Title IX did not give States unambiguous notice that accepting federal funds meant ceding to the federal government power over the day-to-day disciplinary decisions of schools," Kennedy wrote. *(See story, pp 56–61; excerpts, pp. 197–214.)*

Haddle v. Garrison, decided by a 9–0 vote, December 14, 1998; Rehnquist wrote the opinion.

A person fired from a job in retaliation for agreeing to testify in a federal criminal investigation may recover damages under federal civil rights law from those responsible for his termination.

The ruling reinstated a suit by a Georgia man, Michael Haddle, against two officers of a health care company, Healthmaster, Inc., involved in a Medicare fraud investigation. Haddle claimed that the officers, Jeanette Garrison and Dennis Kelly, conspired to have him fired from his job with the company after he agreed to cooperate in the probe and to testify before a federal grand jury. He filed suit under a provision of federal civil rights law, 42 U.S.C. section 1985(2), that allows suits if someone is "injured in his property or person" in retaliation for testifying in a federal court proceeding. But the Eleventh U.S. Circuit Court of Appeals barred the suit, saying that Haddle had no "constitutionally protected interest" in employment because he was an "at will" employee—someone who could be fired for any reason.

In a brief and unanimous opinion, the Court held that the suit stated a valid complaint under the civil rights statute. "Third-party interference with at-will employment relationships . . . has long been a compensable injury under tort law," Rehnquist said.

Hanlon v. Berger, decided by 9–0 and 8–1 votes, May 24, 1999; *per curiam* (unsigned) opinion; Stevens dissented in part.

Federal officers were given a second chance to avoid liability for inviting a television news crew to accompany them on a raid of the grounds and outbuildings of a Montana ranch.

The ruling stemmed from a 1993 raid by agents of the U.S. Fish and Wildlife Service on the grounds and outbuildings of a Montana ranch owned by Paul Berger and his wife. The Bergers filed a suit claiming that the agents violated their constitutional rights by inviting a Cable News Network crew to accompany them on the raid. The Ninth U.S. Circuit Court of Appeals upheld the claim and rejected the agents' effort to invoke the defense of qualified immunity on the ground that their conduct did not violate any rights clearly established at the time. The Court reviewed the ruling along with a similar case, *Wilson v. Layne,* and decided both cases the same day. In *Wilson,* the Court ruled that officers violated the rights of a Maryland couple by allowing news media representatives to accompany them inside a private home, but upheld the officers' qualified immunity defense for the 1992 incident. *(See below.)*

Following that decision, the Court sent the Montana case back to lower federal courts to determine whether the law was any clearer in 1993 when that raid occurred. The ruling also appeared to leave open the question whether it would make any difference that the CNN crew did not go inside the Bergers' home. Stevens said he would have rejected the immunity defense, as he did in *Wilson.*

National Collegiate Athletic Association v. Smith, decided by a 9–0 vote, February 23, 1999; Ginsburg wrote the opinion.

The Court turned aside an effort to apply to the National Collegiate Athletic Association (NCAA) the federal law prohibiting sex discrimination by educational institutions receiving federal assistance. But the ruling allowed a former women's college volleyball player and the federal government a second chance to argue the issue in lower federal courts.

Renee Smith sued under the federal law—known as Title IX of the Education Amendments of 1972—after the NCAA refused to give her a waiver to play on volleyball teams for two colleges where she was enrolled in graduate programs. The NCAA, a private association composed of 1,200 college and university members, cited a rule permitting graduate students to play varsity sports only at colleges they attended as undergraduates. Smith argued that the NCAA applied the rule unevenly, frequently allowing such waivers for male athletes. A federal district court dismissed the complaint, but the Third U.S. Circuit Court of Appeals held the NCAA was subject to Title IX because of the dues paid by member colleges that did receive federal assistance.

In a unanimous decision, the Court held that the dues paid to the NCAA were "insufficient to trigger Title IX coverage." Entities receiving federal aid directly or through an intermediary are subject to the law, Ginsburg said, but "entities that only benefit economically from federal assistance are not."

The decision returned the case to lower courts, however, for rulings on two other claims raised by the federal government and by civil rights groups. They argued that Title IX applied either because the NCAA directly received federal funds for a youth sports program it administered or because it exercised "controlling authority" over federally funded programs at colleges and universities.

Wilson v. Layne, Deputy United States Marshal, decided by 9–0 and 8–1 votes, May 24, 1999; Rehnquist wrote the opinion; Stevens dissented in part.

Police violate the Fourth Amendment and may be held liable for damages by inviting news media representatives to accompany them when executing a warrant inside a private home.

The ruling limited the common but sometimes controversial practice of "media ride-alongs," but gave the officers involved in a 1992 incident in Maryland a chance to avoid liability because the law was not settled at that time.

The case stemmed from an early morning raid by a team of deputy federal marshals and Montgomery County, Maryland, deputy sheriffs, on the private home of Charles and Geraldine Wilson. The officers had an arrest warrant for the Wilsons' son Dominic and had invited a reporter and photographer for the *Washington Post* to accompany them. After an altercation with Charles Wilson, the officers swept through the house, determined that Dominic Wilson was not inside, and departed. The photographer took pictures, but the newspaper published no photos or account of the incident. The Wilsons sued the officers for violation of their constitutional rights by inviting the journalists inside their house. The Fourth U.S. Circuit Court of Appeals declined to decide the Fourth Amendment issue, but granted summary judgment to the officers. It said the officers were entitled to a defense of "qualified immunity" on the ground that their actions did not violate a right clearly established at the time. The Court agreed to review the ruling along with a similar case, *Hanlon v. Berger*, from a different federal appeals court. *(See p. 129.)*

The Court unanimously held that the police violated the Fourth Amendment, but voted 8–1 to uphold the qualified immunity defense. Police violate the Fourth Amendment, Rehnquist wrote, "to bring members of the media or other third parties into a home during the execution of a warrant when the presence of the third parties in the home was not in aid of the execution of the warrant." After reviewing the limited number of judicial opinions on the issue, however, Rehnquist said it was "not unreasonable" for the officers to have thought the action was lawful.

Stevens, in a lone partial dissent, said he would have rejected the qualified immunity defense. "It has long been clearly established that officers may not bring third parties into private homes to witness the execution of a warrant," he wrote.

Disability Rights

Albertsons, Inc. v. Kirkingburg, decided by a 9–0 vote, June 22, 1999; Souter wrote the opinion.

An employer can ordinarily require job applicants with physical impairments to meet standards of federal safety regulations without violating the federal Americans with Disabilities Act (ADA).

The ruling barred a discrimination claim brought by an Oregon truck driver, Hallie Kirkingburg, after the grocery chain Albertsons fired him because he did not meet vision standards set by the federal Department of Transportation (DOT). Kirkingburg asked the company to rehire him under an experimental DOT program waiving the visual standards, but it refused. A lower federal court judge granted summary judgment to Albertsons, but the Ninth U.S. Circuit Court of Appeals reinstated the claim.

Unanimously, the Court held that the disability rights law did not require the company to rehire Kirkingburg under the waiver program. "An employer who requires as a job qualification that an employee meet an otherwise applicable safety regulation," Souter explained, is not required to "justify enforcing the regulation solely because its standard may be waived in an individual case."

All the justices joined that part of Souter's opinion. Stevens and Breyer did not join a section that followed the Court's decision the same day in *Sutton v. United Air Lines, Inc.*, that Kirkingburg's claimed disability had to be determined on the basis of his corrected rather than his uncorrected vision. *(See p. 135.)*

Cedar Rapids Community School District v. Garret F., decided by a 7–2 vote, March 3, 1999; Stevens wrote the opinion; Thomas and Kennedy dissented.

Public schools receiving federal aid for educating children with disabilities may be required to provide students with continuous nursing services if necessary for them to attend school.

The ruling—a significant victory for disability rights advocates and a setback for local school districts—came in a dispute between the mother of a quadriplegic youngster, Garret Frey, and the Cedar Rapids, Iowa, school district. Garret, a high school sophomore by the time of the Court's decision, had been paralyzed from the neck down by a motorcycle accident at the age of four. He was dependent on a ventilator and required continuous nursing services for such functions as urinary catheterization and suctioning of a tracheotomy tube.

Garret's mother, Charlene Frey, said the school district was required to provide those services under the federal Individuals with Disabilities Education Act—sometimes called IDEA. That law authorized federal aid to school districts if they provided special education and "related services" to children with physical or mental disabilities—not including "medical services" other than those required for diagnostic testing and evaluation. The Cedar Rapids district argued the nursing services Garret required were not covered, citing the estimated expense of $18,000 per year. But the school district's argument was rejected by an administrative law judge, a federal district court judge, and the Eighth U.S. Circuit Court of Appeals.

By a 7–2 vote, the Court also agreed that the school district was required to provide the nursing services. "The district must fund such 'related services' in order to help guarantee that students like Garret are integrated into the public schools," Stevens wrote. Stevens based the ruling in part on the Court's earlier decision in a 1984 case that exempted "medical services" from coverage under the law only if they were functions that could be performed only by physicians.

In the dissenting opinion, Thomas, joined by Kennedy, challenged both the earlier decision and the "extension" of the ruling to cover full-time nursing services. "Congress enacted IDEA to increase the *educational* opportunities available to disabled children, not to provide medical care for them," Thomas said. He also said the ruling "blindsides unwary States with fiscal obligations that they could not have anticipated."

Cleveland v. Policy Management Systems Corp., decided by a 9–0 vote, May 24, 1999; Breyer wrote the opinion.

Someone who applies for or receives Social Security disability benefits may also be able to sue an employer over alleged discrimination under the federal Americans with Disabilities Act (ADA).

The ruling was a victory for a stroke victim, Carolyn Cleveland, who received benefits under the Social Security Disability Insurance (SSDI) program and later sued her employer for firing her on account of her disability. The Fifth U.S. Circuit Court of Appeals threw out the discrimination suit. It held that applying for Social Security disability benefits ordinarily barred someone from also claiming that she was qualified to work for purposes of the antidiscrimination law.

Unanimously, the Court reinstated the discrimination suit. "An ADA suit claiming that the plaintiff can perform her job *with* reasonable accommodation," Breyer wrote, "may well prove consistent with an SSDI claim that the plaintiff could not perform her own job (or other jobs) *without* it." But the Court ruled that a plaintiff suing under the antidiscrimination law had to offer an explanation to reconcile an earlier benefits claim. The ruling sent the case back to lower federal courts for further proceedings.

Murphy v. United Parcel Service, Inc., decided by a 7–2 vote, June 22, 1999; O'Connor wrote the opinion; Stevens and Breyer dissented.

The Court rejected a discrimination claim under the Americans with Disabilities Act (ADA) brought by a Kansas man fired from a job as a mechanic because of correctable high blood pressure.

The ruling stemmed from a suit filed by Vaughn Murphy after United Parcel Service fired him from a mechanic's job because he had high blood pressure and did not meet federal Department of Transportation requirements for driving commercial vehicles. A lower federal court and the Tenth U.S. Circuit Court of Appeals both rejected Murphy's suit.

By a 7–2 vote, the Court applied its decision the same day in a comparable case, *Sutton v. United Air Lines, Inc.,* to reject Murphy's claim. *(See p. 135.)* As in *Sutton,* O'Connor said that the determination of a disability under the ADA should take into account any measures to correct or mitigate a physical or mental impairment. Stevens and Breyer dissented, as they did in *Sutton.*

Olmstead, Commissioner, Georgia Department of Human Resources v. L. C., decided by a 6–3 vote, June 22, 1999; Ginsburg wrote the main opinion; Thomas, Rehnquist, and Scalia dissented.

Someone with a mental disability may be entitled to be placed in a community setting rather than an institution if the placement is medically appropriate and can be accommodated within the available mental health treatment resources.

The ruling—a partial victory for disability rights' advocates—sent back for further consideration a suit initiated by two mental health patients in Georgia to win placements in community treatment centers. They claimed the state discriminated against them under the federal Americans with Disabilities Act (ADA) by keeping them in institutions. The state argued that community placement was not required by the law and that the additional cost would "fundamentally alter" the state's program. A lower federal court judge largely ruled in favor of the women, but the Eleventh U.S. Circuit Court of Appeals ordered further proceedings to give the state some opportunity to present its cost defense.

In a fractured decision, the Court agreed that the disability rights law requires community placement under some circumstances, but also gave states greater leeway to show that mandated community treatment would be too expensive or unfair to other mental patients. In the main opinion, Ginsburg said institutionalization would amount to discrimination under the ADA if mental health professionals determined that community placement was "appropriate," if the patient did not oppose transfer to "a less restrictive setting," and if the placement could be "reasonably accommodated, taking into account the resources available . . . and the needs of others with mental disabilities." Four justices—Stevens, O'Connor, Souter, and Breyer—concurred in that standard.

Ginsburg said the case should be sent back to lower courts for the state to have a chance to show that "immediate relief" for plaintiffs in such cases would be "inequitable" toward other mental health patients. Stevens did not join that portion of the opinion; he said he favored upholding the appeals court. In a separate opinion, Kennedy also said the case should be remanded. He warned against the risk that mandatory deinstitutionalization could result in "too little assistance and supervision" for some mental patients. Breyer joined part of Kennedy's opinion.

Writing for the dissenters, Thomas said the two mental health patients had not proved that they were discriminated against "by reason of their disabilities," as the ADA required. "Temporary exclusion from community placement does not amount to 'discrimination' in the traditional sense of the word," he wrote. (See story, pp. 51–56; excerpts, pp. 230–242.)

Sutton v. United Air Lines, Inc., decided by a 7–2 vote, June 22, 1999; O'Connor wrote the opinion; Stevens and Breyer dissented.

Someone is not disabled under the federal Americans with Disabilities Act (ADA) if corrective measures, such as eyeglasses, mean that she is not "substantially limited" in a major life activity.

The ruling—an important victory for employers—rejected a discrimination claim brought by twin sisters, both severely myopic, who unsuccessfully sought to be hired by United Air Lines as pilots in 1992. Although the women had 20/20 vision or better with eyeglasses, the airline rejected their applications because they did not meet its requirement of 20/100 uncorrected vision. A lower federal court and the Tenth U.S. Circuit Court of Appeals both rejected the women's suit. Both courts held that under the ADA's definitions the two women were not disabled or regarded as being disabled.

By a 7 2 vote, the Court agreed that the determination of whether a person is disabled under the ADA should take corrective measures into account. "If a person is taking measures to correct for, or mitigate, a physical or mental impairment," O'Connor wrote, "the effects of those measures . . . must be taken into account when judging whether that person is 'substantially limited' in a major life activity, and thus 'disabled' under the Act." O'Connor also said the women had failed to show that United viewed them as disabled. "The ADA allows employers . . . to establish physical criteria," she wrote.

In a dissenting opinion, Stevens, joined by Breyer, said the Court had adopted "a crabbed vision" of the coverage of the law. The definition of disability, Stevens said, was met by "the existence of an impairment—present or past—that substantially limits, or did so limit, the individual before amelioration." *(See story, pp. 46–51; excerpts, pp. 242–254.)*

Job Discrimination

Kolstad v. American Dental Association, decided by 7–2 and 5–4 votes, June 22, 1999; O'Connor wrote the opinion; Rehnquist and Thomas dissented from one part of the decision; Stevens, Souter, Ginsburg, and Breyer dissented from another part.

Employers can be ordered to pay punitive damages for intentional or reckless job discrimination, but not for actions by a manager that are contrary to the employer's "good faith efforts" to prevent discrimination.

The ruling was a mixed result for civil rights advocates and employers alike in interpreting a recently enacted law that broadened damage remedies for plaintiffs in employment discrimination cases. The Civil Rights Act of 1991 provided that plaintiffs could recover punitive damages if an employer was guilty of intentional discrimination and acted "with malice or with reckless indifference to [the plaintiff's] federally protected rights." A Washington, D.C., woman, Carole Kolstad, invoked that provision in a sex discrimination suit against the American Dental Association after she was passed over for a position as the association's top lobbyist. A jury awarded her back pay of $52,718, but the court refused to allow the panel to consider punitive damages. On appeal, the U.S. Court of Appeals for the District of Columbia Circuit, in a 7–5 decision, held that the law permitted punitive damages only in "extraordinarily egregious cases."

The Court voted 7–2 to reject the appeals court's decision, but by a 5–4 margin adopted a different limitation on employers' liability for punitive damages. The 1991 law, O'Connor wrote, "does not require a showing of egregious or outrageous discrimination independent of the employer's state of mind." But she said that employers cannot be ordered to pay punitive damages for discriminatory decisions by managers if the actions are "contrary to the employer's good faith efforts to comply with" the federal employment discrimination law. The ruling sent the case back for a trial on punitive damages under the new standard.

In a partial dissent, Rehnquist, joined by Thomas, said he agreed with the appeals court's decision to require proof of "egregious" conduct for a punitive damages award. But the two justices joined the section limiting the circumstances for punitive damages for managerial decisions.

In a separate partial dissent, Stevens agreed with the decision to reject an egregiousness requirement for awarding punitive damages. But he called the other part of the opinion "ill advised" because the issue had not been briefed or argued by either side. The Court's other liberal justices—Souter, Ginsburg, and Breyer—joined his opinion. *(See story, pp. 72–76; excerpts, pp. 254–263.)*

West, Secretary of Veterans Affairs v. Gibson, decided by a 5–4 vote, June 14, 1999; Breyer wrote the opinion; Kennedy, Rehnquist, Scalia, and Thomas dissented.

The Equal Employment Opportunity Commission (EEOC) can award compensatory damages as well as back pay and reinstatement in job discrimination claims by federal government employees.

The ruling broadened the application of a 1991 law allowing courts to award compensatory damages in suits under the federal job discrimination law known as Title VII. The new law did not specify whether federal employees could recover damages, but as previously enacted the statute gave the EEOC power to award "appropriate" remedies to federal workers. The issue reached the Court in a sex discrimination claim by an employee of the Department of Veterans Affairs, Michael Gibson, who said he was denied a promotion in favor of a less qualified woman. The EEOC upheld the claim, awarded Gibson back pay, ordered him reinstated, but rejected his effort to recover damages.

By a 5–4 vote, the Court ruled that the 1991 law gave the EEOC authority to award damages. "The meaning of the word 'appropriate' permits its scope to expand to include Title VII remedies that were not appropriate before 1991, but in light of legal changes are appropriate now," Breyer wrote. The ruling sent the case back to a federal appeals court to determine whether Gibson had made a proper request for damages in his claim.

Writing for the dissenters, Kennedy said the EEOC should not be given authority to award damages unless the statute "waives the United States' immunity to the awards in clear and unambiguous terms."

Welfare

Saenz, Director, California Department of Social Services v. Roe, decided by a 7–2 vote, May 17, 1999; Stevens wrote the opinion; Rehnquist and Thomas dissented.

States cannot establish separate welfare benefits for newly arrived residents based on the benefit levels of the state where they previously lived.

The ruling—based on the rarely used Privileges and Immunities Clause of the Fourteenth Amendment—invalidated a 1992 California law that limited welfare benefits for people who moved there from another state to the amounts provided by the other state. Congress in 1996 included a provision authorizing such differentials as part of a broad welfare reform law. Three California residents whose benefits were reduced by the law challenged it on constitutional grounds. The state defended the reductions on the ground that they would save about $10.9 million annually in welfare benefits. A federal district court judge preliminarily enjoined implementation of the law, and the Ninth U.S. Circuit Court of Appeals upheld the injunction.

By a 7–2 vote, the Court said the state law violated the Fourteenth Amendment's clause prohibiting the states from making or enforcing "any law which shall abridge the privileges or immunities of citizens of the United States." Stevens said the law could not be justified by "a purpose to deter welfare applicants from migrating to California" or by "the State's legitimate interest in saving money." As for the federal law, Stevens said that Congress "may not authorize the States to violate the Fourteenth Amendment."

In a dissenting opinion, Rehnquist said he would uphold the benefits limit as "a good-faith residency requirement." Thomas joined Rehnquist's opinion and wrote a separate dissent contending that the Privileges and Immunities Clause should be limited to "fundamental rights, rather than every public benefit established by positive law." Rehnquist joined Thomas's dissent. (See story, pp. 66–71; excerpts, pp. 185–196.)

Labor Law

Arbitration

Wright v. Universal Maritime Service Corp., decided by a 9–0 vote, November 16, 1998; Scalia wrote the opinion.

Employers cannot use a collective bargaining agreement to force employees to arbitrate complaints about job discrimination unless the contract includes an explicit waiver of the right to sue in federal court.

The ruling reinstated a discrimination suit by a South Carolina dock worker, Ceasar Wright, filed against Charleston stevedore companies under the federal Americans with Disabilities Act. The companies sought to dismiss the suit on the ground that Wright had failed to submit the dispute to arbitration under a provision of the contract with the International Longshoremen's Association local. The contract required use of grievance procedures to resolve any "matters under dispute." A lower federal court and the Fourth U.S. Circuit Court of Appeals both agreed with the companies' position.

In a unanimous but narrow opinion, the Court said the arbitration clause was too general to bar an employee from filing suit under a federal antidiscrimination law. The collective bargaining agreement, Scalia wrote, did not contain "a clear and unmistakable waiver of the covered employees' rights to a judicial forum for federal claims of employment discrimination." But Scalia said the Court was leaving open the question whether a more explicit waiver could be enforced.

Federal Employees

National Aeronautics and Space Administration v. Federal Labor Relations Authority, decided by a 5–4 vote, June 17, 1999; Stevens wrote the opinion; Thomas, Rehnquist, O'Connor, and Scalia dissented.

Federal employees are entitled to have a union representative present and allowed to participate in interviews by investigators from the inspector general's office of the agency they work for.

The ruling upheld a finding that NASA and its Office of Inspector General (OIG) committed an unfair labor practice in an investigation involving an employee of the space agency's Marshall Space Flight Center in Huntsville, Alabama. The unidentified employee, invoking a provision of the Federal Service Labor-Management Relations Statute, asked for and was allowed to have a union representative present for the interview. But the inspector general's investigator did not allow the union representative to ask questions. The Federal Labor Relations Authority, which hears complaints of unfair labor practices involving federal workers, agreed with the union that the restriction amounted to an unfair labor practice. In appealing, NASA contended that the federal labor statute did not apply to the interview. It argued that the inspector general's office is statutorily independent of the agency and that the investigator therefore was not a "representative" of the agency as defined by the labor law.

In a closely divided decision, the Court rejected NASA's argument. Stevens said that despite the inspector general's independence, an investigator still was a "representative" of the agency. "The interest in fair treatment for employees under investigation is equally strong," he wrote, "whether they are being questioned by employees in NASA's OIG or by other representatives of the agency."

Writing for the dissenters, Thomas said, "Investigators employed in the Office of Inspector General (OIG) will not represent agency management in the typical case."

National Federation of Federal Employees, Local 1309 v. Department of Interior, decided by a 5–4 vote, March 3, 1999; Breyer wrote the opinion; O'Connor, Rehnquist, Scalia, and Thomas dissented.

Federal agencies may be required to negotiate with labor unions during the term of a collective bargaining agreement.

The ruling returned to the Federal Labor Relations Authority (FLRA) an issue that had put the agency between two federal appeals courts—the District of Columbia Circuit and the Fourth Circuit. The D.C. Circuit had interpreted the Federal Labor Management Relations Statute to require agencies to conduct midterm bargaining with labor unions on request. The Fourth Circuit, however, construed the law to prohibit negotiations until the expiration of a collective bargaining agreement. The issue reached the Court in an effort by the National Federation of Federal Employees, representing employees of the U.S. Geological Survey, to bargain with its parent agency, the Department of the Interior, over a proposed contract clause to permit midterm bargaining. When the Interior Department refused to bargain about the proposed clause, the FLRA ordered it to do so. But the Fourth Circuit set that order aside, prompting both the union and the agency to appeal.

In a closely divided ruling, the Court held that the statute left the issue for the FLRA to decide. Breyer said the statute itself was ambiguous and the issue involved competing policy considerations best resolved by an administrative agency. The statutory ambiguity, he said, justified "the conclusion that Congress delegated to the Authority the power to determine . . . whether, when, where, and what sort of midterm bargaining is required."

Writing for the four dissenters, O'Connor said midterm bargaining would be inconsistent with the federal law. "The Federal Labor Statute contemplates a single end agreement, and not supplementary agreements or modifications," she wrote. O'Connor also disputed the majority's argument for deferring to the FRLA's interpretation of the law. Rehnquist joined that passage, but not Scalia or Thomas.

Pensions and Benefits

Hughes Aircraft Co. v. Jacobson, decided by a 9–0 vote, January 25, 1999; Thomas wrote the opinion.

Employers with pension plans providing fixed benefits to retirees can use any surpluses in those plans for purposes other than increasing benefits or reducing contributions from participants in the plan.

The ruling came in a suit brought by five retirees of the Hughes Aircraft Co. challenging changes the company made to its employee pension plan in 1987. Through 1986, Hughes and the employees each contributed about half of the funds for the plan. The company stopped making contributions after investment gains created a $1 billion surplus. Effective in 1991, Hughes gave workers the option of continuing contributions in the existing plan or joining a new plan with no contributions but reduced benefits. The plan's surplus was used to provide new workers pensions with no required contributions.

The retired workers sued Hughes under the Employee Retirement Income Security Act—known as ERISA. They argued that the changes amounted to a termination of the plan that required distribution of the surplus to workers. Alternatively, they contended that the changes amounted to a violation of ERISA's so-called "anti-inurement" provision, which provides that pension plan funds "shall never inure to the benefit of any employer" and can be used only for pensions and administrative costs. The suit was dismissed by a lower federal court but reinstated by the Ninth U.S. Circuit Court of Appeals.

In a unanimous decision, the Court ruled the retirees had no legal claim under ERISA to block the changes. Pension plan participants "have no entitlement to a share in a plan's surplus," Thomas wrote, "even if it is partially attributable to the investment growth of their contributions." He said Hughes had not violated the anti-inurement provision because it did not use any of the assets "for a purpose other than to pay its obligations to the Plan's beneficiaries."

UNUM Life Insurance Co. of America v. Ward, decided by a 9–0 vote, April 20, 1999; Ginsburg wrote the opinion.

A state law allowing late-filed claims for insurance benefits is not preempted by the federal law governing pensions and health benefits provided by employers.

The ruling favored a California man, John Ward, who filed a claim for disability benefits under an employer-provided policy issued by the

UNUM Life Insurance Co. several months after the deadline set by the policy. The Ninth U.S. Circuit Court of Appeals allowed the claim under a California court ruling that an insurer cannot avoid liability for a late-filed claim unless it shows it was prejudiced by the delay. UNUM contended that the so-called "notice-prejudice" rule was preempted by the federal law governing employee pensions and benefits, the Employee Retirement Income Security Act. The federal law—known as ERISA—supersedes state laws regulating employee benefits, but exempts from preemption "any law of any State which regulates insurance."

Unanimously, the Court ruled that the California notice-prejudice rule was not preempted by ERISA. Ginsburg said the rule "appears to satisfy the common-sense view as a regulation that homes in on the insurance industry."

Public Employees

Central State University v. American Association of University Professors, Central State University Chapter, decided by an 8–1 vote, March 22, 1999; *per curiam* (unsigned) opinion; Stevens dissented.

A state law barring collective bargaining over teaching workload policies for professors at public colleges and universities does not violate the Equal Protection Clause of the U.S. Constitution.

The dispute involved an Ohio law, enacted in 1993, aimed at reversing a decline in the amount of time public university professors devoted to teaching. The law required each of the state's public colleges and universities to adopt policies on instructional workloads and exempted those policies from collective bargaining. The Ohio Supreme Court, ruling in a challenge brought by teachers at Central State University, held that the law violated the equal protection clauses of the Ohio and U.S. constitutions.

In an unsigned decision issued without hearing argument, the Court said the law had a sufficient rational basis to satisfy the requirements of the federal Equal Protection Clause. Ohio's legislature "could properly conclude that collective bargaining would interfere" with the adoption of a uniform workload policy, the Court said.

In a lone dissent, Stevens said the case contained a significant issue over academic freedom and should not have been decided on a summary basis. Stevens in his opinion and Ginsburg, joined by Breyer in a concurring opinion, noted that the Ohio court could reaffirm its decision on remand on the basis of the state constitutional provision.

Unions

Marquez v. Screen Actors Guild, Inc., decided by a 9–0 vote, November 3, 1998; O'Connor wrote the opinion.

Unions do not have to specify in contracts with employers that members do not have to pay fees and dues for union activities outside collective bargaining.

The limited ruling turned aside a claim by a Los Angeles actress that the Screen Actors Guild had breached its duty of fair representation under the National Labor Relations Act. Naomi Marquez lost a part in a television show because she had not joined the guild; she then complained that the "union security clause" in the guild's contract with producers—requiring "membership" in the union as a condition of employment—was misleading because it failed to state that, under Supreme Court precedents, unions cannot require workers to pay for activities outside collective bargaining responsibilities. Two lower federal courts rejected her argument.

In a unanimous opinion, the Court agreed that a union is not required under the act to include the limitation on mandatory fees in a contract with employers. O'Connor said the union security clause followed the language of the statute and was "a shorthand description of workers' legal rights." But she noted that the National Labor Relations Board (NLRB) was considering rules about what steps unions were required to take to notify workers of their rights to withhold portions of dues used to pay for outside activities, such as political activities.

The decision left for trial Marquez's claim that the guild's interpretation of the clause in her case amounted to a breach of the duty of fair representation. Kennedy, in a concurring opinion joined by Thomas, said that the lower court could consider evidence that the security clause had been "used or intended to mislead a potential employer to [Marquez's] detriment."

Workers' Compensation

American Manufacturers Mutual Insurance Co. v. Sullivan, decided by an 8–1 vote, March 3, 1999; Rehnquist wrote the opinion; Stevens dissented in part.

States and private insurers can delay paying workers' compensation benefits pending a review of medical claims without violating workers' rights.

The ruling—an important victory for health insurers—turned back a labor-backed challenge to a claims review procedure the state of Pennsylvania adopted to try to contain medical benefits under its worker compensation system. The scheme, adopted in 1993, allowed insurers to dispute a medical claim by demanding a "utilization review" and to withhold payment of the claim during the thirty-day period for the review. Ten individual workers, a teachers' union, and a coalition of other unions and union workers filed suit, claiming the review process violated due process and property rights protected by the Fourteenth Amendment. The suit was dismissed by a lower federal court, but reinstated by the Third U.S. Circuit Court of Appeals.

In a somewhat fractured opinion, the Court held that the private insurers were not covered by the Due Process Clause and that the withholding of payment of medical claims did not infringe on the workers' property rights. The private insurers were not "state actors" subject to the Due Process Clause, Rehnquist wrote for a seven-justice majority—all but Stevens and Ginsburg. "The state statutory and regulatory scheme leaves the challenged decisions to the judgment of the insurers," he wrote. On the property rights issue, Rehnquist said that the workers "do not have a property interest . . . in having their providers paid for treatment that has yet to be found reasonable and necessary." Four other justices—O'Connor, Kennedy, Souter, and Breyer—joined that part of the opinion.

In a partial concurring opinion, Ginsburg declined to join what she called Rehnquist's "extended endeavor . . . to clean up and rein in our 'state action' precedent." She also said she agreed that the workers had no right to demand "constant payment" of medical claims pending a review, but added that due process "requires fair procedures" of some form. In another partial concurrence, Breyer, joined by Souter, also said workers may have some procedural rights to payment of benefits.

Stevens, dissenting in part, said the appeals court was right to rule that the original review procedure violated due process by not allowing an injured worker to submit evidence in support of the claim. But he noted that Pennsylvania had changed the procedure to give workers an opportunity to justify a claim and, on that basis, agreed that the revised procedure was constitutional.

Property Law

Regulatory Takings

City of Monterey v. Del Monte Dunes at Monterey, Ltd., decided by a 5–4 vote, May 24, 1999; Kennedy wrote the main opinion; Scalia concurred separately; Souter, O'Connor, Ginsburg, and Breyer dissented.

Property owners have a right to a jury trial in federal court in regulatory takings cases brought against state or local governments under the federal civil rights law.

The ruling—an important victory for property rights advocates—upheld a $1.45 million jury award won by a developer against the city of Monterey, California, for blocking a planned oceanfront residential development over a five-year period in the 1980s. The city cited a number of land-use and environmental issues, including the Endangered Species Act, in denying the construction permit. But the developer, Del Monte Dunes, argued the city's action was arbitrary and filed suit under the federal civil rights law known as section 1983 for alleged violations of its property, due process, and equal protection rights. The judge allowed a jury trial over the city's objections. The Ninth U.S. Circuit Court of Appeals agreed that the developer was entitled to a jury trial and upheld the jury's verdict.

By a 5–4 vote, the Court also upheld the damage award. The key issue was whether the Seventh Amendment's guarantee of a jury trial for suits "at common law" applied to so-called regulatory takings suits brought under the federal civil rights statute. In the Court's main opinion, Kennedy said the amendment did apply because the developer had been denied any opportunity for compensation in state courts. "Del Monte Dunes sought . . . damages for the unconstitutional denial of [just] compensation," Kennedy wrote. "Damages for a constitutional violation are a legal remedy."

Three justices joined Kennedy's opinion in full. In a separate concurrence, Scalia said that any plaintiff in a section 1983 suit was entitled to a jury trial. He called "irrelevant" a section of Kennedy's opinion distinguishing between a regulatory takings case and other condemnation cases where there would be no jury trial right.

Writing for the dissenters, Souter said that the Seventh Amendment did not apply because there was no analogous legal action at common law. "At the time of the framing [of the Constitution] the notion of regulatory taking or inverse condemnation was yet to be derived," he wrote.

States

Immunity

Alden v. Maine, decided by a 5–4 vote, June 23, 1999; Kennedy wrote the opinion; Souter, Stevens, Ginsburg, and Breyer dissented.

The Court sharply limited the power of Congress to authorize private citizen suits to enforce federal laws against state governments in state courts.

The ruling—the most important of three major states' rights decisions on the last day of the Court's term—barred a back pay suit by a group of probation officers against the state of Maine for alleged violations of the federal Fair Labor Standards Act. The suit was originally filed in federal court, but was dismissed following the Supreme Court's 1996 decision, *Seminole Tribe of Florida v. Florida,* which barred most private damage suits against states in federal court. When the officers refiled the suit in Maine courts, the state moved to dismiss the action on grounds of state sovereign immunity. A lower court and the Maine Supreme Court both ruled in favor of the state's position.

In a closely divided, exhaustively argued decision, the Court ruled that Congress has only limited power to override a state's sovereign immunity from suits in its own courts. "Federalism requires that Congress accord States the respect and dignity due them as residuary sovereigns," Kennedy wrote. Allowing private damage suits against states without their consent, he continued, could "threaten [their] financial integrity" or "place unwarranted strains on the States' ability to govern in accordance with the will of their citizens." Kennedy said, however, that state governments could be subjected to suits for constitutional violations under the Fourteenth Amendment and that individual state officers as well as local governments could also be sued in state court for federal law violations.

Writing for the dissenters, Souter said the ruling created a "total" barrier to individual enforcement of the federal wage and hours law against state governments. He called the ruling "demonstrably mistaken" and "inconsistent" with both the history and structure of the Constitution. *(See story, pp. 33–39; excerpts, pp. 263–282.)*

College Savings Bank v. Florida Prepaid Postsecondary Education Expense Board, decided by a 5–4 vote, June 23, 1999; Scalia wrote the opinion; Breyer, Stevens, Souter, and Ginsburg dissented.

The Court invalidated an effort by Congress to subject states to federal court suits for trademark violations or false advertising. The decision also overturned a thirty-five-year-old precedent that made it easier to sue states in federal court when they engage in commercial activities.

The ruling—one of three major states' rights decisions on the final day of the Court's term—barred a false advertising suit brought by the New Jersey–based College Savings Bank in federal court against a Florida state agency, the Florida Prepaid Postsecondary Education Expense Board. The bank marketed certificates of deposit designed to cover future costs of college tuition. The bank alleged that Florida Prepaid made false claims about a competing product that the state agency sold to Florida residents. To bring the suit, the bank invoked a 1992 law, the Trademark Remedy Clarification Act, which provided for states to be sued in federal court for false advertising. Florida argued that the law was unconstitutional under the Eleventh Amendment, which generally bars federal court suits against states without a state's consent. The bank also argued that under the Court's 1964 decision, *Parden v. Terminal R. Co. of Ala. Docks Dept.*, the state had waived its sovereign immunity by engaging in commercial activity. A lower federal court in New Jersey and the Third U.S. Circuit Court of Appeals both agreed with the state and barred the suit.

By a 5–4 vote, the Court ruled that the trademark law was unconstitutional in providing for federal court suits against states and that the state could not be subjected to federal court suit merely because it had engaged in commercial activity. Writing for the majority, Scalia said the bank's claimed right to be free from misleading advertising did not amount to a property right that Congress could protect under the Fourteenth Amendment's provision for legislation to prevent deprivations of constitutional rights by the states. Turning to the waiver issue, Scalia "expressly overruled" the *Parden* decision, calling it "ill conceived" and irreconcilable with other rulings on state sovereign immunity.

Writing for the dissenters, Breyer defended both the trademark law and the *Parden* decision. "Congress does possess the authority to abrogate a State's sovereign immunity where 'necessary and proper' to the exercise of its legislative powers," Breyer wrote. As for *Parden*, he said the decision enabled Congress to close "an enforcement gap" that otherwise would disadvantage private companies that compete with states' commercial activities. *(See story, pp. 39–46; excerpts, pp. 283–296.)*

Florida Prepaid Postsecondary Education Expense Board v. College Savings Bank, decided by a 5–4 vote, June 23, 1999; Rehnquist wrote the opinion; Stevens, Souter, Ginsburg, and Breyer dissented.

The Court struck down on state sovereign immunity grounds a federal statute providing that states could be sued in federal courts for patent infringements.

The ruling—one of three major states' rights decisions on the final day of the Court's term—barred a patent infringement suit brought by the New Jersey–based College Savings Bank in federal court against a Florida state agency, the Florida Prepaid Postsecondary Education Expense Board. The bank marketed certificates of deposit designed to cover future costs of college tuition. It claimed that Florida Prepaid infringed its patented financing methodology when the agency began selling a similar product to Florida residents. Florida moved to dismiss the suit on grounds of sovereign immunity under the Eleventh Amendment, which generally bars federal court suits against states. A lower federal court and the U.S. Court of Appeals for the Federal Circuit, which hears appeals in patent cases, both rejected the state's motion. Both courts ruled that Congress had authority under the Fourteenth Amendment when it provided in the Patent Remedy Act of 1992 that states are subject to suit in federal court for patent infringement.

By a 5–4 vote, the Court held that the patent law could not be justified under Congress's powers to enact remedial legislation protecting constitutional rights under the Fourteenth Amendment. Rehnquist said that Congress had little evidence of patent infringements by states and had given no consideration to the availability of legal remedies against states in their own state courts. The "legislative record," Rehnquist wrote, "provides little support for the proposition that Congress sought to remedy a Fourteenth Amendment violation in enacting the Patent Remedy Act."

Writing for the dissenters, Stevens said the law was "an appropriate exercise of Congress's power under section 5 of the Fourteenth Amendment to prevent state deprivations of property without due process of law." He said the ruling would undermine the uniformity of patent law and leave patentholders without effective protection against infringements by state governments. *(See story, pp. 39–46; excerpts, pp. 296–309.)*

Taxation

Arizona Department of Revenue v. Blaze Construction Co., Inc., decided by a 9–0 vote, March 2, 1999; Thomas wrote the opinion.

States may impose nondiscriminatory taxes on contractors hired by the federal government to do work on Indian reservations.

The ruling allowed the state of Arizona to collect a gross receipts tax from a construction company for road construction and repair work performed on Indian reservations in the state. The Arizona Court of Appeals had barred the levy, saying federal law preempted imposition of the tax.

In a brief unanimous opinion, the Court upheld the tax, in line with a 1982 decision, *United States v. New Mexico,* permitting state taxation of federal contractors. Thomas said the same rule applied for work done on

Indian reservations. But he left open the possibility that a tribe might guard a contractor from state taxation under the Indian preemption doctrine if it assumed direct responsibility for work on a reservation.

Jefferson County, Alabama v. Acker, Senior Judge, United States District Court, Northern District of Alabama, decided by a 5–4 vote on a procedural issue and a 7–2 vote on the merits, June 21, 1999; Ginsburg wrote the opinion; Scalia, Rehnquist, Souter, and Thomas dissented on the procedural issue; Breyer and O'Connor dissented on the merits.

The Court upheld application of an Alabama county's "occupational tax" on federal judges.

The ruling stemmed from a suit by Jefferson County (Birmingham), Alabama, to enforce provisions of an occupational tax enacted in 1987 against two federal judges with offices in the county. The judges argued—and the Eleventh U.S. Circuit Court of Appeals agreed—that the tax amounted to a licensing scheme that would violate the so-called intergovernmental tax immunity doctrine. That doctrine sets limits on the ability of the federal government or a state government to tax the operations of the other.

By a 7–2 vote, the Court held that the tax did not violate the intergovernmental tax immunity doctrine. Ginsburg noted that the doctrine had been limited by the Court and then by Congress in the late 1930s to permit the state to impose a nondiscriminatory income tax on federal employees and the federal government to impose a similar levy on state employees. Despite the county's description of the levy as an "occupational" tax, Ginsburg said, the measure "serves a revenue-raising, not a regulatory purpose." In a dissent, Breyer, joined by O'Connor, concluded the measure did establish a license scheme.

The ruling on the merits came after the Court ruled on a preliminary issue: whether the federal judges had properly removed the tax collection case from state to federal court. Five justices—Ginsburg, Stevens, O'Connor, Kennedy, and Breyer—said yes; the other four—Scalia, Rehnquist, Souter, and Thomas—said no.

South Central Bell Telephone Co. v. Alabama, decided by a 9–0 vote, March 23, 1999; Breyer wrote the opinion.

An Alabama tax scheme that resulted in higher levies on out-of-state corporations than on Alabama companies was struck down as an unconstitutional discrimination against interstate commerce.

Alabama corporations were subject to a franchise tax equal to 1 percent of the so-called "par value" of the firm's stock—an amount determined by the corporation itself and usually below the company's actual capitalized value. An out-of-state corporation, on the other hand, had to pay 0.3 percent of the actual value of its capital within the state. South Central Bell Telephone Co. challenged the scheme in state court, saying that it resulted in substantially higher levies on out-of-state corporations. The Alabama Supreme Court rejected the claim, on a 5–4 vote.

In a unanimous decision, the Court held that the tax "facially discriminates against interstate commerce" without justification. "Alabama law gives domestic corporations the ability to reduce their franchise tax liability simply by reducing the par value of their stock," Breyer wrote, "while it denies foreign corporations that same ability."

Torts

Racketeering

Humana Inc. v. Forsyth, decided by a 9–0 vote, January 20, 1999; Ginsburg wrote the opinion.

Insurance companies can be sued for fraud under the federal antiracketeering law despite a separate federal law that generally protects states' authority to regulate insurers.

The ruling allowed Nevada policyholders of the health insurance company Humana Inc. to proceed with a class action suit under a federal law, the Racketeer Influenced and Corrupt Organizations Act, known as RICO. The racketeering law provides triple damages for a pattern of fraudulent conduct. Humana's customers charged that the insurer violated the law by negotiating deep discounts with hospitals but failing to pass on the savings to policyholders in the form of reduced copayments. Humana argued the suit was barred by the McCarran-Ferguson Act, which protects state regulation of insurance from any general federal law that would "invalidate, impair, or supersede" the state law. The Ninth U.S. Circuit Court of Appeals rejected the argument, saying there was no "direct conflict" between Nevada law and the federal racketeering statute.

In a unanimous decision, the Court allowed the suit to proceed, but adopted a standard slightly different from the appeals court. Ginsburg said the McCarran-Ferguson Act did not block the suit because RICO "appears to complement" remedies under Nevada state law. "RICO advances the State's interest in combating insurance fraud, and does not frustrate any articulated Nevada policy," she wrote.

Warsaw Convention

El Al Israel Airlines, Ltd. v. Tseng, decided by an 8–1 vote, January 12, 1999; Ginsburg wrote the opinion; Stevens dissented.

The Court blocked an effort to use state tort remedies to get around limits on lawsuits by international air travel passengers contained in the treaty known as the Warsaw Convention.

The ruling barred a suit by a New York woman, Tsui Yuan Tseng, stemming from a security search before boarding an El Al Israel Airlines flight at Kennedy International Airport in 1993. Tseng filed suit for assault and false imprisonment against the airline in New York state court; she claimed emotional distress but no bodily injury. After removing the case to federal court, El Al argued the 1929 Warsaw Convention—which governs liability for international air transportation—allowed recovery in an airline "accident" only for "bodily injury." A lower federal court agreed, but the Second U.S. Circuit Court of Appeals said the suit could proceed.

In a nearly unanimous decision, the Court said the Warsaw Convention precludes use of state law to recover damages if a claim does not satisfy the treaty's requirements for liability. "Recourse to local law," Ginsburg wrote, "would undermine the uniform regulation of international air carrier liability that the Warsaw Convention was designed to foster."

Ginsburg based her ruling on an interpretation of the treaty's original language, but noted that a new provision, ratified by the U.S. Senate in September 1998, explicitly added such a restriction. Stevens, in a lone dissent, acknowledged the limited effect of the ruling, but argued that an international treaty "should not be construed to preempt state law unless its intent to do so is clear."

Chapter 4

Preview of the 1999–2000 Term

The image of a teenaged girl stares blankly from a billboard at an inner city bus stop. She holds a cigarette in one hand. The message below is subtle but strong: "She'll outgrow all her bad habits. Except one."

This antismoking ad was part of a $5 million campaign launched by the Food and Drug Administration (FDA) in summer 1999 in an effort to reverse a decade-long increase in smoking among young Americans. Other advertisements had blunter messages. A newspaper ad showed images of three youngsters and asked, "What would make you madder? A retailer selling cigarettes to a kid who's (a) 9; (b) 14; (c) yours?" All of the ads—radio and TV spots, print ads, and billboards—closed with the tagline: "Selling cigarettes to children is illegal. For a reason."

The paid advertising campaign represented a departure for the federal government, which had previously limited its public education efforts on smoking to unpaid public service announcements. But the advertising was only a small part of what the FDA had hoped to be doing to try to reduce youth smoking.

Four years earlier, the FDA had claimed for the first time in the agency's ninety-year history that it had the authority under existing law to regulate tobacco. With President Bill Clinton's support, the agency's crusading commissioner, David A. Kessler, had gone to Congress with new evidence of the addictive effects of nicotine and of the tobacco industry's knowledge many years earlier—despite insistent denials—of the habit-forming nature of its products.

Kessler hinted and later warned more directly that he was ready to rule that nicotine was a "drug" and cigarettes a drug-delivery "device" for purposes of invoking the agency's legal charter, the Food, Drug, and Cosmetic Act. Congress listened, gravely, and did nothing. Kessler pro-

President Clinton is joined by Food and Drug Agency Commissioner David Kessler, left, former surgeon general C. Everett Koop, and Vice President Al Gore at a White House briefing in 1997 on legislation aimed at reducing youth smoking. The Supreme Court was to rule in the 1999–2000 term in the tobacco industry's effort to block the FDA from regulating tobacco products.

ceeded to act. With Clinton at his side, Kessler unveiled a proposed regulation at a White House ceremony in August 1995. The rule called for making it a federal offense to sell cigarettes or smokeless tobacco to anyone under the age of eighteen and imposing sweeping new restrictions on the tobacco industry's advertising and marketing practices.

After a voluminous rulemaking proceeding, the FDA adopted the regulation, with a few modifications, in August 1996. The tobacco industry, however, went to court to try to block the rule. It filed suit in federal court in North Carolina, in the heart of tobacco country, claiming that the FDA had overstepped its powers. Two years after the adoption of the rule, the Fourth U.S. Circuit Court of Appeals agreed with the industry's argument. "Congress did not intend to delegate jurisdiction over tobacco products," a divided three-judge panel ruled in August 1998.

Clinton promptly authorized the Justice Department to try to overturn the ruling. In competing filings with the Supreme Court, the Justice Department described the FDA's jurisdictional claim as "thoroughly documented and reasoned," while tobacco companies insisted the agency was seeking to "supplant" Congress's refusal to give it authority over cigarettes. On April 26, 1999, the Court agreed to hear the case, *Food and Drug Administration v. Brown and Williamson Tobacco Corp.*, setting the stage for a showdown in the Court's 1999–2000 term between the administration and an array of public health organizations on one side and the much beleaguered tobacco industry on the other.

The tobacco case was one of twenty-eight disputes that the justices agreed to hear before they began their summer recess at the end of June. The number was the lowest in recent memory. At the start of the decade, the justices began their 1990–1991 term with seventy cases on the calendar. The number had fallen steadily, first into the fifties, and then into the forties. One year earlier, the justices ended the 1997–1998 term with thirty-three cases carried over for the new term.

The Court's calendar grew to a more respectable number—forty-four cases—by the time the new term began on October 4, the traditional first Monday in October. Following a practice that dated from the start of the 1993–1994 term, the justices issued orders granting review in additional cases in September, prior to the opening of the new term. On September 10 the Court agreed to hear six more cases even before all the justices had returned to Washington—a modest additional innovation that raised eyebrows among Court watchers. The justices met in an all-day conference September 27, and the next day the Court issued orders granting review in another nine cases. The Court had also taken on a death penalty case earlier in the month. The new total of forty-four cases almost exactly equaled the number of cases—forty-five—on the Court's calendar as it began the 1997–1998 term. Thus, even with the additional cases, the Court seemed on its way to another relatively low output for the new term.

However thin, the Court's calendar was chock full of legal controversies. The justices were scheduled to pick up where they left off at the end of the 1998–1999 term with four more cases testing the boundaries of federal powers over state governments. The most important appeared to be a Florida case asking whether states could be forced to pay money damages for violating the federal law against age discrimination in employment. Civil rights groups said the case posed an important test of whether the Court would apply its new federalism principles to traditional antidiscrimination laws. Two other cases accepted for review before the summer recess were a challenge to a federal law regulating the use of state driver's license records and an effort by the state of Vermont to block a disgruntled state employee from using a federal law to sue the state for alleged misuse of federal funds.

Women's groups were particularly concerned with the fourth of the federalism cases—a challenge to the constitutionality of a new federal law giving victims of domestic violence the right to file damage suits against their attackers in federal court. The 1994 law, the Violence Against Women Act, had been ruled unconstitutional by the Fourth Circuit appeals court on the ground that there was no basis for federal jurisdiction over such claims. The dispute stemmed from an accusation by a former Virginia Polytechnic University student that she was raped by two of the university's varsity football players at the start of her freshman year in 1994. The student and the government both asked the Court to review the appeals court ruling that barred her federal court suit under the law. The Court's order agreeing to hear the consolidated cases—*United States v. Morrison* and *Brzonkala v. Morrison*—was among those issued on September 28.

The justices in September also agreed to hear arguments in a case testing the validity of new restrictions on protesters outside abortion clinics. The case, *Hill v. Colorado*, involved a state law that makes it a criminal offense to counsel, protest, or demonstrate within 8 feet of a person while within 100 feet of an abortion clinic. The Court also agreed to decide whether health maintenance organizations and their physicians can be sued under the federal law—the Employee Retirement Income Security Act—that regulates health benefits for employees (*Pegram v. Herdrich*). And the justices took up a case challenging the constitutionality of a Washington State law that allowed grandparents or other "third parties" the right to petition a court for visitation rights if visitation would "serve the best interest of the child" (*Troxel v. Granville*).

Earlier, the justices had agreed to hear a Missouri case testing the constitutionality of a state law—akin to the federal campaign finance statute—limiting the amount of money an individual could contribute to a political candidate. A Louisiana case raised the fractious issue of government aid to parochial schools. The justices were also to decide the constitutionality of a federal law regulating sexually explicit programming on cable television and a local ordinance prohibiting nude dancing.

Many of the issues were familiar to the justices even if the precise questions were new. Federalism had been a major theme for the Rehnquist Court for several years, with states emerging with new protections against intrusions on their prerogatives by the federal government. The Court had struggled with campaign finance issues for more than two decades since first ruling, in 1976, that laws setting limits on campaign expenditures violated the First Amendment's free speech provision. The justices had charted an unsteady course in determining the limits of taxpayer funding for church-affiliated schools under the constitutional ban against establishment of religion. And the cable television and nude dancing cases involved precedents from 1996 and 1989 respectively that had divided the justices so badly that no majority opinion was issued in either.

"It's *deja vu* all over again," attorney Theodore Olson remarked to a briefing for reporters in September 1999—borrowing the oft-quoted phrase of baseball great Yogi Berra. Despite the familiarity of the issues, Court watchers and advocates had differing predictions on many of the cases and were hedging their bets on others. The conservative Olson, for example, tentatively predicted that the Court would back the states in the age discrimination case, while such liberals as New York University law professor Burt Neuborne voiced confidence the Court would not limit the enforcement of that or other traditional civil rights laws. The differing forecasts brought to mind another of Yogi's famous aphorisms. The problem with predictions, he said, is that they're in the future.

Tobacco Regulation

In contrast to the other high-profile cases, the FDA's tobacco regulation presented a legal issue both unfamiliar and, in any other context, too technical to generate much interest. The case presented no broad question of constitutional interpretation. Instead, the justices were asked to decide a specific question of statutory construction: whether tobacco products fell within the definition of "drugs" or "devices" in the 1938 Food, Drug, and Cosmetic Act as substances or items "intended to affect the structure of any function of the body."

To fit tobacco within the statute, the agency cited evidence that the nicotine in tobacco products both causes and sustains addiction by directly affecting a part of the brain that rewards the repeated consumption of pleasurable substances. In addition, the FDA said that nicotine can act as a sedative or, in other circumstances, as a stimulant and that it can also contribute to weight loss. Those effects, the FDA argued, were "quintessentially drug-like."

Intent was a more difficult issue. In part, the agency relied on common sense and experience. Because smokers know about nicotine's addictive properties, any manufacturer would foresee many people would use tobacco products to satisfy addiction. Moreover, the FDA said, surveys showed that most tobacco users consume the products primarily because of the addictive, "mood-altering" effects, not for reasons such as taste or social ritual.

The FDA cited evidence discovered in tobacco companies' internal files confirming that the manufacturers had long known of nicotine's effects on the body and had manipulated the nicotine content of cigarettes with those effects in mind. In one memo, researchers for one of the manufacturers described a cigarette as "a dispenser for a dose unit of nicotine."

The FDA issued its rule—covering more than 200 pages in the *Federal Register*—after a rulemaking proceeding that attracted more than 95,000 individual comments representing all sides of the tobacco issue. Despite its length, the regulation ostensibly targeted only one limited issue: youth smoking. Kessler, appearing with Clinton at an election-year White House Rose Garden ceremony, described nicotine addiction as a "pediatric disease that often begins at 12, 13, and 14 only to manifest itself at 16 and 17 when these children find that they cannot quit."

To try to reduce youngsters' access to tobacco products, the FDA's rule required age verification by photo ID of anyone under the age of twenty-seven purchasing cigarettes or smokeless tobacco. In its final form, the rule also banned vending machines or self-service displays except in facilities such as adult-only nightclubs that were completely inaccessible to minors. Originally, the FDA proposed to ban all vending machines, but Clinton decided to soften the restriction somewhat.

The FDA's rule also imposed restrictions aimed at the kinds of advertising most accessible to youngsters. The regulation prohibited all billboards within 1,000 feet of schools or playgrounds and limited other advertising—in stores or inside or outside buses, for example—to black-and-white, text-only messages. The same "tombstone-ad" restrictions were imposed on advertising in print publications with significant youth readership—defined as more than 15 percent or more than 2 million readers under age eighteen. The regulation also banned brand-name sponsorship of sporting or entertainment events and the sale or giveaway of products such as caps or gym bags that carry cigarette or smokeless tobacco brand names or logos.

Tobacco companies filed suits to block the FDA regulations even before the agency adopted the final rule. They contended that the FDA lacked any legal authority over tobacco and that the advertising restrictions in any event violated the First Amendment's protections for commercial speech. Judge William L. Osteen Sr. put the suits on hold until after the FDA completed action. Then, in April 1997, he issued a mixed ruling, holding that the statute gave the agency the authority to regulate access to tobacco but not to regulate marketing or promotion practices.

Both sides appealed, and the case came before a three-judge panel of the predominantly conservative Fourth Circuit appeals court in June 1998. Walter Dellinger, who was leaving his post as U.S. solicitor general, personally argued for the government—an unusual appearance by the government's top appellate advocate in an intermediate-level court. Richard Cooper, a prominent attorney with a well-known Washington firm and a former FDA chief counsel, represented the tobacco industry.

The court's decision two months later gave the tobacco industry a clear-cut victory. In the majority opinion, Judge H. Emory Widener Jr. criticized the FDA for engaging in a "mechanistic" reading of the statute while disregarding Congress's refusal to explicitly give the agency any power to regulate tobacco and its own disclaimers of any such authority for more than fifty years.

An examination of the food and drug law as a whole, Widener said, disclosed half a dozen "internal inconsistencies" in the FDA's position, most notably, the requirement in the law that the agency ban any product found to cause "serious adverse health consequences or death." The dissenting judge said he would have upheld the FDA's regulatory authority over tobacco, including its power to regulate advertising and promotion practices.

The tobacco companies echoed Widener's critique of the FDA in their Supreme Court filings. "Congress gave the FDA no role" when it approved a series of tobacco-specific statutes beginning with the cigarette labeling law in 1965, Cooper wrote. By adopting its own regulation, Cooper continued, "FDA simply seeks to supplant enacted policy by disregarding statutes with which it disagrees and short-circuiting an ongoing political process."

In their briefs, filed in mid-September, the tobacco companies depicted the FDA's position as fundamentally inconsistent with established interpretations of the food and drug law. In examining a product's "intended use" under the statute, they contended, the FDA in the past had

The rock star Madonna exhales a big puff of cigar smoke in an appearance with David Letterman on the CBS *Late Show*. Antismoking groups blamed a rise in youth smoking in part on the increased visibility of smoking by figures in entertainment media.

always looked only to the manufacturer's express claim for the product—and clearly the industry had not marketed cigarettes for their addictive properties. Moreover, the companies argued, the statute simply did not envision the continued marketing of a product that the FDA deemed to be unsafe.

"FDA's assertion of jurisdiction necessarily leads to a ban," Cooper wrote in his brief, "a result contrary to congressional intent and unacceptable even to FDA."

Critics ridiculed what one observer called the industry's "sky-is-falling" argument. "No reputable antismoking organization has proposed or suggested that we should prohibit the sale and use of tobacco products by adults," said John Banzhaf, head of Action for Smoking and Health and a pioneer antismoking activist since the 1960s. For its part, the FDA had rejected a ban on the ground that trying to prohibit cigarettes in a country with 50 million smokers would lead to a widespread underground market in tobacco products.

Banzhaf's group was one of an array of consumer and public health organizations, including the American Cancer Society, that filed or signed friend-of-the-court briefs on the government's side in the case. In addition, forty states—led by Minnesota—urged the justices to uphold the FDA's authority. The tobacco industry had only three groups lined up on its side: the Product Liability Advisory Council and two pro-business public interest litigation centers. "Obviously, tobacco is a controversial issue," said Richard Samp, who wrote one of the pro-industry briefs as chief counsel of the Washington Legal Foundation.

Opposing advocates and Court watchers had relatively little to go on in handicapping the case before the arguments, which were scheduled for December 1. The Court had last dealt with a tobacco issue in 1992 in a fractured ruling, *Cipollone v. Liggett Group*, that gave the industry a partial victory in its effort to use federal preemption doctrine to bar suits in state courts against tobacco manufacturers by smokers or their families. The case gave no useful clue about how the Court would approach the statutory issue posed by the FDA regulation. The opposing briefs in the FDA case cited relatively few Supreme Court precedents directly related to the food and drug statute, only lower court decisions. "It's something of a blank slate," one lawyer in the case remarked.

The case, however, did involve two legal doctrines strongly identified with the Rehnquist Court. One was "plain-meaning" construction of statutes—a view that laws should be interpreted according to the "plain meaning" of the words in the statute, with little if any regard to congressional or legislative intent. The other doctrine took its name from a 1984 case, *Chevron U.S.A. v. Natural Resources Defense Council*, and called for courts to defer to an administrative agency's interpretation of any statute that it was charged with administering or enforcing. The Court's conservatives cited both doctrines often, viewing them as the logical implications of their professed philosophy of judicial restraint.

The government and its allies stressed both doctrines in their briefs urging the justices to uphold the FDA regulation. Some observers saw the issues as posing a potential conflict for the Court's conservatives. "The Court's more conservative justices are likely to have sympathy with the theme of the industry's position," said Peter Rubin, a professor at Georgetown University Law Center. "Yet the doctrines that those justices champion will make it difficult to rule for the industry."

Other observers disagreed. "If you just look at the trees, it's easy to make the FDA's argument," attorney John Roberts remarked about the agency's reading of the statute. "But not if you look at the whole forest."

Both he and Samp argued the Court should not give "*Chevron* deference" to the FDA's interpretation. "The Chevron doctrine is a good idea, but you can have too much of a good thing," Samp said. Upholding the FDA's position, he said, would give the agency "a blank check, and then you have the laws being written by an agency and not by Congress."

Whichever side prevailed at the Court, the tobacco dispute was certain to continue in other forums and perhaps at the FDA as well. A ruling for the FDA on the broad jurisdictional issue would be only a partial victory. The tobacco companies could continue to contest the specific provisions of the regulation in the lower courts. A ruling for the industry, on the other hand, would still leave the industry on the defensive on many fronts, including a new lawsuit filed by the federal government on September 22 seeking billions of dollars from tobacco companies for Medicare health care costs that the government attributed to smoking.

Following are some of the other major cases on the Supreme Court's calendar as it began its 1999–2000 term:

Criminal Law and Procedure

Habeas Corpus. A Virginia inmate's effort to overturn his death sentence because of inadequate legal representation gave the Court a chance to decide how to interpret a key provision of a new law aimed at limiting federal courts' ability to set aside state court convictions or sentences.

The Anti-Terrorism and Effective Death Penalty Act of 1996 included a provision barring federal courts from granting habeas corpus petitions by state inmates on an issue raised in state courts unless the state court decision "was contrary to, or resulted in an unreasonable application of, clearly established Federal law as determined by the Supreme Court of the United States." The federal appeals court for Virginia cited that provision in denying a habeas corpus petition by Terry Williams, who had been sentenced to death in 1986 after being convicted of murder. Williams argued first in a state habeas corpus petition and then in a similar federal plea that his Sixth Amendment right to counsel had been violated because his attorney failed to present any mitigating evidence in the penalty phase of the trial.

The judge who presided over the original trial granted the petition, but the Virginia Supreme Court overturned the decision. Williams then filed a federal petition, arguing that the Virginia Supreme Court had misapplied the U.S. Supreme Court's standards for judging a claim of ineffective assistance of counsel. A federal district court judge agreed, but the Fourth U.S. Circuit Court of Appeals overturned that decision. It said that the Virginia high court's decision was "not unreasonable" and Williams's plea therefore failed under the new habeas corpus law.

In appealing the decision, Williams's attorneys argued the appeals court's interpretation of the 1996 law "does serious damage to the duty of federal courts to interpret and decide questions of constitutional law." Attorneys for the state argued in response that the appeals court had correctly interpreted the law and, in any event, had gone on to reject Williams's plea on the ground that he had failed to show any harm from his lawyer's failure to offer mitigating evidence. (*Williams v. Taylor*)

"Pat-Down" Searches. The Court agreed to decide an important unresolved question of police procedure: whether police can conduct a so-called pat-down search of someone just because he ran away from police in a high crime area.

The case stemmed from the arrest of a Chicago man, William Wardlow, in an area that police said was a center for drug trafficking. Wardlow fled as four police cars converged on the area. When police caught up with him, an officer conducted a pat-down search and found a weapon in a bag he was carrying. Wardlow was convicted of unlawful possession of a firearm and sentenced to two years' imprisonment. But the Illinois Supreme Court reversed the conviction, saying the pat-down search was improper and the evidence should have been suppressed.

In appealing that decision, the Illinois attorney general's office argued the ruling created "an untenable state of affairs." The ruling, the state's lawyers said, "essentially gives citizens the license, when they see a peace officer in a high crime area to just break and run away." Wardlow's attorneys countered, "This is not an 'untenable state of affairs,' but an integral part of personal liberty." (*Illinois v. Wardlow*)

Election Law

Campaign Finance. The state of Missouri asked the Court to reinstate a $1,075 limit on political contributions to candidates for state offices that a federal appeals court ruled to be an unconstitutional restriction on freedom of speech.

The Missouri campaign contribution limit—set at $1,000 in 1994 and indexed to increase with inflation—was challenged by a small political action committee, Shrink Missouri Government PAC, which wanted to make a larger donation to a candidate for state auditor in 1998. In a ruling in November 1998—after the election—the federal appeals court said the state had failed to show that the law was needed to prevent "corruption or a perception thereof."

In appealing the decision, attorneys for the state contended that the limits "indisputably serve a compelling public interest in assuring the integrity of government and of the election process, protecting both from both the appearance and reality of corruption." The state drew support from a handful of liberal public interest groups and from the Justice Department, which noted that the federal campaign finance law sets a similar $1,000 limit on contributions to candidates for federal offices such as senator or representative.

Attorneys for the political action committee argued the appeals court decision was correct. "Missouri has no evidence," they said, "that campaign contributions cause corruption or an objectively reasonable appearance of corruption." (*Nixon v. Shrink Missouri Government PAC*)

Voting Rights Act. The Court scheduled a reargument in a dispute over a school board redistricting plan for Bossier Parish, Louisiana, in order to decide an important issue under the Voting Rights Act: whether a redistricting change violates the law if it intentionally discriminates against minority voters even if it does not leave the minority voters worse off than before.

The redistricting plan adopted by the parish after the 1990 census—like the plan it replaced—gave white voters a majority in all twelve school board districts. The parish submitted the plan—as it was required to do under section 5 of the Voting Rights Act—to a federal court in Washington, and the court approved the plan. On appeal, the Justice Department and a group of African American voters argued the court should have denied preclearance because the county had failed to show—as the law required—that the districting plan did not have "the purpose ... of denying or abridging the right to vote on account of race or color."

The Supreme Court heard arguments in the case on April 26 and then announced on June 23, the final decision day of the term, that it wanted to hear a second round of arguments in the fall. The justices specifically directed the opposing lawyers to address whether section 5's "purpose prong" covered what was called "a discriminatory but non-retrogressive purpose" and, if so, whether the Justice Department or the parish had the burden of proof on the issue.

In its new brief, the Justice Department argued for the more expansive interpretation of the law. It contended, for example, that a new voting practice to prevent registration of black citizens who had previously been prohibited from voting "would have the purpose to deny or abridge black citizens' right to vote . . . even if that voting change was not designed to reduce black voting participation further." But attorneys for the school board insisted that an election law change "abridges voting rights under section 5 only if it provides less voting power than the existing system." (*Reno v. Bossier Parish School Board*; *Price v. Bossier Parish School Board*)

Hawaiian Affairs. The justices agreed to rule on the constitutionality of a Hawaii state law that permits only descendants of the islands' indigenous peoples to vote in elections for a state agency that funds programs intended to benefit "native Hawaiians."

The case involved the Office of Hawaiian Affairs (OHA), an independent state agency funded mainly by revenues from public lands set aside at the time of Hawaii's annexation by the United States in 1898 as well as some state and federal appropriations. Trustees for the agency are elected in statewide balloting, and voting since 1978 has been limited to "native Hawaiians." Harold Rice, a white man whose family settled in Hawaii before its annexation by the United States in 1898, challenged the voting requirement as a violation of the Fifteenth Amendment, which prohibits racial discrimination in voting, and the Fourteenth Amendment, which guarantees "equal protection of the laws." A lower federal court and the Ninth U.S. Circuit Court of Appeals both rejected the challenge. In its decision, the Ninth Circuit said limiting voting to native Hawaiians was constitutional "because Hawaiians are the only group with a stake in the trust and the funds that OHA trustees administer."

In appealing that decision, Rice's attorneys argued that what they called the "stark race-based restriction on the right to vote" was "a direct, open, and undisguised affront to the Fifteenth Amendment." Two national groups opposed to racial preferences also urged the Court to overturn the appeals court decision. But attorneys for the state insisted that the voting scheme was "a reasonable and constitutional effort" to honor the "special trust relationship" Congress had established with indigenous Hawaiians. The Justice Department filed a brief supporting the state's position. (*Rice v. Cayetano*)

Environmental Law

Citizen Suits. A coalition of environmental groups urged the Court to over-turn a federal appeals court decision that they said could have a "devas-tating consequence" for citizen suits to enforce federal antipollution laws.

The environmental groups filed suit in 1992 under the federal Clean Water Act against the operator of a hazardous waste incinerator that released mercury into the North Tyger River near the town of Roebuck in western South Carolina. A lower federal court judge imposed a penal-ty of $405,800, but the Fourth U.S. Circuit Court of Appeals overturned that ruling. It said that because the owner, Laidlaw Environmental Services, had stopped releasing excess mercury after the suit was filed, the case had become moot—legally over. The court said that an injunction would no longer serve a purpose and that the private parties had no stand-ing to seek civil penalties.

In seeking review of that decision, the environmental groups argued that the private suit acted as the "catalyst" for bringing the incinerator into compliance with the clean water law. The appeals court decision, they argued, "would allow defendants to win virtually any citizen suit" by delaying proceedings long enough to come into compliance. The govern-ment, which had not participated in the case earlier, filed a supporting brief also urging reversal of the appeals court decision. In response, attor-neys for Laidlaw urged the justices to uphold the appeals court decision. "A citizen-plaintiff has *no* cognizable legal interest in, and thus *no* stand-ing to prosecute, an action seeking the exaction of a civil penalty payable only to the public treasury," the company's brief read. (*Friends of the Earth v. Laidlaw Environmental Services, Inc.*)

Federal Government

Nursing Homes. The Court took up a dispute spawned by the federal gov-ernment's crackdown on nursing homes and agreed to decide whether the industry can challenge regulations before enforcement actions are brought.

The case stemmed from a federal court suit filed by the Illinois Council on Long Term Care, a trade association representing seventy-five nursing homes in the state, challenging various nursing home regu-lations issued by the Department of Health and Human Services (HHS) to determine eligibility for reimbursement under the Medicare program. The government contended the Medicare act barred any "pre-enforcement" challenges to the regulations and required a nursing home to contest the rules only after being charged with a violation. The federal appeals court for Illinois, however, allowed the industry's challenge to proceed.

In bringing the action, the industry group noted that federal inspectors were finding a significantly higher percentage of violations since the new regulations were adopted in 1987. It blamed what it called "the drastic change in the rate of noncompliance" on "vague" regulations and a "restrictive" appeals process. But the government told the justices the Medicare act was written "to channel all claims through the administrative process as a prerequisite to judicial review." (*Shalala v. Illinois Council on Long Term Care, Inc.*)

First Amendment

Aid to Religious Schools. The Court agreed to rule on the constitutionality of using federal funds to pay for computers, software, and other high-tech instructional aids for use in religiously affiliated schools.

The issue reached the Court in a lawsuit originally filed in 1985 challenging the use of funds under a federal program known as Chapter 2 by parochial schools in Jefferson Parish, Louisiana. The Chapter 2 program, established in 1965, provided grants to states for local school systems to use for textbooks, library resources, and other instructional materials. The program allowed local school systems to use the materials in public schools and also to lend them to nonpublic schools, including religiously affiliated schools. The federal appeals court in New Orleans, acting in a suit brought by a group of Jefferson Parish taxpayers, ruled in August 1998 that the use of the funds in the parish's parochial schools violated separation of church and state principles. It relied in part on Supreme Court decisions that had allowed use of public funds to buy textbooks but not other instructional materials for use in parochial schools.

In appealing the decision, a group of parents of parochial school students said the ruling would "deny technologically sophisticated educational tools to over a million American schoolchildren" and "require discrimination against some schoolchildren solely on the basis of their families' constitutionally protected decision to choose an education under religious auspices." The Clinton administration joined the appeal, stressing that the program contained safeguards against using Chapter 2 materials "for religious purposes." But the taxpayers who brought the suit argued the program was "providing substantial aid to the religious mission of the sectarian school." (*Mitchell v. Helms*)

Student Activity Fees. The University of Wisconsin asked the Court to overturn a federal appeals court decision allowing students to avoid paying a portion of a mandatory fee used to fund student organizations that engage in political advocacy.

The fee—set at $330 in the 1995–1996 school year—funded a variety of student organizations, including some that engaged in election or lobbying activities. A group of conservative Christian students filed a federal court suit claiming that their free speech rights were violated by being forced to help fund organizations that engaged in political advocacy that they opposed. A lower court and the federal appeals court in Chicago agreed.

In appealing the decision, the university argued the students had no constitutional right "to avoid paying for . . . the creation of a forum for robust campus debate and dialogue." The attorneys for the students countered that they "should be able to attend the University without the Board of Regents requiring them to fund student groups who express views they oppose." (*Board of Regents of the University of Wisconsin v. Southworth*)

Nude Dancing. The city of Erie, Pennsylvania, asked the Court to reinstate a local ordinance banning nude dancing after the state's highest court ruled the measure unconstitutional on free speech grounds.

The city enacted the ordinance in 1994 after a number of bars featuring nude female dancers opened in the downtown area. It modeled the ordinance on an Indiana law that the Court had upheld in 1989 by a single vote in a highly fragmented decision, *Barnes v. Glen Theatre, Inc.* The Pennsylvania Supreme Court struck the measure down in a legal challenge brought by the owner of one of the bars, Kandyland. By a 3–2 vote, the state high court reasoned that *Barnes* was not binding because there was no majority position. It went on to conclude that the city law was unconstitutional because it was intended to "suppress the expressive nature of nude dancing."

In seeking review of the decision, the city's lawyers said the Pennsylvania court "refused to acknowledge *Barnes* as binding precedent."

But lawyers for Kandyland said the state court had properly concluded that the ordinance was impermissibly "content-based." They noted that the city had enforced the measure against bars but had permitted a production of the play *Equus*, which includes a nude scene. (*City of Erie, Pennsylvania v. Pap's A.M.*)

"Adult" Cable Channels. The government appealed a lower court ruling striking down a recently enacted federal law requiring cable channels to completely scramble sexually explicit programming.

Congress passed the provision, part of the Telecommunications Act of 1996, because of complaints from some parents that youngsters had access to "indecent programming" as a result of so-called "signal bleed" from incomplete scrambling on the premium subscriber channels. Playboy Entertainment Group, which owned three adult-oriented cable channels, challenged the law before a three-judge federal court as economically burdensome and unnecessarily restrictive of constitutionally protected programming for adults. That court ruled the law unconstitutional. It said the government should instead require cable operators to do more to comply with another part of the law giving subscribers a right to obtain free of charge a "lockbox" to completely block adult channels.

In appealing the decision, the government said the court applied too strict a standard in reviewing the law and came up with an "illogical" hypothetical as a substitute for the scrambling requirement. Lawyers for Playboy countered by reiterating that the law was "more extensive than necessary to serve the government's interest." (*United States v. Playboy Entertainment Group, Inc.*)

States

Age Discrimination. An eight-year-old pay dispute between a group of senior professors and two University of Florida campuses raised the issue whether states can be subjected to private suits for violating the federal Age Discrimination in Employment Act.

The professors filed suit under the law to try to recover a salary adjustment that was aimed at equalizing pay with newer faculty members but then withheld for two years as a cost-cutting measure. The federal appeals court in Atlanta, in a 2–1 decision, barred the suit on Eleventh Amendment grounds. The professors and the federal government both asked the Court to review the decision. The Court granted review in January, but told lawyers to delay filing briefs until after its decisions in the federalism cases already pending in the term: *College Savings Bank v. Florida Prepaid Postsecondary Education Expense Board* and *Florida Prepaid Postsecondary Education Expense Board v. College Savings Bank.* Those two decisions, issued on the last day of the 1998–1999 term, limited Congress's ability to authorize private damage suits against state governments. *(See story, pp. 39–46.)*

In briefs filed in mid-July, lawyers for both the professors and for the government argued that the age discrimination law was a proper exercise of Congress's power under the Fourteenth Amendment to prevent "arbitrary and invidious discrimination." Lawyers for the state university responded that the law exceeded Congress's powers because there was no evidence of widespread age discrimination by the states and no need for preventive legislation because most states had laws on the books prohibiting discrimination on the basis of age anyway. *(Kimel v. Florida Board of Regents; United States v. Florida Board of Regents)*

Whistleblower Suits. The Court agreed to decide whether states could be sued under a Civil War–era law that allowed private citizens to initiate suits for fraudulent use of federal moneys.

The False Claims Act, passed in 1863, prohibited "any person" from presenting a "false or fraudulent claim" to the federal government. It allowed the government or a private citizen acting "in the name of the government" to initiate a suit under the law. The government could take over the suit or allow the citizen to prosecute the claim. In either case, the private citizen was allowed to collect a portion of any penalties imposed. Modern-day "whistleblowers" had been making more frequent use of the law in cases involving state programs receiving federal funds. State governments responded by arguing the suits were barred under the Eleventh Amendment's restriction on private suits against states in federal court.

The issue reached the Court in a case brought by a former Vermont state employee, Jonathan Stevens, who claimed the state's Agency of Natural Resources overstated the staff time devoted to federally financed antipollution programs in order to increase the allocation of matching federal funds. The federal appeals court in New York rejected the state's effort to dismiss the suit.

In its petition for review, the state's lawyers said whistleblower suits against a state allowed private plaintiffs to "disrupt core governmental functions and intrude into the working relationship between two sovereign governments." Stevens's lawyers countered by saying the law provided "a remedy against individual states, state university systems, state administrative agencies, and state research organizations for fraud committed on the public fisc." The Justice Department also filed a brief urging the Court to allow suits against states under the law. (*Vermont Agency of Natural Resources v. United States ex rel. Stevens*)

Driver's License Privacy. The federal government squared off against the states over the constitutionality of a law limiting the release of driver's license information by state motor vehicle departments.

The Driver's Privacy Protection Act, passed by Congress in 1994, generally prohibited states from releasing personal information from driver's license databases without the licenseholder's permission. The law was a response to the widely publicized murder of a film actress in 1989 by a stalker who tracked her down using information from California driver's license records. Many states, however, earned significant revenue by selling their driver's license lists to businesses. A number of states, including South Carolina, challenged the act on federalism grounds. Two federal appeals courts upheld the act, while two others—including the Fourth U.S. Circuit Court of Appeals in the South Carolina case—ruled it unconstitutional.

In urging the Court to uphold the act, the Justice Department said the law was "a wholly proper regulation of interstate commerce that does not impinge on any aspect of state sovereignty protected by the Constitution." But lawyers for South Carolina said the act amounted to "the coerced use of state officials to carry out federal policy choices." (*Reno v. Condon*)

Appendix

Opinion Excerpts

Following are excerpts from some of the most important rulings of the Supreme Court's 1998–1999 term. They appear in the order in which they were announced. Footnotes and legal citations are omitted.

Nos. 98-404 and 98-564

Department of Commerce v. United States House of Representatives
and
Clinton v. Glavin

On appeal from the United States District Court
for the District of Columbia

On appeal from the United States District Court
for the Eastern District of Virginia

[January 25, 1999]

JUSTICE O'CONNOR delivered the opinion of the Court, except as to Part III-B.

The Census Bureau (Bureau) has announced a plan to use two forms of statistical sampling in the 2000 Decennial Census to address a chronic and apparently growing problem of "undercounting" certain identifiable groups of individuals. Two sets of plaintiffs filed separate suits challenging the legality and constitutionality of the Bureau's plan. Convened as three-judge courts, the District Court for the Eastern District of Virginia and the District Court for the District of Columbia each held that the Bureau's plan for the 2000 census violates the Census Act, 13 U.S.C. §1 et seq., and both courts permanently enjoined the Bureau's planned use of statistical sampling to determine the population for purposes of congressional apportionment. (ED Va. 1998); (DC 1998). We noted probable jurisdiction in both cases (1998) and consolidated the cases for oral argument. We now affirm the judgment of the District Court for the Eastern District of Virginia, and we dismiss the appeal from the District Court for the District of Columbia.

I

A

Article 1, §2, cl. 3, of the United States Constitution states that "Representatives . . . shall be apportioned among the several States . . . according to their respective Numbers." It further requires that "[t]he actual Enumeration shall be made within three Years after the first Meeting of the Congress of the United States, and within every subsequent Term of ten Years, in such Manner as they shall by Law direct." Finally, §2 of the Fourteenth Amendment provides that "Representatives shall be apportioned among the several States according to their respective numbers, counting the whole number of persons in each State, excluding Indians not taxed."

Pursuant to this constitutional authority to direct the manner in which the "actual Enumeration" of the population shall be made, Congress enacted the Census Act (hereinafter Census Act or Act), delegating to the Secretary of Commerce (Secretary) authority to conduct the decennial census. §4. The Act provides that the Secretary "shall, in the year 1980 and every 10 years thereafter, take a decennial census of population as of the first day of April of such year." §141(a). It further requires that "[t]he tabulation of total population by States . . . as required for the apportionment of Representatives in Congress among the several States shall be completed within 9 months after the census date and reported by the Secretary to the President of the United States." §141(b). Using this information, the President must then "transmit to the Congress a statement showing the whole number of persons in each State . . . and the number of Representatives to which each State would be entitled." 2 U.S.C. §2a(a). Within 15 days thereafter, the Clerk of the House of Representatives must "send to the executive of each State a certificate of the number of Representatives to which such State is entitled." 2 U.S.C. §2a(b).

The instant dispute centers on the problem of "undercount" in the decennial census. For the last few decades, the Census Bureau has sent census forms to every household, which it asked residents to complete and return. The Bureau followed up on the mailing by sending enumerators to personally visit all households that did not respond by mail. Despite this comprehensive effort to reach every household, the Bureau has always failed to reach—and has thus failed to count—a portion of the population. This shortfall has been labeled the census "undercount."

The Bureau has been measuring the census undercount rate since 1940, and undercount has been the subject of public debate at least since the early 1970's. It has been measured in one of two ways. Under one method, known as "demographic analysis," the Bureau develops an independent estimate of the population using birth, death, immigration, and emigration records. A second method, first used in 1990, involves a large sample survey, called the "Post-Enumeration Survey," that is conducted in conjunction with the decennial census. The Bureau compares the information gathered during the survey with the information obtained in the census and uses the comparison to estimate the number of unenumerated people in the census.

Some identifiable groups—including certain minorities, children, and renters—have historically had substantially higher undercount rates than the population as a whole. Accordingly, in previous censuses, the Bureau sought to increase the number of persons from whom it obtained information. In 1990, for instance, the Bureau attempted to reach out to traditionally undercounted groups by promoting awareness of the census and its importance, providing access to Spanish language forms, and offering a toll free number for those who had questions about the forms. Indeed, the 1990 census was "better designed and executed than any previous census." [Quoting Census Bureau's Census 2000 Report to Congress.] Nonetheless, it was less accurate than its predecessor for the first time since the Bureau began measuring the undercount rate in 1940.

In a further effort to address growing concerns about undercount in the census, Congress passed the Decennial Census Improvement Act of 1991, which instructed the Secretary to contract with the National Academy of Sciences (Academy) to study the "means by which the Government could achieve the most accurate population count possible." Among the issues the Academy was directed to consider was "the appropriateness of using sampling methods, in combination with basic data-collection techniques or otherwise, in the acquisition or refinement of population data." Two of the three panels established by the Academy pursuant to this Act concluded that "[d]ifferential undercount cannot be reduced to acceptable levels at acceptable costs without the use of integrated coverage measurement," a statistical sampling procedure that adjusts census results to account for undercount in the initial enumeration, and all three panels recommended including integrated coverage measurement in the 2000 census. [Citations omitted.]

In light of these studies and other research, the Bureau formulated a plan for the 2000 census that uses statistical sampling to supplement data obtained through traditional census methods. The Bureau plan provides for two types of sampling that are the subject of the instant challenge. First, appellees challenge the proposed use of sampling in the Nonresponse Followup program (NRFU). Under this program, the Bureau would continue to send census forms to all households, as well as make forms available in post offices and in other public places. The Bureau expects that 67 percent of households will return the forms. The Bureau then plans to divide the population into census tracts of approximately 4,000 people that have "homogenous population characteristics, economic status, and living conditions." The Bureau would then visit a randomly selected sample of nonresponding housing units, which would be "statistically representative of all housing units in [a] nonresponding tract." The rate of nonresponse follow-up in a tract would vary with the mail response rate to ensure that the Bureau obtains census data from at least 90 percent of the housing units in each census tract. . . .

The second challenged sampling procedure—which would be implemented after the first is completed—is known as Integrated Coverage Measurement (ICM). ICM employs the statistical technique called Dual System Estimation (DSE) to adjust the census results to account for undercount in the initial enumeration. The plan requires the Bureau to begin by classifying each of the country's 7 million blocks into "strata," which are defined by the characteristics of each block, including state, racial, and ethnic composition, and the proportion of homeowners to renters, as revealed in the 1990 census. The Bureau then plans to select blocks at random from each stratum, for a total of 25,000 blocks, or an estimated 750,000 housing units. Enumerators would then conduct interviews at each of those 750,000 units, and if discrepancies were detected between the pre-ICM response and ICM response, a follow-up interview would be conducted to determine the "true" situation in the home. The information gathered during this stage would be used to assign each person to a poststratum—a group of people who have similar chances of being counted in the initial data collection—which would be defined by state geographic subdivision (*e.g.*, rural or urban), owner or renter, age, sex, race, and Hispanic origin.

In the final stage of the census, the Bureau plans to use DSE to obtain the final count and characteristics of the population. The census plan calls for the Bureau to compare the dual systems of information—that is, the data gathered on the sample blocks during the ICM and the data gathered on those same blocks through the initial phase of the census—to produce an estimation factor for each poststratum. The estimation factors would account for the differences between the ICM numbers and the initial enumeration and would be applied to the initial enumeration to estimate the total population and housing units in each poststratum. The totals for the poststrata would then be summed to determine state and national population totals.

The Bureau's announcement of its plan to use statistical sampling in the 2000 census led to a flurry of legislative activity. Congress amended the Census Act to provide that, "[n]otwithstanding any other provision of law, no sampling or any other statistical procedure, including any statistical adjustment, may be used in any determination of population for purposes of the apportionment of Representatives in Congress among the several States," (1997), but President Clinton vetoed the bill. Congress then passed, and the President signed, a bill providing for the creation of a "comprehensive and detailed plan outlining [the Bureau's] proposed methodologies for conducting the 2000 Decennial Census and available methods to conduct an actual enumeration of the population," including an explanation of any statistical methodologies that may be used. Pursuant to this directive, the Commerce Department issued the Census 2000 Report. After receiving the Report, Congress passed the 1998 Departments of Commerce, Justice, and State, the Judiciary, and Related Agencies Appropriations Act, §209, which provides that the Census 2000 Report and the Bureau's Census 2000 Operational Plan "shall be deemed to constitute final agency action regarding the use of statistical methods in the 2000 decennial census." The Act also permits any person aggrieved by the plan to use statistical sampling in the decennial census to bring a legal action and requires that any action brought under the Act be heard by a three-judge district court. It further provides for review by appeal directly to this Court.

B

The publication of the Bureau's plan for the 2000 census occasioned two separate legal challenges. The first suit, styled *Clinton v. Glavin*, was filed on February 12, 1998, in the District Court for the Eastern District of Virginia by four counties (Cobb County, Georgia; Bucks County, Pennsylvania; Delaware County, Pennsylvania; and DuPage County, Illinois) and residents of 13 States (Arizona, California, Connecticut, Florida, Georgia, Illinois, Indiana, Montana, Nevada, Ohio, Pennsylvania, Virginia, and Wisconsin), who claimed that the Bureau's planned use of statistical sampling to apportion Representatives among the States violates the Census Act and the Census Clause of the Constitution. They sought a declaration that the Bureau's plan is unlawful and/or unconstitutional and an injunction barring use of the NRFU and ICM sampling procedures in the 2000 census.

The District Court held that the case was ripe for review, that the plaintiffs satisfied the requirements for Article III standing, and that the Census Act prohibited use of the challenged sampling procedures to apportion Representatives. The District Court concluded that, because the statute was clear on its face, the court did not need to reach the constitutional questions presented. It thus denied defendants' motion to dismiss, granted plaintiffs' motion for summary judgment, and permanently enjoined the use of the challenged sampling procedures to determine the population for purposes of congressional apportionment. We noted probable jurisdiction on October 9, 1998.

The second challenge was filed by the United States House of Representatives on February 20, 1998, in the District Court for the District of Columbia. The House sought a declaration that the Bureau's proposed use of sampling to determine the population for purposes of apportioning Members of the House of Representatives among the several States violates the Census Act and the Constitution. The House also sought a permanent injunction barring use of the challenged sampling procedures in the apportionment aspect of the 2000 census.

The District Court held that the House had Article III standing, the suit was ripe for review, equitable concerns did not warrant dismissal, the suit did not violate separation of powers principles, and the Census Act does not permit the use of the challenged sampling procedures in counting the population for apportionment. Because it held that the Census Act does not allow for the challenged sampling procedures, it declined to reach the House's constitutional challenge under the Census Clause. The District Court denied the defendants' motion to dismiss, granted the plaintiffs' motion for summary judgment, and issued an injunction preventing defendants from using the challenged sampling methods in the apportionment aspect of the 2000 census. The defendants appealed to this Court and we noted probable jurisdiction on September 10, 1998, and consolidated this case with *Clinton v. Glavin*, No. 98-564, for oral argument.

II

We turn our attention first to the issues presented by *Clinton v. Glavin*, No. 98-564, and we begin our analysis with the threshold issue of justiciability. Congress has eliminated any prudential concerns in this case by providing that "[a]ny person aggrieved by the use of any statistical method in violation of the Constitution or any provision of law (other than this Act), in connection with the 2000 census or any later decennial census, to determine the population for purposes of the apportionment or redistricting of Members in Congress, may in a civil action obtain declaratory, injunctive, and any other appropriate relief against the use of such method." In addition, the District Court below correctly found that the case is ripe for review, and that determination is not challenged here. Thus, the only open justiciability question in this case is whether appellees satisfy the requirements of Article III standing.

We have repeatedly noted that in order to establish Article III standing, "[a] plaintiff must allege personal injury fairly traceable to the defendant's allegedly unlawful conduct and likely to be redressed by the requested relief." . . . Here, the District Court, considering a Rule 56 motion, held that the plaintiffs-appellees, residents from 13 States, had established Article III standing to bring suit challenging the proposed method for conducting the 2000 census because they had made "[g]eneral factual allegations of injury resulting from Defendant's conduct." . . .

. . . [B]ecause the record before us amply supports the conclusion that several of the appellees have met their burden of proof regarding their standing to bring this suit, . . . we affirm the District Court's holding. . . . In support of their motion for summary judgment, appellees submitted the affidavit of Dr. Ronald F. Weber, a professor of government at the University of Wisconsin, which demonstrates that Indiana resident Gary A. Hofmeister has standing to challenge the proposed census 2000 plan. Utilizing data published by the Bureau, Dr. Weber projected year 2000 populations and net undercount rates for all States under the 1990 method of enumeration and under the Department's proposed plan for the 2000 census. He then determined on the basis of these projections how many Representatives would be apportioned to each State under each method and concluded that "it is a virtual certainty that Indiana will lose a seat . . . under the Department's Plan." . . .

Appellee Hofmeister's expected loss of a Representative to the United States Congress undoubtedly satisfies the injury-in-fact requirement of Article III standing. . . . With one fewer Representative, Indiana residents' votes will be diluted. . . . It is clear that if the Bureau is going to alter its plan to use sampling in the 2000 census, it must begin doing so by March 1999. . . . And it is certainly not necessary for this Court to wait until the census has been conducted to consider the issues presented here, because such a pause would result in extreme—possibly irremediable—hardship. . . .

Appellees have also established standing on the basis of the expected effects of the use of sampling in the 2000 census on intrastate redistricting. Dr. Weber indicated in his affidavit that "[i]t is substantially likely that voters in Maricopa County, Arizona, Bergen County, New Jersey, Cumberland County, Pennsylvania, LaSalle County, Illinois, Orange County, California, St. Johns County, Florida, Gallatin County, Montana, Forsyth County, Georgia, and Loudoun County, Virginia, will suffer vote dilution in state and local elections as a result of the [Bureau's] Plan." Several of the appellees reside in these counties, and several of the States in which these counties are located require use of federal decennial census population numbers for their state legislative redistricting. . . . Moreover, States use the population numbers generated by the federal decennial census for federal congressional redistricting. . . . Thus, the appellees who live in the aforementioned counties have a strong claim that they will be injured by the Bureau's plan because their votes will be diluted vis-á-vis residents of counties with larger "undercount" rates. . . .

III

We accordingly arrive at the dispute over the meaning of the relevant provisions of the Census Act. The District Court below examined the plain text and legislative history of the Act and concluded that the proposed use of statistical sampling to determine population for purposes of apportioning congressional seats among the States violates the Act. We agree.

A

An understanding of the historical background of the decennial census and the Act that governs it is essential to a proper interpretation of the Act's present text. From the very first census, the census of 1790, Congress has prohibited the use of statistical sampling in calculating the population for purposes of apportionment. The First Congress enacted legislation requiring census enumerators to swear an oath to make "a just and perfect enumeration" of every person within the division to which they were assigned. Each enumerator was required to compile a schedule of information for his district, listing by family name the number of persons in each family that fell into each of five specified categories. Congress modified this provision in 1810, adding an express statement that "the said enumeration shall be made by an actual inquiry at every dwelling-house, or of the head of every family within each district, and not otherwise," and expanding the number of specifications in the schedule of information. The requirement that census enumerators visit each home in person appeared in statutes governing the next 14 censuses.

The current Census Act was enacted into positive law in 1954. It contained substantially the same language as did its predecessor statutes, requiring enumerators to "visit personally each dwelling house in his subdivision" in order to obtain "every item of information and all particulars required for any census or survey" conducted in connection with the census. Indeed, the first departure from the requirement that the enumerators collect all census information through personal visits to every household in the Nation came in 1957 at the behest of the Secretary. The Secretary asked Congress to amend the Act to permit the Bureau to use statistical sampling in gathering some of the census information. In response, Congress enacted §195, which provided that, "[e]xcept for the determination of population for apportionment purposes, the Secretary may, where he deems it appropriate, authorize the use of the statistical method known as 'sampling' in carrying out the provisions of this title." This provision allowed the Secretary to authorize the use of sampling procedures in gathering supplemental, nonapportionment census information regarding population, unemployment, housing, and other matters collected in conjunction with the decennial census—much of which is now collected through what is known as the "long form"—but it did not authorize the use of sampling procedures in connection with apportionment of Representatives. . . .

In 1964, Congress repealed former §25(c) of the Census Act, which had required that each enumerator obtain "every item of information" by personal visit to each household. The repeal of this section permitted the Bureau to replace the personal visit of the enumerator with a form delivered and returned via the Postal Service. Pursuant to this new authority, census officials conducted approximately 60 percent of the census through a new "mailout-mailback" system for the first time in 1970. The Bureau then conducted follow-up visits to homes that failed to return census forms. Thus, although the legislation permitted the Bureau to conduct a portion of the census through the mail, there was no suggestion from any quarter that this change altered the prohibition in §195 on the use of statistical sampling in determining the population for apportionment purposes.

In 1976, the provisions of the Census Act at issue in this case took their present form. Congress revised §141 of the Census Act, which is now entitled "Population and other census information." It amended subsection (a) to authorize the Secretary to "take a decennial census of population as of the first day of April of such year, which date shall be known as the 'decennial census date,' in such form and content as he may determine, including the use of sampling procedures and special surveys." 13 U.S.C. §141(a). Congress also added several subsections to §141, among them a provision specifying that the term "census of population," as used in §141, "means a census of population, housing, and matters relating to population and housing." §141(g). Together, these revisions provided a broad statement that in collecting a range of demographic information during the decennial census, the Bureau would be permitted to use sampling procedures and special surveys.

This broad grant of authority given in §141(a) is informed, however, by the narrower and more specific §195, which is revealingly entitled, "Use of Sampling." The §141 authorization to use sampling techniques in the decennial census is not necessarily an authorization to use these techniques in collecting all of the information that is gathered during the decennial census. We look to the remainder of the law to determine what portions of the decennial census the authorization covers. When we do, we discover that, as discussed above, §195 directly prohibits the use of sampling in the determination of population for purposes of apportionment.

When Congress amended §195 in 1976, it did not in doing so alter the long-standing prohibition on the use of sampling in matters relating to apportionment. Congress modified the section by changing "apportionment purposes" to "purposes of apportionment of Representatives in Congress among the several States" and changing the phrase "may, where he deems it appropriate" to "shall, if he considers it feasible." The amended section thus reads: "Except for the determination of population for purposes of apportionment of Representatives in Congress among the several States, the Secretary shall, if he considers it feasible, authorize the use of the statistical method known as 'sampling' in carrying out the provisions of this title." 13 U.S.C. §195. As amended, the section now requires the Secretary to use statistical sampling in assembling the myriad demographic data that are collected in connection with the decennial census. But the section maintains its prohibition on the use of statistical sampling in calculating population for purposes of apportionment.

Absent any historical context, the language in the amended §195 might reasonably be read as either permissive or prohibitive with regard to the use of sampling for apportionment purposes. Indeed, appellees and appellants each cite numerous examples of the "except/shall" sentence structure that support their respective interpretations of the statute. . . . But these dueling examples only serve to illustrate that the interpretation of the "except/shall" structure depends primarily on the broader context in which that structure appears. Here, the context is provided by over 200 years during which federal statutes have prohibited the use of statistical sampling where apportionment is concerned. In light of this background, there is only one plausible reading of the amended §195: It prohibits the use of sampling in calculating the population for purposes of apportionment.

In fact, the Bureau itself concluded in 1980 that the Census Act, as amended, "clearly" continued the "historical precedent of using the 'actual Enumeration' for purposes of apportionment, while eschewing estimates based on sampling or other statistical procedures, no matter how sophisticated." That same year, the Solicitor General argued before this Court that "13 U.S.C. 195 prohibits the use of statistical 'sampling methods' in determining the state-by-state population totals.". . . The administration did not adopt the contrary position until 1994, when it first concluded that using statistical sampling to adjust census figures would be consistent with the Census Act. . . .

In holding that the 1976 amendments did not change the prohibition on the use of sampling in determining the population for apportionment purposes, we do not mean to suggest, as JUSTICE STEVENS claims in dissent, that the 1976 amendments had no purpose. Rather, the amendments served a very important purpose: They changed a provision that *permitted* the use of sampling for purposes other than apportionment into one that *required* that sampling be used for such purposes if "feasible." They also added to the existing delegation of authority to the Secretary to carry out the decennial census a statement indicating that despite the move to mandatory use of sampling in collecting non-apportionment information, the Secretary retained substantial authority to determine the manner in which the decennial census is conducted.

B

The conclusion that the Census Act prohibits the use of sampling for apportionment purposes finds support in the debate and discussions surrounding the 1976 revisions to the Census Act. At no point during the debates over these amendments did a single Member of Congress suggest that the amendments would so fundamentally change the manner in which the Bureau could calculate the population for purposes of apportionment. . . . [I]t is hard to imagine that, having explicitly prohibited the use of sampling for apportionment purposes in 1957, Congress would have decided to reverse course on such an important issue by enacting only a subtle change in phraseology.

IV

For the reasons stated, we conclude that the Census Act prohibits the proposed uses of statistical sampling in calculating the population for purposes of apportionment. Because we so conclude, we find it unnecessary to reach the constitutional question presented. . . . Accordingly, we affirm the judgment of the District

Court for the Eastern District of Virginia in *Clinton v. Glavin*, No. 98-564. As this decision also resolves the substantive issues presented by *Department of Commerce v. United States House of Representatives*, No. 98-404, that case no longer presents a substantial federal question. The appeal in that case is therefore dismissed.

It is so ordered.

JUSTICE SCALIA, with whom JUSTICE THOMAS joins, and with whom THE CHIEF JUSTICE and JUSTICE KENNEDY join as to Part II, concurring in part.

I

I join the opinion of the Court, excluding, of course, its resort in Part III-B to what was said by individual legislators and committees of legislators—or more precisely (and worse yet), what was *not* said by individual legislators and committees of legislators. I write separately to respond at somewhat greater length to JUSTICE STEVENS' analysis of 13 U.S.C. §141(a), to add several additional points of textual analysis, and to invoke the doctrine of constitutional doubt, which is a major factor in my decision.

II

Section 141(a) requires the Secretary to conduct a "decennial census of population . . . in such form and content as he may determine, including the use of sampling procedures and special surveys." JUSTICE STEVENS reasons that a reading of §195 that would prohibit sampling for apportionment purposes contradicts this provision. It seems to me there is no conflict at all. [Remainder of passage disputing Stevens's analysis omitted.]

Even if one is not entirely persuaded by the foregoing arguments, and the more substantial analysis contained in the opinion of the Court, I think it must be acknowledged that the statutory intent to permit use of sampling for apportionment purposes is *at least* not clear. In these circumstances, it is our practice to construe the text in such fashion as to avoid serious constitutional doubt. It is in my view unquestionably doubtful whether the constitutional requirement of an "actual Enumeration," Art. I, §2, cl. 3, is satisfied by statistical sampling.

Dictionaries roughly contemporaneous with the ratification of the Constitution demonstrate that an "enumeration" requires an actual counting, and not just an estimation of number. [Dictionary citations omitted.]

One must also be impressed by the facts recited in the opinion of the Court: that the Census Acts of 1790 and 1800 required a listing of persons by family name, and the Census Acts of 1810 through 1950 required census enumerators to visit each home in person. This demonstrates a longstanding tradition of Congress's forbidding the use of estimation techniques in conducting the apportionment census. . . .

JUSTICE STEVENS reasons from the *purpose* of the census clause: "The census is intended to serve the constitutional goal of equal representation. . . . That goal is best served by the use of a 'Manner' that is most likely to be complete and accurate." That is true enough, and would prove the point if either (1) *every* estimate is more accurate than a headcount, or (2) Congress could be relied upon to permit *only* those estimates that are more accurate than headcounts. It is metaphysically certain that the first proposition is false, and morally certain that the second is. To give Congress the power, under the guise of regulating the "Manner" by which the census is taken, to select among various estimation techniques having credible (or even incredible) "expert" support, is to give the party controlling Congress the power to distort representation in its own favor. In other words, genuine enumeration may not be the most accurate way of determining population, but it may be the most accurate way of determining population with minimal possibility of partisan manipulation. The prospect of this Court's reviewing estimation techniques in the future, to determine which of them *so obviously* creates a distortion that it cannot be allowed, is not a happy one. . . . Indeed, it is doubtful whether—separation-of-powers considerations aside—the Court would even have available the raw material to conduct such review effectively. As pointed out by the appellants in the present cases, we will *never* be able to assess the relative accuracy of the sampling system used for the 2000 census by comparing it to the results of a headcount, *for there will have been no headcount.*

For reasons of text and tradition, fully compatible with a constitutional purpose that is entirely sensible, a strong case can be made that an apportionment census conducted with the use of "sampling techniques" is not the "actual Enumeration." . . . And since that is so, the statute before us, which certainly *need not* be interpreted to permit such a census, ought not be interpreted to do so.

JUSTICE BREYER, concurring in part and dissenting in part.

I join Part II of the majority opinion concerning standing, and I join Parts II and III of JUSTICE STEVENS's dissent. I also agree with JUSTICE STEVENS's conclusion in Part I that the plan for the 2000 census presented by the Secretary of Commerce is not barred by the Census Act. In my view, however, the reason that 13 U.S.C. §195 does not bar the statistical sampling at issue here is that §195 focuses upon sampling used as a *substitute* for traditional enumeration methods, while the proposal at the heart of the Secretary's plan for the 2000 census (namely, Integrated Coverage Measurement, or ICM) is not so intended. Rather, ICM uses statistical sampling to *supplement* traditional enumeration methods in order to achieve the very accuracy that the census seeks and the Census Act itself demands. [Remainder of opinion omitted.]

JUSTICE STEVENS, with whom JUSTICE SOUTER and JUSTICE GINSBURG join as to Parts I and II, and with whom JUSTICE BREYER joins as to Parts II and III, dissenting.

The Census Act, 13 U.S.C. §1 *et seq.*, unambiguously authorizes the Secretary of Commerce to use sampling procedures when taking the decennial census. That this authorization is constitutional is equally clear. Moreover, because I am satisfied that at least one of the plaintiffs in each of these cases has standing, I would reverse both District Court judgments.

I

The Census Act, as amended in 1976, contains two provisions that relate to sampling. The first is an unlimited authorization; the second is a limited mandate.

The unlimited authorization is contained in §141(a). As its text plainly states, that section gives the Secretary of Commerce unqualified authority to use sampling procedures when taking the decennial census, the census used to apportion the House of Representatives. [Quotation omitted; see majority opinion.]

The limited mandate is contained in §195. That section commands the Secretary to use sampling, subject to two limitations: he need not do so when determining the population for apportionment purposes, and he need not do so unless he considers it feasible. The command reads as follows:

> "Except for the determination of population for purposes of apportionment of Representatives in Congress among the several States, the Secretary shall, if he considers it feasible, authorize the use of the statistical method known as sampling, in carrying out the provisions of this title." 13 U.S.C. §195.

Although §195 does not command the Secretary to use sampling in the determination of population for apportionment purposes, neither does it prohibit such sampling. Not a word in §195 qualifies the unlimited grant of authority in §141(a). Even if its text were ambiguous, §195 should be construed consistently with §141(a). Moreover, since §141(a) refers specifically to the decennial census, whereas §195 refers to the use of sampling in both the mid-decade and the decennial censuses, the former more specific provision would prevail over the latter if there were any conflict between the two. In my judgment, however, the text of both provisions is perfectly clear: They authorize sampling in both the decennial and the mid-decade census, but they only command its use when the determination is not for apportionment purposes.

A comparison of the text of these provisions with their predecessors in the 1957 Census Act further demonstrates that in 1976 Congress specifically intended to authorize the use of sampling for the purpose of apportioning the House of Representatives. Prior to 1976, the Census Act contained neither an unlimited authorization to use sampling nor a limited mandate to do so. Instead, the 1957 Act merely provided that the Secretary *may* use sampling for any purpose except apportionment. In other words, it contained a limited authorization that was coextensive with the present limited mandate. The 1976 amendments made two changes, each of which is significant. First, Congress added §141(a), which unambiguously told the Secretary to take the decennial census *in such form and content as he may determine, including the use of sampling procedures and special surveys.* Second, Congress changed §195 by replacing the word *may* with the word *shall.* Both amendments unambiguously endorsed the use of sampling. The amendment to §141 gave the Secretary authority that he did not previously possess, and the amendment to §195 changed a limited authorization into a limited command.

The primary purpose of the 1976 enactment was to provide for a mid-decade census to be used for various purposes other than apportionment. Section 141(a), however, is concerned only with the decennial census. The comment in the Senate

Report on the new language in §141(a) states that this provision was intended *to encourage the use of sampling and surveys in the taking of the decennial census.*. . . .

Nevertheless, in an unusual *tour de force*, the Court concludes that the amendments made no change in the scope of the Secretary's authority: Both before and after 1976 he could use sampling for any census-related purpose, other than apportionment. The plurality finds an omission in the legislative history of the 1976 enactment more probative of congressional intent than either the plain text of the statute itself or the pertinent comment in the Senate Report. For the plurality, it is incredible that such an important change in the law would not be discussed in the floor debates. It appears, however, that even though other provisions of the legislation were controversial, no one objected to this change. That the use of sampling has since become a partisan issue sheds no light on the views of the legislators who enacted the authorization to use sampling in 1976. Indeed, the bill was reported out of the House Committee by a unanimous vote, both the House and Senate versions easily passed, and the Conference was unanimous in recommending the revised legislation. Surely we must presume that the legislators who voted for the bill were familiar with its text as well as the several references to sampling in the Committee Reports. Given the general agreement on the proposition that *sampling and surveys* should be encouraged because they can both save money and increase the reliability of the population count, it is not at all surprising that no one objected to what was perceived as an obviously desirable change in the law.

What is surprising is that the Court's interpretation of the 1976 amendment to §141 drains it of any meaning. If the Court is correct, prior to 1976 the Secretary could have used sampling for any census-related purpose except apportionment, and after 1976 he retained precisely the same authority. Why, one must wonder, did Congress make this textual change in 1976? . . .

II

Appellees have argued that the reference in Article I of the Constitution to the apportionment of Representatives and to direct taxes on the basis of an *actual Enumeration* precludes the use of sampling procedures to supplement data obtained through more traditional census methods. U.S. Const., Art 1, §2, cl. 3. There is no merit to their argument.

In 1787, when the Constitution was being drafted, the Framers negotiated the number of Representatives allocated to each State because it was not feasible to conduct a census. They provided, however, that an *actual Enumeration shall be made within three Years after the first Meeting of the Congress of the United States, and within every subsequent Term of ten Years, in such Manner as they shall by Law direct.* U.S. Const., Art. 1, §2, cl. 3. The paramount constitutional principle codified in this clause was the rule of periodic reapportionment by means of a decennial census. The words *actual Enumeration* require post-1787 apportionments to be based on actual population counts, rather than mere speculation or bare estimate, but they do not purport to limit the authority of Congress to direct the *Manner* in which such counts should be made.

The July 1787 debate over future reapportionment of seats in the House of Representatives did not include any dispute about proposed methods of determining the population. Rather, the key questions were whether the rule of reapportionment would be constitutionally fixed and whether subsequent allocations of seats would be based on population or property. . . . The Committee of Style, charged with delivering a polished final version of the Constitution, added the term *actual Enumeration* to the draft reported to the Convention on September 12, 1787—five days before adjournment. This stylistic change did not limit Congress's authority to determine the *Manner* of conducting the census.

The census is intended to serve *the constitutional goal of equal representation. Franklin v. Massachusetts* (1992). That goal is best served by the use of a *Manner* that is most likely to be complete and accurate. As we repeatedly emphasized in our recent decision in *Wisconsin v. City of New York* (1996), our construction of that authorization must respect *the wide discretion bestowed by the Constitution upon Congress.* Methodological improvements have been employed to ease the administrative burden of the census and increase the accuracy of the data collected. The *mailout-mailback* procedure now considered a traditional method of enumeration was itself an innovation of the 1970 census. Requiring a face-to-face headcount would yield absurd results: For example, enumerators unable to gain entry to a large and clearly occupied apartment complex would be required to note zero occupants. For this reason, the 1970 census introduced the Postal Vacancy Check—a form of sampling not challenged here—which uses sample households to impute population figures that have been designated vacant but appear to be occupied. Since it is perfectly clear that the use of sampling will make the census more accurate than an admittedly futile attempt to count every individual by personal inspection, interview, or written interrogatory, the proposed method is a legitimate means of making the *actual Enumeration* that the Constitution commands.

III

I agree with the Court's discussion of the standing of the plaintiffs in No. 98-564. I am also convinced that the House of Representatives has standing to challenge the validity of the process that will determine the size of each State's Congressional delegation. . . . As the District Court in No. 98-404 correctly held, the House has a concrete and particularized *institutional interest in preventing its unlawful composition* that satisfies the injury in fact requirement of Article III. Accordingly, I respectfully dissent in both cases. I would reverse both judgments on the merits.

No. 98-97

Rita L. Saenz, Director, California Department of Social Services, et al., Petitioners v. Brenda Roe and Anna Doe etc.

On writ of certiorari to the United States Court of Appeals
for the Ninth Circuit

[May 17, 1999]

JUSTICE STEVENS delivered the opinion of the Court.

In 1992, California enacted a statute limiting the maximum welfare benefits available to newly arrived residents. The scheme limits the amount payable to a family that has resided in the State for less than 12 months to the amount payable by the State of the family's prior residence. The questions presented by this case are whether the 1992 statute was constitutional when it was enacted and, if not, whether an amendment to the Social Security Act enacted by Congress in 1996 affects that determination.

I

California is not only one of the largest, most populated, and most beautiful States in the Nation; it is also one of the most generous. Like all other States, California has participated in several welfare programs authorized by the Social Security Act and partially funded by the Federal Government. Its programs, however, provide a higher level of benefits and serve more needy citizens than those of most other States. In one year the most expensive of those programs, Aid to Families with Dependent Children (AFDC), which was replaced in 1996 with Temporary Assistance to Needy Families (TANF), provided benefits for an average of 2,645,814 persons per month at an annual cost to the State of $2.9 billion. In California the cash benefit for a family of two—a mother and one child—is $456 a month, but in the neighboring State of Arizona, for example, it is only $275.

In 1992, in order to make a relatively modest reduction in its vast welfare budget, the California Legislature enacted §11450.03 of the state Welfare and Institutions Code. That section sought to change the California AFDC program by limiting new residents, for the first year they live in California, to the benefits they would have received in the State of their prior residence. Because in 1992 a state program either had to conform to federal specifications or receive a waiver from the Secretary of Health and Human Services in order to qualify for federal reimbursement, §11450.03 required approval by the Secretary to take effect. In October 1992, the Secretary issued a waiver purporting to grant such approval.

On December 21, 1992, three California residents who were eligible for AFDC benefits filed an action in the Eastern District of California challenging the constitutionality of the durational residency requirement in §11450.03. Each plaintiff alleged that she had recently moved to California to live with relatives in order to escape abusive family circumstances. One returned to California after living in Louisiana for seven years, the second had been living in Oklahoma for six weeks and the third came from Colorado. Each alleged that her monthly AFDC grant for the ensuing 12 months would be substantially lower under §11450.03 than if the statute were not in effect. Thus, the former residents of Louisiana and Oklahoma would receive $190 and $341 respectively for a family of three even though the full California grant was $641; the former resident of Colorado, who had just one child, was limited to $280 a month as opposed to the full California grant of $504 for a family of two.

The District Court issued a temporary restraining order and, after a hearing, preliminarily enjoined implementation of the statute. District Judge Levi found that the statute "produces substantial disparities in benefit levels and makes no accommodation for the different costs of living that exist in different states." Relying primarily on our decisions in *Shapiro v. Thompson* (1969) and *Zobel v. Williams* (1982), he concluded that the statute placed "a penalty on the decision of new residents to migrate to the State and be treated on an equal basis with existing residents." *Green v. Anderson* (ED Cal. 1993). In his view, if the purpose of the measure was to deter migration by poor people into the State, it would be unconstitutional for that reason. And even if the purpose was only to conserve limited funds, the State had failed to explain why the entire burden of the saving should be imposed on new residents. The Court of Appeals summarily affirmed for the reasons stated by the District Judge. (CA9 1994).

We granted the State's petition for certiorari. (1994) We were, however, unable to reach the merits because the Secretary's approval of §11450.03 had been invalidated in a separate proceeding, and the State had acknowledged that the Act would not be implemented without further action by the Secretary. We vacated the judgment and directed that the case be dismissed. *Anderson v. Green* (1995). Accordingly, §11450.03 remained inoperative until after Congress enacted the Personal Responsibility and Work Opportunity Reconciliation Act of 1996 (PRWORA).

PRWORA replaced the AFDC program with TANF. The new statute expressly authorizes any State that receives a block grant under TANF to "apply to a family the rules (including benefit amounts) of the [TANF] program . . . of another State if the family has moved to the State from the other State and has resided in the State for less than 12 months." 42 U.S.C. §604(c). With this federal statutory provision in effect, California no longer needed specific approval from the Secretary to implement §11450.03. The California Department of Social Services therefore issued an "All County Letter" announcing that the enforcement of §11450.03 would commence on April 1, 1997.

The All County Letter clarifies certain aspects of the statute. Even if members of an eligible family had lived in California all of their lives, but left the State "on January 29th, intending to reside in another state, and returned on April 15th," their benefits are determined by the law of their State of residence from January 29 to April 15, assuming that that level was lower than California's. Moreover, the lower level of benefits applies regardless of whether the family was on welfare in the State of prior residence and regardless of the family's motive for moving to

California. The instructions also explain that the residency requirement is inapplicable to families that recently arrived from another country.

II

On April 1, 1997, the two respondents filed this action in the Eastern District of California making essentially the same claims asserted by the plaintiffs in *Anderson v. Green*, but also challenging the constitutionality of PRWORA's approval of the durational residency requirement. As in *Green*, the District Court issued a temporary restraining order and certified the case as a class action. The Court also advised the Attorney General of the United States that the constitutionality of a federal statute had been drawn into question, but she did not seek to intervene or to file an *amicus* brief. Reasoning that PRWORA permitted, but did not require, States to impose durational residency requirements, Judge Levi concluded that the existence of the federal statute did not affect the legal analysis in his prior opinion in *Green*.

He did, however, make certain additional comments on the parties' factual contentions. He noted that the State did not challenge plaintiffs' evidence indicating that, although California benefit levels were the sixth highest in the Nation in absolute terms, when housing costs are factored in, they rank 18th; that new residents coming from 43 States would face higher costs of living in California; and that welfare benefit levels actually have little, if any, impact on the residential choices made by poor people. On the other hand, he noted that the availability of other programs such as homeless assistance and an additional food stamp allowance of $1 in stamps for every $3 in reduced welfare benefits partially offset the disparity between the benefits for new and old residents. Notwithstanding those ameliorating facts, the State did not disagree with plaintiffs' contention that §11450.03 would create significant disparities between newcomers and welfare recipients who have resided in the State for over one year.

The State relied squarely on the undisputed fact that the statute would save some $10.9 million in annual welfare costs—an amount that is surely significant even though only a relatively small part of its annual expenditures of approximately $2.9 billion for the entire program. It contended that this cost saving was an appropriate exercise of budgetary authority as long as the residency requirement did not penalize the right to travel. The State reasoned that the payment of the same benefits that would have been received in the State of prior residency eliminated any potentially punitive aspects of the measure. Judge Levi concluded, however, that the relevant comparison was not between new residents of California and the residents of their former States, but rather between the new residents and longer term residents of California. He therefore again enjoined the implementation of the statute.

Without finally deciding the merits, the Court of Appeals affirmed his issuance of a preliminary injunction. *Roe v. Anderson* (CA9 1998). It agreed with the District Court's view that the passage of PRWORA did not affect the constitutional analysis, that respondents had established a probability of success on the merits and that class members might suffer irreparable harm if §11450.03 became operative. Although the decision of the Court of Appeals is consistent with the views of other federal courts that have addressed the issue, we granted certiorari because of the importance of the case (1998). We now affirm.

III

The word "travel" is not found in the text of the Constitution. Yet the "constitutional right to travel from one State to another" is firmly embedded in our jurisprudence. *United States v. Guest* (1966). Indeed, as Justice Stewart reminded us in *Shapiro v. Thompson* (1969), the right is so important that it is "assertable against private interference as well as governmental action . . . a virtually unconditional personal right, guaranteed by the Constitution to us all" (concurring opinion).

In *Shapiro*, we reviewed the constitutionality of three statutory provisions that denied welfare assistance to residents of Connecticut, the District of Columbia, and Pennsylvania, who had resided within those respective jurisdictions less than one year immediately preceding their applications for assistance. Without pausing to identify the specific source of the right, we began by noting that the Court had long "recognized that the nature of our Federal Union and our constitutional concepts of personal liberty unite to require that all citizens be free to travel throughout the length and breadth of our land uninhibited by statutes, rules, or regulations which unreasonably burden or restrict this movement." We squarely held that it was "constitutionally impermissible" for a State to enact durational residency requirements for the purpose of inhibiting the migration by needy persons into the State. We further held that a classification that had the effect of imposing a penalty on the exercise of the right to travel violated the Equal Protection Clause "unless shown to be necessary to promote a *compelling* governmental interest," and that no such showing had been made.

In this case California argues that §11450.03 was not enacted for the impermissible purpose of inhibiting migration by needy persons and that, unlike the legislation reviewed in *Shapiro*, it does not penalize the right to travel because new arrivals are not ineligible for benefits during their first year of residence. California submits that, instead of being subjected to the strictest scrutiny, the statute should be upheld if it is supported by a rational basis and that the State's legitimate interest in saving over $10 million a year satisfies that test. Although the United States did not elect to participate in the proceedings in the District Court or the Court of Appeals, it has participated as *amicus curiae* in this Court. It has advanced the novel argument that the enactment of PRWORA allows the States to adopt a "specialized choice-of-law-type provision" that "should be subject to an intermediate level of constitutional review," merely requiring that durational residency requirements be "substantially related to an important governmental objective." The debate about the appropriate standard of review, together with the potential relevance of the federal statute, persuades us that it will be useful to focus on the source of the constitutional right on which respondents rely.

IV

The "right to travel" discussed in our cases embraces at least three different components. It protects the right of a citizen of one State to enter and to leave another State, the right to be treated as a welcome visitor rather than an unfriend-ly alien when temporarily present in the second State, and, for those travelers who elect to become permanent residents, the right to be treated like other citizens of that State.

It was the right to go from one place to another, including the right to cross state borders while en route, that was vindicated in *Edwards v. California* (1941), which invalidated a state law that impeded the free interstate passage of the indi-gent. We reaffirmed that right in *United States v. Guest* (1966), which afforded pro-tection to the "right to travel freely to and from the State of Georgia and to use highway facilities and other instrumentalities of interstate commerce within the State of Georgia." Given that §11450.03 imposed no obstacle to respondents' entry into California, we think the State is correct when it argues that the statute does not directly impair the exercise of the right to free interstate movement. For the purposes of this case, therefore, we need not identify the source of that par-ticular right in the text of the Constitution. . . .

The second component of the right to travel is, however, expressly protected by the text of the Constitution. The first sentence of Article IV, §2, provides:

> "The Citizens of each State shall be entitled to all Privileges and Immu-nities of Citizens in the several States."

Thus, by virtue of a person's state citizenship, a citizen of one State who travels in other States, intending to return home at the end of his journey, is entitled to enjoy the "Privileges and Immunities of Citizens in the several States" that he vis-its. This provision removes "from the citizens of each State the disabilities of alien-age in the other States." *Paul v. Virginia.* (1869). . . . It provides important protec-tions for nonresidents who enter a State whether to obtain employment, *Hicklin v. Orbeck* (1978), to procure medical services, *Doe v. Bolton* (1973), or even to engage in commercial shrimp fishing, *Toomer v. Witsell* (1948). Those protections are not "absolute," but the Clause "does bar discrimination against citizens of other States where there is no substantial reason for the discrimination beyond the mere fact that they are citizens of other States." Id. There may be a substantial reason for requiring the nonresident to pay more than the resident for a hunting license, see *Baldwin v. Fish and Game Comm'n of Mont.* (1978), or to enroll in the state univer-sity, see *Vlandis v. Kline* (1973), but our cases have not identified any acceptable rea-son for qualifying the protection afforded by the Clause for "the citizen of State A who ventures into State B to settle there and establish a home." *Zobel* (O'CON-NOR, J., concurring in judgment). Permissible justifications for discrimination between residents and nonresidents are simply inapplicable to a nonresident's exer-cise of the right to move into another State and become a resident of that State.

What is at issue in this case, then, is this third aspect of the right to travel—the right of the newly arrived citizen to the same privileges and immunities enjoyed by other citizens of the same State. That right is protected not only by the new arrival's status as a state citizen, but also by her status as a citizen of the United States. That additional source of protection is plainly identified in the opening words of the Fourteenth Amendment.

> "All persons born or naturalized in the United States, and subject to the jurisdiction thereof, are citizens of the United States and of the State

wherein they reside. No State shall make or enforce any law which
shall abridge the privileges or immunities of citizens of the United
States. . . ."

Despite fundamentally differing views concerning the coverage of the Privileges
or Immunities Clause of the Fourteenth Amendment, most notably expressed in
the majority and dissenting opinions in the *Slaughter-House Cases* (1873), it has
always been common ground that this Clause protects the third component of the
right to travel. Writing for the majority in the *Slaughter-House Cases,* Justice Miller
explained that one of the privileges conferred by this Clause "is that a citizen of
the United States can, of his own volition, become a citizen of any State of the
Union by a bona fide residence therein, with the same rights as other citizens of
that State." Justice Bradley, in dissent, used even stronger language to make the
same point [Quotation omitted.]

That newly arrived citizens "have two political capacities, one state and one federal" *[U.S. Term Limits, Inc. v. Thompson* (1995) (KENNEDY, J., concurring)] adds
special force to their claim that they have the same rights as others who share their
citizenship. Neither mere rationality nor some intermediate standard of review
should be used to judge the constitutionality of a state rule that discriminates
against some of its citizens because they have been domiciled in the State for less
than a year. The appropriate standard may be more categorical than that articulated in *Shapiro*, but it is surely no less strict.

V

Because this case involves discrimination against citizens who have completed
their interstate travel, the State's argument that its welfare scheme affects the right
to travel only "incidentally" is beside the point. . . .

[S]ince the right to travel embraces the citizen's right to be treated equally in
her new State of residence, the discriminatory classification is itself a penalty.

It is undisputed that respondents and the members of the class that they represent are citizens of California and that their need for welfare benefits is unrelated
to the length of time that they have resided in California. We thus have no occasion to consider what weight might be given to a citizen's length of residence if the
bona fides of her claim to state citizenship were questioned. Moreover, because
whatever benefits they receive will be consumed while they remain in California,
there is no danger that recognition of their claim will encourage citizens of other
States to establish residency for just long enough to acquire some readily portable
benefit, such as a divorce or a college education, that will be enjoyed after they
return to their original domicile. See, e.g., *Sosna v. Iowa* (1975); *Vlandis v. Kline*
(1973).

The classifications challenged in this case—and there are many—are defined
entirely by (a) the period of residency in California and (b) the location of the
prior residences of the disfavored class members. The favored class of beneficiaries includes all eligible California citizens who have resided there for at least one
year, plus those new arrivals who last resided in another country or in a State that
provides benefits at least as generous as California's. Thus, within the broad category of citizens who resided in California for less than a year, there are many who

are treated like lifetime residents. And within the broad sub-category of new arrivals who are treated less favorably, there are many smaller classes whose benefit levels are determined by the law of the States from whence they came. To justify §11450.03, California must therefore explain not only why it is sound fiscal policy to discriminate against those who have been citizens for less than a year, but also why it is permissible to apply such a variety of rules within that class.

These classifications may not be justified by a purpose to deter welfare applicants from migrating to California for three reasons. First, although it is reasonable to assume that some persons may be motivated to move for the purpose of obtaining higher benefits, the empirical evidence reviewed by the District Judge, which takes into account the high cost of living in California, indicates that the number of such persons is quite small—surely not large enough to justify a burden on those who had no such motive. Second, California has represented to the Court that the legislation was not enacted for any such reason. Third, even if it were . . . such a purpose would be unequivocally impermissible.

Disavowing any desire to fence out the indigent, California has instead advanced an entirely fiscal justification for its multitiered scheme. The enforcement of §11450.03 will save the State approximately $10.9 million a year. The question is not whether such saving is a legitimate purpose but whether the State may accomplish that end by the discriminatory means it has chosen. An even-handed, across-the-board reduction of about 72 cents per month for every beneficiary would produce the same result. But our negative answer to the question does not rest on the weakness of the State's purported fiscal justification. It rests on the fact that the Citizenship Clause of the Fourteenth Amendment expressly equates citizenship with residence . . . . It is equally clear that the Clause does not tolerate a hierarchy of 45 subclasses of similarly situated citizens based on the location of their prior residence. Thus, §11450.03 is doubly vulnerable: Neither the duration of respondents' California residence, nor the identity of their prior States of residence, has any relevance to their need for benefits. Nor do those factors bear any relationship to the State's interest in making an equitable allocation of the funds to be distributed among its needy citizens. . . . In short, the State's legitimate interest in saving money provides no justification for its decision to discriminate among equally eligible citizens.

VI

The question that remains is whether congressional approval of durational residency requirements in the 1996 amendment to the Social Security Act somehow resuscitates the constitutionality of §11450.03. That question is readily answered, for we have consistently held that Congress may not authorize the States to violate the Fourteenth Amendment. Moreover, the protection afforded to the citizen by the Citizenship Clause of that Amendment is a limitation on the powers of the National Government as well as the States.

[Remainder of section omitted.]

* * *

Citizens of the United States, whether rich or poor, have the right to choose to be citizens "of the State wherein they reside." U.S. Const., Amdt. 14, §1. The States, however, do not have any right to select their citizens. The Fourteenth Amendment, like the Constitution itself, was, as Justice Cardozo put it, "framed upon the theory that the peoples of the several states must sink or swim together, and that in the long run prosperity and salvation are in union and not division." *Baldwin v. G. A. F. Seelig, Inc.* (1935).

The judgment of the Court of Appeals is affirmed.

It is so ordered.

CHIEF JUSTICE REHNQUIST, with whom JUSTICE THOMAS joins, dissenting.

The Court today breathes new life into the previously dormant Privileges or Immunities Clause of the Fourteenth Amendment—a Clause relied upon by this Court in only one other decision, *Colgate v. Harvey* (1935), overruled five years later by *Madden v. Kentucky* (1940). It uses this Clause to strike down what I believe is a reasonable measure falling under the head of a "good-faith residency requirement." Because I do not think any provision of the Constitution—and surely not a provision relied upon for only the second time since its enactment 130 years ago—requires this result, I dissent.

I

Much of the Court's opinion is unremarkable and sound. The right to travel clearly embraces the right to go from one place to another, and prohibits States from impeding the free interstate passage of citizens. The state law in *Edwards v. California* (1941), which prohibited the transport of any indigent person into California, was a classic barrier to travel or migration and the Court rightly struck it down. Indeed, for most of this country's history, what the Court today calls the first "component" of the right to travel was the entirety of this right. . . . The Court wisely holds that because Cal. Welf. & Inst. Code Ann. §11450.03 imposes no obstacle to respondents' entry into California, the statute does not infringe upon the right to travel. Thus, the traditional conception of the right to travel is simply not an issue in this case.

I also have no difficulty with aligning the right to travel with the protections afforded by the Privileges and Immunities Clause of Article IV, §2, to nonresidents who enter other States "intending to return home at the end of [their] journey." Nonresident visitors of other States should not be subject to discrimination solely because they live out of State. Like the traditional right-to-travel guarantees discussed above, however, this Clause has no application here, because respondents expressed a desire to stay in California and become citizens of that State. Respondents therefore plainly fall outside the protections of Article IV, §2.

Finally, I agree with the proposition that a "citizen of the United States can, of his own volition, become a citizen of any State of the Union by a *bona fide* residence therein, with the same rights as other citizens of that State." *Slaughter-House Cases* (1873).

But I cannot see how the right to become a citizen of another State is a necessary "component" of the right to travel, or why the Court tries to marry these separate and distinct rights. A person is no longer "traveling" in any sense of the word when he finishes his journey to a State which he plans to make his home. Indeed, under the Court's logic, the protections of the Privileges or Immunities Clause recognized in this case come into play only when an individual *stops* traveling with the intent to remain and become a citizen of a new State. The right to travel and the right to become a citizen are distinct, their relationship is not reciprocal, and one is not a "component" of the other. . . .

No doubt the Court has, in the past 30 years, essentially conflated the right to travel with the right to equal state citizenship in striking down durational residence requirements similar to the one challenged here. See, *e.g.*, *Shapiro v. Thompson* (1969) (striking down 1-year residence before receiving any welfare benefit); *Dunn v. Blumstein* (1972) (striking down 1-year residence before receiving the right to vote in state elections); [*Memorial Hospital v.*] *Maricopa County* [(1974)] (striking down 1-year county residence before receiving entitlement to nonemergency hospitalization or emergency care). These cases marked a sharp departure from the Court's prior right-to-travel cases because in none of them was travel itself prohibited. . . .

Instead, the Court in these cases held that restricting the provision of welfare benefits, votes, or certain medical benefits to new citizens for a limited time impermissibly "penalized" them under the Equal Protection Clause of the Fourteenth Amendment for having exercised their right to travel. The Court thus settled for deciding what restrictions amounted to "deprivations of very important benefits and rights" that operated to indirectly "penalize" the right to travel. . . .

The Court today tries to clear much of the underbrush created by these prior right-to-travel cases, abandoning its effort to define what residence requirements deprive individuals of "important rights and benefits" or "penalize" the right to travel. Under its new analytical framework, a State, outside certain ill-defined circumstances, cannot classify its citizens by the length of their residence in the State without offending the Privileges or Immunities Clause of the Fourteenth Amendment. The Court thus departs from *Shapiro* and its progeny, and, while paying lip service to the right to travel, the Court does little to explain how the right to travel is involved at all. Instead, as the Court's analysis clearly demonstrates, this case is only about respondents' right to immediately enjoy all the privileges of being a California citizen in relation to that State's ability to test the good-faith assertion of this right. The Court has thus come full circle by effectively disavowing the analysis of *Shapiro*, segregating the right to travel and the rights secured by Article IV from the right to become a citizen under the Privileges or Immunities Clause, and then testing the residence requirement here against this latter right. For all its misplaced efforts to fold the right to become a citizen into the right to travel, the Court has essentially returned to its original understanding of the right to travel.

II

In unearthing from its tomb the right to become a state citizen and to be treated equally in the new State of residence, however, the Court ignores a State's need to assure that only persons who establish a bona fide residence receive the benefits provided to current residents of the State. . . .

. . . [T]he Court has consistently recognized that while new citizens must have the same opportunity to enjoy the privileges of being a citizen of a State, the States retain the ability to use bona fide residence requirements to ferret out those who intend to take the privileges and run. . . .

While the physical presence element of a bona fide residence is easy to police, the subjective intent element is not. It is simply unworkable and futile to require States to inquire into each new resident's subjective intent to remain. Hence, States employ objective criteria such as durational residence requirements to test a new resident's resolve to remain before these new citizens can enjoy certain in-state benefits. Recognizing the practical appeal of such criteria, this Court has repeatedly sanctioned the State's use of durational residence requirements before new residents receive in-state tuition rates at state universities. *Starns v. Malkerson* (1971) (upholding 1-year residence requirement for in-state tuition); *Sturgis v. Washington* (1973) (same). . . . The Court has done the same in upholding a 1-year residence requirement for eligibility to obtain a divorce in state courts, *Sosna v. Iowa* (1975), and in upholding political party registration restrictions that amounted to a durational residency requirement for voting in primary elections, *Rosario v. Rockefeller* (1973).

If States can require individuals to reside in-state for a year before exercising the right to educational benefits, the right to terminate a marriage, or the right to vote in primary elections that all other state citizens enjoy, then States may surely do the same for welfare benefits. Indeed, there is no material difference between a 1-year residence requirement applied to the level of welfare benefits given out by a State, and the same requirement applied to the level of tuition subsidies at a state university. The welfare payment here and in-state tuition rates are cash subsidies provided to a limited class of people, and California's standard of living and higher education system make both subsidies quite attractive. Durational residence requirements were upheld when used to regulate the provision of higher education subsidies, and the same deference should be given in the case of welfare payments. . . .

The Court today recognizes that States retain the ability to determine the bona fides of an individual's claim to residence, but then tries to avoid the issue. It asserts that because respondents' need for welfare benefits is unrelated to the length of time they have resided in California, it has "no occasion to consider what weight might be given to a citizen's length of residence if the bona fides of her claim to state citizenship were questioned." But I do not understand how the absence of a link between need and length of residency bears on the State's ability to objectively test respondents' resolve to stay in California. There is no link between the need for an education or for a divorce and the length of residence, and yet States may use length of residence as an objective yardstick to channel their benefits to those whose intent to stay is legitimate.

In one respect, the State has a greater need to require a durational residence for welfare benefits than for college eligibility. The impact of a large number of new residents who immediately seek welfare payments will have a far greater impact on a State's operating budget than the impact of new residents seeking to attend a state university. In the case of the welfare recipients, a modest durational residence requirement to allow for the completion of an annual legislative budget cycle gives the State time to decide how to finance the increased obligations.

The Court tries to distinguish education and divorce benefits by contending that the welfare payment here will be consumed in California, while a college education or a divorce produces benefits that are "portable" and can be enjoyed after individuals return to their original domicile. But this "you can't take it with you" distinction is more apparent than real, and offers little guidance to lower courts who must apply this rationale in the future. Welfare payments are a form of insurance, giving impoverished individuals and their families the means to meet the demands of daily life while they receive the necessary training, education, and time to look for a job. The cash itself will no doubt be spent in California, but the benefits from receiving this income and having the opportunity to become employed or employable will stick with the welfare recipient if they stay in California or go back to their true domicile. Similarly, tuition subsidies are "consumed" in-state but the recipient takes the benefits of a college education with him wherever he goes. A welfare subsidy is thus as much an investment in human capital as is a tuition subsidy, and their attendant benefits are just as "portable." More importantly, this foray into social economics demonstrates that the line drawn by the Court borders on the metaphysical, and requires lower courts to plumb the policies animating certain benefits like welfare to define their "essence" and hence their "portability." . . .

I therefore believe that the durational residence requirement challenged here is a permissible exercise of the State's power to "assur[e] that services provided for its residents are enjoyed only by residents." *Martinez* [*v. Bynum* (1983)]. The 1-year period established in §11450.03 is the same period this Court approved in *Starns* and *Sosa*. The requirement does not deprive welfare recipients of all benefits; indeed, the limitation has no effect whatsoever on a recipient's ability to enjoy the full 5-year period of welfare eligibility; to enjoy the full range of employment, training, and accompanying supportive services; or to take full advantage of health care benefits under Medicaid. This waiting period does not preclude new residents from all cash payments, but merely limits them to what they received in their prior State of residence. Moreover, as the Court recognizes, any pinch resulting from this limitation during the 1-year period is mitigated by other programs such as homeless assistance and an increase in food stamp allowance. The 1-year period thus permissibly balances the new resident's needs for subsistence with the State's need to ensure the bona fides of their claim to residence.

Finally, Congress' express approval in 42 U.S.C. §604(c) of durational residence requirements for welfare recipients like the one established by California only goes to show the reasonableness of a law like §11450.03. The National Legislature, where people from Mississippi as well as California are represented, has recognized the need to protect state resources in a time of experimentation and welfare reform. As States like California revamp their total welfare packages, they should have the authority and flexibility to ensure that their new programs are not exploited. Congress has decided that it makes good welfare policy to give the States this power. California has reasonably exercised it through an objective, narrowly tailored residence requirement. I see nothing in the Constitution that should prevent the enforcement of that requirement.

JUSTICE THOMAS, with whom THE CHIEF JUSTICE joins, dissenting.

I join THE CHIEF JUSTICE's dissent. I write separately to address the majority's conclusion that California has violated "the right of the newly arrived citizen to the same privileges and immunities enjoyed by other citizens of the same State." In my view, the majority attributes a meaning to the Privileges or Immunities Clause that likely was unintended when the Fourteenth Amendment was enacted and ratified.

. . . Although the majority appears to breathe new life into the Clause today, it fails to address its historical underpinnings or its place in our constitutional jurisprudence. Because I believe that the demise of the Privileges or Immunities Clause has contributed in no small part to the current disarray of our Fourteenth Amendment jurisprudence, I would be open to reevaluating its meaning in an appropriate case. Before invoking the Clause, however, we should endeavor to understand what the framers of the Fourteenth Amendment thought that it meant. We should also consider whether the Clause should displace, rather than augment, portions of our equal protection and substantive due process jurisprudence. The majority's failure to consider these important questions raises the specter that the Privileges or Immunities Clause will become yet another convenient tool for inventing new rights, limited solely by the "predilections of those who happen at the time to be Members of this Court." *Moore v. East Cleveland* (1977).

I respectfully dissent.

No. 97-843

Aurelia Davis, as Next Friend of LaShonda D., Petitioner v. Monroe County Board of Education et al.

On writ of certiorari to the United States Court of Appeals for the Eleventh Circuit

[May 24, 1999]

JUSTICE O'CONNOR delivered the opinion of the Court.

Petitioner brought suit against the Monroe County Board of Education and other defendants, alleging that her fifth-grade daughter had been the victim of sexual harassment by another student in her class. Among petitioner's claims was a claim for monetary and injunctive relief under Title IX of the Education Amendments of 1972 (Title IX), as amended, 20 U.S.C. §1681 *et seq.* The District Court dismissed petitioner's Title IX claim on the ground that "student-on-student," or peer, harassment provides no ground for a private cause of action under the statute. The Court of Appeals for the Eleventh Circuit, sitting en banc, affirmed. We consider here whether a private damages action may lie against the school board in cases of student-on-student harassment. We conclude that it may, but only where the funding recipient acts with deliberate indifference to known acts of harassment in its programs or activities. Moreover, we conclude that such an action will lie only for harassment that is so severe, pervasive, and objectively offensive that it effectively bars the victim's access to an educational opportunity or benefit.

I

Petitioner's Title IX claim was dismissed under Federal Rule of Civil Procedure 12(b)(6) for failure to state a claim upon which relief could be granted. Accordingly, in reviewing the legal sufficiency of petitioner's cause of action, "we must assume the truth of the material facts as alleged in the complaint." [Citation omitted.]

A

Petitioner's minor daughter, LaShonda, was allegedly the victim of a prolonged pattern of sexual harassment by one of her fifth-grade classmates at Hubbard Elementary School, a public school in Monroe County, Georgia. According to petitioner's complaint, the harassment began in December 1992, when the classmate, G. F., attempted to touch LaShonda's breasts and genital area and made vulgar statements such as "I want to get in bed with you" and "I want to feel your boobs." Similar conduct allegedly occurred on or about January 4 and January 20, 1993. LaShonda reported each of these incidents to her mother and to her classroom teacher, Diane Fort. Petitioner, in turn, also contacted Fort, who allegedly assured petitioner that the school principal, Bill Querry, had been informed of the incidents. Petitioner contends that, notwithstanding these reports, no disciplinary action was taken against G. F.

G. F.'s conduct allegedly continued for many months. In early February, G. F. purportedly placed a door stop in his pants and proceeded to act in a sexually suggestive manner toward LaShonda during physical education class. LaShonda reported G. F.'s behavior to her physical education teacher, Whit Maples. Approximately one week later, G. F. again allegedly engaged in harassing behavior, this time while under the supervision of another classroom teacher, Joyce Pippin. Again, LaShonda allegedly reported the incident to the teacher, and again petitioner contacted the teacher to follow up.

Petitioner alleges that G. F. once more directed sexually harassing conduct toward LaShonda in physical education class in early March, and that LaShonda reported the incident to both Maples and Pippen. In mid-April 1993, G. F. allegedly rubbed his body against LaShonda in the school hallway in what LaShonda considered a sexually suggestive manner, and LaShonda again reported the matter to Fort.

The string of incidents finally ended in mid-May, when G. F. was charged with, and pleaded guilty to, sexual battery for his misconduct. The complaint alleges that LaShonda had suffered during the months of harassment, however; specifically, her previously high grades allegedly dropped as she became unable to concentrate on her studies, and, in April 1993, her father discovered that she had written a suicide note. The complaint further alleges that, at one point, LaShonda told petitioner that she "didn't know how much longer she could keep [G. F.] off her."

Nor was LaShonda G. F.'s only victim; it is alleged that other girls in the class fell prey to G. F.'s conduct. At one point, in fact, a group composed of LaShonda and other female students tried to speak with Principal Querry about G. F.'s behavior. According to the complaint, however, a teacher denied the students' request with the statement, "If [Querry] wants you, he'll call you."

Petitioner alleges that no disciplinary action was taken in response to G. F.'s behavior toward LaShonda. In addition to her conversations with Fort and Pippen, petitioner alleges that she spoke with Principal Querry in mid-May 1993. When petitioner inquired as to what action the school intended to take against G. F., Querry simply stated, "I guess I'll have to threaten him a little bit harder." Yet, petitioner alleges, at no point during the many months of his reported misconduct was G. F. disciplined for harassment. Indeed, Querry allegedly asked petitioner why LaShonda "was the only one complaining."

Nor, according to the complaint, was any effort made to separate G. F. and LaShonda. On the contrary, notwithstanding LaShonda's frequent complaints, only after more than three months of reported harassment was she even permitted to change her classroom seat so that she was no longer seated next to G. F. Moreover, petitioner alleges that, at the time of the events in question, the Monroe County Board of Education (Board) had not instructed its personnel on how to respond to peer sexual harassment and had not established a policy on the issue.

B

On May 4, 1994, petitioner filed suit in the United States District Court for the Middle District of Georgia against the Board, Charles Dumas, the school district's superintendent, and Principal Querry. The complaint alleged that the Board is a recipient of federal funding for purposes of Title IX, that "[t]he persistent sexual advances and harassment by the student G. F. upon [LaShonda] interfered with her ability to attend school and perform her studies and activities," and that "[t]he deliberate indifference by Defendants to the unwelcome sexual advances of a student upon LaShonda created an intimidating, hostile, offensive and abus[ive] school environment in violation of Title IX." The complaint sought compensatory and punitive damages, attorney's fees, and injunctive relief.

The defendants (all respondents here) moved to dismiss petitioner's complaint under Federal Rule of Civil Procedure 12(b)(6) for failure to state a claim upon which relief could be granted, and the District Court granted respondents' motion. (1994). With regard to petitioner's claims under Title IX, the court dismissed the claims against individual defendants on the ground that only federally funded educational institutions are subject to liability in private causes of action under Title IX. As for the Board, the court concluded that Title IX provided no basis for liability absent an allegation "that the Board or an employee of the Board had any role in the harassment."

Petitioner appealed the District Court's decision dismissing her Title IX claim against the Board, and a panel of the Court of Appeals for the Eleventh Circuit reversed. (1996). Borrowing from Title VII law, a majority of the panel determined that student-on-student harassment stated a cause of action against the Board under Title IX. . . .

The Eleventh Circuit granted the Board's motion for rehearing en banc (1996) and affirmed the District Court's decision to dismiss petitioner's Title IX claim against the Board (1998). The en banc court relied, primarily, on the theory that Title IX was passed pursuant to Congress' legislative authority under the Constitution's Spending Clause [Art. I, §8, cl. 1], and that the statute therefore must provide potential recipients of federal education funding with "unambiguous notice of the conditions they are assuming when they accept" it. Title IX, the court reasoned, provides recipients with notice that they must stop their employees from engaging in discriminatory conduct, but the statute fails to provide a recipient with sufficient notice of a duty to prevent student-on-student harassment.

Writing in dissent, four judges urged that the statute, by declining to identify the perpetrator of discrimination, encompasses misconduct by third parties . . . . The plain language, the dissenters reasoned, also provides recipients with sufficient notice that a failure to respond to student-on-student harassment could trigger liability for the district.

We granted certiorari (1998) in order to resolve a conflict in the Circuits over whether, and under what circumstances, a recipient of federal educational funds can be liable in a private damages action arising from student-on-student sexual harassment [citation of other cases omitted]. We now reverse.

II

Title IX provides, with certain exceptions not at issue here, that

> "[n]o person in the United States shall, on the basis of sex, be excluded from participation in, be denied the benefits of, or be subjected to discrimination under any education program or activity receiving Federal financial assistance." 20 U.S.C. §1681(a).

Congress authorized an administrative enforcement scheme for Title IX. Federal departments or agencies with the authority to provide financial assistance are entrusted to promulgate rules, regulations, and orders to enforce the objectives of §1681; and these departments or agencies may rely on "any . . . means authorized by law," including the termination of funding, to give effect to the statute's restrictions.

There is no dispute here that the Board is a recipient of federal education funding for Title IX purposes. Nor do respondents support an argument that student-on-student harassment cannot rise to the level of "discrimination" for purposes of Title IX. Rather, at issue here is the question whether a recipient of federal education funding may be liable for damages under Title IX under any circumstances for discrimination in the form of student-on-student sexual harassment.

A

Petitioner urges that Title IX's plain language compels the conclusion that the statute is intended to bar recipients of federal funding from permitting this form of discrimination in their programs or activities. She emphasizes that the statute prohibits a student from being "*subjected to discrimination* under any education program or activity receiving Federal financial assistance" (emphasis supplied). . . .

Here, however, we are asked to do more than define the scope of the behavior that Title IX proscribes. We must determine whether a district's failure to respond to student-on-student harassment in its schools can support a private suit for money damages. See *Gebser v. Lago Vista Independent School Dist.* (1998). This Court has indeed recognized an implied private right of action under Title IX, see *Cannon v. University of Chicago* (1979), and we have held that money damages are available in such suits, *Franklin v. Gwinnett County Public Schools* (1992). Because we have repeatedly treated Title IX as legislation enacted pursuant to Congress' authority under the Spending Clause, however, private damages actions are available only where recipients of federal funding had adequate notice that they could be liable for the conduct at issue. When Congress acts pursuant to its spending power, it generates legislation "much in the nature of a contract: in return for federal funds, the States agree to comply with federally imposed conditions." *Pennhurst State School and Hospital v. Halderman* (1981). In interpreting language in spending legislation, we thus "insis[t] that Congress speak with a clear voice," recognizing that "[t]here can, of course, be no knowing acceptance [of the terms of the putative contract] if a State is unaware of the conditions [imposed by the legislation] or is unable to ascertain what is expected of it." [Quoting *Pennhurst*.]

Invoking *Pennhurst*, respondents urge that Title IX provides no notice that recipients of federal educational funds could be liable in damages for harm arising from student-on-student harassment. Respondents contend, specifically, that the statute only proscribes misconduct by grant recipients, not third parties. Respondents argue, moreover, that it would be contrary to the very purpose of Spending Clause legislation to impose liability on a funding recipient for the misconduct of third parties, over whom recipients exercise little control.

We agree with respondents that a recipient of federal funds may be liable in damages under Title IX only for its own misconduct. . . .

We disagree with respondents' assertion, however, that petitioner seeks to hold the Board liable for G. F.'s actions instead of its own. Here, petitioner attempts to hold the Board liable for its *own* decision to remain idle in the face of known student-on-student harassment in its schools. In *Gebser*, we concluded that a recipient of federal education funds may be liable in damages under Title IX where it is deliberately indifferent to known acts of sexual harassment by a teacher. In that case, a teacher had entered into a sexual relationship with an eighth grade student, and the student sought damages under Title IX for the teacher's misconduct. . . .

We consider here whether the misconduct identified in *Gebser*—deliberate indifference to known acts of harassment—amounts to an intentional violation of Title IX, capable of supporting a private damages action, when the harasser is a student rather than a teacher. We conclude that, in certain limited circumstances, it does. As an initial matter, in *Gebser* we expressly rejected the use of agency principles in the Title IX context. . . . Additionally, the regulatory scheme surrounding Title IX has long provided funding recipients with notice that they may be liable for their failure to respond to the discriminatory acts of certain non-agents. The Department of Education requires recipients to monitor third parties for discrimination in specified circumstances and to refrain from particular forms of interaction with outside entities that are known to discriminate.

The common law, too, has put schools on notice that they may be held responsible under state law for their failure to protect students from the tortious acts of third parties. In fact, state courts routinely uphold claims alleging that schools have been negligent in failing to protect their students from the torts of their peers. [Citations omitted.]

This is not to say that the identity of the harasser is irrelevant. On the contrary, both the "deliberate indifference" standard and the language of Title IX narrowly circumscribe the set of parties whose known acts of sexual harassment can trigger some duty to respond on the part of funding recipients. Deliberate indifference makes sense as a theory of direct liability under Title IX only where the funding recipient has some control over the alleged harassment. A recipient cannot be directly liable for its indifference where it lacks the authority to take remedial action.

The language of Title IX itself—particularly when viewed in conjunction with the requirement that the recipient have notice of Title IX's prohibitions to be liable for damages—also cabins the range of misconduct that the statute proscribes. The statute's plain language confines the scope of prohibited conduct based on the recipient's degree of control over the harasser and the environment in which the harassment occurs. If a funding recipient does not engage in harassment directly, it may not be liable for damages unless its deliberate indifference "subject[s]" its students to harassment. That is, the deliberate indifference must, at a minimum, "cause [students] to undergo" harassment or "make them liable or vulnerable" to it. [Quoting dictionary definitions of "subject."] Moreover, because the harassment must occur "under" "the operations of" a funding recipient [quoting the statute], the harassment must take place in a context subject to the school district's control. . . .

These factors combine to limit a recipient's damages liability to circumstances wherein the recipient exercises substantial control over both the harasser and the context in which the known harassment occurs. Only then can the recipient be said to "expose" its students to harassment or "cause" them to undergo it "under" the recipient's programs. We agree with the dissent that these conditions are satisfied most easily and most obviously when the offender is an agent of the recipient. We rejected the use of agency analysis in *Gebser*, however, and we disagree that the term "under" somehow imports an agency requirement into Title IX. . . .

Where, as here, the misconduct occurs during school hours and on school grounds—the bulk of G. F.'s misconduct, in fact, took place in the classroom—the misconduct is taking place "under" an "operation" of the funding recipient. . . . In these circumstances, the recipient retains substantial control over the context in which the harassment occurs. More importantly, however, in this setting the Board exercises significant control over the harasser. [Citations omitted.] The common law, too, recognizes the school's disciplinary authority. [Citation omitted.] We thus conclude that recipients of federal funding may be liable for "subject[ing]" their students to discrimination where the recipient is deliberately indifferent to known acts of student-on-student sexual harassment and the harasser is under the school's disciplinary authority.

At the time of the events in question here, in fact, school attorneys and administrators were being told that student-on-student harassment could trigger liability under Title IX. In March 1993, even as the events alleged in petitioner's complaint were unfolding, the National School Boards Association issued a publication . . . which observed that districts could be liable under Title IX for their failure to respond to student-on-student harassment. . . . Although we do not rely on this publication as an "indicium of congressional notice" [quoting the dissent], we do find support for our reading of Title IX in the fact that school attorneys have rendered an analogous interpretation.

Likewise, although they were promulgated too late to contribute to the Board's notice of proscribed misconduct, the Department of Education's Office for Civil Rights (OCR) has recently adopted policy guidelines providing that student-on-student harassment falls within the scope of Title IX's proscriptions. See Department of Education, Office of Civil Rights, Sexual Harassment Guidance: Harassment of Students by School Employees, Other Students, or Third Parties (1997). . . .

We stress that our conclusion here—that recipients may be liable for their deliberate indifference to known acts of peer sexual harassment—does not mean that recipients can avoid liability only by purging their schools of actionable peer harassment or that administrators must engage in particular disciplinary action. We thus disagree with respondents' contention that, if Title IX provides a cause of action for student-on-student harassment, "nothing short of expulsion of every student accused of misconduct involving sexual overtones would protect school systems from liability or damages." See Brief for Respondents. Likewise, the dissent erroneously imagines that victims of peer harassment now have a Title IX right to make particular remedial demands. . . . In fact, as we have previously noted, courts should refrain from second guessing the disciplinary decisions made by school administrators. [Citation omitted.]

School administrators will continue to enjoy the flexibility they require so long as funding recipients are deemed "deliberately indifferent" to acts of student-on-student harassment only where the recipient's response to the harassment or lack thereof is clearly unreasonable in light of the known circumstances. The dissent consistently mischaracterizes this standard to require funding recipients to "remedy" peer harassment and to "ensur[e] that . . . students conform their conduct to" certain rules. Title IX imposes no such requirements. On the contrary, the recipient must merely respond to known peer harassment in a manner that is not clearly unreasonable. This is not a mere "reasonableness" standard, as the dissent assumes. In an appropriate case, there is no reason why courts, on a motion to dismiss, for summary judgment, or for a directed verdict, could not identify a response as not "clearly unreasonable" as a matter of law.

Like the dissent, we acknowledge that school administrators shoulder substantial burdens as a result of legal constraints on their disciplinary authority. To the extent that these restrictions arise from federal statutes, Congress can review these burdens with attention to the difficult position in which such legislation may place our Nation's schools. We believe, however, that the standard set out here is sufficiently flexible to account both for the level of disciplinary authority available to the school and for the potential liability arising from certain forms of disciplinary action. A university might not, for example, be expected to exercise the same degree of control over its students that a grade school would enjoy, and it would be entirely reasonable for a school to refrain from a form of disciplinary action that would expose it to constitutional or statutory claims.

While it remains to be seen whether petitioner can show that the Board's response to reports of G. F.'s misconduct was clearly unreasonable in light of the known circumstances, petitioner may be able to show that the Board "subject[ed]" LaShonda to discrimination by failing to respond in any way over a period of five months to complaints of G. F.'s in-school misconduct from LaShonda and other female students.

B

The requirement that recipients receive adequate notice of Title IX's proscriptions also bears on the proper definition of "discrimination" in the context of a private damages action. . . . Having previously determined that "sexual harassment" is "discrimination" in the school context under Title IX, we are constrained to conclude that student-on-student sexual harassment, if sufficiently severe, can likewise rise to the level of discrimination actionable under the statute. . . . The statute's other prohibitions, moreover, help give content to the term "discrimination" in this context. Students are not only protected from discrimination, but also specifically shielded from being "excluded from participation in" or "denied the benefits of" any "education program or activity receiving Federal financial assistance." [§1681(a).] The statute makes clear that, whatever else it prohibits, students must not be denied access to educational benefits and opportunities on the basis of gender. We thus conclude that funding recipients are properly held liable in damages only where they are deliberately indifferent to sexual harassment, of which they have actual knowledge, that is so severe, pervasive, and objectively offensive that it can be said to deprive the victims of access to the educational opportunities or benefits provided by the school.

The most obvious example of student-on-student sexual harassment capable of triggering a damages claim would thus involve the overt, physical deprivation of access to school resources. Consider, for example, a case in which male students physically threaten their female peers every day, successfully preventing the female students from using a particular school resource—an athletic field or a computer lab, for instance. District administrators are well aware of the daily ritual, yet they deliberately ignore requests for aid from the female students wishing to use the resource. The district's knowing refusal to take any action in response to such behavior would fly in the face of Title IX's core principles, and such deliberate indifference may appropriately be subject to claims for monetary damages. It is not necessary, however, to show physical exclusion to demonstrate that students have been deprived by the actions of another student or students of an educational opportunity on the basis of sex. Rather, a plaintiff must establish sexual harassment of students that is so severe, pervasive, and objectively offensive, and that so undermines and detracts from the victims' educational experience, that the victim-students are effectively denied equal access to an institution's resources and opportunities.

Whether gender-oriented conduct rises to the level of actionable "harassment" thus "depends on a constellation of surrounding circumstances, expectations, and relationships" [quoting *Oncale v. Sundowner Offshore Services, Inc.* (1998)], including, but not limited to, the ages of the harasser and the victim and the number of individuals involved. Courts, moreover, must bear in mind that schools are unlike the adult workplace and that children may regularly interact in a manner that would be unacceptable among adults. . . . Indeed, at least early on, students are still learning how to interact appropriately with their peers. It is thus understandable that, in the school setting, students often engage in insults, banter, teasing, shoving, pushing, and gender-specific conduct that is upsetting to the students subjected to it. Damages are not available for simple acts of teasing and name-calling among school children, however, even where these comments target differences in gender. Rather, in the context of student-on-student harassment, damages are available only where the behavior is so severe, pervasive, and objectively offensive that it denies its victims the equal access to education that Title IX is designed to protect.

The dissent fails to appreciate these very real limitations on a funding recipient's liability under Title IX. It is not enough to show, as the dissent would read this opinion to provide, that a student has been "teased" or "called . . . offensive names." Comparisons to an "overweight child who skips gym class because the other children tease her about her size," the student "who refuses to wear glasses to avoid the taunts of 'four-eyes,' " and "the child who refuses to go to school because the school bully calls him a 'scaredy-cat' at recess" are inapposite and misleading. Nor do we contemplate, much less hold, that a mere "decline in grades is enough to survive" a motion to dismiss. The drop-off in LaShonda's grades provides necessary evidence of a potential link between her education and G. F.'s misconduct, but petitioner's ability to state a cognizable claim here depends equally on the alleged persistence and severity of G. F.'s actions, not to mention the Board's alleged knowledge and deliberate indifference. We trust that the dissent's characterization of our opinion will not mislead courts to impose more sweeping liability than we read Title IX to require.

Moreover, the provision that the discrimination occur "under any education program or activity" suggests that the behavior be serious enough to have the systemic effect of denying the victim equal access to an educational program or activity. . . . Even the dissent suggests that Title IX liability may arise when a funding recipient remains indifferent to severe, gender-based mistreatment played out on a "widespread level" among students. . . .

C

Applying this standard to the facts at issue here, we conclude that the Eleventh Circuit erred in dismissing petitioner's complaint. Petitioner alleges that her daughter was the victim of repeated acts of sexual harassment by G. F. over a 5-month period, and there are allegations in support of the conclusion that G. F.'s misconduct was severe, pervasive, and objectively offensive. The harassment was not only verbal; it included numerous acts of objectively offensive touching, and, indeed, G. F. ultimately pleaded guilty to criminal sexual misconduct. Moreover, the complaint alleges that there were multiple victims who were sufficiently disturbed by G. F.'s misconduct to seek an audience with the school principal. Further, petitioner contends that the harassment had a concrete, negative effect on her daughter's ability to receive an education. The complaint also suggests that petitioner may be able to show both actual knowledge and deliberate indifference on the part of the Board, which made no effort whatsoever either to investigate or to put an end to the harassment.

. . . Accordingly, the judgment of the United States Court of Appeals for the Eleventh Circuit is reversed, and the case is remanded for further proceedings consistent with this opinion.

It is so ordered.

JUSTICE KENNEDY, with whom THE CHIEF JUSTICE, JUSTICE SCALIA, and JUSTICE THOMAS join, dissenting.

The Court has held that Congress' power "to authorize expenditure of public moneys for public purposes is not limited by the direct grants of legislative power found in the Constitution." *South Dakota v. Dole* (1987) [internal quotations omitted]. As a consequence, Congress can use its Spending Clause power to pursue objectives outside of "Article I's enumerated legislative fields" by attaching conditions to the grant of federal funds. So understood, the Spending Clause power, if wielded without concern for the federal balance, has the potential to obliterate distinctions between national and local spheres of interest and power by permitting the federal government to set policy in the most sensitive areas of traditional state concern, areas which otherwise would lie outside its reach.

A vital safeguard for the federal balance is the requirement that, when Congress imposes a condition on the States' receipt of federal funds, it "must do so unambiguously." *Pennhurst State School and Hospital v. Halderman* (1981). . . .

Our insistence that "Congress speak with a clear voice" to "enable the States to exercise their choice knowingly, cognizant of the consequences of their participation" is not based upon some abstract notion of contractual fairness. Rather, it is a concrete safeguard in the federal system. Only if States receive clear notice of the conditions attached to federal funds can they guard against excessive federal intrusion into state affairs and be vigilant in policing the boundaries of federal power. . . . While the majority purports to give effect to these principles, it eviscerates the clear-notice safeguard of our Spending Clause jurisprudence.

Title IX provides:

> "No person in the United States shall, on the basis of sex be [1] excluded from participation in, [2] be denied the benefits of, or [3] be subjected to discrimination under any education program or activity receiving Federal financial assistance." 20 U.S.C. §1681

To read the provision in full is to understand what is most striking about its application in this case: Title IX does not by its terms create any private cause of action whatsoever, much less define the circumstances in which money damages are available. The only private cause of action under Title IX is judicially implied. See *Cannon v. University of Chicago* (1979).

The Court has encountered great difficulty in establishing standards for deciding when to imply a private cause of action under a federal statute which is silent on the subject. We try to conform the judicial judgment to the bounds of likely congressional purpose but, as we observed in *Gebser v. Lago Vista Independent School District* (1998), defining the scope of the private cause of action in general, and the damages remedy in particular, "inherently entails a degree of speculation, since it addresses an issue on which Congress has not specifically spoken."

When the statute at issue is a Spending Clause statute, this element of speculation is particularly troubling because it is in significant tension with the requirement that Spending Clause legislation give States clear notice of the consequences of their acceptance of federal funds. Without doubt, the scope of potential damages liability is one of the most significant factors a school would consider in deciding whether to receive federal funds. Accordingly, the Court must not imply a private cause of action for damages unless it can demonstrate that the congressional purpose to create the implied cause of action is so manifest that the State, when accepting federal funds, had clear notice of the terms and conditions of its monetary liability.

Today the Court fails to heed, or even to acknowledge, these limitations on its authority. The remedial scheme the majority creates today is neither sensible nor faithful to Spending Clause principles. In order to make its case for school liability for peer sexual harassment, the majority must establish that Congress gave grant recipients clear and unambiguous notice that they would be liable in money damages for failure to remedy discriminatory acts of their students. The majority must also demonstrate that the statute gives schools clear notice that one child's harassment of another constitutes "discrimination" on the basis of sex within the meaning of Title IX, and that—as applied to individual cases—the standard for liability will enable the grant recipient to distinguish inappropriate childish behavior from actionable gender discrimination. The majority does not carry these burdens.

Instead, the majority finds statutory clarity where there is none and discovers indicia of congressional notice to the States in the most unusual of places. It treats the issue as one of routine statutory construction alone, and it errs even in this regard. In the end, the majority not only imposes on States liability that was unexpected and unknown, but the contours of which are, as yet, unknowable. The majority's opinion purports to be narrow, but the limiting principles it proposes are illusory. The fence the Court has built is made of little sticks, and it cannot contain the avalanche of liability now set in motion. The potential costs to our schools of today's decision are difficult to estimate, but they are so great that it is most unlikely Congress intended to inflict them.

The only certainty flowing from the majority's decision is that scarce resources will be diverted from educating our children and that many school districts, desperate to avoid Title IX peer harassment suits, will adopt whatever federal code of student conduct and discipline the Department of Education sees fit to impose upon them. The Nation's schoolchildren will learn their first lessons about federalism in classrooms where the federal government is the ever-present regulator. The federal government will have insinuated itself not only into one of the most traditional areas of state concern but also into one of the most sensitive areas of human affairs. This federal control of the discipline of our Nation's schoolchildren is contrary to our traditions and inconsistent with the sensible administration of our schools. Because Title IX did not give States unambiguous notice that accepting federal funds meant ceding to the federal government power over the day-to-day disciplinary decisions of schools, I dissent.

I

... Title IX prohibits only misconduct by grant recipients, not misconduct by third parties. . . . The majority argues, nevertheless, that a school "subjects" its students to discrimination when it knows of peer harassment and fails to respond appropriately.

The mere word "subjected" cannot bear the weight of the majority's argument. . . . The majority does not even attempt to argue that the school's failure to respond to discriminatory acts by students is discrimination by the school itself.

A

In any event, a plaintiff cannot establish a Title IX violation merely by showing that she has been "subjected to discrimination." Rather, a violation of Title IX occurs only if she is "subjected to discrimination under any education program or activity," 20 U.S.C. §1681(a), where "program or activity" is defined as "all of the operations of" a grant recipient, §1687.

Under the most natural reading of this provision, discrimination violates Title IX only if it is authorized by, or in accordance with, the actions, activities, or policies of the grant recipient. . . .

It is not enough, then, that the alleged discrimination occur in a "context subject to the school district's control." The discrimination must actually be "controlled by"—that is, be authorized by, pursuant to, or in accordance with, school policy or actions. . . .

This reading is also consistent with the fact that the discrimination must be "under" the "operations" of the grant recipient. The term "operations" connotes active and affirmative participation by the grant recipient, not merely inaction or failure to respond. . . .

Teacher sexual harassment of students is "under" the school's program or activity in certain circumstances, but student harassment is not. . . .

I am aware of no basis in law or fact . . . for attributing the acts of a student to a school and, indeed, the majority does not argue that the school acts through its students. . . . Discrimination by one student against another therefore cannot be "under" the school's program or activity as required by Title IX. The majority's imposition of liability for peer sexual harassment thus conflicts with the most natural interpretation of Title IX's "under a program or activity" limitation on school liability. . . .

B

1

Quite aside from its disregard for the "under the program" limitation of Title IX, the majority's reading is flawed in other respects. The majority contends that a school's deliberate indifference to known student harassment "subjects" students to harassment—that is, "cause[s] [students] to undergo" harassment. The majority recognizes, however, that there must be some limitation on the third-party conduct that the school can fairly be said to cause. In search of a principle, the majority asserts, without much elaboration, that one causes discrimination when one has some "degree of control" over the discrimination and fails to remedy it.

To state the majority's test is to understand that it is little more than an exercise in arbitrary line-drawing. The majority does not explain how we are to determine what degree of control is sufficient—or, more to the point, how the States were on clear notice that the Court would draw the line to encompass students. . . .

2

The majority nonetheless appears to see no need to justify drawing the "enough control" line to encompass students. In truth, however, a school's control over its students is much more complicated and limited than the majority acknowledges. A public school does not control its students in the way it controls its teachers or those with whom it contracts. Most public schools do not screen or select students, and their power to discipline students is far from unfettered.

[Discussion of legal limitations imposed by state law, the federal Constitution, and the Individuals with Disabilities Education Act omitted.]

The practical obstacles schools encounter in ensuring that thousands of immature students conform their conduct to acceptable norms may be even more significant than the legal obstacles. School districts cannot exercise the same measure of control over thousands of students that they do over a few hundred adult employees. The limited resources of our schools must be conserved for basic educational services. Some schools lack the resources even to deal with serious problems of violence and are already overwhelmed with disciplinary problems of all kinds.

Perhaps even more startling than its broad assumptions about school control over primary and secondary school students is the majority's failure to grapple in any meaningful way with the distinction between elementary and secondary schools, on the one hand, and universities on the other. . . . [T]he majority's holding would appear to apply with equal force to universities, which do not exercise custodial and tutelary control over their adult students.

3

The majority's presentation of its control test illustrates its own discomfort with the rule it has devised. Rather than beginning with the language of Title IX itself, the majority begins with our decision in *Gebser* and appears to discover there a sweeping legal duty . . . for schools to remedy third-party discrimination against students. The majority then finds that the DOE's Title IX regulations and state common law gave States the requisite notice that they would be liable in damages for failure to fulfill this duty. Only then does the majority turn to the language of Title IX itself—not, it appears, to find a duty or clear notice to the States, . . . but rather to suggest a limit on the breathtaking scope of the liability the majority thinks is so clear under the statute. . . .

Our decision in *Gebser* did not, of course, recognize some ill-defined, free-standing legal duty on schools to remedy discrimination by third parties. In particular, *Gebser* gave schools no notice whatsoever that they might be liable on the majority's novel theory that a school "subjects" a student to third-party discrimination if it exercises some measure of control over the third party. . . .

Neither the DOE's Title IX regulations nor state tort law, moreover, could or did provide States the notice required by our Spending Clause principles. [Detailed discussion omitted; Kennedy also discounted the importance of the National School Boards Association pamphlet on sexual harassment as providing notice of potential liability for student-on-student harassment.]

II

Our decision in *Gebser* makes clear that the Spending Clause clear-notice rule requires both that the recipients be on general notice of the kind of conduct the statute prohibits, and—at least when money damages are sought—that they be on notice that illegal conduct is occurring in a given situation. . . .

Title IX, however, gives schools neither notice that the conduct the majority labels peer "sexual harassment" is gender discrimination within the meaning of the Act nor any guidance in distinguishing in individual cases between actionable discrimination and the immature behavior of children and adolescents. The majority thus imposes on schools potentially crushing financial liability for student conduct that is not prohibited in clear terms by Title IX and that cannot, even after today's opinion, be identified by either schools or courts with any precision.

The law recognizes that children—particularly young children—are not fully accountable for their actions because they lack the capacity to exercise mature judgment. . . . It should surprise no one, then, that the schools that are the primary locus of most children's social development are rife with inappropriate behavior by children who are just learning to interact with their peers. The *amici* on the front lines of our schools describe the situation best:

> "Unlike adults in the workplace, juveniles have limited life experiences or familial influences upon which to establish an understanding of appropriate behavior. The real world of school discipline is a rough-and-tumble place where students practice newly learned vulgarities, erupt with anger, tease and embarrass each other, share offensive notes, flirt, push

and shove in the halls, grab and offend." Brief for National School
Boards Association et al. as *Amici Curiae*.

No one contests that much of this "dizzying array of immature or uncontrol-
lable behaviors by students" is inappropriate, even "objectively offensive" at times,
and that parents and schools have a moral and ethical responsibility to help students learn to interact with their peers in an appropriate manner. It is doubtless
the case, moreover, that much of this inappropriate behavior is directed toward
members of the opposite sex, as children in the throes of adolescence struggle to
express their emerging sexual identities.

It is a far different question, however, whether it is either proper or useful to
label this immature, childish behavior gender discrimination. Nothing in Title IX
suggests that Congress even contemplated this question, much less answered it in
the affirmative in unambiguous terms.

The majority, nevertheless, has no problem labeling the conduct of fifth graders
"sexual harassment" and "gender discrimination." . . .

Contrary to the majority's assertion, however, respondents have made a cogent
and persuasive argument that the type of student conduct alleged by petitioner
should not be considered "sexual harassment," much less gender discrimination
actionable under Title IX. . . .

In reality, there is no established body of federal or state law on which courts
may draw in defining the student conduct that qualifies as Title IX gender discrimination. Analogies to Title VII hostile environment harassment are inapposite, because schools are not workplaces and children are not adults. The norms of
the adult workplace that have defined hostile environment sexual harassment are
not easily translated to peer relationships in schools, where teenage romantic relationships and dating are a part of everyday life. Analogies to Title IX teacher sexual harassment of students are similarly flawed. A teacher's sexual overtures toward
a student are always inappropriate; a teenager's romantic overtures to a classmate
(even when persistent and unwelcome) are an inescapable part of adolescence.

The majority admits that, under its approach, "[w]hether gender-oriented conduct rises to the level of actionable harassment . . . depends on a constellation of
surrounding circumstances, expectations, and relationships, including, but not
limited to, the ages of the harasser and the victim and the number of individuals
involved." [Internal quotations omitted.] The majority does not explain how a
school is supposed to discern from this mishmash of factors what is actionable discrimination. Its multifactored balancing test is a far cry from the clarity we
demand of Spending Clause legislation. . . .

The only guidance the majority gives schools in distinguishing between the
"simple acts of teasing and name-calling among school children," said not to be a
basis for suit even when they "target differences in gender," and actionable peer
sexual harassment is, in reality, no guidance at all. The majority proclaims that "in
the context of student-on-student harassment, damages are available only in the
situation where the behavior is so serious, pervasive, and objectively offensive that
it denies its victims the equal access to education that Title IX is designed to protect." The majority does not even purport to explain, however, what constitutes an
actionable denial of "equal access to education." Is equal access denied when a girl
who tires of being chased by the boys at recess refuses to go outside? When she

cannot concentrate during class because she is worried about the recess activities? When she pretends to be sick one day so she can stay home from school? It appears the majority is content to let juries decide.

The majority's reference to a "systemic effect" does nothing to clarify the content of its standard. The majority appears to intend that requirement to do no more than exclude the possibility that a single act of harassment perpetrated by one student on one other student can form the basis for an actionable claim. That is a small concession indeed.

The only real clue the majority gives schools about the dividing line between actionable harassment that denies a victim equal access to education and mere inappropriate teasing is a profoundly unsettling one: On the facts of this case, petitioner has stated a claim because she alleged, in the majority's words, "that the harassment had a concrete, negative effect on her daughter's ability to receive an education." In petitioner's words, the effects that might have been visible to the school were that her daughter's grades "dropped" and her "ability to concentrate on her school work [was] affected." Almost all adolescents experience these problems at one time or another as they mature.

III

The majority's inability to provide any workable definition of actionable peer harassment simply underscores the myriad ways in which an opinion that purports to be narrow is, in fact, so broad that it will support untold numbers of lawyers who will prove adept at presenting cases that will withstand the defendant school districts' pretrial motions. Each of the barriers to run away litigation the majority offers us crumbles under the weight of even casual scrutiny.

For example, the majority establishes what sounds like a relatively high threshold for liability—"denial of equal access" to education—and, almost in the same breath, makes clear that alleging a decline in grades is enough to survive 12(b)(6) and, it follows, to state a winning claim. The majority seems oblivious to the fact that almost every child, at some point, has trouble in school because he or she is being teased by his or her peers. The girl who wants to skip recess because she is teased by the boys is no different from the overweight child who skips gym class because the other children tease her about her size in the locker room; or the child who risks flunking out because he refuses to wear glasses to avoid the taunts of "four-eyes"; or the child who refuses to go to school because the school bully calls him a "scaredy-cat" at recess. Most children respond to teasing in ways that detract from their ability to learn. The majority's test for actionable harassment will, as a result, sweep in almost all of the more innocuous conduct it acknowledges as a ubiquitous part of school life.

The string of adjectives the majority attaches to the word "harassment"— "severe, pervasive, and objectively offensive"—likewise fails to narrow the class of conduct that can trigger liability. . . . Not only is that standard likely to be quite expansive, it also gives schools—and juries—little guidance, requiring them to attempt to gauge the sensitivities of, for instance, the average seven year old.

The majority assures us that its decision will not interfere with school discipline . . . . The problem is that the majority's test, in fact, invites courts and juries to second-guess school administrators in every case, to judge in each instance whether the school's response was "clearly unreasonable." A reasonableness standard, regardless of the modifier, transforms every disciplinary decision into a jury question. . . .

Another professed limitation the majority relies upon is that the recipient will be liable only where the acts of student harassment are "known." The majority's enunciation of the standard begs the obvious question: known to whom? Yet the majority says not one word about the type of school employee who must know about the harassment before it is actionable. . . .

The majority's limitations on peer sexual harassment suits cannot hope to contain the flood of liability the Court today begins. The elements of the Title IX claim created by the majority will be easy not only to allege but also to prove. A female plaintiff who pleads only that a boy called her offensive names, that she told a teacher, that the teacher's response was unreasonable, and that her school performance suffered as a result, appears to state a successful claim.

There will be no shortage of plaintiffs to bring such complaints. Our schools are charged each day with educating millions of children. Of those millions of students, a large percentage will, at some point during their school careers, experience something they consider sexual harassment. A 1993 study by the American Association of University Women Educational Foundation, for instance, found that "fully 4 out of 5 students (81%) report that they have been the target of some form of sexual harassment during their school lives." The number of potential lawsuits against our schools is staggering.

The cost of defending against peer sexual harassment suits alone could overwhelm many school districts, particularly since the majority's liability standards will allow almost any plaintiff to get to summary judgment, if not to a jury. In addition, there are no damages caps on the judicially implied private cause of action under Title IX. As a result, school liability in one peer sexual harassment suit could approach, or even exceed, the total federal funding of many school districts. Petitioner, for example, seeks damages of $500,000 in this case. Respondent school district received approximately $679,000 in federal aid in 1992–1993. . . .

The prospect of unlimited Title IX liability will, in all likelihood, breed a climate of fear that encourages school administrators to label even the most innocuous of childish conduct sexual harassment. It would appear to be no coincidence that, not long after the DOE issued its proposed policy guidance warning that schools could be liable for peer sexual harassment in the fall of 1996, a North Carolina school suspended a 6-year-old boy who kissed a female classmate on the cheek for sexual harassment, on the theory that "[u]nwelcome is unwelcome at any age." A week later, a New York school suspended a second-grader who kissed a classmate and ripped a button off her skirt. The second grader said that he got the idea from his favorite book "Corduroy," about a bear with a missing button. School administrators said only, "We were given guidelines as to why we suspend children. We follow the guidelines."

At the college level, the majority's holding is sure to add fuel to the debate over campus speech codes that, in the name of preventing a hostile educational environment, may infringe students' First Amendment rights. Indeed, under the majority's control principle, schools presumably will be responsible for remedying conduct that occurs even in student dormitory rooms. As a result, schools may well be forced to apply workplace norms in the most private of domains. . . .

Disregarding these state-law remedies for student misbehavior and the incentives that our schools already have to provide the best possible education to all of their students, the majority seeks, in effect, to put an end to student misbehavior by transforming Title IX into a Federal Student Civility Code. I fail to see how federal courts will administer school discipline better than the principals and teachers to whom the public has entrusted that task or how the majority's holding will help the vast majority of students, whose educational opportunities will be diminished by the diversion of school funds to litigation. The private cause of action the Court creates will justify a corps of federal administrators in writing regulations on student harassment. It will also embroil schools and courts in endless litigation over what qualifies as peer sexual harassment and what constitutes a reasonable response.

In the final analysis, this case is about federalism. Yet the majority's decision today says not one word about the federal balance. Preserving our federal system is a legitimate end in itself. It is, too, the means to other ends. It ensures that essential choices can be made by a government more proximate to the people than the vast apparatus of federal power. Defining the appropriate role of schools in teaching and supervising children who are beginning to explore their own sexuality and learning how to express it to others is one of the most complex and sensitive issues our schools face. Such decisions are best made by parents and by the teachers and school administrators who can counsel with them. The delicacy and immense significance of teaching children about sexuality should cause the Court to act with great restraint before it displaces state and local governments.

Heedless of these considerations, the Court rushes onward, finding that the cause of action it creates is necessary to effect the congressional design. It is not. Nothing in Title IX suggests that Congress intended or contemplated the result the Court reaches today, much less dictated it in unambiguous terms. . . .

Perhaps the most grave, and surely the most lasting, disservice of today's decision is that it ensures the Court's own disregard for the federal balance soon will be imparted to our youngest citizens. The Court clears the way for the federal government to claim center stage in America's classrooms. Today's decision mandates to teachers instructing and supervising their students the dubious assistance of federal court plaintiffs and their lawyers and makes the federal courts the final arbiters of school policy and of almost every disagreement between students. Enforcement of the federal right recognized by the majority means that federal influence will permeate everything from curriculum decisions to day-to-day classroom logistics and interactions. After today, Johnny will find that the routine problems of adolescence are to be resolved by invoking a federal right to demand assignment to a desk two rows away.

As its holding makes painfully clear, the majority's watered-down version of the Spending Clause clear-statement rule is no substitute for the real protections of state and local autonomy that our constitutional system requires. If there be any doubt of the futility of the Court's attempt to hedge its holding about with words of limitation for future cases, the result in this case provides the answer. The complaint of this fifth grader survives and the school will be compelled to answer in federal court. We can be assured that like suits will follow—suits, which in cost and number, will impose serious financial burdens on local school districts, the taxpayers who support them, and the children they serve. Federalism and our struggling school systems deserve better from this Court. I dissent.

No. 97-1121

City of Chicago, Petitioner v.
Jesus Morales et al.

On writ of certiorari to the Supreme Court of Illinois

[June 10, 1999]

JUSTICE STEVENS announced the judgment of the Court and delivered the opinion of the Court with respect to Parts I, II, and V, and an opinion with respect to Parts III, IV, and VI, in which JUSTICE SOUTER and JUSTICE GINS-BURG join.

In 1992, the Chicago City Council enacted the Gang Congregation Ordinance, which prohibits "criminal street gang members" from "loitering" with one another or with other persons in any public place. The question presented is whether the Supreme Court of Illinois correctly held that the ordinance violates the Due Process Clause of the Fourteenth Amendment to the Federal Constitution.

I

Before the ordinance was adopted, the city council's Committee on Police and Fire conducted hearings to explore the problems created by the city's street gangs, and more particularly, the consequences of public loitering by gang members. Witnesses included residents of the neighborhoods where gang members are most active, as well as some of the aldermen who represent those areas. Based on that evidence, the council made a series of findings that are included in the text of the ordinance and explain the reasons for its enactment.

The council found that a continuing increase in criminal street gang activity was largely responsible for the city's rising murder rate, as well as an escalation of violent and drug related crimes. It noted that in many neighborhoods throughout the city, "the burgeoning presence of street gang members in public places has intimidated many law abiding citizens." (1997). Furthermore, the council stated that gang members "establish control over identifiable areas" by loitering in those areas and intimidating others from entering those areas; and . . . [m]embers of criminal street gangs avoid arrest by committing no offense punishable under existing laws when they know the police are present. . . ." It further found that "loitering in public places by criminal street gang members creates a justifiable fear for the safety of persons and property in the area" and that "[a]ggressive action is necessary to preserve the city's streets and other public places so that the public may use such places without fear." Moreover, the council concluded that the city "has an interest in discouraging all persons from loitering in public places with criminal gang members."

The ordinance creates a criminal offense punishable by a fine of up to $500, imprisonment for not more than six months, and a requirement to perform up to 120 hours of community service. Commission of the offense involves four predicates. First, the police officer must reasonably believe that at least one of the two or more persons present in a "public place" is a "criminal street gang membe[r]." Second, the persons must be "loitering," which the ordinance defines as "remain[ing] in any one place with no apparent purpose." Third, the officer must then order "all" of the persons to disperse and remove themselves "from the area." Fourth, a person must disobey the officer's order. If any person, whether a gang member or not, disobeys the officer's order, that person is guilty of violating the ordinance.

Two months after the ordinance was adopted, the Chicago Police Department promulgated General Order 92-4 to provide guidelines to govern its enforcement. That order purported to establish limitations on the enforcement discretion of police officers "to ensure that the anti-gang loitering ordinance is not enforced in an arbitrary or discriminatory way." The limitations confine the authority to arrest gang members who violate the ordinance to sworn "members of the Gang Crime Section" and certain other designated officers, and establish detailed criteria for defining street gangs and membership in such gangs. In addition, the order directs district commanders to "designate areas in which the presence of gang members has a demonstrable effect on the activities of law abiding persons in the surrounding community," and provides that the ordinance "will be enforced only within the designated areas." The city, however, does not release the locations of these "designated areas" to the public.

II

During the three years of its enforcement, the police issued over 89,000 dispersal orders and arrested over 42,000 people for violating the ordinance. In the ensuing enforcement proceedings, two trial judges upheld the constitutionality of the ordinance, but eleven others ruled that it was invalid. In respondent Youkhana's case, the trial judge held that the "ordinance fails to notify individuals what conduct is prohibited, and it encourages arbitrary and capricious enforcement by police."

The Illinois Appellate Court affirmed the trial court's ruling in the *Youkhana* case, consolidated and affirmed other pending appeals in accordance with *Youkhana*, and reversed the convictions of respondents Gutierrez, Morales, and others. The Appellate Court was persuaded that the ordinance impaired the freedom of assembly of non-gang members in violation of the First Amendment to the Federal Constitution and Article I of the Illinois Constitution, that it was unconstitutionally vague, that it improperly criminalized status rather than conduct, and that it jeopardized rights guaranteed under the Fourth Amendment.

The Illinois Supreme Court affirmed. It held "that the gang loitering ordinance violates due process of law in that it is impermissibly vague on its face and an arbitrary restriction on personal liberties." The court did not reach the contentions that the ordinance "creates a status offense, permits arrests without probable cause or is overbroad."

In support of its vagueness holding, the court pointed out that the definition of "loitering" in the ordinance drew no distinction between innocent conduct and conduct calculated to cause harm. "Moreover, the definition of 'loiter' provided by the ordinance does not assist in clearly articulating the proscriptions of the ordinance." Furthermore, it concluded that the ordinance was "not reasonably susceptible to a limiting construction which would affirm its validity."

We granted certiorari (1998) and now affirm. Like the Illinois Supreme Court, we conclude that the ordinance enacted by the city of Chicago is unconstitutionally vague.

III

The basic factual predicate for the city's ordinance is not in dispute. As the city argues in its brief, "the very presence of a large collection of obviously brazen, insistent, and lawless gang members and hangers-on on the public ways intimidates residents, who become afraid even to leave their homes and go about their business. That, in turn, imperils community residents' sense of safety and security, detracts from property values, and can ultimately destabilize entire neighborhoods." The findings in the ordinance explain that it was motivated by these concerns. We have no doubt that a law that directly prohibited such intimidating conduct would be constitutional, but this ordinance broadly covers a significant amount of additional activity. Uncertainty about the scope of that additional coverage provides the basis for respondents' claim that the ordinance is too vague.

We are confronted at the outset with the city's claim that it was improper for the state courts to conclude that the ordinance is invalid on its face. The city correctly points out that imprecise laws can be attacked on their face under two different doctrines. First, the overbreadth doctrine permits the facial invalidation of laws that inhibit the exercise of First Amendment rights if the impermissible applications of the law are substantial when "judged in relation to the statute's plainly legitimate sweep." *Broadrick v. Oklahoma* (1973). Second, even if an enactment does not reach a substantial amount of constitutionally protected conduct, it may be impermissibly vague because it fails to establish standards for the police and public that are sufficient to guard against the arbitrary deprivation of liberty interests. *Kolender v. Lawson* (1983).

While we, like the Illinois courts, conclude that the ordinance is invalid on its face, we do not rely on the overbreadth doctrine. We agree with the city's submission that the law does not have a sufficiently substantial impact on conduct protected by the First Amendment to render it unconstitutional. . . .

On the other hand, as the United States recognizes, the freedom to loiter for innocent purposes is part of the "liberty" protected by the Due Process Clause of the Fourteenth Amendment. We have expressly identified this "right to remove from one place to another according to inclination" as "an attribute of personal liberty" protected by the Constitution. *Williams v. Fears* (1900); see also *Papachristou v. Jacksonville* (1972). Indeed, it is apparent that an individual's decision to remain in a public place of his choice is as much a part of his liberty as the freedom of movement inside frontiers that is "a part of our heritage," *Kent v. Dulles* (1958), or the right to move "to whatsoever place one's own inclination may direct" identified in Blackstone's Commentaries. (1765).

There is no need, however, to decide whether the impact of the Chicago ordinance on constitutionally protected liberty alone would suffice to support a facial challenge under the overbreadth doctrine. For it is clear that the vagueness of this enactment makes a facial challenge appropriate. This is . . . a criminal law that contains no *mens rea* requirement, and infringes on constitutionally protected rights. When vagueness permeates the text of such a law, it is subject to facial attack.

Vagueness may invalidate a criminal law for either of two independent reasons. First, it may fail to provide the kind of notice that will enable ordinary people to understand what conduct it prohibits; second, it may authorize and even encourage arbitrary and discriminatory enforcement. Accordingly, we first consider whether the ordinance provides fair notice to the citizen and then discuss its potential for arbitrary enforcement.

IV

. . . The Illinois Supreme Court recognized that the term "loiter" may have a common and accepted meaning, but the definition of that term in this ordinance—"to remain in any one place with no apparent purpose"—does not. It is difficult to imagine how any citizen of the city of Chicago standing in a public place with a group of people would know if he or she had an "apparent purpose." If she were talking to another person, would she have an apparent purpose? If she were frequently checking her watch and looking expectantly down the street, would she have an apparent purpose?

Since the city cannot conceivably have meant to criminalize each instance a citizen stands in public with a gang member, the vagueness that dooms this ordinance is not the product of uncertainty about the normal meaning of "loitering," but rather about what loitering is covered by the ordinance and what is not. The Illinois Supreme Court emphasized the law's failure to distinguish between innocent conduct and conduct threatening harm. Its decision followed the precedent set by a number of state courts that have upheld ordinances that criminalize loitering combined with some other overt act or evidence of criminal intent. However, state courts have uniformly invalidated laws that do not join the term "loitering" with a second specific element of the crime.

The city's principal response to this concern about adequate notice is that loiterers are not subject to sanction until after they have failed to comply with an officer's order to disperse. . . . We find this response unpersuasive for at least two reasons.

First, the purpose of the fair notice requirement is to enable the ordinary citizen to conform his or her conduct to the law. . . . Although it is true that a loiterer is not subject to criminal sanctions unless he or she disobeys a dispersal order, the loitering is the conduct that the ordinance is designed to prohibit. If the loitering is in fact harmless and innocent, the dispersal order itself is an unjustified impairment of liberty. If the police are able to decide arbitrarily which members of the public they will order to disperse, then the Chicago ordinance becomes indistinguishable from the law we held invalid in *Shuttlesworth v. Birmingham* (1965). Because an officer may issue an order only after prohibited conduct has already occurred, it cannot provide the kind of advance notice that will protect the putative loiterer from being ordered to disperse. Such an order cannot retroactively give adequate warning of the boundary between the permissible and the impermissible applications of the law.

Second, the terms of the dispersal order compound the inadequacy of the notice afforded by the ordinance. It provides that the officer "shall order all such persons to disperse and remove themselves from the area." This vague phrasing raises a host of questions. After such an order issues, how long must the loiterers remain apart? How far must they move? If each loiterer walks around the block and they meet again at the same location, are they subject to arrest or merely to being ordered to disperse again? . . .

Lack of clarity in the description of the loiterer's duty to obey a dispersal order might not render the ordinance unconstitutionally vague if the definition of the forbidden conduct were clear, but it does buttress our conclusion that the entire ordinance fails to give the ordinary citizen adequate notice of what is forbidden and what is permitted. . . . This ordinance is therefore vague "not in the sense that it requires a person to conform his conduct to an imprecise but comprehensible normative standard, but rather in the sense that no standard of conduct is specified at all." *Coates v. Cincinnati* (1971).

V

The broad sweep of the ordinance also violates "the requirement that a legislature establish minimal guidelines to govern law enforcement." *Kolender v. Lawson.* There are no such guidelines in the ordinance. In any public place in the city of Chicago, persons who stand or sit in the company of a gang member may be ordered to disperse unless their purpose is apparent. The mandatory language in the enactment directs the police to issue an order without first making any inquiry about their possible purposes. It matters not whether the reason that a gang member and his father, for example, might loiter near Wrigley Field is to rob an unsuspecting fan or just to get a glimpse of Sammy Sosa leaving the ballpark; in either event, if their purpose is not apparent to a nearby police officer, she may—indeed, she "shall"—order them to disperse.

Recognizing that the ordinance does reach a substantial amount of innocent conduct, we turn, then, to its language to determine if it "necessarily entrusts lawmaking to the moment-to-moment judgment of the policeman on his beat." *Kolender v. Lawson.* As we discussed in the context of fair notice, the principal source of the vast discretion conferred on the police in this case is the definition of loitering. . . .

As the Illinois Supreme Court interprets that definition, it "provides absolute discretion to police officers to determine what activities constitute loitering." We have no authority to construe the language of a state statute more narrowly than the construction given by that State's highest court. . . .

Nevertheless, the city disputes the Illinois Supreme Court's interpretation, arguing that the text of the ordinance limits the officer's discretion in three ways. First, it does not permit the officer to issue a dispersal order to anyone who is moving along or who has an apparent purpose. Second, it does not permit an arrest if individuals obey a dispersal order. Third, no order can issue unless the officer reasonably believes that one of the loiterers is a member of a criminal street gang.

Even putting to one side our duty to defer to a state court's construction of the scope of a local enactment, we find each of these limitations insufficient. That the ordinance does not apply to people who are moving—that is, to activity that would not constitute loitering under any possible definition of the term—does not even address the question of how much discretion the police enjoy in deciding which stationary persons to disperse under the ordinance. Similarly, that the ordinance does not permit an arrest until after a dispersal order has been disobeyed does not provide any guidance to the officer deciding whether such an order should issue. The "no apparent purpose" standard for making that decision is inherently subjective because its application depends on whether some purpose is "apparent" to the officer on the scene.

Presumably an officer would have discretion to treat some purposes—perhaps a purpose to engage in idle conversation or simply to enjoy a cool breeze on a warm evening—as too frivolous to be apparent if he suspected a different ulterior motive. Moreover, an officer conscious of the city council's reasons for enacting the ordinance might well ignore its text and issue a dispersal order, even though an illicit purpose is actually apparent.

It is true, as the city argues, that the requirement that the officer reasonably believe that a group of loiterers contains a gang member does place a limit on the authority to order dispersal. That limitation would no doubt be sufficient if the ordinance only applied to loitering that had an apparently harmful purpose or effect, or possibly if it only applied to loitering by persons reasonably believed to be criminal gang members. But this ordinance, for reasons that are not explained in the findings of the city council, requires no harmful purpose and applies to non-gang members as well as suspected gang members. It applies to everyone in the city who may remain in one place with one suspected gang member as long as their purpose is not apparent to an officer observing them. Friends, relatives, teachers, counselors, or even total strangers might unwittingly engage in forbidden loitering if they happen to engage in idle conversation with a gang member. . . .

Finally, in its opinion striking down the ordinance, the Illinois Supreme Court refused to accept the general order issued by the police department as a sufficient limitation on the "vast amount of discretion" granted to the police in its enforcement. We agree. That the police have adopted internal rules limiting their enforcement to certain designated areas in the city would not provide a defense to a loiterer who might be arrested elsewhere. Nor could a person who knowingly loitered with a well-known gang member anywhere in the city safely assume that they would not be ordered to disperse no matter how innocent and harmless their loitering might be.

VI

In our judgment, the Illinois Supreme Court correctly concluded that the ordinance does not provide sufficiently specific limits on the enforcement discretion of the police "to meet constitutional standards for definiteness and clarity." We recognize the serious and difficult problems testified to by the citizens of Chicago that led to the enactment of this ordinance. . . . However, in this instance the city has enacted an ordinance that affords too much discretion to the police and too little notice to citizens who wish to use the public streets.

Accordingly, the judgment of the Supreme Court of Illinois is

Affirmed.

JUSTICE O'CONNOR, with whom JUSTICE BREYER joins, concurring in part and concurring in the judgment.

I agree with the Court that Chicago's Gang Congregation Ordinance, Chicago Municipal Code §8-4-151 (1992) (gang loitering ordinance or ordinance) is unconstitutionally vague. . . . I share JUSTICE THOMAS' concern about the consequences of gang violence, and I agree that some degree of police discretion is necessary to allow the police "to perform their peacekeeping responsibilities satisfactorily." A criminal law, however, must not permit policemen, prosecutors, and juries to conduct "a standardless sweep . . . to pursue their personal predilections." *Kolender v. Lawson* [1983]

The ordinance at issue provides:

> "Whenever a police officer observes a person whom he reasonably believes to be a criminal street gang member loitering in any public place with one or more other persons, he shall order all such persons to disperse and remove themselves from the area. Any person who does not promptly obey such an order is in violation of this section."

To "[l]oiter," in turn, is defined in the ordinance as "to remain in any one place with no apparent purpose." The Illinois Supreme Court declined to adopt a limiting construction of the ordinance and concluded that the ordinance vested "*absolute* discretion to police officers." (1997) (emphasis added). This Court is bound by the Illinois Supreme Court's construction of the ordinance.

As it has been construed by the Illinois court, Chicago's gang loitering ordinance is unconstitutionally vague because it lacks sufficient minimal standards to guide law enforcement officers. In particular, it fails to provide police with any standard by which they can judge whether an individual has an "*apparent* purpose." Indeed, because any person standing on the street has a general "purpose"—even if it is simply to stand—the ordinance permits police officers to choose which purposes are *permissible*. Under this construction the police do not have to decide that an individual is "threaten[ing] the public peace" to issue a dispersal order. [Quoting THOMAS' dissent.] Any police officer in Chicago is free, under the Illinois Supreme Court's construction of the ordinance, to order at his whim any person standing in a public place with a suspected gang member to disperse. Further, as construed by the Illinois court, the ordinance applies to hundreds of thousands of persons who are *not* gang members, standing on any sidewalk or in any park, coffee shop, bar, or "other location open to the public, whether publicly or privately owned."

To be sure, there is no violation of the ordinance unless a person fails to obey promptly the order to disperse. But, a police officer cannot issue a dispersal order until he decides that a person is remaining in one place "with no apparent purpose," and the ordinance provides no guidance to the officer on how to make this antecedent decision. Moreover, the requirement that police issue dispersal orders only when they "reasonably believ[e]" that a group of loiterers includes a gang member fails to cure the ordinance's vague aspects. If the ordinance applied only to persons reasonably believed to be gang members, this requirement might have cured the ordinance's vagueness because it would have directed the manner in which the order was issued by specifying to whom the order could be issued. But, the Illinois Supreme Court did not construe the ordinance to be so limited.

This vagueness consideration alone provides a sufficient ground for affirming the Illinois court's decision, and I agree with Part V of the Court's opinion, which discusses this consideration. . . . Accordingly, there is no need to consider the other issues briefed by the parties and addressed by the plurality. I express no opinion about them.

It is important to courts and legislatures alike that we characterize more clearly the narrow scope of today's holding. As the ordinance comes to this Court, it is unconstitutionally vague. Nevertheless, there remain open to Chicago reasonable alternatives to combat the very real threat posed by gang intimidation and violence. For example, the Court properly and expressly distinguishes the ordinance from laws that require loiterers to have a "harmful purpose," from laws that target only gang members, and from laws that incorporate limits on the area and manner in which the laws may be enforced. In addition, the ordinance here is unlike a law that "directly prohibit[s]" the "presence of a large collection of obviously brazen, insistent, and lawless gang members and hangers-on on the public ways" that "intimidates residents." [Quoting city's brief.] Indeed, as the plurality notes, the city of Chicago has several laws that do exactly this. . . . Specifically, Chicago's general disorderly conduct provision allows the police to arrest those who knowingly "provoke, make or aid in making a breach of peace." . . .

Accordingly, I join Parts I, II, and V of the Court's opinion and concur in the judgment.

JUSTICE KENNEDY, concurring in part and concurring in the judgment.

I join Parts I, II, and V of JUSTICE STEVENS' opinion.

I also share many of the concerns he expresses in Part IV with respect to the sufficiency of notice under the ordinance. As interpreted by the Illinois Supreme Court, the Chicago ordinance would reach a broad range of innocent conduct. For this reason it is not necessarily saved by the requirement that the citizen must disobey a police order to disperse before there is a violation.

. . . The predicate of an order to disperse is not, in my view, sufficient to eliminate doubts regarding the adequacy of notice under this ordinance. A citizen, while engaging in a wide array of innocent conduct, is not likely to know when he may be subject to a dispersal order based on the officer's own knowledge of the identity or affiliations of other persons with whom the citizen is congregating; nor may the citizen be able to assess what an officer might conceive to be the citizen's lack of an apparent purpose.

JUSTICE BREYER, concurring in part and concurring in the judgment.

The ordinance before us creates more than a "*minor* limitation upon the free state of nature." (SCALIA, J., dissenting) (emphasis added). The law authorizes a police officer to order any person to remove himself from any "location open to the public, whether publicly or privately owned," *i.e.*, any sidewalk, front stoop, public park, public square, lakeside promenade, hotel, restaurant, bowling alley, bar, barbershop, sports arena, shopping mall, etc., but with two, and only two, limitations: First, that person must be accompanied by (or must himself be) someone police reasonably believe is a gang member. Second, that person must have remained in that public place "with no apparent purpose."

The first limitation cannot save the ordinance. Though it limits the number of persons subject to the law, it leaves many individuals, gang members and nongang members alike, subject to its strictures. Nor does it limit in any way the range of conduct that police may prohibit. The second limitation is . . . not a limitation at all. Since one always has some apparent purpose, the so-called limitation invites, in fact requires, the policeman to interpret the words "no apparent purpose" as meaning "no apparent purpose except for . . ." And it is in the ordinance's delegation to the policeman of open-ended discretion to fill in that blank that the problem lies. To grant to a policeman virtually standardless discretion to close off major portions of the city to an innocent person is, in my view, to create a major, not a "minor," limitation upon the free state of nature."

JUSTICE SCALIA, dissenting.

The citizens of Chicago were once free to drive about the city at whatever speed they wished. At some point Chicagoans (or perhaps Illinoisans) decided this would not do, and imposed prophylactic speed limits designed to assure safe operation by the average (or perhaps even subaverage) driver with the average (or perhaps even subaverage) vehicle. This infringed upon the "freedom" of all citizens, but was not unconstitutional.

Similarly, the citizens of Chicago were once free to stand around and gawk at the scene of an accident. At some point Chicagoans discovered that this obstructed traffic and caused more accidents. They did not make the practice unlawful, but they did authorize police officers to order the crowd to disperse, and imposed penalties for refusal to obey such an order. Again, this prophylactic measure infringed upon the "freedom" of all citizens, but was not unconstitutional.

Until the ordinance that is before us today was adopted, the citizens of Chicago were free to stand about in public places with no apparent purpose—to engage, that is, in conduct that appeared to be loitering. In recent years, however, the city has been afflicted with criminal street gangs. As reflected in the record before us, these gangs congregated in public places to deal in drugs, and to terrorize the neighborhoods by demonstrating control over their "turf." Many residents of the inner city felt that they were prisoners in their own homes. Once again,

Chicagoans decided that to eliminate the problem it was worth restricting some of the freedom that they once enjoyed. The means they took was similar to the second, and more mild, example given above rather than the first: Loitering was not made unlawful, but when a group of people occupied a public place without an apparent purpose and in the company of a known gang member, police officers were authorized to order them to disperse, and the failure to obey such an order was made unlawful. The minor limitation upon the free state of nature that this prophylactic arrangement imposed upon all Chicagoans seemed to them (and it seems to me) a small price to pay for liberation of their streets.

The majority today invalidates this perfectly reasonable measure by ignoring our rules governing facial challenges, by elevating loitering to a constitutionally guaranteed right, and by discerning vagueness where, according to our usual standards, none exists.

I

Respondents' consolidated appeal presents a facial challenge to the Chicago Ordinance on vagueness grounds. When a facial challenge is successful, the law in question is declared to be unenforceable in *all* its applications, and not just in its particular application to the party in suit. . . .

When our normal criteria for facial challenges are applied, it is clear that the Justices in the majority have transposed the burden of proof. Instead of requiring the respondents, who are challenging the Ordinance, to show that it is invalid in all its applications, they have required the petitioner to show that it is valid in all its applications. Both the plurality opinion and the concurrences display a lively imagination, creating hypothetical situations in which the law's application would (in their view) be ambiguous. But that creative role has been usurped from the petitioner, who can defeat the respondents' facial challenge by conjuring up *a single valid application* of the law. [Remainder of section omitted.]

II

The plurality's explanation for its departure from the usual rule governing facial challenges is seemingly contained in the following statement: "[This] is a criminal law that contains no *mens rea* requirement . . . *and* infringes on constitutionally protected rights. . . . When vagueness permeates the text of *such* a law, it is subject to facial attack." (emphasis added). The proposition is set forth with such assurance that one might suppose that it repeats some well-accepted formula in our jurisprudence: (Criminal law without *mens rea* requirement) + (infringement of constitutionally protected right) + (vagueness) = (entitlement to facial invalidation). There is no such formula; the plurality has made it up for this case. . . .

But no matter. None of the three factors that the plurality relies upon exists anyway. I turn first to the support for the proposition that there is a constitutionally protected right to loiter—or, as the plurality more favorably describes it, for a person to "remain in a public place of his choice." . . .

The plurality tosses around the term "constitutional right" . . . because there is not the slightest evidence for the existence of a genuine constitutional right to loiter. . . . It is simply not maintainable that the right to loiter would have been regarded as an essential attribute of liberty at the time of the framing or at the time of adoption of the Fourteenth Amendment. For the plurality, however, the historical practices of our people are nothing more than a speed bump on the road to the "right" result. . . .

It would be unfair, however, to criticize the plurality's failed attempt to establish that loitering is a constitutionally protected right while saying nothing of the concurrences. The plurality at least makes an attempt. The concurrences, on the other hand, make no pretense at attaching their broad "vagueness invalidates" rule to a liberty interest. As far as appears from JUSTICE O'CONNOR's and JUSTICE BREYER's opinions, *no* police officer may issue *any* order, affecting *any* insignificant sort of citizen conduct . . . unless the standards for the issuance of that order are precise. No modern urban society—and probably none since London got big enough to have sewers—could function under such a rule. . . .

III

I turn next to that element of the plurality's facial-challenge formula which consists of the proposition that this criminal ordinance contains no *mens rea* requirement. The first step in analyzing this proposition is to determine what the *actus reus*, to which that *mens rea* is supposed to be attached, consists of. The majority believes that loitering forms part of (indeed, the essence of) the offense, and must be proved if conviction is to be obtained. That is not what the Ordinance provides. The only part of the Ordinance that refers to loitering is the portion that addresses, not the punishable conduct of the defendant, but what the police officer must observe before he can issue an order to disperse. . . .

The *only* act of a defendant that is made punishable by the Ordinance . . . is his failure to "promptly obey" an order to disperse. The question, then, is whether that *actus reus* must be accompanied by any wrongful intent—and of course it must. . . . No one thinks a defendant could be successfully prosecuted under the Ordinance if he did not hear the order to disperse, or if he suffered a paralysis that rendered his compliance impossible. The willful failure to obey a police order is wrongful intent enough.

IV

Finally, I address the last of the three factors in the plurality's facial-challenge formula: the proposition that the Ordinance is vague. It is not. . . . A law is unconstitutionally vague if its lack of definitive standards either (1) fails to apprise persons of ordinary intelligence of the prohibited conduct, or (2) encourages arbitrary and discriminatory enforcement. . . .

The plurality relies primarily upon the first of these aspects. Since, it reasons, "the loitering is the conduct that the ordinance is designed to prohibit," and "an officer may issue an order only after prohibited conduct has already occurred," the order to disperse cannot itself serve "to apprise persons of ordinary intelligence of the prohibited conduct." What counts for purposes of vagueness analysis, however, is not what the Ordinance is "designed to prohibit," but what it actually subjects to criminal penalty. . . . [T]hat consists of nothing but the refusal to obey a dispersal order, as to which there is no doubt of adequate notice of the prohibited conduct. The plurality's suggestion that even the dispersal *order itself* is unconstitutionally vague, because it does not specify *how far to disperse* (!) scarcely requires a response. If it were true, it would render unconstitutional for vagueness many of the Presidential proclamations issued under that provision of the United States Code which requires the President, before using the militia or the Armed Forces for law enforcement, to issue a proclamation ordering the insurgents to disperse. . . .

For its determination of unconstitutional vagueness, the Court relies secondarily—and JUSTICE O'CONNOR's and JUSTICE BREYER's concurrences exclusively—upon the second aspect of that doctrine, which requires sufficient specificity to prevent arbitrary and discriminatory law enforcement. . . .

The criteria for issuance of a dispersal order under the Chicago Ordinance could hardly be clearer. First, the law requires police officers to "reasonably believ[e]" that one of the group to which the order is issued is a "criminal street gang member." This resembles a probable-cause standard, and the Chicago Police Department's General Order 92-4 (1992)—promulgated to govern enforcement of the Ordinance—makes the probable-cause requirement explicit.

Second, the Ordinance requires that the group be "remain[ing] in one place with no apparent purpose." JUSTICE O'CONNOR's assertion that this applies to "any person standing in a public place" is a distortion. The Ordinance does not apply to "standing," but to "remain[ing]". . . . There may be some ambiguity at the margin, but "remain[ing] in one place" requires more than a temporary stop, and is clear in most of its applications, including all of those represented by the facts surrounding the respondents' arrests described [above]. . . .

V

The plurality points out that Chicago already has several laws that reach the intimidating and unlawful gang-related conduct the Ordinance was directed at. The problem, of course, well recognized by Chicago's City Council, is that the gang members cease their intimidating and unlawful behavior under the watchful eye of police officers, but return to it as soon as the police drive away. The only solution, the council concluded, was to clear the streets of congregations of gangs, their drug customers, and their associates.

JUSTICE O'CONNOR's concurrence proffers the same empty solace of existing laws useless for the purpose at hand, but seeks to be helpful by suggesting some measures *similar* to this ordinance that *would* be constitutional. It says that Chicago could, for example, enact a law that "directly prohibit[s] the presence of a large collection of obviously brazen, insistent, and lawless gang members and hangers-on on the public ways, that intimidates residents." (If the majority considers the present ordinance too vague, it would be fun to see what it makes of "a large collection of obviously brazen, insistent, and lawless gang members.") . . .

The problem, again, is that the intimidation and lawlessness do not occur when the police are in sight.

JUSTICE O'CONNOR's concurrence also proffers another cure: "If the ordinance applied only to persons reasonably believed to be gang members, this requirement might have cured the ordinance's vagueness because it would have directed the manner in which the order was issued by specifying to whom the order could be issued." But the Ordinance already specifies to whom the order can be issued: persons remaining in one place with no apparent purpose in the company of a gang member. And if "remain[ing] in one place with no apparent purpose" is so vague as to give the police unbridled discretion in controlling the conduct of non-gang-members, it surpasses understanding how it ceases to be so vague when applied to gang members *alone*. Surely gang members cannot be decreed to be outlaws, subject to the merest whim of the police as the rest of us are not.

* * *

The fact is that the present ordinance is entirely clear in its application, cannot be violated except with full knowledge and intent, and vests no more discretion in the police than innumerable other measures authorizing police orders to preserve the public peace and safety. . . . [T]he majority's real quarrel with the Chicago Ordinance is simply that it permits (or indeed requires) too much harmless conduct by innocent citizens to be proscribed. . . .

But in our democratic system, how much harmless conduct to proscribe is not a judgment to be made by the courts. So long as constitutionally guaranteed rights are not affected, and so long as the proscription has a rational basis, *all sorts* of perfectly harmless activity by millions of perfectly innocent people can be forbidden—riding a motorcycle without a safety helmet, for example, starting a campfire in a national forest, or selling a safe and effective drug not yet approved by the FDA. All of these acts are entirely innocent and harmless in themselves, but because of the *risk* of harm that they entail, the freedom to engage in them has been abridged. The citizens of Chicago have decided that depriving themselves of the freedom to "hang out" with a gang member is necessary to eliminate pervasive gang crime and intimidation—and that the elimination of the one is worth the deprivation of the other. This Court has no business second-guessing either the degree of necessity or the fairness of the trade.

I dissent from the judgment of the Court.

JUSTICE THOMAS, with whom THE CHIEF JUSTICE and JUSTICE SCALIA join, dissenting.

The duly elected members of the Chicago City Council enacted the ordinance at issue as part of a larger effort to prevent gangs from establishing dominion over the public streets. By invalidating Chicago's ordinance, I fear that the Court has unnecessarily sentenced law-abiding citizens to lives of terror and misery. The ordinance is not vague. "[A]ny fool would know that a particular category of conduct would be within [its] reach." *Kolender v. Lawson* (1983) (White, J., dissenting). Nor does it violate the Due Process Clause. The asserted "freedom to loiter for innocent purposes" is in no way "deeply rooted in this Nation's history and tradition." *Washington v. Glucksberg* (1997). I dissent.

I

The human costs exacted by criminal street gangs are inestimable. In many of our Nation's cities, gangs have "[v]irtually overtak[en] certain neighborhoods, contributing to the economic and social decline of these areas and causing fear and lifestyle changes among law-abiding residents." U.S. Dept. of Justice, Office of Justice Programs, Bureau of Justice Assistance, Monograph: Urban Street Gang Enforcement 3 (1997). Gangs fill the daily lives of many of our poorest and most vulnerable citizens with a terror that the Court does not give sufficient consideration, often relegating them to the status of prisoners in their own homes. . . .

The city of Chicago has suffered the devastation wrought by this national tragedy. Last year, in an effort to curb plummeting attendance, the Chicago Public Schools hired dozens of adults to escort children to school. The youngsters had become too terrified of gang violence to leave their homes alone. The children's fears were not unfounded. In 1996, the Chicago Police Department estimated that there were 132 criminal street gangs in the city. Between 1987 and 1994, these gangs were involved in 63,141 criminal incidents, including 21,689 nonlethal violent crimes and 894 homicides. Many of these criminal incidents and homicides result from gang "turf battles," which take place on the public streets and place innocent residents in grave danger. . . .

Before enacting its ordinance, the Chicago City Council held extensive hearings on the problems of gang loitering. Concerned citizens appeared to testify poignantly as to how gangs disrupt their daily lives. [Thomas quoted from three residents' testimony before the city council's police and fire committee. One of them, eighty-eight-year-old Susan Mary Jackson, said: "We used to have a nice neighborhood. We don't have it anymore. . . . I am scared to go out in the daytime."]

Following these hearings, the council found that "criminal street gangs establish control over identifiable areas . . . by loitering in those areas and intimidating others from entering those areas." It further found that the mere presence of gang members "intimidate[s] many law abiding citizens" and "creates a justifiable fear for the safety of persons and property in the area." It is the product of this democratic process—the council's attempt to address these social ills—that we are asked to pass judgment upon today.

II

As part of its ongoing effort to curb the deleterious effects of criminal street gangs, the citizens of Chicago sensibly decided to return to basics. The ordinance does nothing more than confirm the well-established principle that the police have the duty and the power to maintain the public peace, and, when necessary, to disperse groups of individuals who threaten it. The plurality, however, concludes that the city's commonsense effort to combat gang loitering fails constitutional scrutiny for two separate reasons—because it infringes upon gang members' constitutional right to "loiter for innocent purposes," and because it is vague on its face. A majority of the Court endorses the latter conclusion. I respectfully disagree.

A

... The plurality asserts that "the freedom to loiter for innocent purposes is part of the 'liberty' protected by the Due Process Clause of the Fourteenth Amendment." Yet it acknowledges ... that "antiloitering ordinances have long existed in this country." ...

The plurality's sweeping conclusion that this ordinance infringes upon a liberty interest protected by the Fourteenth Amendment's Due Process Clause withers when exposed to the relevant history: Laws prohibiting loitering and vagrancy have been a fixture of Anglo-American law at least since the time of the Norman Conquest. ... The American colonists enacted laws modeled upon the English vagrancy laws, and at the time of the founding, state and local governments customarily criminalized loitering and other forms of vagrancy. Vagrancy laws were common in the decades preceding the ratification of the Fourteenth Amendment and remained on the books long after.

Tellingly, the plurality cites only three cases in support of the asserted right to "loiter for innocent purposes." Of those, only one—decided more than 100 years after the ratification of the Fourteenth Amendment—actually addressed the validity of a vagrancy ordinance. That case, *Papachristou* [*v. Jacksonville* (1972)], contains some dicta that can be read to support the fundamental right that the plurality asserts. However, the Court in *Papachristou* did not undertake the now-accepted analysis applied in substantive due process cases—it did not look to tradition to define the rights protected by the Due Process Clause. In any event, a careful reading of the opinion reveals that the Court never said anything about a constitutional right. The Court's holding was that the antiquarian language employed in the vagrancy ordinance at issue was unconstitutionally vague. Even assuming, then, that *Papachristou* was correctly decided as an original matter—a doubtful proposition—it does not compel the conclusion that the Constitution protects the right to loiter for innocent purposes. ...

B

The Court concludes that the ordinance is also unconstitutionally vague because it fails to provide adequate standards to guide police discretion and because, in the plurality's view, it does not give residents adequate notice of how to conform their conduct to the confines of the law. I disagree on both counts.

1

At the outset, it is important to note that the ordinance does not criminalize loitering *per se*. Rather, it penalizes loiterers' failure to obey a police officer's order to move along. A majority of the Court believes that this scheme vests too much discretion in police officers. Nothing could be further from the truth. Far from according officers too much discretion, the ordinance merely enables police officers to fulfill one of their traditional functions. ...

In their role as peace officers, the police long have had the authority and the duty to order groups of individuals who threaten the public peace to disperse. ...

The authority to issue dispersal orders continues to play a commonplace and crucial role in police operations, particularly in urban areas. . . . In order to perform their peace-keeping responsibilities satisfactorily, the police inevitably must exercise discretion. Indeed, by empowering them to act as peace officers, the law assumes that the police will exercise that discretion responsibly and with sound judgment. That is not to say that the law should not provide objective guidelines for the police, but simply that it cannot rigidly constrain their every action. By directing a police officer not to issue a dispersal order unless he "observes a person whom he reasonably believes to be a criminal street gang member loitering in any public place," Chicago's ordinance strikes an appropriate balance between those two extremes. Just as we trust officers to rely on their experience and expertise in order to make spur-of-the-moment determinations about amorphous legal standards such as "probable cause" and "reasonable suspicion," so we must trust them to determine whether a group of loiterers contains individuals (in this case members of criminal street gangs) whom the city has determined threaten the public peace. . . . In sum, the Court's conclusion that the ordinance is impermissibly vague because it "necessarily entrusts lawmaking to the moment-to-moment judgment of the policeman on his beat" cannot be reconciled with common sense, longstanding police practice, or this Court's Fourth Amendment jurisprudence.

2

The plurality's conclusion that the ordinance "fails to give the ordinary citizen adequate notice of what is forbidden and what is permitted" is similarly untenable. There is nothing "vague" about an order to disperse. . . . [I]t is safe to assume that the vast majority of people who are ordered by the police to "disperse and remove themselves from the area" will have little difficulty understanding how to comply.

Assuming that we are also obligated to consider whether the ordinance places individuals on notice of what conduct might subject them to such an order, respondents in this facial challenge bear the weighty burden of establishing that the statute is vague in all its applications. . . .

The plurality also concludes that the definition of the term loiter—"to remain in any one place with no apparent purpose"—fails to provide adequate notice. . . . Persons of ordinary intelligence are perfectly capable of evaluating how outsiders perceive their conduct. . . . Members of a group standing on the corner staring blankly into space, for example, are likely well aware that passersby would conclude that they have "no apparent purpose." . . .

* * *

Today, the Court focuses extensively on the "rights" of gang members and their companions. It can safely do so—the people who will have to live with the consequences of today's opinion do not live in our neighborhoods. Rather, the people who will suffer from our lofty pronouncements are people . . . who have seen their neighborhoods literally destroyed by gangs and violence and drugs. They are good, decent people who must struggle to overcome their desperate situation, against all odds, in order to raise their families, earn a living, and remain good citizens. As one resident described, "There is only about maybe one or two percent of the people in the city causing these problems maybe, but it's keeping 98 percent of us in our houses and off the streets and afraid to shop." By focusing exclusively on the imagined "rights" of the two percent, the Court today has denied our most vulnerable citizens the very thing that JUSTICE STEVENS elevates above all else—the "freedom of movement." And that is a shame. I respectfully dissent.

No. 98-536

Tommy Olmstead, Commissioner, Georgia Department of Human Resources, et al., Petitioners v. L. C., by Jonathan Zimring, guardian ad litem and next friend, et al.

On writ of certiorari to the United States Court of Appeals for the Eleventh Circuit

[June 22, 1999]

JUSTICE GINSBURG announced the judgment of the Court and delivered the opinion of the Court with respect to Parts I, II, and III-A, and an opinion with respect to Part III-B, in which O'CONNOR, SOUTER, and BREYER, JJ., joined.

This case concerns the proper construction of the anti-discrimination provision contained in the public services portion (Title II) of the Americans with Disabilities Act of 1990, 42 U.S.C. §12132. Specifically, we confront the question whether the proscription of discrimination may require placement of persons with mental disabilities in community settings rather than in institutions. The answer, we hold, is a qualified yes. Such action is in order when the State's treatment professionals have determined that community placement is appropriate, the transfer from institutional care to a less restrictive setting is not opposed by the affected individual, and the placement can be reasonably accommodated, taking into account the resources available to the State and the needs of others with mental disabilities. In so ruling, we affirm the decision of the Eleventh Circuit in substantial part. We remand the case, however, for further consideration of the appropriate relief, given the range of facilities the State maintains for the care and treatment of persons with diverse mental disabilities, and its obligation to administer services with an even hand.

I

This case, as it comes to us, presents no constitutional question. The complaints filed by plaintiffs-respondents L. C. and E. W. did include such an issue; L. C. and E. W. alleged that defendants-petitioners, Georgia health care officials, failed to afford them minimally adequate care and freedom from undue restraint, in violation of their rights under the Due Process Clause of the Fourteenth Amendment. But neither the District Court nor the Court of Appeals reached those Fourteenth Amendment claims. Instead, the courts below resolved the case solely on statutory grounds. Our review is similarly confined. . . . Mindful that it is a statute we are construing, we set out first the legislative and regulatory prescriptions on which the case turns.

In the opening provisions of the ADA, Congress stated findings applicable to the statute in all its parts. Most relevant to this case, Congress determined that

> (2) historically, society has tended to isolate and segregate individuals with disabilities, and, despite some improvements, such forms of discrimination against individuals with disabilities continue to be a serious and pervasive social problem;
> (3) discrimination against individuals with disabilities persists in such critical areas as . . . institutionalization. . . .
> (5) individuals with disabilities continually encounter various forms of discrimination, including outright intentional exclusion, . . . failure to make modifications to existing facilities and practices, . . . [and] segregation . . . . 42 U.S.C. §12101(a)(2), (3), (5).

Congress then set forth prohibitions against discrimination in employment (Title I), public services furnished by governmental entities (Title II), and public accommodations provided by private entities (Title III). The statute as a whole is intended "to provide a clear and comprehensive national mandate for the elimination of discrimination against individuals with disabilities." §12101(b)(1).

This case concerns Title II, the public services portion of the ADA. The provision of Title II centrally at issue reads:

> "Subject to the provisions of this subchapter, no qualified individual with a disability shall, by reason of such disability, be excluded from participation in or be denied the benefits of the services, programs, or activities of a public entity, or be subjected to discrimination by any such entity." §12132.

Title II's definition section states that "public entity" includes "any State or local government," and "any department, agency, [or] special purpose district." The same section defines "qualified individual with a disability" as

> "an individual with a disability who, with or without reasonable modifications to rules, policies, or practices, the removal of architectural, communication, or transportation barriers, or the provision of auxiliary aids and services, meets the essential eligibility requirements for the receipt of services or the participation in programs or activities provided by a public entity."

On redress for violations of §12132's discrimination prohibition, Congress referred to remedies available under §505 of the Rehabilitation Act of 1973. . . .

Congress instructed the Attorney General to issue regulations implementing provisions of Title II, including §12132's discrimination proscription. . . . The Attorney General's regulations, Congress further directed, "shall be consistent with this chapter and with the coordination regulations . . . applicable to recipients of Federal financial assistance under §504 of the Rehabilitation Act]." One of the §504 regulations requires recipients of federal funds to "administer programs and activities in the most integrated setting appropriate to the needs of qualified handicapped persons."

As Congress instructed, the Attorney General issued Title II regulations, including one modeled on the §504 regulation just quoted; called the "integration regulation," it reads:

> "A public entity shall administer services, programs, and activities in the most integrated setting appropriate to the needs of qualified individuals with disabilities." 28 CFR §35.130 (d) (1998).

The preamble to the Attorney General's Title II regulations defines "the most integrated setting appropriate to the needs of qualified individuals with disabilities" to mean "a setting that enables individuals with disabilities to interact with non-disabled persons to the fullest extent possible." Another regulation requires public entities to "make reasonable modifications" to avoid "discrimination on the basis of disability," unless those modifications would entail a "fundamenta[l] alter[ation]"; called here the "reasonable-modifications regulation," it provides:

> "A public entity shall make reasonable modifications in policies, practices, or procedures when the modifications are necessary to avoid discrimination on the basis of disability, unless the public entity can demonstrate that making the modifications would fundamentally alter the nature of the service, program, or activity." 28 CFR §35.130(b)(7) (1998).

We recite these regulations with the caveat that we do not here determine their validity. While the parties differ on the proper construction and enforcement of the regulations, we do not understand petitioners to challenge the regulatory formulations themselves as outside the congressional authorization.

II

With the key legislative provisions in full view, we summarize the facts underlying this dispute. Respondents L. C. and E. W. are mentally retarded women; L. C. has also been diagnosed with schizophrenia, and E. W., with a personality disorder. Both women have a history of treatment in institutional settings. In May 1992, L. C. was voluntarily admitted to Georgia Regional Hospital at Atlanta (GRH), where she was confined for treatment in a psychiatric unit. By May 1993, her psychiatric condition had stabilized, and L. C.'s treatment team at GRH agreed that her needs could be met appropriately in one of the community-based programs the State supported. Despite this evaluation, L. C. remained institutionalized until February 1996, when the State placed her in a community-based treatment program.

E. W. was voluntarily admitted to GRH in February 1995; like L. C., E. W. was confined for treatment in a psychiatric unit. In March 1995, GRH sought to discharge E. W. to a homeless shelter, but abandoned that plan after her attorney filed an administrative complaint. By 1996, E. W.'s treating psychiatrist concluded that she could be treated appropriately in a community-based setting. She nonetheless remained institutionalized until a few months after the District Court issued its judgment in this case in 1997.

A

In May 1995, when she was still institutionalized at GRH, L. C. filed suit in the United States District Court for the Northern District of Georgia, challenging her continued confinement in a segregated environment. Her complaint invoked 42 U.S.C. §1983 and provisions of the ADA §12131-12134, and named as defendants, now petitioners, the Commissioner of the Georgia Department of Human Resources, the Superintendent of GRH, and the Executive Director of the Fulton County Regional Board (collectively, the State). L. C. alleged that the State's failure to place her in a community-based program, once her treating professionals determined that such placement was appropriate, violated, *inter alia*, Title II of the ADA. L. C.'s pleading requested, among other things, that the State place her in a community care residential program, and that she receive treatment with the ultimate goal of integrating her into the mainstream of society. E. W. intervened in the action, stating an identical claim.

The District Court granted partial summary judgment in favor of L. C. and E. W. The court held that the State's failure to place L. C. and E. W. in an appropriate community-based treatment program violated Title II of the ADA. In so ruling, the court rejected the State's argument that inadequate funding, not discrimination against L. C. and E. W. "by reason of" their disabilities, accounted for their retention at GRH. Under Title II, the court concluded, "unnecessary institutional segregation of the disabled constitutes discrimination *per se*, which cannot be justified by a lack of funding."

In addition to contending that L. C. and E. W. had not shown discrimination "by reason of [their] disabilit[ies]," the State resisted court intervention on the ground that requiring immediate transfers in cases of this order would "fundamentally alter" the State's activity. The State reasserted that it was already using all available funds to provide services to other persons with disabilities. Rejecting the State's "fundamental alteration" defense, the court observed that existing state programs provided community-based treatment of the kind for which L. C. and E. W. qualified, and that the State could "provide services to plaintiffs in the community at considerably *less* cost than is required to maintain them in an institution."

The Court of Appeals for the Eleventh Circuit affirmed the judgment of the District Court, but remanded for reassessment of the State's cost-based defense. As the appeals court read the statute and regulations: When "a disabled individual's treating professionals find that a community-based placement is appropriate for that individual, the ADA imposes a duty to provide treatment in a community setting—the most integrated setting appropriate to that patient's needs"; "[w]here there is no such finding [by the treating professionals], nothing in the ADA requires the deinstitutionalization of th[e] patient."

The Court of Appeals recognized that the State's duty to provide integrated services "is not absolute"; under the Attorney General's Title II regulation, "reasonable modifications" were required of the State, but fundamental alterations were not demanded. The appeals court thought it clear, however, that "Congress wanted to permit a cost defense only in the most limited of circumstances." In conclusion, the court stated that a cost justification would fail "[u]nless the State can prove that requiring it to [expend additional funds in order to provide L. C. and E. W. with integrated services] would be so unreasonable given the demands of the State's mental health budget that it would fundamentally alter the service [the State] provides." Because it appeared that the District Court had entirely ruled out a "lack of funding" justification, the appeals court remanded, repeating that the District Court should consider, among other things, "whether the additional expenditures necessary to treat L. C. and E. W. in community-based care would be unreasonable given the demands of the State's mental health budget."

We granted certiorari in view of the importance of the question presented to the States and affected individuals. (1998).

III

Endeavoring to carry out Congress' instruction to issue regulations implementing Title II, the Attorney General, in the integration and reasonable-modifications regulations, made two key determinations. The first concerned the scope of the ADA's discrimination proscription, 42 U.S.C. §12132; the second concerned the obligation of the States to counter discrimination. As to the first, the Attorney General concluded that unjustified placement or retention of persons in institutions, severely limiting their exposure to the outside community, constitutes a form of discrimination based on disability prohibited by Title II. . . . Regarding the States' obligation to avoid unjustified isolation of individuals with disabilities, the Attorney General provided that States could resist modifications that "would fundamentally alter the nature of the service, program, or activity."

The Court of Appeals essentially upheld the Attorney General's construction of the ADA. . . .

We affirm the Court of Appeals' decision in substantial part. Unjustified isolation, we hold, is properly regarded as discrimination based on disability. But we recognize, as well, the States' need to maintain a range of facilities for the care and treatment of persons with diverse mental disabilities, and the States' obligation to administer services with an even hand. Accordingly, we further hold that the Court of Appeals' remand instruction was unduly restrictive. In evaluating a State's fundamental-alteration defense, the District Court must consider, in view of the resources available to the State, not only the cost of providing community-based care to the litigants, but also the range of services the State provides others with mental disabilities, and the State's obligation to mete out those services equitably.

A

We examine first whether, as the Eleventh Circuit held, undue institutionaliza tion qualifies as discrimination "by reason of . . . disability." The Department of Justice has consistently advocated that it does. Because the Department is the agency directed by Congress to issue regulations implementing Title II, its views warrant respect. . . .

The State argues that L. C. and E. W. encountered no discrimination "by reason of" their disabilities because they were not denied community placement on account of those disabilities. Nor were they subjected to "discrimination," the State contends, because " 'discrimination' necessarily requires uneven treatment of similarly situated individuals," and L. C. and E. W. had identified no comparison class, *i.e.*, no similarly situated individuals given preferential treatment. We are satisfied that Congress had a more comprehensive view of the concept of discrimination advanced in the ADA.

The ADA stepped up earlier measures to secure opportunities for people with developmental disabilities to enjoy the benefits of community living. [Citing the Developmentally Disabled Assistance and Bill of Rights Act of 1975 and the Rehabilitation Act of 1973.] Ultimately, in the ADA, enacted in 1990, Congress not only required all public entities to refrain from discrimination; additionally, in findings applicable to the entire statute, Congress explicitly identified unjustified "segregation" of persons with disabilities as a "for[m] of discrimination." See 42 U.S.C. §12101(a)(2) ("historically, society has tended to isolate and segregate individuals with disabilities, and, despite some improvements, such forms of discrimination against individuals with disabilities continue to be a serious and pervasive social problem"); §12101(a)(5) ("individuals with disabilities continually encounter various forms of discrimination, including . . . segregation").

Recognition that unjustified institutional isolation of persons with disabilities is a form of discrimination reflects two evident judgments. First, institutional placement of persons who can handle and benefit from community settings perpetuates unwarranted assumptions that persons so isolated are incapable or unworthy of participating in community life. . . . Second, confinement in an institution severely diminishes the everyday life activities of individuals, including family relations, social contacts, work options, economic independence, educational advancement, and cultural enrichment. Dissimilar treatment correspondingly exists in this key respect: In order to receive needed medical services, persons with mental disabilities must, because of those disabilities, relinquish participation in community life they could enjoy given reasonable accommodations, while persons without mental disabilities can receive the medical services they need without similar sacrifice.

The State urges that, whatever Congress may have stated as its findings in the ADA, the Medicaid statute "reflected a congressional policy preference for treatment in the institution over treatment in the community." The State correctly used the past tense. Since 1981, Medicaid has provided funding for state-run home and community-based care through a waiver program. Indeed, the United States points out that the Department of Health and Human Services (HHS) "has a policy of encouraging States to take advantage of the waiver program, and often approves more waiver slots than a State ultimately uses." [Citing Justice Department Brief and noting that it also observed that by 1996 "HHS approved up to 2109 waiver slots for Georgia, but Georgia used only 700."]

We emphasize that nothing in the ADA or its implementing regulations condones termination of institutional settings for persons unable to handle or benefit from community settings. Title II provides only that "qualified individual[s] with a disability" may not "be subjected to discrimination." "Qualified individuals," the ADA further explains, are persons with disabilities who, "with or without reasonable modifications to rules, policies, or practices, . . . mee[t] the essential eligibility requirements for the receipt of services or the participation in programs or activities provided by a public entity."

Consistent with these provisions, the State generally may rely on the reasonable assessments of its own professionals in determining whether an individual "meets the essential eligibility requirements" for habilitation in a community-based program. Absent such qualification, it would be inappropriate to remove a patient from the more restrictive setting. . . . In this case, however, there is no genuine dispute concerning the status of L. C. and E. W. as individuals "qualified" for non-institutional care: The State's own professionals determined that community-based treatment would be appropriate for L. C. and E. W., and neither woman opposed such treatment.

B

The State's responsibility, once it provides community-based treatment to qualified persons with disabilities, is not boundless. The reasonable-modifications regulation speaks of "reasonable modifications" to avoid discrimination, and allows States to resist modifications that entail a "fundamenta[l] alter[ation]" of the States' services and programs. The Court of Appeals construed this regulation to permit a cost-based defense "only in the most limited of circumstances," and remanded to the District Court to consider, among other things, "whether the additional expenditures necessary to treat L. C. and E. W. in community-based care would be unreasonable given the demands of the State's mental health budget."

The Court of Appeals' construction of the reasonable-modifications regulation is unacceptable for it would leave the State virtually defenseless once it is shown that the plaintiff is qualified for the service or program she seeks. If the expense entailed in placing one or two people in a community-based treatment program is properly measured for reasonableness against the State's entire mental health budget, it is unlikely that a State, relying on the fundamental-alteration defense, could ever prevail. . . . Sensibly construed, the fundamental-alteration component of the reasonable-modifications regulation would allow the State to show that, in the allocation of available resources, immediate relief for the plaintiffs would be inequitable, given the responsibility the State has undertaken for the care and treatment of a large and diverse population of persons with mental disabilities.

When it granted summary judgment for plaintiffs in this case, the District Court compared the cost of caring for the plaintiffs in a community-based setting with the cost of caring for them in an institution. That simple comparison showed that community placements cost less than institutional confinements. As the United States recognizes, however, a comparison so simple overlooks costs the State cannot avoid; most notably, a "State . . . may experience increased overall expenses by funding community placements without being able to take advantage of the savings associated with the closure of institutions."

As already observed, the ADA is not reasonably read to impel States to phase out institutions, placing patients in need of close care at risk. Nor is it the ADA's mission to drive States to move institutionalized patients into an inappropriate setting, such as a homeless shelter, a placement the State proposed, then retracted, for E. W. Some individuals, like L. C. and E. W. in prior years, may need institutional care from time to time "to stabilize acute psychiatric symptoms." . . . For other individuals, no placement outside the institution may ever be appropriate. . . .

To maintain a range of facilities and to administer services with an even hand, the State must have more leeway than the courts below understood the fundamental-alteration defense to allow. If, for example, the State were to demonstrate that it had a comprehensive, effectively working plan for placing qualified persons with mental disabilities in less restrictive settings, and a waiting list that moved at a reasonable pace not controlled by the State's endeavors to keep its institutions fully populated, the reasonable-modifications standard would be met. . . . In such circumstances, a court would have no warrant effectively to order displacement of persons at the top of the community-based treatment waiting list by individuals lower down who commenced civil actions.

* * *

For the reasons stated, we conclude that, under Title II of the ADA, States are required to provide community-based treatment for persons with mental disabilities when the State's treatment professionals determine that such placement is appropriate, the affected persons do not oppose such treatment, and the placement can be reasonably accommodated, taking into account the resources available to the State and the needs of others with mental disabilities. The judgment of the Eleventh Circuit is therefore affirmed in part and vacated in part, and the case is remanded for further proceedings consistent with this opinion.

It is so ordered.

JUSTICE STEVENS, concurring in part and concurring in the judgment.

Unjustified disparate treatment, in this case, "unjustified institutional isolation," constitutes discrimination under the Americans with Disabilities Act of 1990. If a plaintiff requests relief that requires modification of a State's services or programs, the State may assert, as an affirmative defense, that the requested modification would cause a fundamental alteration of a State's services and programs. In this case, the Court of Appeals appropriately remanded for consideration of the State's affirmative defense. On remand, the District Court rejected the State's "fundamental-alteration defense." If the District Court was wrong in concluding that costs unrelated to the treatment of L. C. and E. W. do not support such a defense in this case, that arguable error should be corrected either by the Court of Appeals or by this Court in review of that decision. In my opinion, therefore, we should simply affirm the judgment of the Court of Appeals. But because there are not five votes for that disposition, I join JUSTICE GINSBURG's judgment and Parts I, II, and III-A of her opinion.

JUSTICE KENNEDY, with whom JUSTICE BREYER joins as to Part I, concurring in the judgment.

I

. . . Beginning in the 1950's, many victims of severe mental illness were moved out of state-run hospitals, often with benign objectives. According to one estimate, when adjusted for population growth, "the actual decrease in the numbers of people with severe mental illnesses in public psychiatric hospitals between 1955 and 1995 was 92 percent." This was not without benefit or justification. The so-called "deinstitutionalization" has permitted a substantial number of mentally disabled persons to receive needed treatment with greater freedom and dignity. It may be, moreover, that those who remain institutionalized are indeed the most severe cases. With reference to this case, . . . it is undisputed that the State's own treating professionals determined that community-based care was medically appropriate for respondents. Nevertheless, the depopulation of state mental hospitals has its dark side. According to one expert:

> "For a substantial minority . . . deinstitutionalization has been a psychiatric *Titanic*. Their lives are virtually devoid of 'dignity' or 'integrity of body, mind, and spirit.' 'Self-determination' often means merely that the person has a choice of soup kitchens. The 'least restrictive setting' frequently turns out to be a cardboard box, a jail cell, or a terror-filled existence plagued by both real and imaginary enemies." [Quoting E. Torrey, *Out of the Shadows* (1997)].

It must be remembered that for the person with severe mental illness who has no treatment the most dreaded of confinements can be the imprisonment inflicted by his own mind, which shuts reality out and subjects him to the torment of voices and images beyond our own powers to describe.

It would be unreasonable, it would be a tragic event, then, were the Americans with Disabilities Act of 1990 (ADA) to be interpreted so that States had some incentive, for fear of litigation, to drive those in need of medical care and treatment out of appropriate care and into settings with too little assistance and supervision. The opinion of a responsible treating physician in determining the appropriate conditions for treatment ought to be given the greatest of deference. It is a common phenomenon that a patient functions well with medication, yet, because of the mental illness itself, lacks the discipline or capacity to follow the regime the medication requires. This is illustrative of the factors a responsible physician will consider in recommending the appropriate setting or facility for treatment. JUSTICE GINSBURG's opinion takes account of this background. It is careful, and quite correct, to say that it is not "the ADA's mission to drive States to move institutionalized patients into an inappropriate setting, such as a homeless shelter. . . ."

In light of these concerns, if the principle of liability announced by the Court is not applied with caution and circumspection, States may be pressured into attempting compliance on the cheap, placing marginal patients into integrated settings devoid of the services and attention necessary for their condition. This danger is in addition to the federalism costs inherent in referring state decisions regarding the administration of treatment programs and the allocation of resources to the reviewing authority of the federal courts. It is of central importance, then, that courts apply today's decision with great deference to the medical decisions of the responsible, treating physicians and, as the Court makes clear, with appropriate deference to the program funding decisions of state policymakers.

II

With these reservations made explicit, in my view we must remand the case for a determination of the questions the Court poses and for a determination whether respondents can show a violation of 42 U.S.C. §12132's ban on discrimination based on the summary judgment materials on file or any further pleadings and materials properly allowed. . . .

Putting aside issues of animus or unfair stereotype, I agree with JUSTICE THOMAS that on the ordinary interpretation and meaning of the term, one who alleges discrimination must show that she "received differential treatment vis-à-vis members of a different group on the basis of a statutorily described characteristic." In my view, however, discrimination so defined might be shown here. . . .

. . . [I]f respondents could show that Georgia (i) provides treatment to individuals suffering from medical problems of comparable seriousness, (ii) as a general matter, does so in the most integrated setting appropriate for the treatment of those problems (taking medical and other practical considerations into account), but (iii) without adequate justification, fails to do so for a group of mentally disabled persons (treating them instead in separate, locked institutional facilities), I believe it would demonstrate discrimination on the basis of mental disability.

Of course, it is a quite different matter to say that a State without a program in place is required to create one. No State has unlimited resources and each must make hard decisions on how much to allocate to treatment of diseases and disabilities. If, for example, funds for care and treatment of the mentally ill, including the severely mentally ill, are reduced in order to support programs directed to the treatment and care of other disabilities, the decision may be unfortunate. The judgment, however, is a political one and not within the reach of the statute. . . . It is not reasonable to read the ADA to permit court intervention in these decisions. In addition, as the Court notes, by regulation a public entity is required only to make "reasonable modifications in policies, practices, or procedures" when necessary to avoid discrimination and is not even required to make those if "the modifications would fundamentally alter the nature of the service, program, or activity." It follows that a State may not be forced to create a community-treatment program where none exists. . . .

The possibility . . . remains that, on the facts of this case, respondents would be able to support a claim under §12132 by showing that they have been subject to discrimination by Georgia officials on the basis of their disability. This inquiry would not be simple. Comparisons of different medical conditions and the corresponding treatment regimens might be difficult, as would be assessments of the degree of integration of various settings in which medical treatment is offered. For example, the evidence might show that, apart from services for the mentally disabled, medical treatment is rarely offered in a community setting but also is rarely offered in facilities comparable to state mental hospitals. Determining the relevance of that type of evidence would require considerable judgment and analysis. However, as petitioners observe, "[i]n this case, no class of similarly situated individuals was even identified, let alone shown to be given preferential treatment." Without additional information regarding the details of state-provided medical services in Georgia, we cannot address the issue in the way the statute demands. As a consequence, the judgment of the courts below, granting partial summary judgment to respondents, ought not to be sustained. In addition, as JUSTICE GINSBURG's opinion is careful to note, it was error in the earlier proceedings to restrict the relevance and force of the State's evidence regarding the comparative costs of treatment. The State is entitled to wide discretion in adopting its own systems of cost analysis, and, if it chooses, to allocate health care resources based on fixed and overhead costs for whole institutions and programs. . . .

I would remand the case to the Court of Appeals or the District Court for it to determine in the first instance whether a statutory violation is sufficiently alleged and supported in respondents' summary judgment materials and, if not, whether they should be given leave to replead and to introduce evidence and argument along the lines suggested above.

JUSTICE THOMAS, with whom THE CHIEF JUSTICE and JUSTICE SCALIA join, dissenting.

Title II of the Americans with Disabilities Act of 1990 (ADA), 42 .S.C. §12132 provides:

> "Subject to the provisions of this subchapter, no qualified individual with a disability shall, *by reason of such disability*, be excluded from participation in or be denied the benefits of the services, programs, or activities of a public entity, *or be subjected to discrimination* by any such entity." (Emphasis added.)

The majority concludes that petitioners "discriminated" against respondents—as a matter of law—by continuing to treat them in an institutional setting after they became eligible for community placement. I disagree. Temporary exclusion from community placement does not amount to "discrimination" in the traditional sense of the word, nor have respondents shown that petitioners "discriminated" against them "by reason of" their disabilities.

Until today, this Court has never endorsed an interpretation of the term "discrimination" that encompassed disparate treatment among members of the *same* protected class. Discrimination, as typically understood, requires a showing that a claimant received differential treatment vis-à-vis members of a different group on the basis of a statutorily described characteristic. This interpretation comports with dictionary definitions of the term discrimination, which means to "distinguish," to "differentiate," or to make a "distinction in favor of or against, a person or thing based on the group, class, or category to which that person or thing belongs rather than on individual merit." Random House Dictionary 564 (2d ed.

1987); see also Webster's Third New International Dictionary 648 (1981) (defining "discrimination" as "the making or perceiving of a distinction or difference" or as "the act, practice, or an instance of discriminating categorically rather than individually").

Our decisions construing various statutory prohibitions against "discrimination" have not wavered from this path. [Discussion of case law under Title VII of the Civil Rights Act of 1964 and §504 of the Rehabilitation Act of 1973 omitted.]

Despite this traditional understanding, the majority derives a more "capacious" definition of "discrimination," as that term is used in Title II of the ADA, one that includes "institutional isolation of persons with disabilities." It chiefly relies on certain congressional findings contained within the ADA. To be sure, those findings appear to equate institutional isolation with segregation, and thereby discrimination. . . . The congressional findings, however, are written in general, hortatory terms and provide little guidance to the interpretation of the specific language of §12132. . . . In my view, the vague congressional findings upon which the majority relies simply do not suffice to show that Congress sought to overturn a well-established understanding of a statutory term (here, "discrimination"). Moreover, the majority fails to explain why terms in the findings should be given a medical content, pertaining to the place where a mentally retarded person is treated. When read in context, the findings instead suggest that terms such as "segregation" were used in a more general sense, pertaining to matters such as access to employment, facilities, and transportation. Absent a clear directive to the contrary, we must read "discrimination" in light of the common understanding of the term. We cannot expand the meaning of the term "discrimination" in order to invalidate policies we may find unfortunate. . . .

Elsewhere in the ADA, Congress chose to alter the traditional definition of discrimination. Title I of the ADA, §12112(b)(1), defines discrimination to include "limiting, segregating, or classifying a job applicant or employee in a way that adversely affects the opportunities or status of such applicant or employee." Notably, however, Congress did not provide that this definition of discrimination, unlike other aspects of the ADA, applies to Title II. Ordinary canons of construction require that we respect the limited applicability of this definition of "discrimination" and not import it into other parts of the law where Congress did not see fit. . . .

At bottom, the type of claim approved of by the majority does not concern a prohibition against certain conduct (the traditional understanding of discrimination), but rather imposition of a standard of care. As such, the majority can offer no principle limiting this new species of "discrimination" claim apart from an affirmative defense because it looks merely to an individual in isolation, without comparing him to otherwise similarly situated persons, and determines that discrimination occurs merely because that individual does not receive the treatment he wishes to receive. By adopting such a broad view of discrimination, the majority drains the term of any meaning other than as a proxy for decisions disapproved of by this Court.

Further, I fear that the majority's approach imposes significant federalism costs, directing States how to make decisions about their delivery of public services. We previously have recognized that constitutional principles of federalism erect limits on the Federal Government's ability to direct state officers or to interfere with the functions of state governments. We have suggested that these principles specifically apply to whether States are required to provide a certain level of benefits to individuals with disabilities. As noted in *Alexander* [*v. Choate* (1985)], in rejecting a similar theory under §504 of the Rehabilitation Act: "[N]othing . . . suggests that Congress desired to make major inroads on the States' longstanding discretion to choose the proper mix of amount, scope, and duration limitations on services.". . . The majority's affirmative defense will likely come as cold comfort to the States that will now be forced to defend themselves in federal court every time resources prevent the immediate placement of a qualified individual. In keeping with our traditional deference in this area, the appropriate course would be to respect the States' historical role as the dominant authority responsible for providing services to individuals with disabilities.

Finally, it is also clear petitioners did not "discriminate" against respondents "by reason of [their] disabili[ties]," as §12132 requires. We have previously interpreted the phrase "by reason of" as requiring proximate causation. . . . This statute should be read as requiring proximate causation as well. Respondents do not contend that their disabilities constituted the proximate cause for their exclusion. Nor could they—community placement simply is not available to those without disabilities. Continued institutional treatment of persons who, though now deemed treatable in a community placement, must wait their turn for placement, does not establish that the denial of community placement occurred "by reason of" their disability. Rather, it establishes no more than the fact that petitioners have limited resources.

For the foregoing reasons, I respectfully dissent.

No. 97-1943

Karen Sutton and Kimberly Hinton, Petitioners
v. United Air Lines, Inc.

On writ of certiorari to the United States Court of Appeals
for the Tenth Circuit

[June 22, 1999]

JUSTICE O'CONNOR delivered the opinion of the Court.

The Americans with Disabilities Act of 1990 (ADA or Act), 42 U.S.C. §12101 *et seq.*, prohibits certain employers from discriminating against individuals on the basis of their disabilities. See §12112(a). Petitioners challenge the dismissal of their ADA action for failure to state a claim upon which relief can be granted. We conclude that the complaint was properly dismissed. In reaching that result, we hold that the determination of whether an individual is disabled should be made with reference to measures that mitigate the individual's impairment, including, in this instance, eyeglasses and contact lenses. In addition, we hold that petitioners failed to allege properly that respondent "regarded" them as having a disability within the meaning of the ADA.

I

Petitioners' amended complaint was dismissed for failure to state a claim upon which relief could be granted. Accordingly, we accept the allegations contained in their complaint as true for purposes of this case.

Petitioners are twin sisters, both of whom have severe myopia. Each petitioner's uncorrected visual acuity is 20/200 or worse in her right eye and 20/400 or worse in her left eye, but "[w]ith the use of corrective lenses, each . . . has vision that is 20/20 or better." [Quoting complaint.] Consequently, without corrective lenses, each "effectively cannot see to conduct numerous activities such as driving a vehicle, watching television or shopping in public stores," but with corrective measures, such as glasses or contact lenses, both "function identically to individuals without a similar impairment."

In 1992, petitioners applied to respondent for employment as commercial airline pilots. They met respondent's basic age, education, experience, and FAA certification qualifications. After submitting their applications for employment, both petitioners were invited by respondent to an interview and to flight simulator tests. Both were told during their interviews, however, that a mistake had been made in inviting them to interview because petitioners did not meet respondent's minimum vision requirement, which was uncorrected visual acuity of 20/100 or better. Due to their failure to meet this requirement, petitioners' interviews were terminated, and neither was offered a pilot position.

In light of respondent's proffered reason for rejecting them, petitioners filed a charge of disability discrimination under the ADA with the Equal Employment Opportunity Commission (EEOC). After receiving a right to sue letter, petitioners filed suit in the United States District Court for the District of Colorado, alleging that respondent had discriminated against them "on the basis of their disability, or because [respondent] regarded [petitioners] as having a disability" in violation of the ADA. Specifically, petitioners alleged that due to their severe myopia they actually have a substantially limiting impairment or are regarded as having such an impairment, and are thus disabled under the Act.

The District Court dismissed petitioners' complaint for failure to state a claim upon which relief could be granted. Because petitioners could fully correct their visual impairments, the court held that they were not actually substantially limited in any major life activity and thus had not stated a claim that they were disabled within the meaning of the ADA. The court also determined that petitioners had not made allegations sufficient to support their claim that they were "regarded" by the respondent as having an impairment that substantially limits a major life activity. The court observed that "[t]he statutory reference to a substantial limitation indicates . . . that an employer regards an employee as handicapped in his or her ability to work by finding the employee's impairment to foreclose generally the type of employment involved." But petitioners had alleged only that respondent regarded them as unable to satisfy the requirements of a particular job, global airline pilot. Consequently, the court held that petitioners had not stated a claim that they were regarded as substantially limited in the major life activity of working. Employing similar logic, the Court of Appeals for the Tenth Circuit affirmed the District Court's judgment (1997).

The Tenth Circuit's decision is in tension with the decisions of other Courts of Appeals. [Citations omitted.] We granted certiorari (1999) and now affirm.

II

The ADA prohibits discrimination by covered entities, including private employers, against qualified individuals with a disability. Specifically, it provides that no covered employer "shall discriminate against a qualified individual with a disability because of the disability of such individual in regard to job application procedures, the hiring, advancement, or discharge of employees, employee compensation, job training, and other terms, conditions, and privileges of employment." 42 U.S.C. §12112(a). . . . A "qualified individual with a disability" is identified as "an individual with a disability who, with or without reasonable accommodation, can perform the essential functions of the employment position that such individual holds or desires." §12111(8). In turn, a "disability" is defined as:

> "(A) a physical or mental impairment that substantially limits one or more of the major life activities of such individual;
> "(B) a record of such an impairment; or
> "(C) being regarded as having such an impairment." §12102(2).

Accordingly, to fall within this definition one must have an actual disability (subsection (A)), have a record of a disability (subsection (B)), or be regarded as having one (subsection (C)).

The parties agree that the authority to issue regulations to implement the Act is split primarily among three Government agencies. According to the parties, the EEOC has authority to issue regulations to carry out the employment provisions in Title I of the ADA, §12111-12117, pursuant to §12116. . . . The Attorney General is granted authority to issue regulations with respect to Title II, subtitle A, §12131-12134, which relates to public services. . . . Finally, the Secretary of Transportation has authority to issue regulations pertaining to the transportation provisions of Titles II and III. . . .

No agency, however, has been given authority to issue regulations implementing the generally applicable provisions of the ADA, see §12101-12102, which fall outside Titles I-V. Most notably, no agency has been delegated authority to interpret the term "disability." . . . The EEOC has, nonetheless, issued regulations to provide additional guidance regarding the proper interpretation of this term. . . .

The agencies have also issued interpretive guidelines to aid in the implementation of their regulations. For instance, at the time that it promulgated the above regulations, the EEOC issued an "Interpretive Guidance," which provides that "[t]he determination of whether an individual is substantially limited in a major life activity must be made on a case by case basis, without regard to mitigating measures such as medicines, or assistive or prosthetic devices." (1998) The Department of Justice has issued a similar guideline. . . .

III

With this statutory and regulatory framework in mind, we turn first to the question whether petitioners have stated a claim under subsection (A) of the disability definition, that is, whether they have alleged that they possess a physical impairment that substantially limits them in one or more major life activities. Because petitioners allege that with corrective measures their vision "is 20/20 or better," they are not actually disabled within the meaning of the Act if the "disability" determination is made with reference to these measures. Consequently, with respect to subsection (A) of the disability definition, our decision turns on whether disability is to be determined with or without reference to corrective measures.

Petitioners maintain that whether an impairment is substantially limiting should be determined without regard to corrective measures. They argue that, because the ADA does not directly address the question at hand, the Court should defer to the agency interpretations of the statute, which are embodied in the agency guidelines issued by the EEOC and the Department of Justice. These guidelines specifically direct that the determination of whether an individual is substantially limited in a major life activity be made without regard to mitigating measures.

Respondent, in turn, maintains that an impairment does not substantially limit a major life activity if it is corrected. It argues that the Court should not defer to the agency guidelines cited by petitioners because the guidelines conflict with the plain meaning of the ADA. The phrase "substantially limits one or more major life activities," it explains, requires that the substantial limitations actually and presently exist. Moreover, respondent argues, disregarding mitigating measures taken by an individual defies the statutory command to examine the effect of the impairment on the major life activities "of such individual." And even if the statute is ambiguous, respondent claims, the guidelines' directive to ignore mitigating measures is not reasonable, and thus this Court should not defer to it.

We conclude that respondent is correct that the approach adopted by the agency guidelines—that persons are to be evaluated in their hypothetical uncorrected state—is an impermissible interpretation of the ADA. Looking at the Act as a whole, it is apparent that if a person is taking measures to correct for, or mitigate, a physical or mental impairment, the effects of those measures—both positive and negative—must be taken into account when judging whether that person is "substantially limited" in a major life activity and thus "disabled" under the Act. The dissent relies on the legislative history of the ADA for the contrary proposition that individuals should be examined in their uncorrected state. Because we decide that, by its terms, the ADA cannot be read in this manner, we have no reason to consider the ADA's legislative history.

Three separate provisions of the ADA, read in concert, lead us to this conclusion. The Act defines a "disability" as "a physical or mental impairment that *sub-*

stantially limits one or more of the major life activities" of an individual (emphasis added). Because the phrase "substantially limits" appears in the Act in the present indicative verb form, we think the language is properly read as requiring that a person be presently—not potentially or hypothetically—substantially limited in order to demonstrate a disability. A "disability" exists only where an impairment "substantially limits" a major life activity, not where it "might," "could," or "would" be substantially limiting if mitigating measures were not taken. A person whose physical or mental impairment is corrected by medication or other measures does not have an impairment that presently "substantially limits" a major life activity. To be sure, a person whose physical or mental impairment is corrected by mitigating measures still has an impairment, but if the impairment is corrected it does not "substantially limi[t]" a major life activity.

The definition of disability also requires that disabilities be evaluated "with respect to an individual" and be determined based on whether an impairment substantially limits the "major life activities of such individual." Thus, whether a person has a disability under the ADA is an individualized inquiry. . . .

The agency guidelines' directive that persons be judged in their uncorrected or unmitigated state runs directly counter to the individualized inquiry mandated by the ADA. The agency approach would often require courts and employers to speculate about a person's condition and would, in many cases, force them to make a disability determination based on general information about how an uncorrected impairment usually affects individuals, rather than on the individual's actual condition. For instance, under this view, courts would almost certainly find all diabetics to be disabled, because if they failed to monitor their blood sugar levels and administer insulin, they would almost certainly be substantially limited in one or more major life activities. A diabetic whose illness does not impair his or her daily activities would therefore be considered disabled simply because he or she has diabetes. Thus, the guidelines approach would create a system in which persons often must be treated as members of a group of people with similar impairments, rather than as individuals. This is contrary to both the letter and the spirit of the ADA.

The guidelines approach could also lead to the anomalous result that in determining whether an individual is disabled, courts and employers could not consider any negative side effects suffered by an individual resulting from the use of mitigating measures, even when those side effects are very severe. . . . This result is also inconsistent with the individualized approach of the ADA.

Finally, and critically, findings enacted as part of the ADA require the conclusion that Congress did not intend to bring under the statute's protection all those whose uncorrected conditions amount to disabilities. Congress found that "some 43,000,000 Americans have one or more physical or mental disabilities, and this number is increasing as the population as a whole is growing older." §12101(a)(1). This figure is inconsistent with the definition of disability pressed by petitioners. [Discussion of origin of 43 million figure omitted.]

Regardless of its exact source, however, the 43 million figure reflects an understanding that those whose impairments are largely corrected by medication or other devices are not "disabled" within the meaning of the ADA. . . .

Because it is included in the ADA's text, the finding that 43 million individuals are disabled gives content to the ADA's terms, specifically the term "disability."

Had Congress intended to include all persons with corrected physical limitations among those covered by the Act, it undoubtedly would have cited a much higher number of disabled persons in the findings. That it did not is evidence that the ADA's coverage is restricted to only those whose impairments are not mitigated by corrective measures.

The dissents suggest that viewing individuals in their corrected state will exclude from the definition of "disab[led]" those who use prosthetic limbs or take medicine for epilepsy or high blood pressure. This suggestion is incorrect. The use of a corrective device does not, by itself, relieve one's disability. Rather, one has a disability under subsection A if, notwithstanding the use of a corrective device, that individual is substantially limited in a major life activity. For example, individuals who use prosthetic limbs or wheelchairs may be mobile and capable of functioning in society but still be disabled because of a substantial limitation on their ability to walk or run. The same may be true of individuals who take medicine to lessen the symptoms of an impairment so that they can function but nevertheless remain substantially limited. Alternatively, one whose high blood pressure is "cured" by medication may be regarded as disabled by a covered entity, and thus disabled under subsection C of the definition. The use or nonuse of a corrective device does not determine whether an individual is disabled; that determination depends on whether the limitations an individual with an impairment *actually* faces are in fact substantially limiting.

Applying this reading of the Act to the case at hand, we conclude that the Court of Appeals correctly resolved the issue of disability in respondent's favor. As noted above, petitioners allege that with corrective measures, their visual acuity is 20/20, and that they "function identically to individuals without a similar impairment." In addition, petitioners concede that they "do not argue that the use of corrective lenses in itself demonstrates a substantially limiting impairment." Accordingly, because we decide that disability under the Act is to be determined with reference to corrective measures, we agree with the courts below that petitioners have not stated a claim that they are substantially limited in any major life activity.

IV

Our conclusion that petitioners have failed to state a claim that they are actually disabled under subsection (A) of the disability definition does not end our inquiry. Under subsection (C), individuals who are "regarded as" having a disability are disabled within the meaning of the ADA. . . . There are two apparent ways in which individuals may fall within this statutory definition: (1) a covered entity mistakenly believes that a person has a physical impairment that substantially limits one or more major life activities, or (2) a covered entity mistakenly believes that an actual, nonlimiting impairment substantially limits one or more major life activities. In both cases, it is necessary that a covered entity entertain misperceptions about the individual—it must believe either that one has a substantially limiting impairment that one does not have or that one has a substantially limiting impairment when, in fact, the impairment is not so limiting. . . .

There is no dispute that petitioners are physically impaired. Petitioners do not make the obvious argument that they are regarded due to their impairments as substantially limited in the major life activity of seeing. They contend only that respondent mistakenly believes their physical impairments substantially limit them in the major life activity of working. To support this claim, petitioners allege that respondent has a vision requirement, which is allegedly based on myth and stereotype. Further, this requirement substantially limits their ability to engage in the major life activity of working by precluding them from obtaining the job of global airline pilot, which they argue is a "class of employment." In reply, respondent argues that the position of global airline pilot is not a class of jobs and therefore petitioners have not stated a claim that they are regarded as substantially limited in the major life activity of working.

Standing alone, the allegation that respondent has a vision requirement in place does not establish a claim that respondent regards petitioners as substantially limited in the major life activity of working. . . . By its terms, the ADA allows employers to prefer some physical attributes over others and to establish physical criteria. An employer runs afoul of the ADA when it makes an employment decision based on a physical or mental impairment, real or imagined, that is regarded as substantially limiting a major life activity. Accordingly, an employer is free to decide that physical characteristics or medical conditions that do not rise to the level of an impairment—such as one's height, build, or singing voice—are preferable to others, just as it is free to decide that some limiting, but not *substantially* limiting, impairments make individuals less than ideally suited for a job.

Considering the allegations of the amended complaint in tandem, petitioners have not stated a claim that respondent regards their impairment as *substantially limiting* their ability to work. . . .

When the major life activity under consideration is that of working, the statutory phrase "substantially limits" requires, at a minimum, that plaintiffs allege they are unable to work in a broad class of jobs. Reflecting this requirement, the EEOC uses a specialized definition of the term "substantially limits" when referring to the major life activity of working:

> "[S]ignificantly restricted in the ability to perform either a class of jobs or a broad range of jobs in various classes as compared to the average person having comparable training, skills and abilities. The inability to perform a single, particular job does not constitute a substantial limitation in the major life activity of working."

The EEOC further identifies several factors that courts should consider when determining whether an individual is substantially limited in the major life activity of working, including the geographical area to which the individual has reasonable access, and "the number and types of jobs utilizing similar training, knowledge, skills or abilities, within the geographical area, from which the individual is also disqualified." To be substantially limited in the major life activity of working, then, one must be precluded from more than one type of job, a specialized job, or a particular job of choice. If jobs utilizing an individual's skills (but perhaps not his or her unique talents) are available, one is not precluded from a substantial class of jobs. Similarly, if a host of different types of jobs are available, one is not precluded from a broad range of jobs.

Assuming without deciding that working is a major life activity and that the EEOC regulations interpreting the term "substantially limits" are reasonable, petitioners have failed to allege adequately that their poor eyesight is regarded as an impairment that substantially limits them in the major life activity of working. They allege only that respondent regards their poor vision as precluding them from holding positions as a "global airline pilot." Because the position of global airline pilot is a single job, this allegation does not support the claim that respondent regards petitioners as having a *substantially limiting* impairment. . . . Indeed, there are a number of other positions utilizing petitioners' skills, such as regional pilot and pilot instructor to name a few, that are available to them. Even under the EEOC's Interpretative Guidance. . . , "an individual who cannot be a commercial airline pilot because of a minor vision impairment, but who can be a commercial airline co-pilot or a pilot for a courier service, would not be substantially limited in the major life activity of working."

Petitioners also argue that if one were to assume that a substantial number of airline carriers have similar vision requirements, they would be substantially limited in the major life activity of working. Even assuming for the sake of argument that the adoption of similar vision requirements by other carriers would represent a substantial limitation on the major life activity of working, the argument is nevertheless flawed. It is not enough to say that if the physical criteria of a single employer were *imputed* to all similar employers one would be regarded as substantially limited in the major life activity of working *only as a result of this imputation*. An otherwise valid job requirement, such as a height requirement, does not become invalid simply because it *would* limit a person's employment opportunities in a substantial way *if* it were adopted by a substantial number of employers. Because petitioners have not alleged, and cannot demonstrate, that respondent's vision requirement reflects a belief that petitioners' vision substantially limits them, we agree with the decision of the Court of Appeals affirming the dismissal of petitioners' claim that they are regarded as disabled.

For these reasons, the decision of the Court of Appeals for the Tenth Circuit is affirmed.

It is so ordered.

JUSTICE GINSBURG, concurring.

I agree that 42 U.S.C. §12102(2)(A) does not reach the legions of people with correctable disabilities. The strongest clues to Congress' perception of the domain of the Americans with Disabilities Act (ADA), as I see it, are legislative findings that "some 43,000,000 Americans have one or more physical or mental disabilities," §12101(a)(1), and that "individuals with disabilities are a discrete and insular minority," persons "subjected to a history of purposeful unequal treatment, and relegated to a position of political powerlessness in our society." §12101(a)(7). These declarations are inconsistent with the enormously embracing definition of disability petitioners urge. As the Court demonstrates, the inclusion of correctable disabilities within the ADA's domain would extend the Act's coverage to far more than 43 million people. And persons whose uncorrected eyesight is poor, or who rely on daily medication for their well-being, can be found in every social and economic class; they do not cluster among the politically powerless, nor do they coalesce as historical victims of discrimination. In short, in no sensible way can one rank the large numbers of diverse individuals with corrected disabilities as a "discrete and insular minority.". . .

JUSTICE STEVENS, with whom JUSTICE BREYER joins, dissenting.

When it enacted the Americans with Disabilities Act in 1990, Congress certainly did not intend to require United Air Lines to hire unsafe or unqualified pilots. Nor, in all likelihood, did it view every person who wears glasses as a member of a "discrete and insular minority." Indeed, by reason of legislative myopia it may not have foreseen that its definition of "disability" might theoretically encompass, not just "some 43,000,000 Americans," 42 U.S.C. §12101(a)(1), but perhaps two or three times that number. Nevertheless, if we apply customary tools of statutory construction, it is quite clear that the threshold question whether an individual is "disabled" within the meaning of the Act—and, therefore, is entitled to the basic assurances that the Act affords—focuses on her past or present physical condition without regard to mitigation that has resulted from rehabilitation, self-improvement, prosthetic devices, or medication. One might reasonably argue that the general rule should not apply to an impairment that merely requires a nearsighted person to wear glasses. But I believe that, in order to be faithful to the remedial purpose of the Act, we should give it a generous, rather than a miserly, construction. . . .

I

[Stevens began by quoting the definition of "disability" from §12102(2); see majority opinion.] The three parts of this definition do not identify mutually exclusive, discrete categories. On the contrary, they furnish three overlapping formulas aimed at ensuring that individuals who now have, or ever had, a substantially limiting impairment are covered by the Act.

An example of a rather common condition illustrates this point: There are many individuals who have lost one or more limbs in industrial accidents, or perhaps in the service of their country in places like Iwo Jima. With the aid of prostheses, coupled with courageous determination and physical therapy, many of these hardy individuals can perform all of their major life activities just as efficiently as an average couch potato. If the Act were just concerned with their present ability to participate in society, many of these individuals' physical impairments would not be viewed as disabilities. Similarly, if the statute were solely concerned with whether these individuals viewed themselves as disabled—or with whether a majority of employers regarded them as unable to perform most jobs—many of these individuals would lack statutory protection from discrimination based on their prostheses.

The sweep of the statute's three-pronged definition, however, makes it pellucidly clear that Congress intended the Act to cover such persons. The fact that a prosthetic device, such as an artificial leg, has restored one's ability to perform major life activities surely cannot mean that subsection (A) of the definition is inapplicable. Nor should the fact that the individual considers himself (or actually is) "cured," or that a prospective employer considers him generally employable, mean that subsections (B) or (C) are inapplicable. But under the Court's emphasis on "the present indicative verb form" used in subsection (A), that subsection presumably would not apply. And under the Court's focus on the individual's "presen[t]—not potentia[l] or hypothetica[l]"—condition, and on whether a person is "precluded from a broad range of jobs," subsections (B) and (C) presumably would not apply.

In my view, when an employer refuses to hire the individual "because of" his prosthesis, and the prosthesis in no way affects his ability to do the job, that employer has unquestionably discriminated against the individual in violation of the Act. Subsection (B) of the definition, in fact, sheds a revelatory light on the question whether Congress was concerned only about the corrected or mitigated status of a person's impairment. If the Court is correct that "[a] 'disability' exists only where" a person's "present" or "actual" condition is substantially impaired, there would be no reason to include in the protected class those who were once disabled but who are now fully recovered.

The three prongs of the statute, rather, are most plausibly read together not to inquire into whether a person is currently "functionally" limited in a major life activity, but only into the existence of an impairment—present or past—that substantially limits, or did so limit, the individual before amelioration. This reading avoids the counterintuitive conclusion that the ADA's safeguards vanish when individuals make themselves more employable by ascertaining ways to overcome their physical or mental limitations.

To the extent that there may be doubt concerning the meaning of the statutory text, ambiguity is easily removed by looking at the legislative history. [In a lengthy passage, Stevens noted that both the Senate and the House committee reports specified that "whether a person has a disability should be assessed without regard to the availability of mitigating measures, such as reasonable accommodations or auxiliary aids."]

In addition, each of the three Executive agencies charged with implementing the Act has consistently interpreted the Act as mandating that the presence of disability turns on an individual's uncorrected state. . . .

In my judgment, the Committee Reports and the uniform agency regulations merely confirm the message conveyed by the text of the Act—at least insofar as it applies to impairments such as the loss of a limb, the inability to hear, or any condition such as diabetes that is substantially limiting without medication. The Act generally protects individuals who have "correctable" substantially limiting impairments from unjustified employment discrimination on the basis of those impairments. The question, then, is whether the fact that Congress was specifically concerned about protecting a class that included persons characterized as a "discrete and insular minority" and that it estimated that class to include "some 43,000,000 Americans" means that we should construe the term "disability" to exclude individuals with impairments that Congress probably did not have in mind.

II

. . . If a narrow reading of the term "disability" were necessary in order to avoid the danger that the Act might otherwise force United to hire pilots who might endanger the lives of their passengers, it would make good sense to use the

"43,000,000 Americans" finding to confine its coverage. There is, however, no such danger in this case. If a person is "disabled" within the meaning of the Act, she still cannot prevail on a claim of discrimination unless she can prove that the employer took action "because of" that impairment, and that she can, "with or without reasonable accommodation, . . . perform the essential functions" of the job of a commercial airline pilot. Even then, an employer may avoid liability if it shows that the criteria of having uncorrected visual acuity of at least 20/100 is "job-related and consistent with business necessity" or if such vision (even if correctable to 20/20) would pose a health or safety hazard. §12113(a) and (b).

This case, in other words, is not about whether petitioners are genuinely qualified or whether they can perform the job of an airline pilot without posing an undue safety risk. The case just raises the threshold question whether petitioners are members of the ADA's protected class. It simply asks whether the ADA lets petitioners in the door in the same way as the Age Discrimination in Employment Act of 1967 does for every person who is at least 40 years old, and as Title VII of the Civil Rights Act of 1964 does for every single individual in the work force. Inside that door lies nothing more than basic protection from irrational and unjustified discrimination because of a characteristic that is beyond a person's control. Hence, this particular case, at its core, is about whether, assuming that petitioners can prove that they are "qualified," the airline has any duty to come forward with some legitimate explanation for refusing to hire them because of their uncorrected eyesight, or whether the ADA leaves the airline free to decline to hire petitioners on this basis even if it is acting purely on the basis of irrational fear and stereotype.

. . . [I]t seems to me eminently within the purpose and policy of the ADA to require employers who make hiring and firing decisions based on individuals' uncorrected vision to clarify why having, for example, 20/100 uncorrected vision or better is a valid job requirement. So long as an employer explicitly makes its decision based on an impairment that in some condition is substantially limiting, it matters not under the structure of the Act whether that impairment is widely shared or so rare that it is seriously misunderstood. Either way, the individual has an impairment that is covered by the purpose of the ADA, and she should be protected against irrational stereotypes and unjustified disparate treatment on that basis.

I do not mean to suggest, of course, that the ADA should be read to prohibit discrimination on the basis of, say, blue eyes, deformed fingernails, or heights of less than six feet. Those conditions, to the extent that they are even "impairments," do not substantially limit individuals in any condition and thus are different in kind from the impairment in the case before us. While not all eyesight that can be enhanced by glasses is substantially limiting, having 20/200 vision in one's better eye is, without treatment, a significant hindrance. Only two percent of the population suffers from such myopia. Such acuity precludes a person from driving, shopping in a public store, or viewing a computer screen from a reasonable distance. Uncorrected vision, therefore, can be "substantially limiting" in the same way that unmedicated epilepsy or diabetes can be. Because Congress obviously intended to include individuals with the latter impairments in the Act's protected class, we should give petitioners the same protection.

III

... Instead of including petitioners within the Act's umbrella, however, the Court decides, in this opinion and its companion, to expel all individuals who, by using "measures [to] mitigate [their] impairment[s]," are able to overcome substantial limitations regarding major life activities. The Court, for instance, holds that severe hypertension that is substantially limiting without medication is not a "disability," *Murphy v. United Parcel Service, Inc.*, and—perhaps even more remarkably—indicates (directly contrary to the Act's legislative history) that diabetes that is controlled only with insulin treatments is not a "disability" either.

The Court claims that this rule is necessary to avoid requiring courts to "speculate" about a person's "hypothetical" condition and to preserve the Act's focus on making "individualized inquiries" into whether a person is disabled. The Court also asserts that its rejection of the general rule of viewing individuals in their unmitigated state prevents distorting the scope of the Act's protected class to cover a "much higher number" of persons than Congress estimated in its findings. And, I suspect, the Court has been cowed by respondent's persistent argument that viewing all individuals in their unmitigated state will lead to a tidal wave of lawsuits. None of the Court's reasoning, however, justifies a construction of the Act that will obviously deprive many of Congress' intended beneficiaries of the legal protection it affords. [Remainder of section omitted.]

IV

Occupational hazards characterize many trades. The farsighted pilot may have as much trouble seeing the instrument panel as the near sighted pilot has in identifying a safe place to land. The vision of appellate judges is sometimes subconsciously obscured by a concern that their decision will legalize issues best left to the private sphere or will magnify the work of an already-overburdened judiciary. Although these concerns may help to explain the Court's decision to chart its own course—rather than to follow the one that has been well marked by Congress, by the overwhelming consensus of circuit judges, and by the Executive officials charged with the responsibility of administering the ADA—they surely do not justify the Court's crabbed vision of the territory covered by this important statute.

Accordingly, although I express no opinion on the ultimate merits of petitioners' claim, I am persuaded that they have a disability covered by the ADA. I therefore respectfully dissent.

JUSTICE BREYER, dissenting.

We must draw a statutory line that either (1) will include within the category of persons authorized to bring suit under the Americans with Disabilities Act of 1990 some whom Congress may not have wanted to protect (those who wear ordinary eyeglasses), or (2) will exclude from the threshold category those whom Congress certainly did want to protect (those who successfully use corrective devices or medicines, such as hearing aids or prostheses or medicine for epilepsy). Faced with this dilemma, the statute's language, structure, basic purposes, and history require us to choose the former statutory line, as JUSTICE STEVENS (whose opinion I join) well explains. I would add that, if the more generous choice of threshold led to too many lawsuits that ultimately proved without merit or otherwise drew too much time and attention away from those whom Congress clearly sought to protect, there is a remedy. The Equal Employment Opportunity Commission (EEOC), through regulation, might draw finer definitional lines, excluding some of those who wear eyeglasses (say, those with certain vision impairments who readily can find corrective lenses), thereby cabining the overly broad extension of the statute that the majority fears. . . .

No. 98-208

Carole Kolstad, Petitioner v. American Dental Association

On writ of Certiorari to the United States Court of Appeals for the District of Columbia Circuit
[June 22, 1999]

JUSTICE O'CONNOR delivered the opinion of the Court.

Under the terms of the Civil Rights Act of 1991 (1991 Act), punitive damages are available in claims under Title VII of the Civil Rights Act of 1964 (Title VII), as amended, 42 U.S.C. §2000e *et seq.*, and the Americans with Disabilities Act of 1990, 42 U.S.C. §12101 *et seq.* Punitive damages are limited, however, to cases in which the employer has engaged in intentional discrimination and has done so "with malice or with reckless indifference to the federally protected rights of an aggrieved individual," 42 U.S.C. §1981a(b)(1). We here consider the circumstances under which punitive damages may be awarded in an action under Title VII.

I

A

In September 1992, Jack O'Donnell announced that he would be retiring as the Director of Legislation and Legislative Policy and Director of the Council on Government Affairs and Federal Dental Services for respondent, American Dental Association. Petitioner, Carole Kolstad, was employed with O'Donnell in respondent's Washington, D.C., office, where she was serving as respondent's Director of Federal Agency Relations. When she learned of O'Donnell's retirement, she expressed an interest in filling his position. Also interested in replacing O'Donnell was 'Tom Spangler, another employee in respondent's Washington office. At this time, Spangler was serving as the Association's Legislative Counsel, a position that involved him in respondent's legislative lobbying efforts. Both petitioner and Spangler had worked directly with O'Donnell, and both had received "distinguished" performance ratings by the acting head of the Washington office, Leonard Wheat.

Both petitioner and Spangler formally applied for O'Donnell's position, and Wheat requested that Dr. William Allen, then serving as respondent's Executive Director in the Association's Chicago office, make the ultimate promotion decision. After interviewing both petitioner and Spangler, Wheat recommended that Allen select Spangler for O'Donnell's post. Allen notified petitioner in December 1992 that he had, in fact, selected Spangler to serve as O'Donnell's replacement. Petitioner's challenge to this employment decision forms the basis of the instant action.

B

After first exhausting her avenues for relief before the Equal Employment Opportunity Commission, petitioner filed suit against the Association in Federal District Court, alleging that respondent's decision to promote Spangler was an act of employment discrimination proscribed under Title VII. In petitioner's view, the entire selection process was a sham. Counsel for petitioner urged the jury to conclude that Allen's stated reasons for selecting Spangler were pretext for gender discrimination, and that Spangler had been chosen for the position before the formal selection process began. Among the evidence offered in support of this view, there was testimony to the effect that Allen modified the description of O'Donnell's post to track aspects of the job description used to hire Spangler. In petitioner's view, this "preselection" procedure suggested an intent by the Association to discriminate on the basis of sex. Petitioner also introduced testimony at trial that Wheat told sexually offensive jokes and that he had referred to certain prominent professional women in derogatory terms. Moreover, Wheat allegedly refused to meet with petitioner for several weeks regarding her interest in O'Donnell's position. Petitioner testified, in fact, that she had historically experienced difficulty gaining access to meet with Wheat. Allen, for his part, testified that he conducted informal meetings regarding O'Donnell's position with both petitioner and Spangler, although petitioner stated that Allen did not discuss the position with her.

The District Court denied petitioner's request for a jury instruction on punitive damages. The jury concluded that respondent had discriminated against petitioner on the basis of sex and awarded her backpay totaling $52,718. Although the District Court subsequently denied respondent's motion for judgment as a matter of law on the issue of liability, the court made clear that it had not been persuaded that respondent had selected Spangler over petitioner on the basis of sex, and the court denied petitioner's requests for reinstatement and for attorney's fees. (DC 1996).

Petitioner appealed from the District Court's decisions denying her requested jury instruction on punitive damages and her request for reinstatement and attorney's fees. Respondent cross-appealed from the denial of its motion for judgment as a matter of law. In a split decision, a panel of the Court of Appeals for the District of Columbia Circuit reversed the District Court's decision denying petitioner's request for an instruction on punitive damages. (1997). In so doing, the court rejected respondent's claim that punitive damages are available under Title VII only in "extraordinarily egregious cases." . . .

The Court of Appeals subsequently agreed to rehear the case en banc, limited to the punitive damages question. In a divided opinion, the court affirmed the decision of the District Court. (1998). The en banc majority concluded that, "before the question of punitive damages can go to the jury, the evidence of the defendant's culpability must exceed what is needed to show intentional discrimination." Based on the 1991 Act's structure and legislative history, the court determined, specifically, that a defendant must be shown to have engaged in some "egregious" misconduct before the jury is permitted to consider a request for punitive damages. Although the court declined to set out the "egregiousness" requirement in any detail, it concluded that petitioner failed to make the requisite showing in the instant case. Judge Randolph concurred, relying chiefly on §1981a's structure as evidence of a congressional intent to "limi[t] punitive damages to exceptional cases." Judge Tatel wrote in dissent for five judges, who agreed generally with the panel majority.

We granted certiorari (1998) to resolve a conflict among the Federal Courts of Appeals concerning the circumstances under which a jury may consider a request for punitive damages under §1981a(b)(1). . . .

II

A

Prior to 1991, only equitable relief, primarily backpay, was available to prevailing Title VII plaintiffs; the statute provided no authority for an award of punitive or compensatory damages. With the passage of the 1991 Act, Congress provided for additional remedies, including punitive damages, for certain classes of Title VII and ADA violations.

The 1991 Act limits compensatory and punitive damages awards, however, to cases of "intentional discrimination"—that is, cases that do not rely on the "disparate impact" theory of discrimination. Section 1981a(b)(1) further qualifies the availability of punitive awards:

> "A complaining party may recover punitive damages under this section against a respondent (other than a government, government agency or political subdivision) if the complaining party demonstrates that the respondent engaged in a discriminatory practice or discriminatory practices *with malice or with reckless indifference to the federally protected rights of an aggrieved individual.*" (Emphasis added.)

The very structure of §1981a suggests a congressional intent to authorize punitive awards in only a subset of cases involving intentional discrimination. Section 1981a(a)(1) limits compensatory and punitive awards to instances of intentional discrimination, while §1981a(b)(1) requires plaintiffs to make an additional "demonstrat[ion]" of their eligibility for punitive damages. Congress plainly sought to impose two standards of liability—one for establishing a right to compensatory damages and another, higher standard that a plaintiff must satisfy to qualify for a punitive award.

The Court of Appeals sought to give life to this two-tiered structure by limiting punitive awards to cases involving intentional discrimination of an "egregious" nature. We credit the en banc majority's effort to effectuate congressional intent, but, in the end, we reject its conclusion that eligibility for punitive damages can only be described in terms of an employer's "egregious" misconduct. The terms "malice" and "reckless" ultimately focus on the actor's state of mind. . . . While egregious misconduct is evidence of the requisite mental state, §1981a does not limit plaintiffs to this form of evidence, and the section does not require a showing of egregious or outrageous discrimination independent of the employer's state of mind. Nor does the statute's structure imply an independent role for "egregiousness" in the face of congressional silence. On the contrary, the view that §1981a provides for punitive awards based solely on an employer's state of mind is consistent with the 1991 Act's distinction between equitable and compensatory relief. Intent determines which remedies are open to a plaintiff here as well; compensatory awards are available only where the employer has engaged in "*intentional* discrimination." §1981a(a)(1) (emphasis added).

Moreover, §1981a's focus on the employer's state of mind gives some effect to Congress' apparent intent to narrow the class of cases for which punitive awards are available to a subset of those involving intentional discrimination. The employer must act with "malice or with reckless indifference *to [the plaintiff's] federally protected rights.*" §1981a(b)(1) (emphasis added). The terms "malice" or "reckless indifference" pertain to the employer's knowledge that it may be acting in violation of federal law, not its awareness that it is engaging in discrimination. . . .

There will be circumstances where intentional discrimination does not give rise to punitive damages liability under this standard. In some instances, the employer may simply be unaware of the relevant federal prohibition. There will be cases, moreover, in which the employer discriminates with the distinct belief that its discrimination is lawful. The underlying theory of discrimination may be novel or otherwise poorly recognized, or an employer may reasonably believe that its discrimination satisfies a bona fide occupational qualification defense or other statutory exception to liability. . . .

At oral argument, respondent urged that the common law tradition surrounding punitive awards includes an "egregious misconduct" requirement. . . . We assume that Congress, in legislating on punitive awards, imported common law principles governing this form of relief. Moreover, some courts and commentators have described punitive awards as requiring both a specified state of mind and egregious or aggravated misconduct. . . .

Most often, however, eligibility for punitive awards is characterized in terms of a defendant's motive or intent. . . .

Egregious misconduct is often associated with the award of punitive damages, but the reprehensible character of the conduct is not generally considered apart from the requisite state of mind.

Conduct warranting punitive awards has been characterized as "egregious," for example, *because* of the defendant's mental state. . . . That conduct committed with the specified mental state may be characterized as egregious, however, is not to say that employers must engage in conduct with some independent, "egregious" quality before being subject to a punitive award.

To be sure, egregious or outrageous acts may serve as evidence supporting an inference of the requisite "evil motive." . . . Again, however, respondent has not shown that the terms "reckless indifference" and "malice," in the punitive damages context, have taken on a consistent definition including an independent, "egregiousness" requirement. . . .

B

The inquiry does not end with a showing of the requisite "malice or . . . reckless indifference" on the part of certain individuals, however. The plaintiff must impute liability for punitive damages to respondent. The en banc dissent recognized that agency principles place limits on vicarious liability for punitive damages. Likewise, the Solicitor General as *amicus* acknowledged during argument that common law limitations on a principal's liability in punitive awards for the acts of its agents apply in the Title VII context.

JUSTICE STEVENS urges that we should not consider these limitations here. [See opinion concurring in part and dissenting in part.] While we decline to engage in any definitive application of the agency standards to the facts of this case, it is important that we address the proper legal standards for imputing liability to an employer in the punitive damages context. This issue is intimately bound up with the preceding discussion on the evidentiary showing necessary to qualify for a punitive award, and it is easily subsumed within the question on which we granted certiorari—namely, "[i]n what circumstances may punitive damages be awarded under Title VII of the 1964 Civil Rights Act, as amended, for unlawful intentional discrimination?" . . . Here, moreover, limitations on the extent to which principals may be liable in punitive damages for the torts of their agents was the subject of discussion by both the en banc dissent and majority, and substantial questioning at oral argument. Nor did respondent discount the notion that agency principles may place limits on an employer's vicarious liability for punitive damages. In fact, respondent advanced the general position "that the higher agency principles, under common law, would apply to punitive damages." [Quoting transcript of oral argument.] Accordingly, we conclude that these potential limitations on the extent of respondent's liability are properly considered in the instant case.

The common law has long recognized that agency principles limit vicarious liability for punitive awards. [Citations omitted.] This is a principle, moreover, that this Court historically has endorsed. [Citations omitted.] Courts of Appeals, too, have relied on these liability limits in interpreting 42 U.S.C. §1981a. [Citations omitted.]

We have observed that, "[i]n express terms, Congress has directed federal courts to interpret Title VII based on agency principles." *Burlington Industries, Inc. v. Ellerth* (1998); see also *Meritor Savings Bank, FSB v. Vinson* (1986) (noting that, in interpreting Title VII, "Congress wanted courts to look to agency principles for guidance"). Observing the limits on liability that these principles impose is especially important when interpreting the 1991 Act. In promulgating the Act, Congress conspicuously left intact the "limits of employer liability" established in *Meritor.* . . .

Although jurisdictions disagree over whether and how to limit vicarious liability for punitive damages, . . . our interpretation of Title VII is informed by "the general common law of agency, rather than . . . the law of any particular State." The common law as codified in the Restatement (Second) of Agency provides a useful starting point for defining this general common law. . . . The Restatement of Agency places strict limits on the extent to which an agent's misconduct may be imputed to the principal for purposes of awarding punitive damages:

> "Punitive damages can properly be awarded against a master or other principal because of an act by an agent if, but only if:
> "(a) the principal authorized the doing and the manner of the act, or
> "(b) the agent was unfit and the principal was reckless in employing him, or
> "(c) the agent was employed in a managerial capacity and was acting in the scope of employment, or
> "(d) the principal or a managerial agent of the principal ratified or approved the act."

See also Restatement (Second) of Torts.

Holding employers liable for punitive damages when they engage in good faith efforts to comply with Title VII, however, is in some tension with the very principles underlying common law limitations on vicarious liability for punitive damages—that it is "improper ordinarily to award punitive damages against one who himself is personally innocent and therefore liable only vicariously." Restatement (Second) of Torts. Where an employer has undertaken such good faith efforts at Title VII compliance, it "demonstrat[es] that it never acted in reckless disregard of federally protected rights." [Quoting Judge Tatel's dissent in Court of Appeals decision.] . . .

Applying the Restatement of Agency's "scope of employment" rule in the Title VII punitive damages context, moreover, would reduce the incentive for employers to implement antidiscrimination programs. In fact, such a rule would likely exacerbate concerns among employers that §1981a's "malice" and "reckless indifference" standard penalizes those employers who educate themselves and their employees on Title VII's prohibitions. . . . Dissuading employers from implementing programs or policies to prevent discrimination in the workplace is directly contrary to the purposes underlying Title VII. The statute's "primary objective" is "a prophylactic one;" it aims, chiefly, "not to provide redress but to avoid harm." [Quoting prior Court decisions.] . . . The purposes underlying Title VII are . . . advanced where employers are encouraged to adopt antidiscrimination policies and to educate their personnel on Title VII's prohibitions.

In light of the perverse incentives that the Restatement's "scope of employment" rules create, we are compelled to modify these principles to avoid undermining the objectives underlying Title VII. . . . Recognizing Title VII as an effort to promote prevention as well as remediation, and observing the very principles underlying the Restatements' strict limits on vicarious liability for punitive damages, we agree that, in the punitive damages context, an employer may not be vicariously liable for the discriminatory employment decisions of managerial agents where these decisions are contrary to the employer's "good-faith efforts to comply with Title VII." [Tatel, J., dissenting]. As the dissent recognized, "[g]iving punitive damages protection to employers who make good-faith efforts to prevent discrimination in the workplace accomplishes" Title VII's objective of "motivat[ing] employers to detect and deter Title VII violations."

We have concluded that an employer's conduct need not be independently "egregious" to satisfy §1981a's requirements for a punitive damages award, although evidence of egregious misconduct may be used to meet the plaintiff's burden of proof. We leave for remand the question whether petitioner can identify facts sufficient to support an inference that the requisite mental state can be imputed to respondent. The parties have not yet had an opportunity to marshal the record evidence in support of their views on the application of agency principles in the instant case, and the en banc majority had no reason to resolve the issue because it concluded that petitioner had failed to demonstrate the requisite "egregious" misconduct. Although trial testimony established that Allen made the ultimate decision to promote Spangler while serving as petitioner's interim executive director, respondent's highest position, it remains to be seen whether petitioner can make a sufficient showing that Allen acted with malice or reckless indifference to petitioner's Title VII rights. Even if it could be established that Wheat effectively selected O'Donnell's replacement, moreover, several questions would remain, e.g., whether Wheat was serving in a "managerial capacity" and whether he behaved with malice or reckless indifference to petitioner's rights. It may also be necessary to determine whether the Association had been making good faith efforts to enforce an antidiscrimination policy. We leave these issues for resolution on remand.

For the foregoing reasons, the decision of the Court of Appeals is vacated, and the case is remanded for proceedings consistent with this opinion.

It is so ordered.

CHIEF JUSTICE REHNQUIST, with whom JUSTICE THOMAS joins, concurring in part and dissenting in part.

For the reasons stated by Judge Randolph in his concurring opinion in the Court of Appeals, I would hold that Congress' two-tiered scheme of Title VII monetary liability implies that there is an egregiousness requirement that reserves punitive damages only for the worst cases of intentional discrimination. Since the Court has determined otherwise, however, I join that portion of Part II-B of the Court's opinion holding that principles of agency law place a significant limitation, and in many foreseeable cases a complete bar, on employer liability for punitive damages.

JUSTICE STEVENS, with whom JUSTICE SOUTER, JUSTICE GINSBURG, and JUSTICE BREYER join, concurring in part and dissenting in part.

The Court properly rejects the Court of Appeals' holding that defendants in Title VII actions must engage in "egregious" misconduct before a jury may be permitted to consider a request for punitive damages. Accordingly, I join Parts I and II-A of its opinion. I write separately, however, because I strongly disagree with the Court's decision to volunteer commentary on an issue that the parties have not briefed and that the facts of this case do not present. I would simply remand for a trial on punitive damages.

I

In enacting the Civil Rights Act of 1991 (1991 Act), Congress established a three-tiered system of remedies for a broad range of discriminatory conduct, including violations of Title VII of the Civil Rights Act of 1964, 42 U.S.C. §2000e *et seq.*, as well as some violations of the Americans with Disabilities Act of 1990 (ADA), 42 U.S.C. §12101 *et seq.* Equitable remedies are available for disparate impact violations; compensatory damages for intentional disparate treatment; and punitive damages for intentional discrimination "with malice or with reckless indifference to the federally protected rights of an aggrieved individual." §1981a(b)(1). . . .

Construing §1981a(b)(1) to impose a purely mental standard is perfectly consistent with the structure and purpose of the 1991 Act. . . . [T]he 1991 Act's "willful" or "reckless disregard" standard respects the Act's "two-tiered" damages scheme while deterring future intentionally unlawful discrimination. There are, for reasons the Court explains, numerous instances in which an employer might intentionally treat an individual differently because of her race, gender, religion, or disability without knowing that it is violating Title VII or the ADA. In order to recover compensatory damages under the 1991 Act, victims of unlawful disparate treatment must prove that the defendants' *conduct* was intentional, but they need not prove that the defendants either knew or should have known that they were *violating the law*. It is the additional element of willful or reckless disregard of the law that justifies a penalty of . . . punitive damages in the broad range of cases covered by the 1991 Act.

It is of course true that as our society moves closer to the goal of eliminating intentional, invidious discrimination, the core mandates of Title VII and the ADA are becoming increasingly ingrained in employers' minds. As more employers come to appreciate the importance and the proportions of those statutes' mandates, the number of federal violations will continue to decrease accordingly. But at the same time, one could reasonably believe, as Congress did, that as our national resolve against employment discrimination hardens, deliberate violations of Title VII and the ADA become increasingly blameworthy and more properly the subject of "societal condemnation" in the form of punitive damages. Indeed, it would have been rather perverse for Congress to conclude that the increasing acceptance of antidiscrimination laws in the workplace somehow mitigates willful violations of those laws such that only those violations that are accompanied by particularly outlandish acts warrant special deterrence. . . .

If we accept the jury's appraisal of the evidence in this case and draw, as we must when reviewing the denial of a jury instruction, all reasonable inferences in petitioner's favor, there is ample evidence from which the jury could have concluded that respondent willfully violated Title VII. Petitioner emphasized, at trial and in her briefs to this Court, that respondent took "a tangible employment action" against her in the form of denying a promotion. Evidence indicated that petitioner was the more qualified of the two candidates for the job. Respondent's decisionmakers, who were senior executives of the Association, were known occasionally to tell sexually offensive jokes and referred to professional women in derogatory terms. The record further supports an inference that these executives not only deliberately refused to consider petitioner fairly and to promote her because she is a woman, but they manipulated the job requirements and conducted a "sham" selection procedure in an attempt to conceal their misconduct.

There is no claim that respondent's decisionmakers violated any company policy; that they were not acting within the scope of their employment; or that respondent has ever disavowed their conduct. Neither the respondent nor its two decisionmakers claimed at trial any ignorance of Title VII's requirements, nor did either offer any "good-faith" reason for believing that being a man was a legitimate requirement for the job. Rather, at trial respondent resorted to false, pretextual explanations for its refusal to promote petitioner.

The record, in sum, contains evidence from which a jury might find that respondent acted with reckless indifference to petitioner's federally protected rights. It follows, in my judgment, that the three-judge panel of the Court of Appeals correctly decided to remand the case to the district court for a trial on punitive damages. To the extent that the Court's opinion fails to direct that disposition, I respectfully dissent.

II

In Part II-B of its opinion, the Court discusses the question "whether liability for punitive damages may be imputed to respondent" under "agency principles." That is a question that neither of the parties has ever addressed in this litigation and that respondent, at least, has expressly disavowed. When prodded at oral argument, counsel for respondent twice stood firm on this point. "[W]e all agree," he twice repeated, "that that precise issue is not before the Court." Nor did any of the 11 judges in the Court of Appeals believe that it was applicable to the dispute at hand—presumably because promotion decisions are quintessential "company acts," (quoting Court of Appeals opinion), and because the two executives who made this promotion decision were the executive director of the Association and the acting head of its Washington office. (Quoting Judge Tatel's dissenting opinion.) Judge Tatel, who the Court implies raised the agency issue, in fact explicitly (and correctly) concluded that "[t]his case does not present these or analogous circumstances."

The absence of briefing or meaningful argument by the parties makes this Court's gratuitous decision to volunteer an opinion on this nonissue particularly ill advised. It is not this Court's practice to consider arguments—specifically, alternative defenses of the judgment under review—that were not presented in the brief in opposition to the petition for certiorari. See this Court's Rule 15.2. Indeed, on two occasions in this very Term, we refused to do so despite the fact that the issues were briefed and argued by the parties. See *South Central Bell Telephone Co. v. Alabama* (1999); *Roberts v. Galen of Virginia, Inc.* (1999). If we declined to reach alternate defenses under those circumstances, surely we should do so here.

Nor is it accurate for the Court to imply that the Solicitor General as *amicus* advocates a course similar to that which the Court takes regarding the agency question. The Solicitor General, like the parties, did not brief any agency issue. At oral argument, he correspondingly stated that the issue "is not really presented here." He then responded to the Court's questions by stating that the Federal Government believes that whenever a tangible employment consequence is involved §1981a incorporates the "managerial capacity" principles espoused by §217C of the Restatement (Second) of Agency. But to the extent that the Court tinkers with the Restatement's standard, it is rejecting the Government's view of its own statute without giving it an opportunity to be heard on the issue.

Accordingly, while I agree with the Court's rejection of the en banc majority's holding on the only issue that it confronted, I respectfully dissent from the Court's failure to order a remand for trial on the punitive damages issue.

No. 98-436

John H. Alden, et al., Petitioners v. Maine

On writ of certiorari to the Supreme Judicial Court of Maine

[June 23, 1999]

JUSTICE KENNEDY delivered the opinion of the Court.

In 1992, petitioners, a group of probation officers, filed suit against their employer, the State of Maine, in the United States District Court for the District of Maine. The officers alleged the State had violated the overtime provisions of the Fair Labor Standards Act of 1938 (FLSA), 29 U.S.C. §201 *et seq.*, and sought compensation and liquidated damages. While the suit was pending, this Court decided *Seminole Tribe of Fla. v. Florida* (1996), which made it clear that Congress lacks power under Article I to abrogate the States' sovereign immunity from suits commenced or prosecuted in the federal courts. Upon consideration of *Seminole Tribe*, the District Court dismissed petitioners' action, and the Court of Appeals affirmed. *Mills v. Maine* (CA1 1997). Petitioners then filed the same action in state court. The state trial court dismissed the suit on the basis of sovereign immunity, and the Maine Supreme Judicial Court affirmed. (1998).

The Maine Supreme Judicial Court's decision conflicts with the decision of the Supreme Court of Arkansas, *Jacoby v. Arkansas Dept. of Ed.* (1998), and calls into question the constitutionality of the provisions of the FLSA purporting to authorize private actions against States in their own courts without regard for consent,

see 29 U.S.C. §216(b), 203(x). In light of the importance of the question presented and the conflict between the courts, we granted certiorari. (1998). The United
States intervened as a petitioner to defend the statute.

We hold that the powers delegated to Congress under Article I of the United
States Constitution do not include the power to subject nonconsenting States
to private suits for damages in state courts. We decide as well that the State of
Maine has not consented to suits for overtime pay and liquidated damages under
the FLSA. On these premises we affirm the judgment sustaining dismissal of the
suit.

I

The Eleventh Amendment makes explicit reference to the States' immunity
from suits "commenced or prosecuted against one of the United States by Citizens
of another State, or by Citizens or Subjects of any Foreign State." We have, as a
result, sometimes referred to the States' immunity from suit as "Eleventh
Amendment immunity." The phrase is convenient shorthand but something of a
misnomer, for the sovereign immunity of the States neither derives from nor is
limited by the terms of the Eleventh Amendment. Rather, as the Constitution's
structure, and its history, and the authoritative interpretations by this Court make
clear, the States' immunity from suit is a fundamental aspect of the sovereignty
which the States enjoyed before the ratification of the Constitution, and which
they retain today (either literally or by virtue of their admission into the Union
upon an equal footing with the other States) except as altered by the plan of the
Convention or certain constitutional Amendments.

A

Although the Constitution establishes a National Government with broad,
often plenary authority over matters within its recognized competence, the founding document "specifically recognizes the States as sovereign entities." *Seminole
Tribe of Fla. v. Florida.* . . . Various textual provisions of the Constitution assume
the States' continued existence and active participation in the fundamental
processes of governance. See *Printz v. United States* (1997) (citing Art. III, §2; Art.
IV, §2-4; Art. V). The limited and enumerated powers granted to the Legislative,
Executive, and Judicial Branches of the National Government, moreover, under-
score the vital role reserved to the States by the constitutional design, see, *e.g.*, Art.
I, §8; Art. II, §2-3; Art. III, §2. Any doubt regarding the constitutional role of the
States as sovereign entities is removed by the Tenth Amendment, which, like the
other provisions of the Bill of Rights, was enacted to allay lingering concerns
about the extent of the national power. The Amendment confirms the promise
implicit in the original document: "The powers not delegated to the United States
by the Constitution, nor prohibited by it to the States, are reserved to the States
respectively, or to the people."

The States thus retain "a residuary and inviolable sovereignty." The Federalist
No. 39 [Madison]. They are not relegated to the role of mere provinces or political corporations, but retain the dignity, though not the full authority, of sovereignty.

B

The generation that designed and adopted our federal system considered immunity from private suits central to sovereign dignity. When the Constitution was ratified, it was well established in English law that the Crown could not be sued without consent in its own courts. . . .

Although the American people had rejected other aspects of English political theory, the doctrine that a sovereign could not be sued without its consent was universal in the States when the Constitution was drafted and ratified. . . .

The ratification debates, furthermore, underscored the importance of the States' sovereign immunity to the American people. Grave concerns were raised by the provisions of Article III which extended the federal judicial power to controversies between States and citizens of other States or foreign nations. . . . The leading advocates of the Constitution assured the people in no uncertain terms that the Constitution would not strip the States of sovereign immunity. [Quotations omitted from *Federalist* No. 81, written by Hamilton, and from Madison and John Marshall during debates at the Virginia ratifying convention.] Although the state conventions which addressed the issue of sovereign immunity in their formal ratification documents sought to clarify the point by constitutional amendment, they made clear that they, like Hamilton, Madison, and Marshall, understood the Constitution as drafted to preserve the States' immunity from private suits. . . .

Despite the persuasive assurances of the Constitution's leading advocates and the expressed understanding of the only state conventions to address the issue in explicit terms, this Court held, just five years after the Constitution was adopted, that Article III authorized a private citizen of another State to sue the State of Georgia without its consent. *Chisholm v. Georgia* (1793). [Discussion of justices' opinions omitted.]

The States . . . responded with outrage to the decision. The Massachusetts Legislature, for example, denounced the decision as "repugnant to the first principles of a federal government," and called upon the State's Senators and Representatives to take all necessary steps to "remove any clause or article of the Constitution, which can be construed to imply or justify a decision, that, a State is compellable to answer in any suit by an individual or individuals in any Court of the United States." Georgia's response was more intemperate: Its House of Representatives passed a bill providing that anyone attempting to enforce the *Chisholm* decision would be "guilty of felony and shall suffer death, without benefit of clergy, by being hanged."

An initial proposal to amend the Constitution was introduced in the House of Representatives the day after *Chisholm* was announced; the proposal adopted as the Eleventh Amendment was introduced in the Senate promptly following an intervening recess. Congress turned to the latter proposal with great dispatch; little more than two months after its introduction it had been endorsed by both Houses and forwarded to the States.

Each House spent but a single day discussing the Amendment, and the vote in each House was close to unanimous. . . . All attempts to weaken the Amendment were defeated. . . .

It might be argued that the *Chisholm* decision was a correct interpretation of the constitutional design and that the Eleventh Amendment represented a deviation from the original understanding. This, however, seems unsupportable. First, . . . the majority failed to address either the practice or the understanding that prevailed in the States at the time the Constitution was adopted. Second, even a casual reading of the opinions suggests the majority suspected the decision would be unpopular and surprising. . . .

[T]he swiftness and near unanimity with which the Eleventh Amendment was adopted suggest "either that the Court had not captured the original understanding, or that the country had changed its collective mind most rapidly." D. Currie, *The Constitution in the Supreme Court: The First Century* (1985). The more reasonable interpretation, of course, is that regardless of the views of four Justices in *Chisholm*, the country as a whole—which had adopted the Constitution just five years earlier—had not understood the document to strip the States of their immunity from private suits. . . .

C

The Court has been consistent in interpreting the adoption of the Eleventh Amendment as conclusive evidence "that the decision in *Chisholm* was contrary to the well-understood meaning of the Constitution," *Seminole Tribe*, and that the views expressed by Hamilton, Madison, and Marshall during the ratification debates, and by Justice Iredell in his dissenting opinion in *Chisholm* reflect the original understanding of the Constitution. [Citations omitted.] In accordance with this understanding, we have recognized a "presumption that no anomalous and unheard-of proceedings or suits were intended to be raised up by the Constitution—anomalous and unheard of when the constitution was adopted." *Hans*. As a consequence, we have looked to "history and experience, and the established order of things," rather than "[a]dhering to the mere letter" of the Eleventh Amendment in determining the scope of the States' constitutional immunity from suit.

Following this approach, the Court has upheld States' assertions of sovereign immunity in various contexts falling outside the literal text of the Eleventh Amendment. In *Hans v. Louisiana* [1890], the Court held that sovereign immunity barred a citizen from suing his own State under the federal-question head of jurisdiction. The Court was unmoved by the petitioner's argument that the Eleventh Amendment, by its terms, applied only to suits brought by citizens of other States. . . . Later decisions rejected similar requests to conform the principle of sovereign immunity to the strict language of the Eleventh Amendment in holding that nonconsenting States are immune from suits brought by federal corporations, *Smith v. Reeves* (1900), foreign nations, *Principality of Monaco* [1934], or Indian tribes, *Blatchford v. Native Village of Noatak* (1991), and in concluding that sovereign immunity is a defense to suits in admiralty, though the text of the Eleventh Amendment addresses only suits "in law or equity," *Ex parte New York* (1921).

These holdings reflect a settled doctrinal understanding, consistent with the views of the leading advocates of the Constitution's ratification, that sovereign immunity derives not from the Eleventh Amendment but from the structure of the original Constitution itself. [Citations omitted.] The Eleventh Amendment confirmed rather than established sovereign immunity as a constitutional principle; it follows that the scope of the States' immunity from suit is demarcated not by the text of the Amendment alone but by fundamental postulates implicit in the constitutional design. . . .

II

. . . While the constitutional principle of sovereign immunity does pose a bar to federal jurisdiction over suits against nonconsenting States, this is not the only structural basis of sovereign immunity implicit in the constitutional design. Rather, "[t]here is also the postulate that States of the Union, still possessing attributes of sovereignty, shall be immune from suits, without their consent, save where there has been 'a surrender of this immunity in the plan of the convention.' " *Principality of Monaco* (quoting The Federalist No. 81). This separate and distinct structural principle is not directly related to the scope of the judicial power established by Article III, but inheres in the system of federalism established by the Constitution. In exercising its Article I powers Congress may subject the States to private suits in their own courts only if there is "compelling evidence" that the States were required to surrender this power to Congress pursuant to the constitutional design. *Blatchford.*

A

Petitioners contend the text of the Constitution and our recent sovereign immunity decisions establish that the States were required to relinquish this portion of their sovereignty. We turn first to these sources.

1

Article I, §8 grants Congress broad power to enact legislation in several enumerated areas of national concern. The Supremacy Clause, furthermore, provides:

> "This Constitution, and the Laws of the United States which shall be made in Pursuance thereof . . . shall be the supreme Law of the Land; and the Judges in every State shall be bound thereby, any Thing in the Constitution or Laws of any state to the Contrary notwithstanding." U.S. Const., Art. VI.

It is contended that, by virtue of these provisions, where Congress enacts legislation subjecting the States to suit, the legislation by necessity overrides the sovereign immunity of the States.

As is evident from its text, however, the Supremacy Clause enshrines as "the supreme Law of the Land" only those federal Acts that accord with the constitutional design. Appeal to the Supremacy Clause alone merely raises the question whether a law is a valid exercise of the national power. . . .

The Constitution, by delegating to Congress the power to establish the supreme law of the land when acting within its enumerated powers, does not foreclose a State from asserting immunity to claims arising under federal law merely because that law derives not from the State itself but from the national power. . . . When a State asserts its immunity to suit, the question is not the primacy of federal law but the implementation of the law in a manner consistent with the constitutional sovereignty of the States.

Nor can we conclude that the specific Article I powers delegated to Congress necessarily include, by virtue of the Necessary and Proper Clause or otherwise, the incidental authority to subject the States to private suits as a means of achieving objectives otherwise within the scope of the enumerated powers.

Although some of our decisions had endorsed this contention, see *Parden v. Terminal R. Co. of Ala. Docks Dept.* (1964); *Pennsylvania v. Union Gas Co.* (1989) (plurality opinion), they have since been overruled, see *Seminole Tribe*; *College Savings Bank v. Florida Prepaid Postsecondary Ed. Expense Bd.* [1999]. . . .

The cases we have cited, of course, came at last to the conclusion that neither the Supremacy Clause nor the enumerated powers of Congress confer authority to abrogate the States' immunity from suit in federal court. The logic of the decisions, however, does not turn on the forum in which the suits were prosecuted but extends to state-court suits as well.

The dissenting opinion seeks to reopen these precedents, contending that state sovereign immunity must derive either from the common law (in which case the dissent contends it is defeasible by statute) or from natural law (in which case the dissent believes it cannot bar a federal claim). As should be obvious to all, this is a false dichotomy. The text and the structure of the Constitution protect various rights and principles. Many of these, such as the right to trial by jury and the prohibition on unreasonable searches and seizures, derive from the common law. The common-law lineage of these rights does not mean they are defeasible by statute or remain mere common-law rights, however. They are, rather, constitutional rights, and form the fundamental law of the land.

Although the sovereign immunity of the States derives at least in part from the common-law tradition, the structure and history of the Constitution make clear that the immunity exists today by constitutional design. The dissent has provided no persuasive evidence that the founding generation regarded the States' sovereign immunity as defeasible by federal statute. . . .

2

There are isolated statements in some of our cases suggesting that the Eleventh Amendment is inapplicable in state courts. [Citations omitted.] This, of course, is a truism as to the literal terms of the Eleventh Amendment. As we have explained, however, the bare text of the Amendment is not an exhaustive description of the States' constitutional immunity from suit. The cases, furthermore, do not decide the question presented here—whether the States retain immunity from private suits in their own courts notwithstanding an attempted abrogation by the Congress. [Remainder of subsection omitted.]

B

Whether Congress has authority under Article I to abrogate a State's immunity from suit in its own courts is, then, a question of first impression. In determining whether there is "compelling evidence" that this derogation of the States' sovereignty is "inherent in the constitutional compact," *Blatchford*, we continue our discussion of history, practice, precedent, and the structure of the Constitution.

1

We look first to evidence of the original understanding of the Constitution. Petitioners contend that because the ratification debates and the events surrounding the adoption of the Eleventh Amendment focused on the States' immunity from suit in federal courts, the historical record gives no instruction as to the founding generation's intent to preserve the States' immunity from suit in their own courts.

We believe, however, that the founders' silence is best explained by the simple fact that no one, not even the Constitution's most ardent opponents, suggested the document might strip the States of the immunity. In light of the overriding concern regarding the States' war-time debts, together with the well known creativity, foresight, and vivid imagination of the Constitution's opponents, the silence is most instructive. It suggests the sovereign's right to assert immunity from suit in its own courts was a principle so well established that no one conceived it would be altered by the new Constitution. . . . [Remainder of subsection omitted.]

2

Our historical analysis is supported by early congressional practice. . . . Although early Congresses enacted various statutes authorizing federal suits in state court, we have discovered no instance in which they purported to authorize suits against nonconsenting States in these fora. . . . It thus appears early Congresses did not believe they had the power to authorize private suits against the States in their own courts.

Not only were statutes purporting to authorize private suits against nonconsenting States in state courts not enacted by early Congresses, statutes purporting to authorize such suits in any forum are all but absent from our historical experience. The first statute we confronted that even arguably purported to subject the States to private actions was the [Federal Employers' Liability Act]. . . . As we later recognized, however, even this statute did not clearly create a cause of action against the States. The provisions of the FLSA at issue here . . . are among the first statutory enactments purporting in express terms to subject nonconsenting States to private suits. Although similar statutes have multiplied in the last generation, "they are of such recent vintage that they are no more probative than the [FLSA] of a constitutional tradition that lends meaning to the text. Their persuasive force is far outweighed by almost two centuries of apparent congressional avoidance of the practice." [Quoting *Printz*.]

Even the recent statutes, moreover, do not provide evidence of an understanding that Congress has a greater power to subject States to suit in their own courts than in federal courts. On the contrary, the statutes purport to create causes of actions against the States which are enforceable in federal, as well as state, court. To the extent recent practice thus departs from longstanding tradition, it reflects not so much an understanding that the States have surrendered their immunity from suit in their own courts as the erroneous view, perhaps inspired by *Parden* and *Union Gas*, that Congress may subject nonconsenting States to private suits in any forum.

3

The theory and reasoning of our earlier cases suggest the States do retain a constitutional immunity from suit in their own courts. We have often described the States' immunity in sweeping terms, without reference to whether the suit was prosecuted in state or federal court. [Citations omitted.]

We have said on many occasions, furthermore, that the States retain their immunity from private suits prosecuted in their own courts. [Citations omitted.]

We have also relied on the States' immunity in their own courts as a premise in our Eleventh Amendment rulings. . . .

In particular, the exception to our sovereign immunity doctrine recognized in *Ex parte Young* (1908) is based in part on the premise that sovereign immunity bars relief against States and their officers in both state and federal courts, and that certain suits for declaratory or injunctive relief against state officers must therefore be permitted if the Constitution is to remain the supreme law of the land. . . . Had we not understood the States to retain a constitutional immunity from suit in their own courts, the need for the *Ex parte Young* rule would have been less pressing, and the rule would not have formed so essential a part of our sovereign immunity doctrine. . . .

4

Our final consideration is whether a congressional power to subject nonconsenting States to private suits in their own courts is consistent with the structure of the Constitution. We look both to the essential principles of federalism and to the special role of the state courts in the constitutional design.

Although the Constitution grants broad powers to Congress, our federalism requires that Congress treat the States in a manner consistent with their status as residuary sovereigns and joint participants in the governance of the Nation. . . .

Petitioners contend that immunity from suit in federal court suffices to preserve the dignity of the States. Private suits against nonconsenting States, however, present "the indignity of subjecting a State to the coercive process of judicial tribunals at the instance of private parties," *In re Ayers* [1887], regardless of the forum. Not only must a State defend or default but also it must face the prospect of being thrust, by federal fiat and against its will, into the disfavored status of a debtor, subject to the power of private citizens to levy on its treasury or perhaps even government buildings or property which the State administers on the public's behalf.

In some ways, of course, a congressional power to authorize private suits against nonconsenting States in their own courts would be even more offensive to state sovereignty than a power to authorize the suits in a federal forum. Although the immunity of one sovereign in the courts of another has often depended in part on comity or agreement, the immunity of a sovereign in its own courts has always been understood to be within the sole control of the sovereign itself. A power to press a State's own courts into federal service to coerce the other branches of the State, furthermore, is the power first to turn the State against itself and ultimately to commandeer the entire political machinery of the State against its will and at the behest of individuals. Such plenary federal control of state governmental processes denigrates the separate sovereignty of the States.

It is unquestioned that the Federal Government retains its own immunity from suit not only in state tribunals but also in its own courts. In light of our constitutional system recognizing the essential sovereignty of the States, we are reluctant to conclude that the States are not entitled to a reciprocal privilege.

Underlying constitutional form are considerations of great substance. Private suits against nonconsenting States—especially suits for money damages—may threaten the financial integrity of the States. It is indisputable that, at the time of the founding, many of the States could have been forced into insolvency but for their immunity from private suits for money damages. Even today, an unlimited congressional power to authorize suits in state court to levy upon the treasuries of the States for compensatory damages, attorney's fees, and even punitive damages could create staggering burdens, giving Congress a power and a leverage over the States that is not contemplated by our constitutional design. The potential national power would pose a severe and notorious danger to the States and their resources.

A congressional power to strip the States of their immunity from private suits in their own courts would pose more subtle risks as well. . . . When the States' immunity from private suits is disregarded, "the course of their public policy and the administration of their public affairs" may become "subject to and controlled by the mandates of judicial tribunals without their consent, and in favor of individual interests." *In re Ayers.* While the States have relinquished their immunity from suit in some special contexts. . . , this surrender carries with it substantial costs to the autonomy, the decisionmaking ability, and the sovereign capacity of the States.

A general federal power to authorize private suits for money damages would place unwarranted strain on the States' ability to govern in accordance with the will of their citizens. Today, as at the time of the founding, the allocation of scarce resources among competing needs and interests lies at the heart of the political process. While the judgment creditor of the State may have a legitimate claim for compensation, other important needs and worthwhile ends compete for access to the public fisc. Since all cannot be satisfied in full, it is inevitable that difficult decisions involving the most sensitive and political of judgments must be made. If the principle of representative government is to be preserved to the States, the balance between competing interests must be reached after deliberation by the political process established by the citizens of the State, not by judicial decree mandated by the Federal Government and invoked by the private citizen. . . .

The asserted authority would blur not only the distinct responsibilities of the State and National Governments but also the separate duties of the judicial and political branches of the state governments. . . . A State is entitled to order the processes of its own governance, assigning to the political branches, rather than the courts, the responsibility for directing the payment of debts. . . . If Congress could displace a State's allocation of governmental power and responsibility, the judicial branch of the State, whose legitimacy derives from fidelity to the law, would be compelled to assume a role not only foreign to its experience but beyond its competence as defined by the very constitution from which its existence derives.

Congress cannot abrogate the States' sovereign immunity in federal court; were the rule to be different here, the National Government would wield greater power in the state courts than in its own judicial instrumentalities. . . .

The resulting anomaly cannot be explained by reference to the special role of the state courts in the constitutional design. Although Congress may not require the legislative or executive branches of the States to enact or administer federal regulatory programs, it may require state courts . . . "to enforce federal prescriptions, insofar as those prescriptions relat[e] to matters appropriate for the judicial power," *Printz*. It would be an unprecedented step, however, to infer from the fact that Congress may declare federal law binding and enforceable in state courts the further principle that Congress' authority to pursue federal objectives through the state judiciaries exceeds not only its power to press other branches of the State into its service but even its control over the federal courts themselves. The conclusion would imply that Congress may in some cases act only through instrumentalities of the States. . . .

We have recognized that Congress may require state courts to hear only "matters appropriate for the judicial power," *Printz*. Our sovereign immunity precedents establish that suits against nonconsenting States are not "properly susceptible of litigation in courts," *Hans*, and, as a result, that "[t]he 'entire judicial power granted by the Constitution' does not embrace authority to entertain such suits in the absence of the State's consent." *Principality of Monaco* (quoting *Ex parte New York*). . . . We are aware of no constitutional precept that would admit of a congressional power to require state courts to entertain federal suits which are not within the judicial power of the United States and could not be heard in federal courts. . . .

In light of history, practice, precedent, and the structure of the Constitution, we hold that the States retain immunity from private suit in their own courts, an immunity beyond the congressional power to abrogate by Article I legislation.

III

The constitutional privilege of a State to assert its sovereign immunity in its own courts does not confer upon the State a concomitant right to disregard the Constitution or valid federal law. The States and their officers are bound by obligations imposed by the Constitution and by federal statutes that comport with the constitutional design. We are unwilling to assume the States will refuse to honor the Constitution or obey the binding laws of the United States. . . .

Sovereign immunity, moreover, does not bar all judicial review of state compliance with the Constitution and valid federal law. Rather, certain limits are implicit in the constitutional principle of state sovereign immunity.

The first of these limits is that sovereign immunity bars suits only in the absence of consent. Many States, on their own initiative, have enacted statutes consenting to a wide variety of suits. . . . Nor, subject to constitutional limitations, does the Federal Government lack the authority or means to seek the States' voluntary consent to private suits. . . .

The States have consented, moreover, to some suits pursuant to the plan of the Convention or to subsequent constitutional amendments. In ratifying the Constitution, the States consented to suits brought by other States or by the Federal Government. A suit which is commenced and prosecuted against a State in the name of the United States by those who are entrusted with the constitutional duty to "take Care that the Laws be faithfully executed," U.S. Const., Art. II, §3, differs in kind from the suit of an individual: While the Constitution contemplates suits among the members of the federal system as an alternative to extralegal measures, the fear of private suits against nonconsenting States was the central reason given by the founders who chose to preserve the States' sovereign immunity. Suits brought by the United States itself require the exercise of political responsibility for each suit prosecuted against a State, a control which is absent from a broad delegation to private persons to sue nonconsenting States.

We have held also that in adopting the Fourteenth Amendment, the people required the States to surrender a portion of the sovereignty that had been preserved to them by the original Constitution, so that Congress may authorize private suits against nonconsenting States pursuant to its §5 enforcement power.... When Congress enacts appropriate legislation to enforce this Amendment, federal interests are paramount, and Congress may assert an authority over the States which would be otherwise unauthorized by the Constitution.

The second important limit to the principle of sovereign immunity is that it bars suits against States but not lesser entities. The immunity does not extend to suits prosecuted against a municipal corporation or other governmental entity which is not an arm of the State. [Citations omitted.] Nor does sovereign immunity bar all suits against state officers. ... The rule ... does not bar certain actions against state officers for injunctive or declaratory relief. [Citations omitted.] Even a suit for money damages may be prosecuted against a state officer in his individual capacity for unconstitutional or wrongful conduct fairly attributable to the officer himself, so long as the relief is sought not from the state treasury but from the officer personally. [Citations omitted.]

The principle of sovereign immunity as reflected in our jurisprudence strikes the proper balance between the supremacy of federal law and the separate sovereignty of the States. Established rules provide ample means to correct ongoing violations of law and to vindicate the interests which animate the Supremacy Clause. That we have, during the first 210 years of our constitutional history, found it unnecessary to decide the question presented here suggests a federal power to subject nonconsenting States to private suits in their own courts is unnecessary to uphold the Constitution and valid federal statutes as the supreme law.

IV

The sole remaining question is whether Maine has waived its immunity. The State of Maine "regards the immunity from suit as 'one of the highest attributes inherent in the nature of sovereignty,' " and adheres to the general rule that "a specific authority conferred by an enactment of the legislature is requisite if the sovereign is to be taken as having shed the protective mantle of immunity" [quoting Maine court decisions]. Petitioners have not attempted to establish a waiver of immunity under this standard. ... The State, we conclude, has not consented to suit.

V

This case at one level concerns the formal structure of federalism, but in a Constitution as resilient as ours form mirrors substance. Congress has vast power but not all power. When Congress legislates in matters affecting the States, it may not treat these sovereign entities as mere prefectures or corporations. Congress must accord States the esteem due to them as joint participants in a federal system, one beginning with the premise of sovereignty in both the central Government and the separate States. Congress has ample means to ensure compliance with valid federal laws, but it must respect the sovereignty of the States.

In apparent attempt to disparage a conclusion with which it disagrees, the dissent attributes our reasoning to natural law. We seek to discover, however, only what the Framers and those who ratified the Constitution sought to accomplish when they created a federal system. We appeal to no higher authority than the Charter which they wrote and adopted. Theirs was the unique insight that freedom is enhanced by the creation of two governments, not one. We need not attach a label to our dissenting colleagues' insistence that the constitutional structure adopted by the founders must yield to the politics of the moment. Although the Constitution begins with the principle that sovereignty rests with the people, it does not follow that the National Government becomes the ultimate, preferred mechanism for expressing the people's will. The States exist as a refutation of that concept. In choosing to ordain and establish the Constitution, the people insisted upon a federal structure for the very purpose of rejecting the idea that the will of the people in all instances is expressed by the central power, the one most remote from their control. The Framers of the Constitution did not share our dissenting colleagues' belief that the Congress may circumvent the federal design by regulating the States directly when it pleases to do so, including by a proxy in which individual citizens are authorized to levy upon the state treasuries absent the States' consent to jurisdiction.

The case before us depends upon these principles. The State of Maine has not questioned Congress' power to prescribe substantive rules of federal law to which it must comply. Despite an initial good-faith disagreement about the requirements of the FLSA, it is conceded by all that the State has altered its conduct so that its compliance with federal law cannot now be questioned. The Solicitor General of the United States has appeared before this Court, however, and asserted that the federal interest in compensating the States' employees for alleged past violations of federal law is so compelling that the sovereign State of Maine must be stripped of its immunity and subjected to suit in its own courts by its own employees. Yet, despite specific statutory authorization, see 29 U.S.C. §216(c), the United States apparently found the same interests insufficient to justify sending even a single attorney to Maine to prosecute this litigation. The difference between a suit by the United States on behalf of the employees and a suit by the employees implicates a rule that the National Government must itself deem the case of sufficient importance to take action against the State; and history, precedent, and the structure of the Constitution make clear that, under the plan of the Convention, the States have consented to suits of the first kind but not of the second. The judgment of the Supreme Judicial Court of Maine is

Affirmed.

JUSTICE SOUTER, with whom JUSTICE STEVENS, JUSTICE GINS-BURG, and JUSTICE BREYER join, dissenting.

In *Seminole Tribe of Fla. v. Florida* (1996), a majority of this Court invoked the Eleventh Amendment to declare that the federal judicial power under Article III of the Constitution does not reach a private action against a State, even on a federal question. In the Court's conception, however, the Eleventh Amendment was understood as having been enhanced by a "background principle" of state sovereign immunity (understood as immunity to suit) that operated beyond its limited codification in the Amendment, dealing solely with federal citizen-state diversity jurisdiction. To the *Seminole Tribe* dissenters, of whom I was one, the Court's enhancement of the Amendment was at odds with constitutional history and at war with the conception of divided sovereignty that is the essence of American federalism.

Today's issue arises naturally in the aftermath of the decision in *Seminole Tribe*. The Court holds that the Constitution bars an individual suit against a State to enforce a federal statutory right under the Fair Labor Standards Act of 1938 (FLSA), 29 U.S.C. §201 *et seq.*, when brought in the State's courts over its objection. In thus complementing its earlier decision, the Court of course confronts the fact that the state forum renders the Eleventh Amendment beside the point, and it has responded by discerning a simpler and more straightforward theory of state sovereign immunity than it found in *Seminole Tribe*: a State's sovereign immunity from all individual suits is a "fundamental aspect" of state sovereignty "confirm[ed]" by the Tenth Amendment. As a consequence, *Seminole Tribe*'s contorted reliance on the Eleventh Amendment and its background was presumably unnecessary; the Tenth would have done the work with an economy that the majority in *Seminole Tribe* would have welcomed. Indeed, if the Court's current reasoning is correct, the Eleventh Amendment itself was unnecessary. Whatever Article III may originally have said about the federal judicial power, the embarrassment to the State of Georgia occasioned by attempts in federal court to enforce the State's war debt could easily have been avoided if only the Court that decided *Chisholm v. Georgia* (1793) had understood a State's inherent, Tenth Amendment right to be free of any judicial power, whether the court be state or federal, and whether the cause of action arise under state or federal law.

The sequence of the Court's positions prompts a suspicion of error, and skepticism is confirmed by scrutiny of the Court's efforts to justify its holding. There is no evidence that the Tenth Amendment constitutionalized a concept of sovereign immunity as inherent in the notion of statehood, and no evidence that any concept of inherent sovereign immunity was understood historically to apply when the sovereign sued was not the font of the law. Nor does the Court fare any better with its subsidiary lines of reasoning, that the state-court action is barred by the scheme of American federalism, a result supposedly confirmed by a history largely devoid of precursors to the action considered here. The Court's federalism ignores the accepted authority of Congress to bind States under the FLSA and to provide for enforcement of federal rights in state court. The Court's history simply disparages the capacity of the Constitution to order relationships in a Republic that has changed since the founding.

On each point the Court has raised it is mistaken, and I respectfully dissent from its judgment.

I

The Court rests its decision principally on the claim that immunity from suit was "a fundamental aspect of the sovereignty which the States enjoyed before the ratification of the Constitution," an aspect which the Court understands to have survived the ratification of the Constitution in 1788 and to have been "confirm[ed]" and given constitutional status by the adoption of the Tenth Amendment in 1791. If the Court truly means by "sovereign immunity," what that term meant at common law, its argument would be insupportable. While sovereign immunity entered many new state legal systems as a part of the common law selectively received from England, it was not understood to be indefeasible or to have been given any such status by the new National Constitution, which did not mention it. Had the question been posed, state sovereign immunity could not have been thought to shield a State from suit under federal law on a subject committed to national jurisdiction by Article I of the Constitution. Congress exercising its conceded Article I power may unquestionably abrogate such immunity. I set out this position at length in my dissent in *Seminole Tribe* and will not repeat it here.

The Court does not, however, offer today's holding as a mere corollary to its reasoning in *Seminole Tribe*, substituting the Tenth Amendment for the Eleventh as the occasion demands, and it is fair to read its references to a "fundamental aspect" of state sovereignty as referring not to a prerogative inherited from the Crown, but to a conception necessarily implied by statehood itself. The conception is thus not one of common law so much as of natural law, a universally applicable proposition discoverable by reason. This, I take it, is the sense in which the Court so emphatically relies on Alexander Hamilton's reference in The Federalist No. 81 to the States' sovereign immunity from suit as an "inherent" right, a characterization that does not require, but is at least open to, a natural law reading.

I understand the Court to rely on the Hamiltonian formulation with the object of suggesting that its conception of sovereign immunity as a "fundamental aspect" of sovereignty was a substantially popular, if not the dominant, view in the periods of Revolution and Confederation. There is, after all, nothing else in the Court's opinion that would suggest a basis for saying that the ratification of the Tenth Amendment gave this "fundamental aspect" its constitutional status and protection against any legislative tampering by Congress. The Court's principal rationale for today's result, then, turns on history: was the natural law conception of sovereign immunity as inherent in any notion of an independent State widely held in the United States in the period preceding the ratification of 1788 (or the adoption of the Tenth Amendment in 1791)?

The answer is certainly no. There is almost no evidence that the generation of the Framers thought sovereign immunity was fundamental in the sense of being unalterable. Whether one looks at the period before the framing, to the ratification controversies, or to the early republican era, the evidence is the same. Some Framers thought sovereign immunity was an obsolete royal prerogative inapplicable in a republic; some thought sovereign immunity was a common-law power defeasible, like other common-law rights, by statute; and perhaps a few thought, in keeping with a natural law view distinct from the common-law conception, that immunity was inherent in a sovereign because the body that made a law could not logically be bound by it. Natural law thinking on the part of a doubtful few will not, however, support the Court's position.

A, B

[In two sections dealing with the American history before the Constitutional Convention, Souter argued that sovereign immunity was not well established either in the American colonies or in the new states immediately after independence. "The American Colonies did not enjoy sovereign immunity, that being a privilege understood in English law to be reserved for the Crown alone," Souter wrote. He noted that several colonial charters "expressly specified that the corporate body established thereunder could sue and be sued." After independence, Souter continued, "some States appear to have understood themselves to be without immunity from suit in their own courts. . . ." Others "understood themselves to be inheritors of the Crown's common-law sovereign immunity," but also enacted statutes "authorizing legal remedies against the State" parallel to procedures available in England.

"Around the time of the Constitutional Convention," Souter concluded, "there existed among the States some diversity of practice with respect to sovereign immunity; but despite a tendency among the state constitutions to announce and declare certain inalienable and natural rights of men and even of the collective people of a State, . . . no State declared that sovereign immunity was one of those rights. To the extent that States were thought to possess immunity, it was perceived as a prerogative of the sovereign under common law. And where sovereign immunity was recognized as barring suit, provisions for recovery from the State were in order, just as they had been at common law in England."]

C

At the Constitutional Convention, the notion of sovereign immunity, whether as natural law or as common law, was not an immediate subject of debate, and the sovereignty of a State in its own courts seems not to have been mentioned. This comes as no surprise, for although the Constitution required state courts to apply federal law, the Framers did not consider the possibility that federal law might bind States, say, in their relations with their employees. In the subsequent ratification debates, however, the issue of jurisdiction over a State did emerge in the question whether States might be sued on their debts in federal court, and on this point, too, a variety of views emerged and the diversity of sovereign immunity conceptions displayed itself. [Remainder of subsection omitted.]

D

At the close of the ratification debates, the issue of the sovereign immunity of the States under Article III had not been definitively resolved. . . . Several state ratifying conventions proposed amendments and issued declarations that would have exempted States from subjection to suit in federal court. [Souter noted that the New York and Rhode Island conventions proposed amendments to bar federal court jurisdiction over "any suit by any person against a state," and that the Virginia and North Carolina conventions proposed amendments eliminating federal jurisdiction over any controversies between a state and citizens of another state.]

At all events, the state ratifying conventions' felt need for clarification on the question of state suability demonstrates that uncertainty surrounded the matter even at the moment of ratification. . . .

E

If the natural law conception of sovereign immunity as an inherent characteristic of sovereignty enjoyed by the States had been broadly accepted at the time of the founding, one would expect to find it reflected somewhere in the five opinions delivered by the Court in *Chisholm v. Georgia* (1793). Yet that view did not appear in any of them. And since a bare two years before *Chisholm*, the Bill of Rights had been added to the original Constitution, if the Tenth Amendment had been understood to give federal constitutional status to state sovereign immunity so as to endue it with the equivalent of the natural law conception, one would be certain to find such a development mentioned somewhere in the *Chisholm* writings. In fact, however, not one of the opinions espoused the natural law view, and not one of them so much as mentioned the Tenth Amendment. Not even Justice Iredell, who alone among the Justices thought that a State could not be sued in federal court, echoed Hamilton or hinted at a constitutionally immutable immunity doctrine.

F [OMITTED]

II

The Court's rationale for today's holding based on a conception of sovereign immunity as somehow fundamental to sovereignty or inherent in statehood fails for the lack of any substantial support for such a conception in the thinking of the founding era. The Court . . . has a second line of argument looking not to a clause-based reception of the natural law conception or even to its recognition as a "background principle," but to a structural basis in the Constitution's creation of a federal system. Immunity, the Court says, "inheres in the system of federalism established by the Constitution[.]" . . . That is, the Court believes that the federal constitutional structure itself necessitates recognition of some degree of state autonomy broad enough to include sovereign immunity from suit in a State's own courts, regardless of the federal source of the claim asserted against the State. If one were to read the Court's federal structure rationale in isolation from the preceding portions of the opinion, it would appear that the Court's position on state sovereign immunity might have been rested entirely on federalism alone. If it had been, however, I would still be in dissent, for the Court's argument that state court sovereign immunity on federal questions is inherent in the very concept of federal structure is demonstrably mistaken.

A

. . . [T]the general scheme of delegated sovereignty as between the two component governments of the federal system was clear, and was succinctly stated by Chief Justice Marshall: "In America, the powers of sovereignty are divided between the government of the Union, and those of the States. They are each sovereign, with respect to the objects committed to it, and neither sovereign with respect to the objects committed to the other." *McCulloch* v. Maryland (1819).

Hence the flaw in the Court's appeal to federalism. The State of Maine is not sovereign with respect to the national objective of the FLSA. It is not the authority that promulgated the FLSA, on which the right of action in this case depends. That authority is the United States acting through the Congress, whose legislative power under Article I of the Constitution to extend FLSA coverage to state employees has already been decided, see *Garcia v. San Antonio Metropolitan Transit Authority* (1985), and is not contested here.

Nor can it be argued that because the State of Maine creates its own court system, it has authority to decide what sorts of claims may be entertained there, and thus in effect to control the right of action in this case. Maine has created state courts of general jurisdiction; once it has done so, the Supremacy Clause of the Constitution, Art. VI, cl. 2, which requires state courts to enforce federal law and state-court judges to be bound by it, requires the Maine courts to entertain this federal cause of action. . . . The Court's insistence that the federal structure bars Congress from making States susceptible to suit in their own courts is, then, [a] plain mistake.

B

It is symptomatic of the weakness of the structural notion proffered by the Court that it seeks to buttress the argument by relying on "the dignity and respect afforded a State, which the immunity is designed to protect" (quoting *Idaho v. Coeur d'Alene Tribe of Idaho* (1997)), and by invoking the many demands on a State's fisc. Apparently beguiled by Gilded Era language describing private suits against States as "neither becoming nor convenient" (quoting *In re Ayers* (1887)), the Court calls "immunity from private suits central to sovereign dignity," and assumes that this "dignity" is a quality easily translated from the person of the King to the participatory abstraction of a republican State. . . . It would be hard to imagine anything more inimical to the republican conception, which rests on the understanding of its citizens precisely that the government is not above them, but of them, its actions being governed by law just like their own. Whatever justification there may be for an American government's immunity from private suit, it is not dignity

It is equally puzzling to hear the Court say that "federal power to authorize private suits for money damages would place unwarranted strain on the States' ability to govern in accordance with the will of their citizens." So long as the citizens' will, expressed through state legislation, does not violate valid federal law, the strain will not be felt; and to the extent that state action does violate federal law, the will of the citizens of the United States already trumps that of the citizens of the State: the strain then is not only expected, but necessarily intended.

Least of all does the Court persuade by observing that "other important needs" than that of the "judgment creditor" compete for public money. The "judgment creditor" in question is not a dunning bill-collector, but a citizen whose federal rights have been violated, and a constitutional structure that stints on enforcing federal rights out of an abundance of delicacy toward the States has substituted politesse in place of respect for the rule of law.

III

If neither theory nor structure can supply the basis for the Court's conceptions of sovereign immunity and federalism, then perhaps history might. The Court apparently believes that because state courts have not historically entertained Commerce Clause-based federal-law claims against the States, such an innovation carries a presumption of unconstitutionality.... At the outset, it has to be noted that this approach assumes a more cohesive record than history affords. In *Hilton v. South Carolina Public Railways Comm'n* (1991) (KENNEDY, J.), ... we held that a state-owned railroad could be sued in state court under the Federal Employers' Liability Act, 45 U.S.C. §§51-60, notwithstanding the lack of an express congressional statement, because "the Eleventh Amendment does not apply in state courts." But even if the record were less unkempt, the problem with arguing from historical practice in this case is that past practice, even if unbroken, provides no basis for demanding preservation when the conditions on which the practice depended have changed in a constitutionally relevant way.

It was at one time, though perhaps not from the framing, believed that "Congress' authority to regulate the States under the Commerce Clause" was limited by "certain underlying elements of political sovereignty ... deemed essential to the States' separate and independent existence." [Quoting from *Garcia*.] ... As a consequence it was rare, if not unknown, for state courts to confront the situation in which federal law enacted under the Commerce Clause provided the authority for a private right of action against a State in state court. The question of state immunity from a Commerce Clause-based federal-law suit in state court thus tended not to arise for the simple reason that acts of Congress authorizing such suits did not exist.

Today, however, in light of *Garcia*, ... the law is settled that federal legislation enacted under the Commerce Clause may bind the States without having to satisfy a test of undue incursion into state sovereignty.... Because the commerce power is no longer thought to be circumscribed, the dearth of prior private federal claims entertained against the States in state courts does not tell us anything, and reflects nothing but an earlier and less expansive application of the commerce power.

Least of all is it to the point for the Court to suggest that because the Framers would be surprised to find States subjected to a federal-law suit in their own courts under the commerce power, the suit must be prohibited by the Constitution.... The Framers' intentions and expectations count so far as they point to the meaning of the Constitution's text or the fair implications of its structure, but they do not hover over the instrument to veto any application of its principles to a world that the Framers could not have anticipated.

If the Framers would be surprised to see States subjected to suit in their own courts under the commerce power, they would be astonished by the reach of Congress under the Commerce Clause generally. The proliferation of Government, State and Federal, would amaze the Framers, and the administrative state with its reams of regulations would leave them rubbing their eyes. But the Framers' surprise at, say, the FLSA, or the Federal Communications Commission, or the Federal Reserve Board is no threat to the constitutionality of any one of them....

IV

A

If today's decision occasions regret at its anomalous versions of history and federal theory, it is the more regrettable in being the second time the Court has suddenly changed the course of prior decision in order to limit the exercise of authority over a subject now concededly within the Article I jurisdiction of the Congress. The FLSA, which requires employers to pay a minimum wage, was first enacted in 1938, with an exemption for States acting as employers. In 1966, it was amended to remove the state employer exemption so far as it concerned workers in hospitals, institutions, and schools. In [*Maryland v*]. *Wirtz* [1968], the Court upheld the amendment. . . .

In 1974, Congress again amended the FLSA, this time "extend[ing] the minimum wage and maximum hour provisions to almost all public employees employed by the States and by their various political subdivisions." This time the Court went the other way: in *National League of Cities*, the Court held the extension of the Act to these employees an unconstitutional infringement of state sovereignty; for good measure, the Court overturned *Wirtz*, dismissing its reasoning as no longer authoritative.

But *National League of Cities* was not the last word. In *Garcia*, decided some nine years later, the Court addressed the question whether a municipally owned mass-transit system was exempt from the FLSA. In holding that it was not, the Court overruled *National League of Cities*, this time taking the position that Congress was not barred by the Constitution from binding the States as employers under the Commerce Clause. As already mentioned, the Court held that whatever protection the Constitution afforded to the States' sovereignty lay in the constitutional structure, not in some substantive guarantee. *Garcia* remains good law, its reasoning has not been repudiated, and it has not been challenged here.

The FLSA has not, however, fared as well in practice as it has in theory. The Court in *Seminole Tribe* created a significant impediment to the statute's practical application by rendering its damages provisions unenforceable against the States by private suit in federal court. Today's decision blocking private actions in state courts makes the barrier to individual enforcement a total one.

B

The Court might respond to the charge that in practice it has vitiated *Garcia* by insisting, as counsel for Maine argued, that the United States may bring suit in federal court against a State for damages under the FLSA. . . . It is true, of course, that the FLSA does authorize the Secretary of Labor to file suit seeking damages, see 29 U.S.C. §216(c), but unless Congress plans a significant expansion of the National Government's litigating forces to provide a lawyer whenever private litigation is barred by today's decision and *Seminole Tribe*, the allusion to enforcement of private rights by the National Government is probably not much more than whimsy. Facing reality, Congress specifically found, as long ago as 1974, "that the enforcement capability of the Secretary of Labor is not alone sufficient to provide redress in all or even a substantial portion of the situations where compliance is not forthcoming voluntarily." [Quoting Senate Report.] One hopes that such voluntary compliance will prove more popular than it has in Maine, for there is no reason today to suspect that enforcement by the Secretary of Labor alone would likely prove adequate to assure compliance with this federal law in the multifarious circumstances of some 4.7 million employees of the 50 States of the Union.

The point is not that the difficulties of enforcement should drive the Court's decision, but simply that where Congress has created a private right to damages, it is implausible to claim that enforcement by a public authority without any incentive beyond its general enforcement power will ever afford the private right a traditionally adequate remedy. No one would think the remedy adequate if private tort claims against a State could only be brought by the National Government: the tradition of private enforcement, as old as the common law itself, is the benchmark. But wage claims have a lineage of private enforcement just as ancient, and a claim under the FLSA is a claim for wages due on work performed. Denying private enforcement of an FLSA claim is thus on par with closing the courthouse door to state tort victims unaccompanied by a lawyer from Washington. . . .

V

The Court has swung back and forth with regrettable disruption on the enforceability of the FLSA against the States, but if the present majority had a defensible position one could at least accept its decision with an expectation of stability ahead. As it is, any such expectation would be naive. The resemblance of today's state sovereign immunity to the *Lochner* era's industrial due process is striking. The Court began this century by imputing immutable constitutional status to a conception of economic self-reliance that was never true to industrial life and grew insistently fictional with the years, and the Court has chosen to close the century by conferring like status on a conception of state sovereign immunity that is true neither to history nor to the structure of the Constitution. I expect the Court's late essay into immunity doctrine will prove the equal of its earlier experiment in laissez-faire, the one being as unrealistic as the other, as indefensible, and probably as fleeting.

No. 98-149

College Savings Bank, Petitioner v. Florida Prepaid Postsecondary Education Expense Board et al.

On writ of certiotari to the United States Court of Appeals
for the Third Circuit

[June 23,1999]

JUSTICE SCALIA delivered the opinion of the Court.

The Trademark Remedy Clarification Act (TRCA) subjects the States to suits brought under §43(a) of the Trademark Act of 1946 (Lanham Act) for false and misleading advertising, 15 U.S.C. §1125(a). The question presented in this case is whether that provision is effective to permit suit against a State for its alleged misrepresentation of its own product—either because the TRCA effects a constitutionally permissible abrogation of state sovereign immunity, or because the TRCA operates as an invitation to waiver of such immunity which is automatically accepted by a State's engaging in the activities regulated by the Lanham Act.

I

In *Chisholm v. Georgia* (1793), we asserted jurisdiction over an action in assumpsit brought by a South Carolina citizen against the State of Georgia. In so doing, we reasoned that Georgia's sovereign immunity was qualified by the general jurisdictional provisions of Article III, and, most specifically, by the provision extending the federal judicial power to controversies "between a State and Citizens of another State." The "shock of surprise" created by this decision prompted the immediate adoption of the Eleventh Amendment, which provides:

> "The Judicial power of the United States shall not be construed to extend to any suit in law or equity, commenced or prosecuted against one of the United States by Citizens of another State, or by Citizens or Subjects of any Foreign State."

Though its precise terms bar only federal jurisdiction over suits brought against one State by citizens of another State or foreign state, we have long recognized that the Eleventh Amendment accomplished much more: It repudiated the central premise of *Chisholm* that the jurisdictional heads of Article III superseded the sovereign immunity that the States possessed before entering the Union. This has been our understanding of the Amendment since the landmark case of *Hans v. Louisiana* (1890). [Other citations omitted.]

While this immunity from suit is not absolute, we have recognized only two circumstances in which an individual may sue a State. First, Congress may authorize such a suit in the exercise of its power to enforce the Fourteenth Amendment—an Amendment enacted after the Eleventh Amendment and specifically designed to alter the federal-state balance. Second, a State may waive its sovereign immunity by consenting to suit. This case turns on whether either of these two circumstances is present.

II

Section 43(a) of the Lanham Act, enacted in 1946, created a private right of action against "[a]ny person" who uses false descriptions or makes false representations in commerce. The TRCA amends §43(a) by defining "any person" to include "any State, instrumentality of a State or employee of a State or instrumentality of a State acting in his or her official capacity." §3(c) The TRCA further amends the Lanham Act to provide that such state entities "shall not be immune, under the eleventh amendment of the Constitution of the United States or under any other doctrine of sovereign immunity, from suit in Federal court by any person, including any governmental or nongovernmental entity for any violation under this Act," and that remedies shall be available against such state entities "to the same extent as such remedies are available . . . in a suit against" a nonstate entity. §3(b) (codified in 15 U.S.C. §1122).

Petitioner College Savings Bank is a New Jersey chartered bank located in Princeton, New Jersey. Since 1987, it has marketed and sold CollegeSure certificates of deposit designed to finance the costs of college education. College Savings holds a patent upon the methodology of administering its CollegeSure certificates. Respondent Florida Prepaid Postsecondary Education Expense Board (Florida Prepaid) is an arm of the State of Florida. Since 1988, it has administered a tuition prepayment program designed to provide individuals with sufficient funds to cover future college expenses. College Savings brought a patent infringement action against Florida Prepaid in United States District Court in New Jersey. That action is the subject of today's decision in *Florida Prepaid Postsecondary Ed. Expense Bd. v. College Savings Bank*. In addition, and in the same court, College Savings filed the instant action alleging that Florida Prepaid violated §43(a) of the Lanham Act by making misstatements about its own tuition savings plans in its brochures and annual reports.

Florida Prepaid moved to dismiss this action on the ground that it was barred by sovereign immunity. It argued that Congress had not abrogated sovereign immunity in this case because the TRCA was enacted pursuant to Congress's powers under Article I of the Constitution and, under our decisions in *Seminole Tribe* [*of Fla. v. Florida* (1996)] and *Fitzpatrick* [*v. Bitzer* (1976)], Congress can abrogate state sovereign immunity only when it legislates to enforce the Fourteenth Amendment. The United States intervened to defend the constitutionality of the TRCA. Both it and College Savings argued that, under the doctrine of constructive waiver articulated in *Parden v. Terminal R. Co. of Ala. Docks Dept.* (1964), Florida Prepaid had waived its immunity from Lanham Act suits by engaging in the interstate marketing and administration of its program after the TRCA made clear that such activity would subject Florida Prepaid to suit. College Savings also argued that Congress's purported abrogation of Florida Prepaid's sovereign immunity in the TRCA was effective, since it was enacted not merely pursuant to Article I but also to enforce the Due Process Clause of the Fourteenth Amendment. The District Court rejected both of these arguments and granted Florida Prepaid's motion to dismiss. (N.J. 1996). The Court of Appeals affirmed. (CA3 1997). We granted certiorari. (1999).

III

We turn first to the contention that Florida's sovereign immunity was validly abrogated. Our decision three Terms ago in *Seminole Tribe* held that the power "to regulate Commerce" conferred by Article I of the Constitution gives Congress no authority to abrogate state sovereign immunity. As authority for the abrogation in the present case, petitioner relies upon §5 of the Fourteenth Amendment, which we held in *Fitzpatrick v. Bitzer* and reaffirmed in *Seminole Tribe*, could be used for that purpose.

Section 1 of the Fourteenth Amendment provides that no State shall "deprive any person of . . . property . . . without due process of law." Section 5 provides that "[t]he Congress shall have power to enforce, by appropriate legislation, the provisions of this article." We made clear in *City of Boerne v. Flores* (1997), that the term "enforce" is to be taken seriously—that the object of valid §5 legislation must be the carefully delimited remediation or prevention of constitutional violations. Petitioner claims that, with respect to §43(a) of the Lanham Act, Congress enacted the TRCA to remedy and prevent state deprivations without due process of two species of "property" rights: (1) a right to be free from a business competitor's false advertising about its own product, and (2) a more generalized right to be secure in one's business interests. Neither of these qualifies as a property right protected by the Due Process Clause.

As to the first: The hallmark of a protected property interest is the right to exclude others. . . . That is why the right that we all possess to use the public lands is not the "property" right of anyone. . . . The Lanham Act may well contain provisions that protect constitutionally cognizable property interests—notably, its provisions dealing with infringement of trademarks, which are the "property" of the owner because he can exclude others from using them. . . . The Lanham Act's false-advertising provisions, however, bear no relationship to any right to exclude; and Florida Prepaid's alleged misrepresentations concerning its own products intruded upon no interest over which petitioner had exclusive dominion.

Unsurprisingly, petitioner points to no decision of this Court (or of any other court, for that matter) recognizing a property right in freedom from a competitor's false advertising about its own products. . . .

Petitioner argues that the common-law tort of unfair competition "by definition" protects property interests, and thus the TRCA "by definition" is designed to remedy and prevent deprivations of such interests in the false-advertising context. Even as a logical matter, that does not follow, since not everything which *protects* property interests is designed to remedy or prevent *deprivations* of those property interests. A municipal ordinance prohibiting billboards in residential areas protects the property interests of homeowners, although erecting billboards would ordinarily not deprive them of property. To sweep within the Fourteenth Amendment the elusive property interests that are "by definition" protected by unfair-competition law would violate our frequent admonition that the Due Process Clause is not merely a "font of tort law."

Petitioner's second assertion of a property interest rests upon an argument similar to the one just discussed, and suffers from the same flaw. Petitioner argues that businesses are "property" within the meaning of the Due Process Clause, and that

Congress legislates under §5 when it passes a law that prevents state interference with business (which false advertising does). The assets of a business (including its good will) unquestionably are property, and any state taking of those assets is unquestionably a "deprivation" under the Fourteenth Amendment. But business in the sense of *the activity of doing business,* or *the activity of making a profit* is not property in the ordinary sense—and it is only *that,* and not any business asset, which is impinged upon by a competitors' false advertising.

Finding that there is no deprivation of property at issue here, we need not pursue the follow-on question that *City of Boerne* would otherwise require us to resolve: whether the prophylactic measure taken under purported authority of §5 (viz., prohibition of States' sovereign-immunity claims, which are not in themselves a violation of the Fourteenth Amendment) was genuinely necessary to prevent violation of the Fourteenth Amendment. We turn next to the question whether Florida's sovereign immunity, though not abrogated, was voluntarily waived.

IV

We have long recognized that a State's sovereign immunity is "a personal privilege which it may waive at pleasure." The decision to waive that immunity, however, "is altogether voluntary on the part of the sovereignty." *Beers v. Arkansas* (1858). Accordingly, our "test for determining whether a State has waived its immunity from federal-court jurisdiction is a stringent one." *Atascadero State Hospital v. Scanlon* (1985). Generally, we will find a waiver either if the State voluntarily invokes our jurisdiction, or else if the State makes a "clear declaration" that it intends to submit itself to our jurisdiction. . . . Thus, a State does not consent to suit in federal court merely by consenting to suit in the courts of its own creation. Nor does it consent to suit in federal court merely by stating its intention to "sue and be sued," or even by authorizing suits against it "in any court of competent jurisdiction." We have even held that a State may, absent any contractual commitment to the contrary, alter the conditions of its waiver and apply those changes to a pending suit.

There is no suggestion here that respondent Florida Prepaid expressly consented to being sued in federal court. Nor is this a case in which the State has affirmatively invoked our jurisdiction. Rather, petitioner College Savings and the United States both maintain that Florida Prepaid has "impliedly" or "constructively" waived its immunity from Lanham Act suit. They do so on the authority of *Parden v. Terminal R. Co. of Ala. Docks Dept.* (1964)—an elliptical opinion that stands at the nadir of our waiver (and, for that matter, sovereign immunity) jurisprudence. In *Parden,* we permitted employees of a railroad owned and operated by Alabama to bring an action under the Federal Employers' Liability Act (FELA) against their employer. Despite the absence of any provision in the statute specifically referring to the States, we held that the Act authorized suits against the States by virtue of its general provision subjecting to suit "[e]very common carrier by railroad . . . engaging in commerce between . . . the several States." We further held that Alabama had waived its immunity from FELA suit even though Alabama law expressly disavowed any such waiver:

> "By enacting the [FELA] . . . Congress conditioned the right to operate a railroad in interstate commerce upon amenability to suit in federal court as provided by the Act; by thereafter operating a railroad in interstate commerce, Alabama must be taken to have accepted that condition and thus to have consented to suit."

The four dissenting Justices in *Parden* refused to infer a waiver because Congress had not "expressly declared" that a *State* operating in commerce would be subject to liability, but they went on to acknowledge—in a concession that, strictly speaking, was not necessary to their analysis—that Congress possessed the power to effect such a waiver of the State's constitutionally protected immunity so long as it did so with clarity.

Only nine years later, in *Employees of Dept. of Public Health and Welfare of Mo. v. Department of Public Health and Welfare of Mo.* (1973), we began to retreat from *Parden*. That case held—in an opinion written by one of the *Parden* dissenters over the solitary dissent of *Parden*'s author—that the State of Missouri was immune from a suit brought under the Fair Labor Standards Act by employees of its state health facilities. Although the statute specifically covered the state hospitals in question, and such coverage was unquestionably enforceable in federal court by the United States, we did not think that the statute expressed with clarity Congress's intention to supersede the States' immunity from suits brought by individuals. . . .

The next year, we observed (in dictum) that there is "no place" for the doctrine of constructive waiver in our sovereign-immunity jurisprudence, and we emphasized that we would "find waiver only where stated by the most express language or by such overwhelming implications from the text as [will] leave no room for any other reasonable construction." *Edelman v. Jordan* (1974). Several Terms later, in *Welch v. Texas Dept. of Highways and Public Transp.* (1987), although we expressly avoided addressing the constitutionality of Congress's conditioning a State's engaging in Commerce-Clause activity upon the State's waiver of sovereign immunity, we said there was "no doubt that *Parden*'s discussion of congressional intent to negate Eleventh Amendment immunity is no longer good law," and overruled *Parden* "to the extent [it] is inconsistent with the requirement that an abrogation of Eleventh Amendment immunity by Congress must be expressed in unmistakably clear language."

College Savings and the United States concede, as they surely must, that these intervening decisions have seriously limited the holding of *Parden*. They maintain, however, that *Employees* and *Welch* are distinguishable, and that a core principle of *Parden* remains good law. A *Parden*-style waiver of immunity, they say, is still possible . . . so long as the following two conditions are satisfied: First, Congress must provide unambiguously that the State will be subject to suit if it engages in certain specified conduct governed by federal regulation. Second, the State must voluntarily elect to engage in the federally regulated conduct that subjects it to suit. In this latter regard, their argument goes, a State is never deemed to have constructively waived its sovereign immunity by engaging in activities that it cannot realistically choose to abandon, such as the operation of a police force; but constructive waiver is appropriate where a State runs an enterprise for profit, operates in a field traditionally occupied by private persons or corporations, engages in activities sufficiently removed from "core [state] functions," or otherwise acts as a "mar-

ket participant" in interstate commerce. On this theory, Florida Prepaid constructively waived its immunity from suit by engaging in the voluntary and nonessen-
tial activity of selling and advertising a for-profit educational investment vehicle in
interstate commerce after being put on notice by the clear language of the TRCA
that it would be subject to Lanham Act liability for doing so.

We think that the constructive-waiver experiment of *Parden* was ill conceived,
and see no merit in attempting to salvage any remnant of it. As we explain below
in detail, *Parden* broke sharply with prior cases, and is fundamentally incompatible with later ones. We have never applied the holding of *Parden* to another
statute, and in fact have narrowed the case in every subsequent opinion in which
it has been under consideration. In short, *Parden* stands as an anomaly in the
jurisprudence of sovereign immunity, and indeed in the jurisprudence of constitutional law. Today, we drop the other shoe: Whatever may remain of our decision
in *Parden* is expressly overruled.

To begin with, we cannot square *Parden* with our cases requiring that a State's
express waiver of sovereign immunity be unequivocal. The whole point of requiring a "clear declaration" *by the State* of its waiver is to be certain that the State in
fact consents to suit. But there is little reason to assume actual consent based upon
the State's mere presence in a field subject to congressional regulation. There is a
fundamental difference between a State's expressing unequivocally that it waives
its immunity, and Congress's expressing unequivocally its intention that if the
State takes certain action it shall be deemed to have waived that immunity. . . .

Indeed, *Parden*-style waivers are simply unheard of in the context of *other* constitutionally protected privileges. . . . For example, imagine if Congress amended
the securities laws to provide with unmistakable clarity that anyone committing
fraud in connection with the buying or selling of securities in interstate commerce
would not be entitled to a jury in any federal criminal prosecution of such fraud.
Would persons engaging in securities fraud after the adoption of such an amendment be deemed to have "constructively waived" their constitutionally protected
rights to trial by jury in criminal cases? . . . The answer, of course, is no. . . . State
sovereign immunity, no less than the right to trial by jury in criminal cases, is constitutionally protected. And in the context of *federal* sovereign immunity—obviously the closest analogy to the present case—it is well established that waivers are
not implied. [Citations omitted.] We see no reason why the rule should be different with respect to state sovereign immunity.

Given how anomalous it is to speak of the "constructive waiver" of a constitutionally protected privilege, it is not surprising that the very cornerstone of the
Parden opinion was the notion that state sovereign immunity is not constitutionally grounded. [Excerpt from opinion omitted.] Our more recent decision in *Seminole Tribe* expressly repudiates that proposition, and in formally overruling *Parden*
we do no more than make explicit what that case implied.

Recognizing a congressional power to exact constructive waivers of sovereign
immunity through the exercise of Article I powers would also, as a practical matter, permit Congress to circumvent the antiabrogation holding of *Seminole Tribe*.
Forced waiver and abrogation are not even different sides of the same coin—they
are the same side of the same coin. . . . There is little more than a verbal distinction between saying that Congress can make Florida liable to private parties for

false or misleading advertising in interstate commerce of its prepaid tuition program, and saying the same thing but adding at the end "if Florida chooses to engage in such advertising." As further evidence that constructive waiver is little more than abrogation under another name, consider the revealing facts of this case: The statutory provision relied upon to demonstrate that Florida constructively waived its sovereign immunity is the very same provision that purported to abrogate it.

Nor do we think that the constitutionally grounded principle of state sovereign immunity is any less robust where, as here, the asserted basis for constructive waiver is conduct that the State realistically could choose to abandon, that is undertaken for profit, that is traditionally performed by private citizens and corporations, and that otherwise resembles the behavior of "market participants." Permitting abrogation or constructive waiver of the constitutional right only when these conditions exist would of course limit the evil—but it is hard to say that that limitation has any more support in text or tradition than, say, limiting abrogation or constructive waiver to the last Friday of the month. Since sovereign immunity itself was not traditionally limited by these factors, and since they have no bearing upon the voluntariness of the waiver, there is no principled reason why they should enter into our waiver analysis. . . .

V

The principal thrust of JUSTICE BREYER's dissent is an attack upon the very legitimacy of state sovereign immunity itself. In this regard, JUSTICE BREYER and the other dissenters proclaim that they are "not *yet* ready" (emphasis added) to adhere to the still-warm precedent of *Seminole Tribe* and to the 110-year-old decision in *Hans* that supports it. . . . On this score, we think nothing further need be said except two minor observations peculiar to this case.

First, JUSTICE BREYER and the other dissenters have adopted a decidedly perverse theory of *stare decisis*. While finding themselves entirely unconstrained by a venerable precedent such as *Hans*, . . . they cling desperately to an anomalous and severely undermined decision (*Parden*) from the 1960's. Surely this approach to *stare decisis* is exactly backwards. . . . Second, . . . we find it puzzling that JUSTICE BREYER would choose this occasion to criticize our sovereign-immunity jurisprudence as being ungrounded in constitutional text, since the present lawsuit that he would allow to go forward—having apparently been commenced against a State (Florida) by a citizen of another State (College Savings Bank of New Jersey)—seems to fall four square within the literal text of the Eleventh Amendment: "The Judicial power of the United States shall not be construed to extend to *any* suit in law or equity, commenced or prosecuted against one of the United States by Citizens of another State. . . ." (emphasis added).

* * *

Concluding, for the foregoing reasons, that the sovereign immunity of the State of Florida was neither validly abrogated by the Trademark Remedy Clarification Act, nor voluntarily waived by the State's activities in interstate commerce, we hold that the federal courts are without jurisdiction to entertain this suit against an arm of the State of Florida. The judgment of the Third Circuit dismissing the action is affirmed.

It is so ordered.

JUSTICE STEVENS, dissenting.

This case has been argued and decided on the basis of assumptions that may not be entirely correct. Accepting them, *arguendo*, the judgment of the Court of Appeals should be reversed for the reasons set forth in JUSTICE BREYER's dissent, which I have joined. I believe, however, that the importance of this case and the other two "states rights" cases decided today merits this additional comment.

The procedural posture of this case requires the Court to assume that Florida Prepaid is an "arm of the State" of Florida because its activities relate to the State's educational programs. But the validity of that assumption is doubtful if the Court's jurisprudence in this area is to be based primarily on present-day assumptions about the status of the doctrine of sovereign immunity in the 18th century. Sovereigns did not then play the kind of role in the commercial marketplace that they do today. In future cases, it may therefore be appropriate to limit the coverage of state sovereign immunity by treating the commercial enterprises of the States like the commercial activities of foreign sovereigns under the Foreign Sovereign Immunities Act of 1976.

The majority also assumes that petitioner's complaint has alleged a violation of the Lanham Act, but not one that is sufficiently serious to amount to a "deprivation" of its property. I think neither of those assumptions is relevant to the principal issue raised in this case, namely, whether Congress had the constitutional power to authorize suits against States and state instrumentalities for such a violation. In my judgment the Constitution granted it ample power to do so. Section 5 of the Fourteenth Amendment authorizes Congress to enact appropriate legislation to prevent deprivations of property without due process. Unlike the majority, I am persuaded that the Trademark Remedy Clarification Act was a valid exercise of that power, even if Florida Prepaid's allegedly false advertising in this case did not violate the Constitution. My conclusion rests on two premises that the Court rejects.

First, in my opinion "the activity of doing business," or "the activity of making a profit," is a form of property. . . . A State's deliberate destruction of a going business is surely a deprivation of property within the meaning of the Due Process Clause.

Second, the validity of a congressional decision to abrogate sovereign immunity in a category of cases does not depend on the strength of the claim asserted in a particular case within that category. Instead, the decision depends on whether Congress had a reasonable basis for concluding that abrogation was necessary to prevent violations that would otherwise occur. Given the presumption of validity that supports all federal statutes, I believe the Court must shoulder the burden of demonstrating why the judgment of the Congress of the United States should not command our respect. It has not done so.

For these reasons, as well as those expressed by JUSTICE BREYER, I respectfully dissent.

JUSTICE BREYER, with whom JUSTICE STEVENS, JUSTICE SOUTER, and JUSTICE GINSBURG join, dissenting.

The Court holds that Congress, in the exercise of its commerce power, cannot require a State to waive its immunity from suit in federal court even where the State engages in activity from which it might readily withdraw, such as federally regulated commercial activity. This Court has previously held to the contrary. *Parden v. Terminal R. Co. of Ala. Docks Dept.* (1964). I would not abandon that precedent.

I

Thirty-five years ago this Court unanimously subscribed to the holding that the Court today overrules. Justice White, writing for four Members of the Court who dissented on a different issue, succinctly described that holding as follows:

> "[I]t is within the power of Congress to condition a State's permit to engage in the interstate transportation business on a waiver of the State's sovereign immunity from suits arising out of such business. Congress might well determine that allowing regulable conduct such as the operation of a railroad to be undertaken by a body legally immune from liability directly resulting from these operations is so inimical to the purposes of its regulation that the State must be put to the option of either foregoing participation in the conduct or consenting to legal responsibility for injury caused thereby." (Opinion of White, J., joined by Douglas, Harlan, and Stewart, JJ.).

The majority, seeking to justify the overruling of so clear a precedent, describes *Parden*'s holding as a constitutional "anomaly" that "broke sharply with prior cases," that is "fundamentally incompatible with later ones," and that has been "narrowed . . . in every subsequent opinion." *Parden* is none of those things.

Far from being anomalous, *Parden*'s holding finds support in reason and precedent. When a State engages in ordinary commercial ventures, it acts like a private person, outside the area of its "core" responsibilities, and in a way unlikely to prove essential to the fulfillment of a basic governmental obligation. A Congress that decides to regulate those state commercial activities rather than to exempt the State likely believes that an exemption, by treating the State differently from identically situated private persons, would threaten the objectives of a federal regulatory program aimed primarily at private conduct. . . . And a Congress that includes the State not only within its substantive regulatory rules but also (expressly) within a related system of private remedies likely believes that a remedial exemption would similarly threaten that program. See *Florida Prepaid Postsecondary Ed. Expense Bd. v. College Savings Bank* (STEVENS, J., dissenting). It thereby avoids an enforcement gap which, when allied with the pressures of a competitive marketplace, could place the State's regulated private competitors at a significant disadvantage.

These considerations make Congress' need to possess the power to condition entry into the market upon a waiver of sovereign immunity (as "necessary and proper" to the exercise of its commerce power) unusually strong, for to deny Congress that power would deny Congress the power effectively to regulate *private* conduct. At the same time they make a State's need to exercise sovereign immunity unusually weak, for the State is unlikely to *have to* supply what private firms already supply, nor may it fairly demand special treatment, even to protect the public purse, when it does so. Neither can one easily imagine what the Constitution's founders would have thought about the assertion of sovereign immunity in this special context. These considerations, differing in kind or degree from those that would support a general congressional "abrogation" power, indicate that *Parden*'s holding is sound, irrespective of this Court's decisions in *Seminole Tribe of Fla. v. Florida* (1996) and *Alden v. Maine.*

Neither did *Parden* break "sharply with prior cases." *Parden* itself cited authority that found related "waivers" in at least roughly comparable circumstances. *United States v. California* (1936), for example, held that a State, "by engaging in interstate commerce by rail, has subjected itself to the commerce power," which amounted to a waiver of a (different though related) substantive immunity. *Parden* also relied on authority holding that States seeking necessary congressional approval for an interstate compact had, "by venturing into the [federal] realm, 'assume[d] the [waiver of sovereign immunity] conditions . . . attached.' " Earlier case law had found a waiver of sovereign immunity in a State's decision to bring a creditor's claim in bankruptcy. *Gardner v. New Jersey* (1947). Later case law, suggesting that a waiver may be found in a State's acceptance of a federal grant, see *Atascadero State Hospital v .Scanlon* (1985), supports *Parden*'s conclusion. Where is the sharp break?

The majority has only one answer to this question. It believes that this Court's case law requires any "waiver" to be "express" and "unequivocal." But the cases to which I have just referred show that is not so. The majority tries to explain some of those cases away with the statement that "what is attached to the refusal to waive" in those cases is "the forgoing of some federal beneficence," while what is involved here is "the exclusion of the State from [an] otherwise lawful activity." This statement does not explain away a difference. It simply states a difference that demands an explanation.

The statement does appeal to an intuition, namely, that it is somehow easier for the State, and hence more voluntary, to forgo "federal beneficence" than to refrain from "otherwise lawful activity," or that it is somehow more compelling or oppressive for Congress to forbid the State to perform an "otherwise lawful" act than to withhold "beneficence." But the force of this intuition depends upon the example that one chooses as its illustration; and realistic examples suggest the intuition is not sound in the present context. Given the amount of money at stake, it may be harder, not easier, for a State to refuse highway funds than to refrain from entering the investment services business. . . . It is more compelling and oppressive for Congress to threaten to withhold from a State funds needed to educate its children than to threaten to subject it to suit when it competes directly with a private investment company. The distinction that the majority seeks to make—drawn in terms of gifts and entitlements—does not exist.

The majority is also wrong to say that this Court has "narrowed" *Parden* in its "subsequent opinion[s]," at least in any way relevant to today's decision. *Parden* considered two separate issues: (1) Does Congress have the *power* to require a State to waive its immunity? (2) How *clearly* must Congress speak when it does so? The Court has narrowed *Parden* only in respect to the second issue, not the first;

but today we are concerned only with the first. The Court in *Employees of Dept. of Public Health and Welfare of Mo. v. Department of Public Health and Welfare of Mo.* (1973), for example, discussed whether Congress *had, or had not,* "lift[ed]" sovereign immunity, not whether it *could, or could not,* have done so. . . . And *Employees'* limitation of *Parden,* to "the area where private persons and corporations normally ran the enterprise," took place in the context of *clarity,* not *power.* . . .

The remaining cases the majority mentions offer it no greater support. [Discussion omitted of *Welch v. Texas Dept. of Highways and Public Transp.* (1987), *Atascadero State Hospital v. Scanlon* (1985), and *Edelman v. Jordan* (1974).] Even *Seminole Tribe* carefully avoided calling *Parden* into question. While specifying that Congress cannot, in the exercise of its Article I powers, "abrogate unilaterally the States' immunity from suit," it left open the scope of the term "unilaterally" by referring to *Parden,* without criticism, as standing for the "unremarkable, and completely unrelated, proposition that the States may waive their sovereign immunity." In short, except for those in today's majority, no member of this Court had ever questioned the holding of *Parden* that the Court today discards because it cannot find "merit in attempting to salvage any remnant of it."

Parden had never been questioned because, *Seminole Tribe* or not, it still makes sense. The line the Court today rejects has been drawn by this Court to place States outside the ordinary dormant Commerce Clause rules when they act as "market participants." [Citations omitted.] And Congress has drawn this same line in the related context of foreign state sovereign immunity. In doing so, Congress followed the modern trend . . . regarding foreign state sovereign immunity. . . . Indeed, given the widely accepted view among modern nations that when a State engages in ordinary commercial activity sovereign immunity has no significant role to play, it is today's holding, not *Parden,* that creates the legal "anomaly."

II

I resist all the more strongly the Court's extension of *Seminole Tribe* in this case because, although I accept this Court's pre-*Seminole Tribe* sovereign immunity decisions, I am not yet ready to adhere to the proposition of law set forth in *Seminole Tribe.* In my view, Congress does possess the authority to abrogate a State's sovereign immunity where "necessary and proper" to the exercise of an Article I power. My reasons include those that JUSTICES STEVENS and SOUTER already have described in detail.

(1) Neither constitutional text nor the surrounding debates support *Seminole Tribe's* view that Congress lacks the Article I power to abrogate a State's sovereign immunity in federal question cases, (unlike diversity cases). . . .

(2) The precedents that offer important legal support for the doctrine of sovereign immunity do not help the *Seminole Tribe* majority. They all focus upon a critically different question, namely, whether *courts,* acting without legislative support, can abrogate state sovereign immunity, not whether Congress, acting legislatively, can do so.

(3) Sovereign immunity is a common-law doctrine. The new American Nation received common-law doctrines selectively, accepting some, abandoning others, and frequently modifying those it accepted in light of the new Nation's special needs and circumstances. The new Nation's federalist lodestar, Dual Sovereignty

(of State and Nation), demanded modification of the traditional single-sovereign immunity doctrine, thereby permitting Congress to narrow or abolish state sovereign immunity where necessary.

(a) Dual Sovereignty undercuts the doctrine's traditional "logical and practical" justification, namely (in the words of Justice Holmes), that "there can be no legal right as against the authority that makes the law on which the right depends." When a State is sued for violating federal law, the "authority" that would assert the immunity, the State, is not the "authority" that made the (federal) law. This point remains true even if the Court treats sovereign immunity as a principle of natural law.

(b) Dual Sovereignty, by granting Congress the power to create substantive rights that bind States (despite their sovereignty), must grant Congress the subsidiary power to create related private remedies that bind States (despite their sovereignty).

(c) Dual Sovereignty means that Congress may need that lesser power lest States (if they are not subject to federal remedies) ignore the substantive federal law that binds them, thereby disabling the National Government and weakening the very Union that the Constitution creates.

(4) By interpreting the Constitution as rendering immutable this one common-law doctrine (sovereign immunity), Seminole Tribe threatens the Nation's ability to enact economic legislation needed for the future in much the way that *Lochner v. New York* (1905) threatened the Nation's ability to enact social legislation over 90 years ago.

I shall elaborate upon this last-mentioned point. The similarity to *Lochner* lies in the risk that *Seminole Tribe* and the Court's subsequent cases will deprive Congress of necessary legislative flexibility. Their rules will make it more difficult for Congress to create, for example, a decentralized system of individual private remedies, say a private remedial system needed to protect intellectual property, including computer-related educational materials, irrespective of the need for, or importance of, such a system in a 21st century advanced economy. Cf. *Florida Prepaid Postsecondary Ed. Expense Bd. v. College Savings Bank* (STEVENS, J., dissenting) (illustrating the harm the rules work to the patent system). Similarly, those rules will inhibit the creation of innovative legal regimes, say, incentive-based or decentralized regulatory systems, that deliberately take account of local differences by assigning roles, powers, or responsibility, not just to federal administrators, but to citizens, at least if such a regime must incorporate a private remedy against a State (e.g., a State as water polluter) to work effectively. Yet, ironically, Congress needs this kind of flexibility if it is to achieve one of federalism's basic objectives.

That basic objective should not be confused with the details of any particular federalist doctrine, for the contours of federalist doctrine have changed over the course of our Nation's history. . . .

But those changing doctrines reflect at least one unchanging goal: the protection of liberty. Federalism helps to protect liberty not simply in our modern sense of helping the individual remain free of restraints imposed by a distant government, but more directly by promoting the sharing among citizens of governmental decisionmaking authority. The ancient world understood the need to divide sovereign power among a nation's citizens, thereby creating government in which all would exercise that power. . . . Our Nation's founders understood the same, for they wrote a Constitution that divided governmental authority, retained great power at state and local levels, and which foresaw, indeed assumed, democratic citizen participation in government at all levels, including levels that facilitated citizen participation closer to a citizen's home.

In today's world, legislative flexibility is necessary if we are to protect this kind of liberty. Modern commerce and the technology upon which it rests needs large markets and seeks government large enough to secure trading rules that permit industry to compete in the global market place, to prevent pollution that crosses borders, and to assure adequate protection of health and safety by discouraging a regulatory "race to the bottom." Yet local control over local decisions remains necessary. Uniform regulatory decisions about, for example, chemical waste disposal, pesticides, or food labeling, will directly affect daily life in every locality. But they may reflect differing views among localities about the relative importance of the wage levels or environmental preferences that underlie them. Local control can take account of such concerns and help to maintain a sense of community despite global forces that threaten it. Federalism matters to ordinary citizens seeking to maintain a degree of control, a sense of community, in an increasingly interrelated and complex world.

Courts can remain sensitive to these needs when they interpret statutes and apply constitutional provisions, for example, the dormant Commerce Clause. But courts cannot easily draw the proper basic lines of authority. The proper local/national/international balance is often highly context specific. And judicial rules that would allocate power are often far too broad. Legislatures, however, can write laws that more specifically embody that balance. Specific regulatory schemes, for example, can draw lines that leave certain local authority untouched, or that involve States, local communities, or citizens directly through the grant of funds, powers, rights, or privileges. Depending upon context, Congress may encourage or require interaction among citizens working at various levels of government. That is why the modern substantive federalist problem demands a flexible, context-specific legislative response (and it does not help to constitutionalize an ahistoric view of sovereign immunity that, by freezing its remedial limitations, tends to place the State beyond the reach of law).

I recognize the possibility that Congress may achieve its objectives in other ways. *Ex parte Young* (1908) is still available, though effective only where damages remedies are not important. Congress, too, might create a federal damages-collecting "enforcement" bureaucracy charged with responsibilities that Congress would prefer to place in the hands of States or private citizens. Or perhaps Congress will be able to achieve the results it seeks (including decentralization) by embodying the necessary state "waivers" in federal funding programs—in which case, the Court's decisions simply impose upon Congress the burden of rewriting legislation, for no apparent reason.

But none of these alternatives is satisfactory. Unfortunately, *Seminole Tribe*, and today's related decisions, separate one formal strand from the federalist skein—a strand that has been understood as anti-Republican since the time of Cicero—and they elevate that strand to the level of an immutable constitutional principle more akin to the thought of James I than of James Madison. They do so when the role sovereign immunity once played in helping to assure the States that their political independence would remain even after joining the Union no longer holds center stage. They do so when a federal court's ability to enforce its judgment against a

State is no longer a major concern. And they do so without adequate legal support grounded in either history or practical need. To the contrary, by making that doctrine immune from congressional Article I modification, the Court makes it more difficult for Congress to decentralize governmental decisionmaking and to provide individual citizens, or local communities, with a variety of enforcement powers. By diminishing congressional flexibility to do so, the Court makes it somewhat more difficult to satisfy modern federalism's more important liberty-protecting needs. In this sense, it is counterproductive.

III

I do not know whether the State has engaged in false advertising or unfair competition as College Savings Bank alleges. But this case was dismissed at the threshold. Congress has clearly said that College Savings Bank may bring a Lanham Act suit in these circumstances. For the reasons set forth in this opinion, I believe Congress has the constitutional power so to provide. I would therefore reverse the judgment of the Court of Appeals.

No. 98-531

Florida Prepaid Postsecondary Education Expense Board, Petitioner v. College Savings Bank and United States

On writ of certiorari to the United States Court of Appeals for the Federal Circuit

[June 23, 1999]

CHIEF JUSTICE REHNQUIST delivered the opinion of the Court.

In 1992, Congress amended the patent laws and expressly abrogated the States' sovereign immunity from claims of patent infringement. Respondent College Savings then sued the State of Florida for patent infringement, and the Court of Appeals held that Congress had validly abrogated the State's sovereign immunity from infringement suits pursuant to its authority under §5 of the Fourteenth Amendment. We hold that, under *City of Boerne v. Flores* (1997), the statute cannot be sustained as legislation enacted to enforce the guarantees of the Fourteenth Amendment's Due Process Clause, and accordingly reverse the decision of the Court of Appeals.

I

Since 1987, respondent College Savings Bank, a New Jersey chartered savings bank located in Princeton, New Jersey, has marketed and sold certificates of deposit known as the CollegeSure CD, which are essentially annuity contracts for financing future college expenses. College Savings obtained a patent for its financing methodology, designed to guarantee investors sufficient funds to cover the costs of tuition for colleges. Petitioner Florida Prepaid Postsecondary Education Expenses Board (Florida Prepaid) is an entity created by the State of Florida that administers similar tuition prepayment contracts available to Florida residents and their children. College Savings claims that, in the course of administering its tuition prepayment program, Florida Prepaid directly and indirectly infringed College Savings' patent.

College Savings brought an infringement action under 35 U.S.C. §271(a) against Florida Prepaid in the United States District Court for the District of New Jersey in November 1994. By the time College Savings filed its suit, Congress had already passed the Patent and Plant Variety Protection Remedy Clarification Act (Patent Remedy Act), 35 U.S.C. §§271(h), 296(a). Before this legislation, the patent laws stated only that "whoever" without authority made, used, or sold a patented invention infringed the patent. Applying this Court's decision in *Atascadero State Hosp. v. Scanlon* (1985), the Federal Circuit had held that the patent laws failed to contain the requisite statement of intent to abrogate state sovereign immunity from infringement suits. See, *e.g., Chew v. California* (1989). In response to *Chew* and similar decisions, Congress enacted the Patent Remedy Act to "clarify that States, instrumentalities of States, and officers and employees of States acting in their official capacity, are subject to suit in Federal court by any person for infringement of patents and plant variety protections." [Quoting preamble to statute.] Section 271(h) now states: "As used in this section, the term 'whoever' includes any State, any instrumentality of a State, and any officer or employee of a State or instrumentality of a State acting in his official capacity." Section 296(a) addresses the sovereign immunity issue even more specifically:

> "Any State, any instrumentality of a State, and any officer or employee of a State or instrumentality of a State acting in his official capacity, shall not be immune, under the eleventh amendment of the Constitution of the United States or under any other doctrine of sovereign immunity, from suit in Federal court by any person . . . for infringement of a patent under section 271, or for any other violation under this title."

Relying on these provisions, College Savings alleged that Florida Prepaid had willfully infringed its patent under §271, as well as contributed to and induced infringement. College Savings sought declaratory and injunctive relief as well as damages, attorney's fees, and costs.

After this Court decided *Seminole Tribe of Fla. v. Florida* (1996), Florida Prepaid moved to dismiss the action on the grounds of sovereign immunity. Florida Prepaid argued that the Patent Remedy Act was an unconstitutional attempt by Congress to use its Article I powers to abrogate state sovereign immunity. College Savings responded that Congress had properly exercised its power pursuant to §5 of the Fourteenth Amendment to enforce the guarantees of the Due Process Clause in §1 of the Amendment. The United States intervened to defend the constitutionality of the statute. Agreeing with College Savings, the District Court denied Florida Prepaid's motion to dismiss (N.J. 1996), and the Federal Circuit affirmed (1998).

The Federal Circuit held that Congress had clearly expressed its intent to abrogate the States' immunity from suit in federal court for patent infringement, and that Congress had the power under §5 of the Fourteenth Amendment to do so. The court reasoned that patents are property subject to the protections of the Due Process Clause and that Congress' objective in enacting the Patent Remedy Act was permissible because it sought to prevent States from depriving patent owners of this property without due process. The court rejected Florida Prepaid's argument that it and other States had not deprived patent owners of their property *without due process*, and refused to "deny Congress the authority to subject all states to suit for patent infringement in the federal courts, regardless of the extent of procedural due process that may exist at any particular time." Finally, the court held that the Patent Remedy Act was a proportionate response to state infringement and an appropriate measure to protect patent owners' property under this Court's decision in *City of Boerne*. The court concluded that significant harm results from state infringement of patents, and "[t]here is no sound reason to hold that Congress cannot subject a state to the same civil consequences that face a private party infringer." We granted certiorari (1999), and now reverse.

II

The Eleventh Amendment provides:

> "The Judicial Power of the United States shall not be construed to extend to any suit in law or equity, commenced or prosecuted against one of the United States by Citizens of another State, or by Citizens or Subjects of any Foreign State."

As the Court recently explained in *Seminole Tribe*:

> "Although the text of the Amendment would appear to restrict only the Article III diversity jurisdiction of the federal courts, 'we have understood the Eleventh Amendment to stand not so much for what it says, but for the presupposition . . . which it confirms.' That presupposition, first observed over a century ago in *Hans v. Louisiana* (1890), has two parts: first, that each State is a sovereign entity in our federal system; and second, that '[i]t is inherent in the nature of sovereignty not to be amenable to the suit of an individual without its consent.' [Quoting the *Federalist* No. 81.] . . . For over a century we have reaffirmed that federal jurisdiction over suits against unconsenting States 'was not contemplated by the Constitution when establishing the judicial power of the United States.' "

Here, College Savings sued the State of Florida in federal court and it is undisputed that Florida has not expressly consented to suit. College Savings and the United States argue that Florida has impliedly waived its immunity under *Parden v. Terminal R. Co. of Ala. Docks Dept.* (1964). That argument, however, is foreclosed by our decision in the companion case overruling the constructive waiver theory announced in *Parden.* See *College Savings Bank v. Florida Prepaid Postsecondary Ed. Expense Bd.* (1999).

College Savings and the United States nonetheless contend that Congress' enactment of the Patent Remedy Act validly abrogated the States' sovereign immunity. To determine the merits of this proposition, we must answer two questions: "first, whether Congress has 'unequivocally expresse[d] its intent to abrogate the immunity,' . . . and second, whether Congress has acted 'pursuant to a valid exercise of power.' " *Seminole Tribe.* We agree with the parties and the Federal Circuit that in enacting the Patent Remedy Act, Congress has made its intention to abrogate the States' immunity "unmistakably clear in the language of the statute.' " Indeed, Congress' intent to abrogate could not have been any clearer. . . .

Whether Congress had the power to compel States to surrender their sovereign immunity for these purposes, however, is another matter. Congress justified the Patent Remedy Act under three sources of constitutional authority: the Patent Clause, Art. I, §8, cl. 8; the Interstate Commerce Clause, Art. I, §8, cl. 3; and §5 of the Fourteenth Amendment. In *Seminole Tribe,* of course, this Court overruled the plurality opinion in *Pennsylvania v. Union Gas Co.* (1989), our only prior case finding congressional authority to abrogate state sovereign immunity pursuant to an Article I power (the Commerce Clause). *Seminole Tribe* makes clear that Congress may not abrogate state sovereign immunity pursuant to its Article I powers; hence the Patent Remedy Act cannot be sustained under either the Commerce Clause or the Patent Clause. The Federal Circuit recognized this, and College Savings and the United States do not contend otherwise.

Instead, College Savings and the United States argue that the Federal Circuit properly concluded that Congress enacted the Patent Remedy Act to secure the Fourteenth Amendment's protections against deprivations of property without due process of law. The Fourteenth Amendment provides in relevant part:

> "Section 1. . . . No State shall . . . deprive any person of life, liberty, or property, without due process of law.
> . . ."Section 5. The Congress shall have power to enforce, by appropriate legislation, the provisions of this article."

While reaffirming the view that state sovereign immunity does not yield to Congress' Article I powers, this Court in *Seminole Tribe* also reaffirmed its holding in *Fitzpatrick v. Bitzer* (1976) that Congress retains the authority to abrogate state sovereign immunity pursuant to the Fourteenth Amendment. . . .

College Savings and the United States are correct in suggesting that "appropriate" legislation pursuant to the Enforcement Clause of the Fourteenth Amendment could abrogate state sovereignty. Congress itself apparently thought the Patent Remedy Act could be so justified:

> "[T]he bill is justified as an acceptable method of enforcing the provisions of the fourteenth amendment. The Court in *Lemelson v. Ampex Corp.* (ND Ill. 1974) recognized that a patent is a form of property, holding that a right to compensation exists for patent infringement. Additionally, because courts have continually recognized patent rights as

property, the fourteenth amendment prohibits a State from depriving a person of property without due process of law." [Citing Senate committee report.]

We have held that "[t]he 'provisions of this article,' to which §5 refers, include the Due Process Clause of the Fourteenth Amendment." *City of Boerne v. Flores.*

But the legislation must nonetheless be "appropriate" under §5 as that term was construed in *City of Boerne*. There, this Court held that the Religious Freedom Restoration Act of 1993 (RFRA) exceeded Congress' authority under §5 of the Fourteenth Amendment, insofar as RFRA was made applicable to the States. RFRA was enacted "in direct response to" this Court's decision in *Employment Div., Dept. of Human Resources of Ore. v. Smith* (1990), which construed the Free Exercise Clause of the First Amendment to hold that "neutral, generally applicable laws may be applied to religious practices even when not supported by a compelling governmental interest." Through RFRA, Congress reinstated the compelling governmental interest test eschewed by *Smith* by requiring that a generally applicable law placing a "substantial burden" on the free exercise of religion must be justified by a "compelling governmental interest" and must employ the "least restrictive means" of furthering that interest.

In holding that RFRA could not be justified as "appropriate" enforcement legislation under §5, the Court emphasized that Congress' enforcement power is "remedial" in nature. We recognized that "[l]egislation which deters or remedies constitutional violations can fall within the sweep of Congress' enforcement power even if in the process it prohibits conduct which is not itself unconstitutional and intrudes into 'legislative spheres of autonomy previously reserved to the States.' " We also noted, however, that " '[a]s broad as the congressional enforcement power is, it is not unlimited,' " and held that "Congress does not enforce a constitutional right by changing what the right is. It has been given the power 'to enforce,' not the power to determine what constitutes a constitutional violation." Canvassing the history of the Fourteenth Amendment and case law examining the propriety of Congress' various voting rights measures, the Court explained:

> "While the line between measures that remedy or prevent unconstitutional actions and measures that make a substantive change in the governing law is not easy to discern, and Congress must have wide latitude in determining where it lies, the distinction exists and must be observed. There must be a congruence and proportionality between the injury to be prevented or remedied and the means adopted to that end. Lacking such a connection, legislation may become substantive in operation and effect."

We thus held that for Congress to invoke §5, it must identify conduct transgressing the Fourteenth Amendment's substantive provisions, and must tailor its legislative scheme to remedying or preventing such conduct.

RFRA failed to meet this test because there was little support in the record for the concerns that supposedly animated the law. And, unlike the measures in the voting rights cases, RFRA's provisions were "so out of proportion to a supposed remedial or preventive object" that it could not be understood "as responsive to, or designed to prevent, unconstitutional behavior.". . .

Can the Patent Remedy Act be viewed as remedial or preventive legislation aimed at securing the protections of the Fourteenth Amendment for patent owners? Following *City of Boerne*, we must first identify the Fourteenth Amendment "evil" or "wrong" that Congress intended to remedy, guided by the principle that the propriety of any §5 legislation "must be judged with reference to the historical experience . . . it reflects." The underlying conduct at issue here is state infringement of patents and the use of sovereign immunity to deny patent owners compensation for the invasion of their patent rights. . . . It is this conduct then—unremedied patent infringement by the States—that must give rise to the Fourteenth Amendment violation that Congress sought to redress in the Patent Remedy Act.

In enacting the Patent Remedy Act, however, Congress identified no pattern of patent infringement by the States, let alone a pattern of constitutional violations. Unlike the undisputed record of racial discrimination confronting Congress in the voting rights cases, Congress came up with little evidence of infringing conduct on the part of the States. The House Report acknowledged that "many states comply with patent law" and could provide only two examples of patent infringement suits against the States. The Federal Circuit in its opinion identified only eight patent-infringement suits prosecuted against the States in the 110 years between 1880 and 1990.

Testimony before the House Subcommittee in favor of the bill acknowledged that "states are willing and able to respect patent rights. The fact that there are so few reported cases involving patent infringement claims against states underlies the point." [Citations of testimony omitted.] The Senate Report, as well, contains no evidence that unremedied patent infringement by States had become a problem of national import. At most, Congress heard testimony that patent infringement by States might increase in the future, and acted to head off this speculative harm.

College Savings argues that by infringing a patent and then pleading immunity to an infringement suit, a State not only infringes the patent, but deprives the patentee of property without due process of law and "takes" the property in the patent without paying the just compensation required by the Fifth Amendment. The United States declines to defend the Act as based on the Just Compensation Clause, but joins in College Savings' defense of the Act as designed to prevent a State from depriving a patentee of property without due process of law. Florida Prepaid contends that Congress may not invoke §5 to protect property interests that it has created in the first place under Article 1. Patents, however, have long been considered a species of property. [Citations omitted.] As such, they are surely included within the "property" of which no person may be deprived by a State without due process of law. And if the Due Process Clause protects patents, we know of no reason why Congress might not legislate against their deprivation without due process under §5 of the Fourteenth Amendment.

Though patents may be considered "property" for purposes of our analysis, the legislative record still provides little support for the proposition that Congress sought to remedy a Fourteenth Amendment violation in enacting the Patent Remedy Act. The Due Process Clause provides, "nor shall any State deprive any person of life, liberty, or property, *without due process of law*" (emphasis added). This Court has accordingly held that "[i]n procedural due process claims, the deprivation by state action of a constitutionally protected interest . . . is not in itself unconstitutional; what is unconstitutional is the deprivation of such an interest without due process of law." *Zinermon v. Burch* (1990).

Thus, under the plain terms of the Clause and the clear import of our precedent, a State's infringement of a patent, though interfering with a patent owner's right to exclude others, does not by itself violate the Constitution. Instead, only where the State provides no remedy, or only inadequate remedies, to injured patent owners for its infringement of their patent could a deprivation of property without due process result. . . .

Congress, however, barely considered the availability of state remedies for patent infringement and hence whether the States' conduct might have amounted to a constitutional violation under the Fourteenth Amendment. It did hear a limited amount of testimony to the effect that the remedies available in some States were uncertain.

The primary point made by these witnesses, however, was not that state remedies were constitutionally inadequate, but rather that they were less convenient than federal remedies, and might undermine the uniformity of patent law. . . .

Congress itself said nothing about the existence or adequacy of state remedies in the statute or in the Senate Report, and made only a few fleeting references to state remedies in the House Report, essentially repeating the testimony of the witnesses. [Citing Senate report references to "tenuous" remedies in states and goal of "national uniformity in our patent system."] The need for uniformity in the construction of patent law is undoubtedly important, but that is a factor which belongs to the Article I patent-power calculus, rather than to any determination of whether a state plea of sovereign immunity deprives a patentee of property without due process of law.

We have also said that a state actor's negligent act that causes unintended injury to a person's property does not "deprive" that person of property within the meaning of the Due Process Clause. [Citation omitted.] Actions predicated on direct patent infringement, however, do not require any showing of intent to infringe; instead, knowledge and intent are considered only with respect to damages. . . . Congress did not focus on instances of intentional or reckless infringement on the part of the States. Indeed, the evidence before Congress suggested that most state infringement was innocent or at worst negligent. . . . Such negligent conduct, however, does not violate the Due Process Clause of the Fourteenth Amendment.

The legislative record thus suggests that the Patent Remedy Act does not respond to a history of "widespread and persisting deprivation of constitutional rights" of the sort Congress has faced in enacting proper prophylactic §5 legislation. *City of Boerne.* Instead, Congress appears to have enacted this legislation in response to a handful of instances of state patent infringement that do not necessarily violate the Constitution. Though the lack of support in the legislative record is not determinative, identifying the targeted constitutional wrong or evil is still a critical part of our §5 calculus because "[s]trong measures appropriate to address one harm may be an unwarranted response to another, lesser one." *Id.* Here, the record at best offers scant support for Congress' conclusion that States were depriving patent owners of property without due process of law by pleading sovereign immunity in federal-court patent actions.

Because of this lack, the provisions of the Patent Remedy Act are "so out of proportion to a supposed remedial or preventive object that [they] cannot be understood as responsive to, or designed to prevent, unconstitutional behavior." *Id.* An unlimited range of state conduct would expose a State to claims of direct, induced, or contributory patent infringement, and the House Report itself cited testimony acknowledging " 'it[']s difficult for us to identify a patented product or process which might not be used by a state.' " Despite subjecting States to this expansive liability, Congress did nothing to limit the coverage of the Act to cases involving arguable constitutional violations, such as where a State refuses to offer any state-court remedy for patent owners whose patents it had infringed. Nor did it make any attempt to confine the reach of the Act by limiting the remedy to certain types of infringement, such as nonnegligent infringement or infringement authorized pursuant to state policy; or providing for suits only against States with questionable remedies or a high incidence of infringement.

Instead, Congress made all States immediately amenable to suit in federal court for all kinds of possible patent infringement and for an indefinite duration. Our opinion in *City of Boerne* discussed with approval the various limits that Congress imposed in its voting rights measures, and noted that where "a congressional enactment pervasively prohibits constitutional state action in an effort to remedy or to prevent unconstitutional state action, limitations of this kind tend to ensure Congress' means are proportionate to ends legitimate under §5." The Patent Remedy Act's indiscriminate scope offends this principle, and is particularly incongruous in light of the scant support for the predicate unconstitutional conduct that Congress intended to remedy. In sum, it simply cannot be said that "many of [the acts of infringement] affected by the congressional enactment have a significant likelihood of being unconstitutional."

The historical record and the scope of coverage therefore make it clear that the Patent Remedy Act cannot be sustained under §5 of the Fourteenth Amendment. The examples of States avoiding liability for patent infringement by pleading sovereign immunity in a federal-court patent action are scarce enough, but any plausible argument that such action on the part of the State deprived patentees of property and left them without a remedy under state law is scarcer still. The statute's apparent and more basic aims were to provide a uniform remedy for patent infringement and to place States on the same footing as private parties under that regime. These are proper Article I concerns, but that Article does not give Congress the power to enact such legislation after *Seminole Tribe.*

The judgment of the Court of Appeals is reversed, and the case is remanded for proceedings consistent with this opinion.

It is so ordered.

JUSTICE STEVENS, with whom JUSTICE SOUTER, JUSTICE GINS-BURG, and JUSTICE BREYER join, dissenting.

The Constitution vests Congress with plenary authority over patents and copyrights. U.S. Const., Art. I, §8, cl.8. Nearly 200 years ago, Congress provided for exclusive jurisdiction of patent infringement litigation in the federal courts. In 1992 Congress clarified that jurisdictional grant by an amendment to the patent law that unambiguously authorizes patent infringement actions against States, state instrumentalities, and any officer or employee of a State acting in his official capacity. 35 U.S.C. §271(h). Given the absence of effective state remedies for patent infringement by States and the statutory pre-emption of such state remedies, the 1992 Patent and Plant Variety Protection Remedy Clarification Act (Patent Remedy Act) was an appropriate exercise of Congress' power under §5 of the Fourteenth Amendment to prevent state deprivations of property without due process of law.

This Court's recent decision in *City of Boerne v. Flores* (1997) amply supports congressional authority to enact the Patent Remedy Act, whether one assumes that States seldom infringe patents, or that patent infringements potentially permeate an "unlimited range of state conduct." Before discussing *City of Boerne*, however, I shall comment briefly on the principle that undergirds all aspects of our patent system: national uniformity.

I

... Sound reasons support both Congress' authority over patents and its subsequent decision in 1800 to vest exclusive jurisdiction over patent infringement litigation in the federal courts. The substantive rules of law that are applied in patent infringement cases are entirely federal. From the beginning, Congress has given the patentee the right to bring an action for patent infringement. There is, accordingly, a strong federal interest in an interpretation of the patent statutes that is both uniform and faithful to the constitutional goals of stimulating invention and rewarding the disclosure of novel and useful advances in technology. Federal interests are threatened, not only by inadequate protection for patentees, but also when overprotection may have an adverse impact on a competitive economy. Therefore, consistency, uniformity, and familiarity with the extensive and relevant body of patent jurisprudence are matters of overriding significance in this area of the law.

Patent infringement litigation often raises difficult technical issues that are unfamiliar to the average trial judge. That consideration, as well as the divergence among the federal circuits in their interpretation of patent issues, provided support for the congressional decision in 1982 to consolidate appellate jurisdiction of patent appeals in the Court of Appeals for the Federal Circuit. Although that court has jurisdiction over all appeals from federal trial courts in patent infringement cases, it has no power to review state court decisions on questions of patent law. The reasons that motivated the creation of the Federal Circuit would be undermined by any exception that allowed patent infringement claims to be brought in state court.

Today the Court first acknowledges that the "need for uniformity in the construction of patent law is undoubtedly important," but then discounts its significance as merely "a factor which belongs to the Article I patent-power calculus, rather than to any determination of whether a state plea of sovereign immunity deprives a patentee of property without due process of law." But the "Article I patent-power calculus" is directly relevant to this case because it establishes the constitutionality of the congressional decision to vest exclusive jurisdiction over patent infringement cases in the federal courts. That basic decision was unquestionably appropriate. It was equally appropriate for Congress to abrogate state sovereign immunity in patent infringement cases in order to close a potential loophole in the uniform federal scheme, which, if undermined, would necessarily decrease the efficacy of the process afforded to patent holders.

II

Our recent decision in *City of Boerne v. Flores* sets out the general test for determining whether Congress has enacted "appropriate" legislation pursuant to §5 of the Fourteenth Amendment. "There must be a congruence and proportionality between the injury to be prevented or remedied and the means adopted to that end." The first step of the inquiry, then, is to determine what injury Congress sought to prevent or remedy with the relevant legislation.

As the Court recognizes, Congress' authority under §5 of the Fourteenth Amendment extends to enforcing the Due Process Clause of that Amendment. Congress decided, and I agree, that the Patent Remedy Act was a proper exercise of this power.

The Court acknowledges, as it must, that patents are property. . . . The Court suggests, however, that a State's infringement of a patent does not necessarily constitute a "deprivation" within the meaning of the Due Process Clause, because the infringement may be done negligently.

As part of its attempt to stem the tide of prisoner litigation, and to avoid making "the Fourteenth Amendment a font of tort law to be superimposed upon whatever systems may already be administered by the States," *Daniels v. Williams* (1986), this Court has drawn a constitutional distinction between negligent and intentional misconduct. Injuries caused by the mere negligence of state prison officials—in leaving a pillow on the stairs of the jail, for example—do not "deprive" anyone of liberty or property within the meaning of the Due Process Clause of that Amendment. On the other hand, willful misconduct, and perhaps "recklessness or gross negligence," may give rise to such a deprivation.

While I disagree with the Court's assumption that this standard necessarily applies to deprivations of patent rights, the *Daniels* line of cases has only marginal relevance to this case: Respondent College Savings Bank has alleged that petitioner's infringement was willful. The question presented by this case, then, is whether the Patent Remedy Act, which clarified Congress' intent to subject state infringers to suit in federal court, may be applied to willful infringement.

As I read the Court's opinion, its negative answer to that question has nothing to do with the facts of this case. Instead, it relies entirely on perceived deficiencies in the evidence reviewed by Congress before it enacted the clarifying amendment. "In enacting the Patent Remedy Act . . . Congress identified no pattern of patent infringement by the States, let alone a pattern of constitutional violations." [Quoting Court's opinion.]

It is quite unfair for the Court to strike down Congress' Act based on an absence of findings supporting a requirement this Court had not yet articulated. The legislative history of the Patent Remedy Act makes it abundantly clear that Congress was attempting to hurdle the then-most-recent barrier this Court had erected in the Eleventh Amendment course—the "clear statement" rule of *Atascadero State Hospital v. Scanlon* (1985).

Nevertheless, Congress did hear testimony about inadequate state remedies for patent infringement when considering the Patent Remedy Act. The leading case referred to in the congressional hearing was *Chew v. California* (CA Fed. 1990). In fact, *Chew* prompted Congress to consider the legislation that became the Patent Remedy Act. The Federal Circuit held in that case that congressional intent to abrogate state sovereign immunity under the patent laws was not "unmistakably clear," as this Court had required in *Atascadero*.

The facts of *Chew* clearly support both Congress' decision and authority to enact the Patent Remedy Act. Marian Chew had invented a method for testing automobile engine exhaust emissions and secured a patent on her discovery. Her invention was primarily used by States and other governmental entities. In 1987, Chew, an Ohio resident, sued the State of California in federal court for infringing her patent. California filed a motion to dismiss on Eleventh Amendment grounds, which the District Court granted. The Federal Circuit affirmed, expressly stating that the question whether Chew had a remedy under California law "is a question not before us." Nevertheless, it implied that its decision would have been the same even if Chew were left without any remedy. During its hearing on the Patent Remedy Act, Congress heard testimony about the *Chew* case. Professor Merges stated that Chew might not have been able to draft her infringement suit as a tort claim. "This might be impossible, o[r] at least difficult, under California law. Consequently, relief under [state statutes] may be not be a true alternative avenue of recovery." [Citing House hearing.]

Congress heard other general testimony that state remedies would likely be insufficient to compensate inventors whose patents had been infringed. . . . The legislative record references several cases of patent infringement involving States. [Citations omitted.]

In addition, Congress found that state infringement of patents was likely to increase. The Court's opinion today dismisses this rationale: "At most, Congress heard testimony that patent infringement by States might increase in the future and acted to head off this speculative harm." In fact, States and their instrumentalities, especially state universities, have been involved in many patent cases since 1992. [Citation of six cases omitted.]

Furthermore, States and their instrumentalities are heavily involved in the federal patent system. The United States Patent and Trademark Office issued more than 2,000 patents to universities (both public and private) in 1986 alone. Royalty earnings from licenses at United States universities totaled $273.5 million in 1995, a 12 percent increase over the prior year. The State of Florida has obtained over 200 United States patents since the beginning of 1995. All 50 States own or have obtained patents.

It is true that, when considering the Patent Remedy Act, Congress did not review the remedies available in each State for patent infringements and surmise what kind of recovery a plaintiff might obtain in a tort suit in all 50 jurisdictions. But, it is particularly ironic that the Court should view this fact as support for its holding. Given that Congress had long ago pre-empted state jurisdiction over patent infringement cases, it was surely reasonable for Congress to assume that such remedies simply did not exist. Furthermore, it is well known that not all

States have waived their sovereign immunity from suit, and among those States that have, the contours of this waiver vary widely.

Even if such remedies might be available in theory, it would have been "appropriate" for Congress to conclude that they would not guarantee patentees due process in infringement actions against state defendants. State judges have never had the exposure to patent litigation that federal judges have experienced for decades, and, unlike infringement actions brought in federal district courts, their decisions would not be reviewable in the Court of Appeals for the Federal Circuit. Surely this Court would not undertake the task of reviewing every state court decision that arguably misapplied patent law. And even if 28 U.S.C. §1338 is amended or construed to permit state courts to entertain infringement actions when a State is named as a defendant, given the Court's opinion in *Alden v. Maine*, it is by no means clear that state courts could be required to hear these cases at all.

Even if state courts elected to hear patent infringement cases against state entities, the entire category of such cases would raise questions of impartiality. This concern underlies both the constitutional authorization of diversity jurisdiction and the statutory provisions for removal of certain cases from state to federal courts. The same concern justified John Marshall's narrow construction of the Eleventh Amendment *Cohens v. Virginia* (1821). As he there noted, when there is a conflict between a State's interest and a federal right, it "would be hazarding too much to assert, that the judicatures of the states will be exempt from the prejudices by which the legislatures and people are influenced, and will constitute perfectly impartial tribunals."

Finally, this Court has never mandated that Congress must find " 'widespread and persisting deprivation of constitutional rights,' " in order to employ its §5 authority. It is not surprising, therefore, that Congress did not compile an extensive legislative record analyzing the due process (or lack thereof) that each State might afford for a patent infringement suit retooled as an action in tort. In 1992, Congress had no reason to believe it needed to do such a thing; indeed, it should not have to do so today.

III

In my view, Congress had sufficient evidence of due process violations, whether actual or potential, to meet the requirement we expressed in *City of Boerne* that Congress can act under §5 only to "remedy or prevent unconstitutional actions." The Court's opinion today threatens to read Congress' power to pass prophylactic legislation out of §5 altogether; its holding is unsupported by *City of Boerne* and in fact conflicts with our reasoning in that case.

In *City of Boerne* we affirmed the well-settled principle that the broad sweep of Congress' enforcement power encompasses legislation that deters or remedies constitutional violations, even if it prohibits conduct that is not itself unconstitutional, and even if it intrudes into spheres of autonomy previously reserved to the States. Nevertheless, we held that the enactment of the Religious Freedom Restoration Act of 1993 (RFRA) was not an "appropriate" exercise of Congress' enforcement power under §5 of the Fourteenth Amendment. . . .

The difference between the harm targeted by RFRA and the harm that motivated the enactment of the Patent Remedy Act is striking. In RFRA Congress sought to overrule this Court's interpretation of the First Amendment. The Patent Remedy Act, however, was passed to prevent future violations of due process, based on the substantiated fear that States would be unable or unwilling to provide adequate remedies for their own violations of patent-holders' rights. Congress' "wide latitude" in determining remedial or preventive measures [quoting from *City of Boerne*] has suddenly become very narrow indeed.

City of Boerne also identified a "proportionality" component to "appropriate" legislation under §5. Our opinion expressly recognized that "preventive rules are sometimes appropriate" if there is

> "a congruence between the means used and the ends to be achieved. The appropriateness of remedial measures must be considered in light of the evil presented.... Strong measures appropriate to address one harm may be an unwarranted response to another, lesser one."

In RFRA we found no such congruence, both because of the absence of evidence of widespread violations that were in need of redress, and because the sweeping coverage of the statute ensured "its intrusion at every level of government, displacing laws and prohibiting official actions of almost every description and regardless of subject matter."

Again, the contrast between RFRA and the Act at issue in this case could not be more stark. The sole purpose of this amendment is to abrogate the States' sovereign immunity as a defense to a charge of patent infringement. It has no impact whatsoever on any substantive rule of state law, but merely effectuates settled federal policy to confine patent infringement litigation to federal judges. There is precise congruence between "the means used" (abrogation of sovereign immunity in this narrow category of cases) and "the ends to be achieved" (elimination of the risk that the defense of sovereign immunity will deprive some patentees of property without due process of law).

That congruence is equally precise whether infringement of patents by state actors is rare or frequent. If they are indeed unusual, the statute will operate only in those rare cases. But if such infringements are common, or should become common as state activities in the commercial arena increase, the impact of the statute will likewise expand in precise harmony with the growth of the problem that Congress anticipated and sought to prevent. In either event the statute will have no impact on the States' enforcement of their own laws. None of the concerns that underlay our decision in *City of Boerne* are even remotely implicated in this case.

The Patent Remedy Act merely puts States in the same position as all private users of the patent system, and in virtually the same posture as the United States.... Recognizing the injustice of sovereign immunity in this context, the United States has waived its immunity from suit for patent violations. In 1910, Congress enacted a statute entitled, "An Act to provide additional protection for owners of patents of the United States." The Act provided that owners of patents infringed by the United States "may recover reasonable compensation for such use by suit in the Court of Claims." The United States has consistently maintained this policy for the last 90 years. See 28 U.S.C. §1498.

In my judgment, the 1992 Act is a paradigm of an appropriate exercise of Congress' §5 power.

IV

For these reasons, I am convinced that the 1992 Act should be upheld even if full respect is given to the Court's recent cases cloaking the States with increasing protection from congressional legislation. I do, however, note my continuing dissent from the Court's aggressive sovereign immunity jurisprudence; today, this Court once again demonstrates itself to be the champion of States' rights. In this case, it seeks to guarantee rights the States themselves did not express any particular desire in possessing: during Congress' hearings on the Patent Remedy Act, although invited to do so, the States chose not to testify in opposition to the abrogation of their immunity.

The statute that the Court invalidates today was only one of several "clear statements" that Congress enacted in response to the decision in *Atascadero State Hospital v. Scanlon* (1985). In each of those clarifications Congress was fully justified in assuming that it had ample authority to abrogate sovereign immunity defenses to federal claims, an authority that the Court squarely upheld in *Pennsylvania v. Union Gas Co.* (1989). It was that *holding*—not just the "plurality opinion"—that was overruled in *Seminole Tribe of Fla. v. Florida* (1996). The full reach of that case's dramatic expansion of the judge-made doctrine of sovereign immunity is unpredictable; its dimensions are defined only by the present majority's perception of constitutional penumbras rather than constitutional text. [Citing statement in Court's opinion: "We have understood the Eleventh Amendment to stand not so much for what it says."] Until this expansive and judicially crafted protection of States' rights runs its course, I shall continue to register my agreement with the views expressed in the *Seminole* dissents and in the scholarly commentary on that case.

I respectfully dissent.

How the Court Works

The Constitution makes the Supreme Court the final arbiter in "cases" and "controversies" arising under the Constitution or the laws of the United States. As the interpreter of the law, the Court often is viewed as the least mutable and most tradition-bound of the three branches of the federal government. But the Court has undergone innumerable changes in its history, some of which have been mandated by law. Some of these changes are embodied in Court rules; others are informal adaptations to needs and circumstances.

The Schedule of the Term

Annual Terms

By law the Supreme Court begins its regular annual term on the first Monday in October, and the term lasts approximately nine months. This session is known as the October term. The summer recess, which is not determined by statute or Court rules, generally begins in late June or early July of the following year. This system—staying in continuous session throughout the year, with periodic recesses—makes it unnecessary to convene a special term to deal with matters arising in the summer.

The justices actually begin work before the official opening of the term. They hold their initial conference during the last week in September. When the justices formally convene on the first Monday in October, oral arguments begin.

Arguments and Conferences

At least four justices must request that a case be argued before it can be accepted. Arguments are heard on Monday, Tuesday, and Wednesday for seven two-week sessions, beginning in the first week in October and ending in mid-April. Recesses of two weeks or longer occur between the sessions of oral arguments so that justices can consider the cases and deal with other Court business.

The schedule for oral arguments is 10:00 a.m. to noon and 1 p.m. to 3 p.m. Because most cases receive one hour apiece for argument, the Court can hear up to twelve cases a week.

The Court holds conferences on the Friday just before the two-week oral argument periods and on Wednesday and Friday during the weeks when oral arguments are scheduled. The conferences are designed for consideration of cases already heard in oral argument.

Before each of the Friday conferences, the chief justice circulates a "discuss" list—a list of cases deemed important enough for discussion and a vote. Appeals are placed on the discuss list almost automatically, but as many as three-quarters of the petitions for certiorari are denied. No case is denied review during conference, however, without an initial examination by the justices and their law clerks. Any justice can have a case placed on the Court's conference agenda for review. Most of the cases scheduled for the discuss list also are denied review in the end but only after discussion by the justices during the conference.

Although the last oral arguments have been heard by mid-April each year, the conferences of the justices continue until the end of the term to consider cases remaining on the Court's agenda. All conferences are held in secret, with no legal assistants or other staff present. The attendance of six justices constitutes a quorum. Conferences begin with handshakes all around. In discussing a case, the chief justice speaks first, followed by each justice in order of seniority.

Decision Days

Opinions are released on Tuesdays and Wednesdays during the weeks that the Court is hearing oral arguments; during other weeks, they are released on Mondays. In addition to opinions, the Court also releases an "orders" list—the summary of the Court's action granting or denying review. The orders list is posted at the beginning of the Monday session. It is not announced orally but can be obtained from the clerk and the public information officer. When urgent or important matters arise, the Court's summary orders may be made available on a day other than Monday.

Unlike its orders, decisions of the Court are announced orally in open Court. The justice who wrote the opinion announces the Court's decision, and justices writing concurring or dissenting opinions may state their

---

Visiting the Supreme Court

The Supreme Court building has six levels, two of which—the ground and main floors—are accessible to the public. The basement contains a parking garage, a printing press, and offices for security guards and maintenance personnel. On the ground floor are the John Marshall statue, the exhibition area, the public information office, and a cafeteria. The main corridor, known as the Great Hall, the courtroom, and justices' offices are on the main floor. The second floor contains dining rooms, the justices' reading room, and other offices; the third floor, the Court library; and the fourth floor, the gym and storage areas.

From October to mid-April, the Court hears oral arguments Monday through Wednesday for about two weeks a month. These sessions begin at 10 a.m. and continue until 3 p.m., with a one-hour recess starting at noon. They are open to the public on a first-come, first-served basis.

Visitors may inspect the Supreme Court chamber any time the Court is not in session. Historical exhibits and a free motion picture on how the Court works also are available throughout the year. The Supreme Court building is open from 9 a.m. to 4:30 p.m. Monday through Friday, except for legal holidays. When the Court is not in session, lectures are given in the courtroom every hour on the half hour between 9:30 a.m. and 3:30 p.m.

---

views as well. When more than one decision is to be rendered, the justices who wrote the opinion make their announcements in reverse order of seniority. Occasionally, all or a large portion of the opinion is read aloud. More often the author summarizes the opinion or simply announces the result and states that a written opinion has been filed.

Reviewing Cases

In determining whether to accept a case for review, the Court has considerable discretion, subject only to the restraints imposed by the Constitution and Congress. Article III, section 2, of the Constitution provides that "In all Cases affecting Ambassadors, other public Ministers and Consuls, and those in which a State shall be Party, the supreme Court shall have original Jurisdiction. In all the other Cases . . . the supreme Court shall have appellate Jurisdiction, both as to Law and Fact, with such Exceptions, and under such Regulations as the Congress shall make."

Original jurisdiction refers to the right of the Supreme Court to hear a case before any other court does. Appellate jurisdiction is the right to review the decision of a lower court. The vast majority of cases reaching the Supreme Court are appeals from rulings of the lower courts; generally only a handful of original jurisdiction cases are filed each term.

After enactment of the Judiciary Act of 1925, the Supreme Court gained broad discretion to decide for itself what cases it would hear. In 1988 Congress virtually eliminated the Court's mandatory jurisdiction, which obliged it to hear most appeals. Since then that discretion has been nearly unlimited.

Methods of Appeal

Cases come to the Supreme Court in several ways: through petitions for writs of certiorari, appeals, and requests for certification.

In petitioning for a writ of certiorari, a litigant who has lost a case in a lower court sets out the reasons why the Supreme Court should review the case. If a writ is granted, the Court requests a certified record of the case from the lower court.

The main difference between the certiorari and appeal routes is that the Court has complete discretion to grant a request for a writ of certiorari but is under more obligation to accept and decide a case that comes to it on appeal.

Most cases reach the Supreme Court by means of the writ of certiorari. In the relatively few cases to reach the Court by means of appeal, the appellant must file a jurisdictional statement explaining why the case qualifies for review and why the Court should grant it a hearing. Often the justices dispose of these cases by deciding them summarily, without oral argument or formal opinion.

Those whose petitions for certiorari have been granted must pay the Court's standard $300 fee for docketing the case. The U.S. government does not have to pay these fees, nor do persons too poor to afford them. The latter may file in forma pauperis (in the character or manner of a pauper) petitions. Another, seldom used, method of appeal is certification, the request by a lower court—usually a court of appeals—for a final answer to questions of law in a particular case. The Court, after examining the certificate, may order the case argued before it.

Process of Review

In recent terms the Court has been asked to review around 7,000 cases. All petitions are examined by the staff of the clerk of the Court; those found to be in reasonably proper form are placed on the docket and given a number. All cases, except those falling within the Court's original jurisdiction, are placed on a single docket, known simply as "the docket." Only in the numbering of the cases is a distinction made between prepaid and in forma pauperis cases on the docket. The first case filed in the 1996–1997 term, for example, would be designated 96–1. In forma pauperis cases contain the year and begin with the number 5001. The second in forma pauperis case filed in the 1996–1997 term would thus be number 96–5002.

Each justice, aided by law clerks, is responsible for reviewing all cases on the docket. In recent years a number of justices have used a "cert pool" system in this review. Their clerks work together to examine cases, writing a pool memo on several petitions. The memo then is given to the justices who determine if more research is needed. Other justices may prefer to review each petition themselves or have their clerks do it.

Petitions on the docket vary from elegantly printed and bound documents, of which multiple copies are submitted to the Court, to single sheets of prison stationery scribbled in pencil. The decisions to grant or deny review of cases are made in conferences, which are held in the conference room adjacent to the chief justice's chambers. Justices are summoned to the conference room by a buzzer, usually between 9:30 and 10:00 a.m. They shake hands with each other and take their appointed seats, and the chief justice then begins the discussion.

Discuss and Orders Lists

A few days before the conference convenes, the chief justice compiles the discuss list of cases deemed important enough for discussion and a vote. As many as three-quarters of the petitions for certiorari are denied a place on the list and thus rejected without further consideration. Any justice can have a case placed on the discuss list simply by requesting that it be placed there.

Only the justices attend conferences; no legal assistants or staff are present. The junior associate justice acts as doorkeeper and messenger, sending for reference material and receiving messages and data. Unlike with other parts of the federal government, few leaks have occurred about what transpires during the conferences.

At the start of the conference, the chief justice makes a brief statement outlining the facts of each case. Then each justice, beginning with the senior associate justice, comments on the case, usually indicating in the course of the comments how he or she intends to vote. A traditional but unwritten rule is that four affirmative votes puts a case on the schedule for oral argument.

Petitions for certiorari, appeals, and in forma pauperis motions that are approved for review or denied review during conference are placed on a certified orders list to be released the next Monday in open court.

Arguments

Once the Court announces it will hear a case, the clerk of the Court arranges the schedule for oral argument. Cases are argued roughly in the order in which they were granted review, subject to modification if more time is needed to acquire all the necessary documents. Cases generally are heard not sooner than three months after the Court has agreed to review them. Under special circumstances the date scheduled for oral argument can be advanced or postponed.

Well before oral argument takes place, the justices receive the briefs and records from counsel in the case. The measure of attention the brief receives—from a thorough and exhaustive study to a cursory glance—depends both on the nature of the case and the work habits of the justice.

As one of the two public functions of the Court, oral arguments are viewed by some as very important. Others dispute the significance of oral arguments, contending that by the time a case is heard most of the justices already have made up their minds.

Time Limits

The time allowed each side for oral argument is thirty minutes. Because the time allotted must accommodate any questions the justices may wish to ask, the actual time for presentation may be considerably shorter than thirty minutes. Under the current rules of the Court, one counsel only will be heard for each side, except by special permission.

An exception is made for an amicus curiae, a "friend of the court," a person who volunteers or is invited to take part in matters before a court but is not a party in the case. Counsel for an amicus curiae may participate in oral argument if the party supported by the amicus allows use of part of its argument time or the Court grants a motion permitting argument by this counsel. The motion must show, the rules state, that the amicus's argument "is thought to provide assistance to the Court not otherwise available." The Court is generally unreceptive to such motions.

Court rules provide advice to counsel presenting oral arguments before the Court: "Oral argument should emphasize and clarify the written arguments appearing in the briefs on the merits." That same rule warns—with italicized emphasis—that the Court "looks with disfavor on oral argument read from a prepared text." Most attorneys appearing before the Court use an outline or notes to make sure they cover the important points.

Circulating the Argument

The Supreme Court has tape-recorded oral arguments since 1955. In 1968 the Court, in addition to its own recording, began contracting with private firms to tape and transcribe all oral arguments. The contract stipulates that the transcript "shall include everything spoken in argument, by Court, counsel, or others, and nothing shall be omitted from the transcript unless the Chief Justice or Presiding Justice so directs." But "the names of Justices asking questions shall not be recorded or transcribed; questions shall be indicated by the letter 'Q.'"

The marshal of the Court keeps the tapes during the term, and their use usually is limited to the justices and their law clerks. At the end of the term, the tapes are sent to the National Archives. Persons wishing to listen to the tapes or buy a copy of a transcript can apply to the Archives for permission to do so.

Transcripts made by a private firm can be acquired more quickly. These transcripts usually are available a week after arguments are heard. Transcripts can be read in the Court's library or public information office. Those who purchase the transcripts must agree that they will not be photographically reproduced. In addition, transcripts of oral arguments are available on the Westlaw electronic data retrieval system.

Proposals have been made to tape arguments for television and radio use or to permit live broadcast coverage of arguments. The Court has rejected these proposals.

Use of Briefs

The brief of the petitioner or appellant must be filed within forty-five days of the Court's announced decision to hear the case. Except for in forma pauperis cases, forty copies of the brief must be filed with the Court. For in forma pauperis proceedings, the Court requires only that documents be legible. The opposing brief from the respondent or appellee is to be filed within thirty days of receipt of the brief of the petitioner or appellant. Either party may appeal to the clerk for an extension of time in filing the brief.

Court Rule 24 sets forth the elements that a brief should contain. These are: the questions presented for review; a list of all parties to the proceeding; a table of contents and table of authorities; citations of the opinions and judgments delivered in the lower courts; "a concise statement of the grounds on which the jurisdiction of this Court is invoked"; constitutional provisions, treaties, statutes, ordinances, and regulations involved; "a concise statement of the case containing all that is material to the consideration of the questions presented"; a summary of argument; the argument, which exhibits "clearly the points of fact and of law being presented and citing the authorities and statutes relied upon"; and a conclusion "specifying with particularity the relief which the party seeks."

The form and organization of the brief are covered by rules 33 and 34. The rules limit the number of pages in various types of briefs. The rules also set out a color code for the covers of different kinds of briefs. Petitions are white; motions opposing them are orange. Petitioner's briefs on the merits are light blue, while those of respondents are red. Reply briefs are yellow; amicus curiae, green; and documents filed by the United States, gray.

Questioning

During oral argument the justices may interrupt with questions or remarks as often as they wish. Unless counsel has been granted special permission extending the thirty-minute limit, he or she can continue talking after the time has expired only to complete a sentence.

The frequency of questioning, as well as the manner in which questions are asked, depends on the style of the justices and their interest in a particular case. Of the current justices, all but Clarence Thomas participate, more or less actively, in questioning during oral arguments; Thomas asks questions very, very rarely.

Questions from the justices may upset and unnerve counsel by interrupting a well-rehearsed argument and introducing an unexpected element. Nevertheless, questioning has several advantages. It serves to alert counsel about what aspects of the case need further elaboration or more information. For the Court, questions can bring out weak points in an argument—and sometimes strengthen it.

Conferences

Cases for which oral arguments have been heard are then dealt with in conference. During the Wednesday afternoon conference, the cases that were argued the previous Monday are discussed and decided. At the all-day Friday conference, the cases argued on the preceding Tuesday and Wednesday are discussed and decided. Justices also consider new motions, appeals, and petitions while in conference.

Conferences are conducted in complete secrecy. No secretaries, clerks, stenographers, or messengers are allowed into the room. This practice began many years ago when the justices became convinced that decisions were being disclosed prematurely.

The justices meet in an oak-paneled, book-lined conference room adjacent to the chief justice's suite. Nine chairs surround a large rectangular table, each chair bearing the nameplate of the justice who sits there. The chief justice sits at the east end of the table, and the senior associate justice at the west end. The other justices take their places in order of seniority. The junior justice is charged with sending for and receiving documents or other information the Court needs.

On entering the conference room the justices shake hands with each other, a symbol of harmony that began in the 1880s. The chief justice begins the conference by calling the first case to be decided and discussing it. When the chief justice is finished, the senior associate justice speaks, followed by the other justices in order of seniority.

The justices can speak for as long as they wish, but they practice restraint because of the amount of business to be completed. By custom each justice speaks without interruption. Other than these procedural arrangements, little is known about what transpires in conference. Although discussions generally are said to be polite and orderly, occasionally they can be acrimonious. Likewise, consideration of the issues in a particular case may be full and probing, or perfunctory, leaving the real debate on the question until later when the written drafts of opinions are circulated up and down the Court's corridors between chambers.

Generally the discussion of the case clearly indicates how a justice plans to vote on it. A majority vote is needed to decide a case—five votes if all nine justices are participating.

Opinions

After the justices have voted on a case, the writing of the opinion or opinions begins. An opinion is a reasoned argument explaining the legal issues in the case and the precedents on which the opinion is based. Soon after a case is decided in conference, the task of writing the majority opinion is assigned. When in the majority, the chief justice designates the writer. When the chief justice is in the minority, the senior associate justice voting with the majority assigns the job of writing the majority opinion.

Any justice may write a separate opinion. If in agreement with the Court's decision but not with some of the reasoning in the majority opinion, the justice writes a concurring opinion giving his or her reasoning. If in disagreement with the majority, the justice writes a dissenting opinion or simply goes on record as a dissenter without an opinion. More than one justice can sign a concurring opinion or a dissenting opinion.

The amount of time between the vote on a case and the announcement of the decision varies from case to case. In simple cases where few points of law are at issue, the opinion sometimes can be written and cleared by the other justices in a week or less. In more complex cases, especially those with several dissenting or concurring opinions, the process can take six months or more. Some cases may have to be reargued or the initial decision reversed after the drafts of opinions have been circulated.

The assigning justice may consider the points made by majority justices during the conference discussion, the workload of the other justices, the need to avoid the more extreme opinions within the majority, and expertise in the particular area of law involved in a case.

The style of writing a Court opinion—majority, concurring, or dissenting—depends primarily on the individual justice. In some cases, the justice may prefer to write a restricted and limited opinion; in others, he or she may take a broader approach to the subject. The decision likely is to be influenced by the need to satisfy the other justices in the majority.

When a justice is satisfied that the written opinion is conclusive or "unanswerable," it goes into print. Draft opinions are circulated, revised, and printed on a computerized typesetting system. The circulation of the drafts—whether computer-to-computer or on paper—provokes further discussion in many cases. Often the suggestions and criticisms require the writer to juggle opposing views. To retain a majority, the author of the draft opinion frequently feels obliged to make major emendations to satisfy justices who are unhappy with the initial draft. Some opinions have to be rewritten several times.

One reason for the secrecy surrounding the circulation of drafts is that some of the justices who voted with the majority may find the majority draft opinion so unpersuasive—or one or more of the dissenting drafts so convincing—that they change their vote. If enough justices alter their

votes, the majority may shift, so that a former dissent becomes the majority opinion. When a new majority emerges from this process, the task of
writing, printing, and circulating a new majority draft begins all over again.

When the drafts of an opinion—including dissents and concurring
views—have been written, circulated, discussed, and revised, if necessary,
the final versions then are printed. Before the opinion is produced the
reporter of decisions adds a "headnote" or syllabus summarizing the decision and a "lineup" showing how the justices voted.

Two hundred copies of the "bench opinion" are made. As the decision
is announced in Court, the bench opinion is distributed to journalists and
others in the public information office. Another copy, with any necessary
corrections noted on it, is sent to the U.S. Government Printing Office,
which prints 3,397 "slip" opinions, which are distributed to federal and
state courts and agencies. The Court receives 400 of these, and they are
available to the public free through the Public Information Office as long
as supplies last. The Government Printing Office also prints the opinion
for inclusion in United States Reports, the official record of Supreme
Court opinions.

The Court also makes opinions available electronically, through its so-
called Hermes system, to a number of large legal publishers, the Government Printing Office, and other information services. These organizations allow redistribution of the opinions to their own subscribers and
users. Opinions are available on the Internet through Case Western
Reserve University. The Hermes system was established as a pilot project
in 1991 and expanded and made permanent in 1993.

In 1996 the Court also established its own electronic bulletin board system (BBS) that provides anyone with a personal computer online access to
the Court's opinions, docket, argument calendar, and other information and
publications. The telephone number for the Court's BBS is (202) 554-2570.

The public announcement of opinions in Court probably is the Court's
most dramatic function. It may also be the most expendable. Depending
on who delivers the opinion and how, announcements can take a considerable amount of the Court's time. Opinions are given simultaneously to
the public information officer for distribution. Nevertheless, those who
are in the courtroom to hear the announcement of a ruling are participating in a very old tradition. The actual delivery may be tedious or exciting,
depending on the nature of the case, the eloquence of the opinion, and the
style of its oral delivery.

Brief Biographies

William Hubbs Rehnquist

Born: October 1, 1924, Milwaukee, Wisconsin.

Education: Stanford University, B.A., Phi Beta Kappa, and M.A., 1948; Harvard University, M.A., 1949; Stanford University Law School, LL.B., 1952.

Family: Married Natalie Cornell, 1953; died, 1991; two daughters, one son.

Career: Law clerk to Justice Robert H. Jackson, U.S. Supreme Court, 1952–1953; practiced law, 1953–1969; assistant U.S. attorney general, Office of Legal Counsel, 1969–1971.

Supreme Court Service: Nominated as associate justice of the U.S. Supreme Court by President Richard Nixon, October 21, 1971; confirmed, 68–26, December 10, 1971; nominated as chief justice of the United States by President Ronald Reagan, June 17, 1986; confirmed, 65–33, September 17, 1986.

President Reagan's appointment of William H. Rehnquist as chief justice in 1986 was a deliberate effort to shift the Court to the right. Since his early years as an associate justice in the 1970s, Rehnquist had been the Court's strongest conservative voice. And as chief justice, Rehnquist has helped move the Court to the right in a number of areas, including criminal law, states' rights, civil rights, and church-state issues.

Rehnquist, the fourth associate justice to become chief, argues that the original intent of the Framers of the Constitution and the Bill of Rights is the proper standard for interpreting those documents today. He also takes a literal approach to individual rights. These beliefs have led him to dissent from the Court's rulings protecting a woman's privacy-based right to abortion, to argue that no constitutional barrier exists to school prayer, and to side with police and prosecutors on questions of criminal law. In 1991 he wrote the Court's decision upholding an administration ban on abortion counseling at publicly financed clinics. The next year he vigorously dissented from the Court's affirmation of *Roe v. Wade*, the 1973 opinion that made abortion legal nationwide.

A native of Milwaukee, Rehnquist attended Stanford University, where he earned both a B.A. and an M.A. He received a second M.A. from Harvard before returning to Stanford for law school. His classmates there recalled him as an intelligent student with already well-entrenched conservative views.

After graduating from law school in 1952, Rehnquist came to Washington, D.C., to serve as a law clerk to Supreme Court justice Robert H. Jackson. There he wrote a memorandum that later came back to haunt him during his Senate confirmation hearings. In the memo Rehnquist favored separate but equal schools for blacks and whites. Asked about those views by the Senate Judiciary Committee in 1971, Rehnquist repudiated them, declaring that they were Justice Jackson's, not his own.

Following his clerkship, Rehnquist decided to practice law in the Southwest. He moved to Phoenix and immediately became immersed in Arizona Republican politics. From his earliest days in the state, he was associated with the party's conservative wing. A 1957 speech denouncing the liberalism of the Warren Court typified his views at the time.

During the 1964 presidential race, Rehnquist campaigned ardently for Barry Goldwater. It was then that Rehnquist met and worked with Richard G. Kleindienst, who later, as President Richard Nixon's deputy attorney general, appointed Rehnquist to head the Justice Department's Office of Legal Counsel as an assistant attorney general. In 1971 Nixon nominated him to the Supreme Court.

Rehnquist drew opposition from liberals and civil rights organizations before winning confirmation and again before being approved as chief justice in 1986. The Senate voted to approve his nomination in December 1971 by a vote of 68–26 at the same time that another Nixon nominee, Lewis F. Powell Jr., was winning nearly unanimous confirmation.

In 1986 Rehnquist faced new accusations of having harassed voters as a Republican poll watcher in Phoenix in the 1950s and 1960s. He was also found to have accepted anti-Semitic restrictions in a property deed to a Vermont home. Despite the charges, the Senate approved his appointment as chief justice 65–33. Liberal Democratic senators cast most of the no votes in both confirmations.

Despite his strong views, Rehnquist is popular among his colleagues and staff. When he was nominated for chief justice, Justice William J. Brennan Jr., the leader of the Court's liberal bloc, said Rehnquist would be "a splendid chief justice." After becoming chief justice, Rehnquist was credited with speeding up the Court's conferences, in which the justices decide what cases to hear, vote on cases, and assign opinions.

Rehnquist was married to Natalie Cornell, who died in 1991. They had two daughters and a son.

John Paul Stevens

Born: April 20, 1920, Chicago, Illinois.

Education: University of Chicago, B.A., Phi Beta Kappa, 1941; Northwestern University School of Law, J.D., 1947.

Family: Married Elizabeth Jane Sheeren, 1942; three daughters, one son; divorced 1979; married Maryan Mulholland Simon, 1980.

Career: Law clerk to Justice Wiley B. Rutledge, U.S. Supreme Court, 1947–1948; practiced law, Chicago, 1949–1970; judge, U.S. Court of Appeals for the Seventh Circuit, 1970–1975.

Supreme Court Service: Nominated as associate justice of the U.S. Supreme Court by President Gerald R. Ford, November 28, 1975; confirmed, 98–0, December 17, 1975.

When President Gerald R. Ford nominated federal appeals court judge John Paul Stevens to the Supreme Court seat vacated by veteran liberal William O. Douglas in 1975, Court observers struggled to pin an ideological label on the new nominee. The consensus that finally emerged was that Stevens was neither a doctrinaire liberal nor conservative, but a judicial centrist. His subsequent opinions bear out this description, although in recent years he has moved steadily toward the liberal side.

Stevens is a soft-spoken, mild-mannered man who often sports a bow tie under his judicial robes. A member of a prominent Chicago family, he had a long record of excellence in scholarship, graduating Phi Beta Kappa from the University of Chicago in 1941. He earned the Bronze Star during a wartime stint in the navy and then returned to Chicago to enter Northwestern University Law School, from which he was graduated magna cum laude in 1947. From there Stevens left for Washington, where he served as a law clerk to Supreme Court justice Wiley B. Rutledge. He returned to Chicago to join the prominent law firm of Poppenhusen, Johnston, Thompson & Raymond, which specialized in antitrust law. Stevens developed a reputation as a pre-eminent antitrust lawyer and three years later in 1952 formed his own firm, Rothschild, Stevens, Barry & Myers. He remained there, engaging in private practice and teaching part-time at Northwestern and the University of Chicago law schools, until his appointment by President Richard Nixon in 1970 to the U.S. Court of Appeals for the Seventh Circuit.

Stevens developed a reputation as a political moderate during his undergraduate days at the University of Chicago, then an overwhelmingly liberal campus. Although he is a registered Republican, he has never been active in partisan politics. Nevertheless, Stevens served as Republican counsel in 1951 to the House Judiciary Subcommittee on the Study of Monopoly Power. He also served from 1953 to 1955, during the Eisenhower administration, as a member of the attorney general's committee to study antitrust laws.

In his five years on the federal appeals court, Stevens earned a reputation as an independent-minded judicial craftsman. President Ford, who took office after Nixon's forced resignation, wanted to nominate a moderate of impeccable legal reputation to help restore confidence in government after the Watergate scandals. Stevens was confirmed without dissent, 98–0, on December 17, 1975, and took office two days later.

Stevens has frequently dissented from the most conservative rulings of the Burger and Rehnquist Courts. For example, he dissented from the Burger Court's 1986 decision upholding state antisodomy laws and the Rehnquist Court's 1989 decision permitting states to execute someone for committing a murder at the age of sixteen or seventeen. He has taken liberal positions on abortion rights, civil rights, and church-state issues.

In his second full term on the Court, Stevens wrote the main opinion in a case upholding the right of the Federal Communications Commission to penalize broadcasters for airing indecent material at times when children are in the audience. But in 1997, he led the Court in a major victory for First Amendment interests by striking down a newly enacted law aimed at blocking sexually explicit materials from children on the Internet. In the same year, he wrote the opinion holding that presidents have no immunity while in office from civil suits for private conduct unrelated to their office.

In 1942 Stevens married Elizabeth Jane Sheeren. They have four children. They were divorced in 1979. Stevens subsequently married Maryan Mulholland Simon, a longtime neighbor in Chicago.

Sandra Day O'Connor

Born: March 26, 1930, El Paso, Texas.
Education: Stanford University, B.A., 1950; Stanford University Law School, LL.B., 1952.
Family: Married John J. O'Connor III, 1952; three sons.
Career: Deputy county attorney, San Mateo, California, 1952–1953; assistant attorney general, Arizona, 1965–1969; Arizona state senator, 1969–1975; Arizona Senate majority leader, 1972–1975; judge, Maricopa County Superior Court, 1974–1979; judge, Arizona Court of Appeals, 1979–1981.
Supreme Court Service: Nominated as associate justice of the U.S. Supreme Court by President Ronald Reagan August 19, 1981; confirmed, 99–0, September 21, 1981.

Sandra Day O'Connor, the first woman to serve on the Court, has been a pivotal figure in forming a conservative majority on a range of issues but has also moderated the Rehnquist Court's stance on some questions, including abortion rights and affirmative action.

Pioneering came naturally to O'Connor. Her grandfather left Kansas in 1880 to take up ranching in the desert land that eventually became the state of Arizona. O'Connor, born in El Paso, Texas, where her mother's parents lived, was raised on the Lazy B Ranch, the 198,000-acre spread that her grandfather founded in southeastern Arizona near Duncan. She spent her school years in El Paso, living with her grandmother. She graduated from high school at age sixteen and then entered Stanford University.

Six years later, in 1952, Sandra Day had won degrees with great distinction, both from the university, in economics, and from Stanford Law School. At Stanford she met John J. O'Connor III, her future husband, and William H. Rehnquist, a future colleague on the Supreme Court. While in law school, Sandra Day was an editor of the *Stanford Law Review* and a member of Order of the Coif, the academic honor society.

Despite her record, O'Connor had difficulty finding a job as an attorney in 1952 when relatively few women were practicing law. She applied, among other places, to the firm in which William French Smith—first attorney general in the Reagan administration—was a partner, only to be offered a job as a secretary.

After she completed a short stint as deputy county attorney for San Mateo County (California) while her new husband completed law school at Stanford, the O'Connors moved with the U.S. Army to Frankfurt, Germany. There Sandra O'Connor worked as a civilian attorney for the army, while John O'Connor served his tour of duty. In 1957 they returned to Phoenix, where, during the next eight years, their three sons were born. O'Connor's life was a mix of parenthood, homemaking, volunteer work, and some "miscellaneous legal tasks" on the side.

In 1965 she resumed her legal career on a full-time basis, taking a job as an assistant attorney general for Arizona. After four years in that post she was appointed to fill a vacancy in the state Senate, where she served on the judiciary committee. In 1970 she was elected to the same body and two years later was chosen its majority leader, the first woman in the nation to hold such a post. O'Connor was active in Republican Party politics, serving as co-chair of the Arizona Committee for the Re-election of the President in 1972.

In 1974 she was elected to the Superior Court for Maricopa County, where she served for five years. Then in 1979 Democratic governor Bruce Babbitt appointed O'Connor to the Arizona Court of Appeals. It was from that post that President Reagan chose her as his first nominee to the Supreme Court, succeeding Potter Stewart, who retired. Reagan described her as "a person for all seasons." The Senate confirmed her on September 21, 1981, by a vote of 99–0.

O'Connor brings to the Court a conservative viewpoint and a cautious, case-by-case decisionmaking style. On criminal law issues, she has generally voted to give broader discretion to police, uphold death penalty cases, and restrict the use of federal habeas corpus to challenge state court convictions. She was a strong supporter of limiting punitive damage awards in state courts and relaxing restrictions on government support for religion.

In two important areas, however, O'Connor's cautious approach has disappointed conservatives. While she voted in many decisions in the 1980s to limit abortion rights, she joined in 1992 with two other Republican-appointed justices, Anthony M. Kennedy and David H. Souter, to form a majority for preserving a modified form of the Court's original abortion rights ruling, *Roe v. Wade*. In a jointly authored opinion the three justices said that *Roe*'s "essential holding"—guaranteeing a woman's right to an abortion during most of her pregnancy—should be reaffirmed. But the joint opinion also said that states could regulate abortion procedures as long as they did not impose "an undue burden" on a woman's choice— a test that O'Connor had advocated in previous opinions.

O'Connor has also voted to limit racial preferences in employment and government contracting and wrote the Court's first opinion restricting the use of race in drawing legislative and congressional districts. But she also joined the majority in a critical 1987 case upholding voluntary affirmative action by government employers to remedy past discrimination against women. And she has refused to limit all consideration of race in redistricting cases.

Antonin Scalia

Born: March 11, 1936, Trenton, New Jersey.

Education: Georgetown University, A.B., 1957; Harvard University Law School, LL.B., 1960.

Family: Married Maureen McCarthy, 1960; five sons, four daughters.

Career: Practiced law, Cleveland, 1960–1967; taught at the University of Virginia, 1967–1971; general counsel, White House Office of Telecommunications Policy, 1971–1972; chairman, Administrative Conference of the United States, 1972–1974; head, Justice Department Office of Legal Counsel, 1974–1977; taught at the University of Chicago Law School, 1977–1982; judge, U.S. Court of Appeals for the District of Columbia Circuit, 1982–1986.

Supreme Court Service: Nominated as associate justice of the U.S. Supreme Court by President Ronald Reagan June 17, 1986; confirmed, 98–0, September 17, 1986.

After Warren E. Burger retired from the Court and Ronald Reagan named William H. Rehnquist to succeed him as chief justice, the president's next move—appointing Antonin Scalia as associate justice—was not surprising. On issues dear to Reagan, Scalia clearly met the president's tests for conservatism. Scalia, whom Reagan had named to the U.S. Court of Appeals for the District of Columbia Circuit in 1982, became the first Supreme Court justice of Italian ancestry. A Roman Catholic, he opposes abortion. He has also strongly opposed "affirmative action" preferences for minorities.

In contrast to the heated debate over Rehnquist's nomination as chief justice, only a few, brief speeches were given before the Senate confirmed the equally conservative Scalia, 98–0. He has since become the scourge of some members of Congress because of his suspicion of committee reports, floor speeches, and other elements of legislative history that courts traditionally use to interpret statutes.

Born in Trenton, New Jersey, March 11, 1936, Scalia grew up in Queens, New York. His father was a professor of Romance languages at Brooklyn College, and his mother was a schoolteacher. He was first in his graduating class at an all-male military academy in Manhattan, St. Francis Xavier, and class valedictorian at Georgetown University, where he graduated in 1957. He received his law degree in 1960 from Harvard Law School, where he served as note editor of the *Harvard Law Review*. He worked for six years for the firm of Jones, Day, Cockley & Reavis in Cleveland and then taught contract, commercial, and comparative law at the University of Virginia Law School.

Scalia was a specialist in administrative law and a strong advocate of deregulation. He served as general counsel of the White House Office of Telecommunications Policy from 1971 to 1972. He then headed the Administrative Conference of the United States, a group that advises the government on questions of administrative law and procedure. From 1974 through the Ford administration he headed the Justice Department's Office of Legal Counsel, a post Rehnquist had held three years earlier. Scalia then returned to academia to teach at the University of Chicago Law School. From 1977 to 1982 he was editor of the magazine *Regulation*, published by the American Enterprise Institute for Public Policy Research.

President Ronald Reagan appointed Scalia to the U.S. Court of Appeals for the District of Columbia Circuit in 1982. There, Scalia showed himself to be a hard worker, an aggressive interrogator, and an articulate advocate. He had a marked impatience with what he saw as regulatory or judicial overreaching. In 1983 he dissented from a ruling requiring the Food and Drug Administration (FDA) to consider whether drugs used for lethal injections met FDA standards as safe and effective. The Supreme Court agreed, reversing the appeals court in 1985.

Scalia was thought to be the principal author of an unsigned decision in 1986 that declared major portions of the Gramm-Rudman-Hollings budget-balancing act unconstitutional. The Supreme Court upheld the decision later in the year.

On the Supreme Court Scalia quickly became a forceful voice for conservative positions. He joined in conservative decisions limiting procedural rights in criminal cases and in a series of rulings in 1989 limiting remedies in employment discrimination cases. He also strongly dissented from rulings upholding affirmative action and reaffirming abortion rights. In 1997, he wrote an important decision that struck down on states' rights grounds a federal law requiring state and local law enforcement agencies to conduct background checks on prospective gun purchasers.

In many of his constitutional law opinions, Scalia argued for an "original intent" approach that limited rights to those intended when the Constitution was adopted. He also sharply challenged the use of legislative history in interpreting statutes. He argued that judges should look only to the words of the statute itself.

Scalia expressed his conservative views in aggressive questioning from the bench and in frequently acerbic opinions, especially in dissent.

Anthony McLeod Kennedy

Born: July 23, 1936, Sacramento, California.

Education: Stanford University, A.B., Phi Beta Kappa, 1958; Harvard University Law School, LL.B., 1961.

Family: Married Mary Davis, 1963; two sons, one daughter.

Career: Practiced law, San Francisco, 1961–1963, Sacramento, 1963–1975; professor of constitutional law, McGeorge School of Law, University of the Pacific, 1965–1988; judge, U.S. Court of Appeals for the Ninth Circuit, 1975–1988.

Supreme Court Service: Nominated as associate justice of the U.S. Supreme Court by President Ronald Reagan November 11, 1987; confirmed, 97–0, February 3, 1988.

Quiet, scholarly Anthony M. Kennedy, President Reagan's third choice for his third appointment to the Supreme Court, helped form a conservative majority on many issues in his initial years after joining the Court in 1988. While he adheres to generally conservative views, Kennedy has taken moderate stands on some issues that often make him a pivotal vote between the Court's conservative and liberal blocs.

Before Kennedy's nomination in November 1987, the Senate and the country had agonized through Reagan's two unsuccessful attempts to replace retiring Justice Lewis F. Powell Jr., first with Robert H. Bork and then with Douglas H. Ginsburg. The Senate rejected Bork's nomination after contentious hearings, where opponents depicted the federal appeals court judge as a conservative ideologue. Reagan then turned to Ginsburg, a colleague of Bork's on the federal appeals court in Washington, but he withdrew his name amid controversy about his admitted past use of marijuana.

A quiet sense of relief prevailed when Reagan finally selected a nominee who could be confirmed without another wrenching confrontation. Kennedy spent twelve years as a judge on the U.S. Court of Appeals for the Ninth Circuit. But unlike Bork, who wrote and spoke extensively for twenty years, Kennedy's record was confined mostly to his approximately five hundred judicial opinions, where he generally decided issues narrowly instead of using his opinions as a testing ground for constitutional theories. The Senate voted to confirm him without dissent, 97–0, on February 3, 1988.

A native Californian, Kennedy attended Stanford University from 1954 to 1957 and the London School of Economics from 1957 to 1958. He received an A.B. from Stanford in 1958 and an LL.B. from Harvard Law School in 1961. Admitted to the California bar in 1962, he was in private law practice until 1975, when President Gerald R. Ford appointed him to the appeals court. From 1965 to 1988 he taught constitutional law at McGeorge School of Law, University of the Pacific.

In his first full term on the Court, Kennedy provided a crucial fifth vote for the Court's conservative wing in a number of civil rights cases. He generally favored law enforcement in criminal cases. And in a closely watched abortion-rights case, he voted along with Chief Justice William H. Rehnquist and Justices Byron R. White and Antonin Scalia to overturn the 1973 ruling, *Roe v. Wade*, that first established a constitutional right to abortion.

Many observers viewed Kennedy's arrival as ushering in a new conservative era. But in 1992 he sorely disappointed conservatives in two major cases. In one he provided the critical fifth vote and wrote the majority opinion in a decision barring officially sponsored prayers at public high school graduation ceremonies. In the other he reversed himself on the abortion issue, joining with Justices Sandra Day O'Connor and David H. Souter in an opinion that upheld a modified version of *Roe v. Wade*.

Kennedy has proved to be a strong free speech advocate in First Amendment cases. In 1989 he helped form the 5–4 majority that overturned state laws against burning or desecrating the U.S. flag. The former constitutional law professor has also displayed a special interest in equal protection and federalism issues. He has voted with other conservatives in rulings that limited racially motivated congressional districting and backed states in disputes over federal power. But he was the swing vote in a 1995 decision to bar the states from imposing term limits on members of Congress. And in 1996 he wrote the opinion striking down Colorado's anti-gay rights amendment prohibiting enactment of any laws to bar discrimination against homosexuals.

David Hackett Souter

Born: September 17, 1939, Melrose, Massachusetts.

Education: Harvard College, B.A., 1961; Rhodes scholar, Oxford University, 1961–1963; Harvard University Law School, LL.B., 1966.

Family: Unmarried.

Career: Private law practice, Concord, New Hampshire, 1966–1968; assistant attorney general, New Hampshire, 1968–1971; deputy attorney general, New Hampshire, 1971–1976; attorney general, New Hampshire, 1976–1978; associate justice, New Hampshire Superior Court, 1978–1983; associate justice, New Hampshire Supreme Court, 1983–1990; judge, U.S. Court of Appeals for the First Circuit, 1990.

Supreme Court Service: Nominated as associate justice of the U.S. Supreme Court by President George Bush July 23, 1990; confirmed, 90–9, October 2, 1990.

At first the Senate did not know what to make of David H. Souter, a cerebral, button-down nominee who was President Bush's first appointment to the Court. Souter was little known outside his home state of New Hampshire, where he had been attorney general, a trial judge, and a state supreme court justice. He had virtually no scholarly writings to dissect and little federal court experience to scrutinize. Only three months earlier Bush had appointed him to the U.S. Court of Appeals for the First Circuit. Souter had yet to write a legal opinion on the appeals court.

During his confirmation hearings, the Harvard graduate and former Rhodes scholar demonstrated intellectual rigor and a masterly approach to constitutional law. His earlier work as state attorney general and New Hampshire Supreme Court justice had a conservative bent, but he came across as more moderate during the hearings.

Under persistent questioning from Democratic senators, Souter refused to say how he would vote on the issue of abortion rights. Abortion rights supporters feared he would provide a fifth vote for overturning the 1973 *Roe v. Wade* decision. Senators in both parties, however, said they were impressed with his legal knowledge. He was confirmed by the Senate 90–9; dissenting senators cited his refusal to take a stand on abortion.

On the bench Souter proved to be a tenacious questioner but reserved in his opinions. He generally voted with the Court's conservative majority in his first term. But in the 1991–1992 term he staked out a middle ground with Justices Sandra Day O'Connor and Anthony M. Kennedy in two crucial cases. In a closely watched abortion case Souter joined with the other two Republican-appointed justices in writing the main opinion reaffirming the "essential holding" of *Roe v. Wade*. The three also joined in forming a 5–4 majority to prohibit school-sponsored prayers at public high school graduation ceremonies.

In the Court's next several terms Souter moved markedly to the left. He joined with liberals in dissenting from cases that restricted racial redistricting. He also voted with the Court's liberal bloc on church-state and some criminal law issues.

Despite his experience in state government, Souter has proved to be a strong supporter of federal power in cases affecting states' rights. He joined the dissenters in a 1995 decision striking down on states' rights grounds a federal law banning the possession of guns near schools. And in 1996 he wrote a massive and scholarly dissent from the Court's decision limiting Congress's power to authorize private citizens to sue states in federal courts to enforce federal law.

Souter is known for his intensely private, ascetic life. He was born September 17, 1939, in Melrose, Massachusetts. An only child, he moved with his parents to Weare, New Hampshire, at age eleven. Except for college, he lived in Weare until 1990.

Graduating from Harvard College in 1961, Souter attended Oxford University on a Rhodes Scholarship from 1961 to 1963, then returned to Cambridge for Harvard Law School. Graduating in 1966, he worked for two years in a Concord law firm. In 1968 he became an assistant attorney general, rose to deputy attorney general in 1971, and in 1976 was appointed attorney general. Souter served as attorney general until 1978, when he was named to the state's trial court. Five years later Gov. John H. Sununu appointed Souter to the state supreme court. Sununu was Bush's chief of staff when Souter was named to the U.S. Supreme Court.

Souter, a bachelor, is a nature enthusiast and avid hiker.

Clarence Thomas

Born: June 23, 1948, Savannah, Georgia.

Education: Immaculate Conception Seminary, 1967–1968; Holy Cross College, B.A., 1971; Yale University Law School, J.D., 1974.

Family: Married Kathy Grace Ambush, 1971; one son; divorced 1984; married Virginia Lamp, 1987.

Career: Assistant attorney general, Missouri, 1974–1977; attorney, Monsanto Co., 1977–1979; legislative assistant to Sen. John C. Danforth, R-Mo., 1979–1981; assistant secretary of education for civil rights, 1981–1982; chairman, Equal Employment Opportunity Commission, 1982–1990; judge, U.S. Court of Appeals for the District of Columbia Circuit, 1990–1991.

Supreme Court Service: Nominated as associate justice of the U.S. Supreme Court by President George Bush July 1, 1991; confirmed, 52–48, October 15, 1991.

Clarence Thomas won a narrow confirmation to the Supreme Court in 1991 after surviving dramatic accusations of sexual harassment. He generated continuing controversy with outspoken conservative views as a justice.

The Senate's 52–48 vote on Thomas was the closest Supreme Court confirmation vote in more than a century. It followed a tumultuous nomination process that included close scrutiny of Thomas's judicial philosophy and sensational charges of sexual harassment brought by a former aide. Thomas denied the charges and accused the Senate Judiciary Committee of conducting a "high-tech lynching."

President George Bush nominated Thomas to succeed Thurgood Marshall, the Court's first black justice and a pioneer of the civil rights movement. Thomas came to prominence as a black conservative while serving as chairman of the Equal Employment Opportunity Commission during the Reagan and Bush administrations. Bush appointed him to the U.S. Court of Appeals for the District of Columbia Circuit in 1990.

Thomas was only forty-three at the time of his nomination to the Court, and senators noted that he likely would be affecting the outcome of major constitutional rulings well into the twenty-first century. Democratic senators closely questioned him on a range of constitutional issues— in particular, abortion. Thomas declined to give his views on abortion, saying he had never discussed the issue.

The committee decided to end its hearings even though it had received an allegation from a University of Oklahoma law professor, Anita Hill, that Thomas had sexually harassed her while she worked for him at the U.S. Department of Education and the EEOC. When the accusation leaked out, the Judiciary Committee reopened the hearing to take testimony from Hill, Thomas, and other witnesses.

In the end most senators said they could not resolve the conflict between Hill's detailed allegations and Thomas's categorical denials. Instead, senators fell back on their previous positions. Supporters praised his determined character and rise from poverty in rural Georgia. Opponents questioned whether Thomas had been candid with the committee in discussing his judicial philosophy.

After joining the Court, Thomas became one of the Court's most conservative members. He closely aligned himself with fellow conservative Antonin Scalia, voting with Scalia about 90 percent of the time. In 1992 he voted as his opponents had warned to overturn the 1973 abortion rights ruling, *Roe v. Wade*, but the Court reaffirmed the decision by a 5–4 vote.

In later cases Thomas wrote lengthy opinions sharply challenging existing legal doctrines. In 1994 he called for scrapping precedents that allowed courts to order the creation of majority-black districts for legislative or congressional seats. In 1995 he authored opinions that called for restricting the basis for Congress to regulate interstate commerce and for re-examining federal courts' role in desegregating public schools. In a campaign finance case in 1996, he urged the Court to overturn all laws limiting political contributions as an infringement on the First Amendment.

Thomas graduated from Yale Law School in 1974 and became an assistant attorney general of Missouri and, three years later, a staff attorney for Monsanto Company. He worked for Sen. John C. Danforth, R-Mo., as a legislative assistant and served in the Department of Education as assistant secretary for civil rights for one year before being named chairman of the EEOC.

Thomas's wife, the former Virginia Lamp, is a lawyer who served as a legislative official with the U.S. Department of Labor during the Bush administration and since 1993 as a senior policy analyst with the House Republican Conference. They were married in 1987. He has a son from his first marriage, which ended in divorce in 1984.

Ruth Bader Ginsburg

Born: March 15, 1933, Brooklyn, New York.

Education: Cornell University, B.A., 1954; attended Harvard University Law School, 1956–1958; graduated Columbia Law School, J.D., 1959.

Family: Married Martin D. Ginsburg, 1954; one daughter, one son.

Career: Law clerk to U.S. District Court Judge Edmund L. Palmieri, 1959–1961; Columbia Law School Project on International Procedure, 1961–1963; professor, Rutgers University School of Law, 1963–1972; director, Women's Rights Project, American Civil Liberties Union, 1972–1980; professor, Columbia Law School, 1972–1980; judge, U.S. Court of Appeals for the District of Columbia Circuit, 1980–1993.

Supreme Court Service: Nominated as associate justice of the U.S. Supreme Court by President Bill Clinton, June 22, 1993; confirmed, 96–3, August 3, 1993.

Ruth Bader Ginsburg's path to the U.S. Supreme Court is a classic American story of overcoming obstacles and setbacks through intelligence, persistence, and quiet hard work. Her achievements as a student, law teacher, advocate, and judge came against a background of personal adversity and institutional discrimination against women. Ginsburg not only surmounted those hurdles for herself but also charted the legal strategy in the 1970s that helped broaden opportunities for women by establishing constitutional principles limiting sex discrimination in the law.

Born into a Jewish family of modest means in Brooklyn, Ruth Bader was greatly influenced by her mother, Celia, who imparted a love of learning and a determination to be independent. Celia Bader died of cancer on the eve of her daughter's high school graduation in 1948.

Ruth Bader attended Cornell University, where she graduated first in her class and met her future husband, Martin Ginsburg, who became a tax lawyer and later a professor at Georgetown University Law Center in Washington.

At Harvard Law School Ruth Bader Ginsburg made law review, cared for an infant daughter, and then helped her husband complete his studies after he was diagnosed with cancer. He recovered, graduated, and got a job in New York, and she transferred to Columbia for her final year of law school.

Although she was tied for first place in her class when she graduated, Ginsburg was unable to land a Supreme Court clerkship or job with a top New York law firm. Instead, she won a two-year clerkship with a federal district court judge. She then accepted a research position at Columbia that took her to Sweden, where she studied civil procedure and began to be stirred by feminist thought.

Ginsburg taught at Rutgers law school in New Jersey from 1963 to 1972. She also worked with the New Jersey affiliate of the American Civil Liberties Union (ACLU), where her caseload included several early sex discrimination complaints. In 1972 Ginsburg became the first woman to be named to a tenured position on the Columbia Law School faculty. As director of the national ACLU's newly established Women's Rights Project, she also handled the cases that over the course of several years led the Supreme Court to require heightened scrutiny of legal classifications based on sex. Ginsburg won five of the six cases she argued before the Court.

President Jimmy Carter named Ginsburg to the U.S. Court of Appeals for the District of Columbia Circuit in 1980. There she earned a reputation as a judicial moderate on a sharply divided court. When Justice Byron R. White announced plans for his retirement in March 1993, Ginsburg was among the large field of candidates President Bill Clinton considered for the vacancy. Clinton considered and passed over two other leading candidates for the position before deciding to interview Ginsburg. White House aides told reporters later that Clinton had been especially impressed with Ginsburg's life story. Reaction to the nomination was overwhelmingly positive.

In three days of confirmation hearings before the Senate Judiciary Committee, Ginsburg depicted herself as an advocate of judicial restraint, but she also said courts sometimes had a role to play in bringing about social change. On specific issues she strongly endorsed abortion rights, equal rights for women, and the constitutional right to privacy. But she declined to give her views on many other issues, including capital punishment. Some senators said that she had been less than forthcoming, but the committee voted unanimously to recommend her for confirmation. The full Senate confirmed her four days later by a vote of 96–3.

Ginsburg was sworn in August 10, 1993, as the Court's second female justice—joining Justice Sandra Day O'Connor—and the first Jewish justice since 1969.

In her first weeks on the bench, Ginsburg startled observers and drew some criticism with her unusually active questioning, but she eased up later. In her voting, she took liberal positions on women's rights, civil rights, church-state, states' rights, and First Amendment issues, but she had a more mixed record in other areas, including criminal law. In 1996 she wrote the Court's opinion in an important sex discrimination case, requiring the all-male Virginia Military Institute to admit women or give up its public funding.

Stephen Gerald Breyer

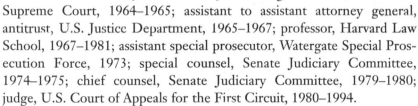

Born: August 15, 1938, San Francisco, California.

Education: Stanford University, A.B., Phi Beta Kappa, 1959; Oxford University, B.A. (Marshall scholar), 1961; Harvard Law School, LL.B., 1964.

Family: Married Joanna Hare, 1967; two daughters, one son.

Career: Law clerk to Justice Arthur J. Goldberg, U.S. Supreme Court, 1964–1965; assistant to assistant attorney general, antitrust, U.S. Justice Department, 1965–1967; professor, Harvard Law School, 1967–1981; assistant special prosecutor, Watergate Special Prosecution Force, 1973; special counsel, Senate Judiciary Committee, 1974–1975; chief counsel, Senate Judiciary Committee, 1979–1980; judge, U.S. Court of Appeals for the First Circuit, 1980–1994.

Supreme Court Service: Nominated as associate justice of the U.S. Supreme Court by President Bill Clinton May 17, 1994; confirmed, 87–9, July 29, 1994.

When President Bill Clinton introduced Stephen G. Breyer, his second Supreme Court nominee, at a White House ceremony on May 16, 1994, he described the federal appeals court judge as a "consensus-builder." The reaction to the nomination proved his point. Senators from both parties quickly endorsed Breyer. The only vocal dissents came from a few liberals and consumer advocates, who said Breyer was too probusiness.

Breyer, chosen to replace the retiring liberal justice Harry A. Blackmun, won a reputation as a centrist in fourteen years on the federal appeals court in Boston and two earlier stints as a staff member for the Senate Judiciary Committee. Breyer's work crossed ideological lines. He played a critical role in enacting airline deregulation in the 1970s and writing federal sentencing guidelines in the 1980s.

Born in 1938 to a politically active family in San Francisco, Breyer earned degrees from Stanford University and Harvard Law School. He clerked for Supreme Court Justice Arthur J. Goldberg and helped draft Goldberg's influential opinion in the 1965 case establishing the right of married couples to use contraceptives. Afterward he served two years in the Justice Department's antitrust division and then took a teaching position at Harvard Law School in 1967.

Breyer took leave from Harvard to serve as an assistant prosecutor in the Watergate investigation in 1973, special counsel to the Judiciary Committee's Administrative Practices Subcommittee from 1974 to 1975, and the full committee's chief counsel from 1979 to 1980. He worked for Sen. Edward Kennedy, D-Mass., but also had good relationships with Republican committee members. His ties to senators paid off when President Jimmy Carter nominated him for the federal appeals court in November 1980. Even though Ronald Reagan had been elected president, GOP senators allowed a vote on Breyer's nomination.

As a judge, Breyer was regarded as scholarly, judicious, and open-minded, with generally conservative views on economic issues and more liberal views on social questions. He wrote two books on regulatory reform that criticized economic regulations as anticompetitive and questioned priorities in some environmental and health rulemaking. He also served as a member of the newly created United States Sentencing Commission from 1985 to 1989. Later he defended the commission's guidelines against criticism from judges and others who viewed them as overly restrictive.

President Clinton interviewed Breyer before his first Supreme Court appointment in 1993 but chose Ruth Bader Ginsburg instead. He picked Breyer in 1994 after Senate Majority Leader George Mitchell took himself out of consideration and problems developed with two other leading candidates.

In his confirmation hearings before the Senate Judiciary Committee, Breyer defused two potential controversies by saying that he accepted Supreme Court precedents upholding abortion rights and capital punishment. The only contentious issue in the confirmation process concerned Breyer's investment in the British insurance syndicate Lloyd's of London. Some senators said Breyer should have recused himself from several environmental pollution cases because of the investment. Breyer told the committee that the cases could not have affected his holdings but also promised to get out of Lloyd's as soon as possible. The panel went on to recommend the nomination unanimously.

One Republican senator, Indiana's Richard Lugar, raised the Lloyd's issue during debate, but Breyer was strongly supported by senators from both parties. The Senate voted to confirm Breyer 87–9. Breyer disposed of his investment in Lloyd's shortly after taking office.

Breyer has compiled a moderately liberal record on the Court. He dissented from several conservative rulings on race and religion and wrote the dissenting opinion for the four liberal justices in a decision that struck down a federal law prohibiting the possession of firearms near schools. But he had a more conservative record on criminal law issues and joined the Court's 1995 opinion permitting random drug testing of high school athletes.

Breyer joined Ginsburg as the Court's second Jewish justice. The Court had two Jewish members only once before, in the 1930s when Louis Brandeis and Benjamin Cardozo served together for six years.

Glossary of Legal Terms

Accessory. In criminal law, a person not present at the commission of an offense who commands, advises, instigates, or conceals the offense.

Acquittal. A person is acquitted when a jury returns a verdict of not guilty. A person also may be acquitted when a judge determines that insufficient evidence exists to convict him or that a violation of due process precludes a fair trial.

Adjudicate. To determine finally by the exercise of judicial authority, to decide a case.

Affidavit. A voluntary written statement of facts or charges affirmed under oath.

A fortiori. With stronger force, with more reason.

Amicus curiae. Friend of the court; a person, not a party to litigation, who volunteers or is invited by the court to give his or her views on a case.

Appeal. A legal proceeding to ask a higher court to review or modify a lower court decision. In a civil case, either the plaintiff or the defendant can appeal an adverse ruling. In criminal cases a defendant can appeal a conviction, but the Double Jeopardy Clause prevents the government from appealing an acquittal. In Supreme Court practice an appeal is a case that falls within the Court's mandatory jurisdiction as opposed to a case that the Court agrees to review under the discretionary writ of certiorari. With the virtual elimination of the Court's mandatory jurisdiction in 1988, the Court now hears very few true appeals, but petitions for certiorari are often referred to imprecisely as appeals.

Appellant. The party who appeals a lower court decision to a higher court.

Appellee. One who has an interest in upholding the decision of a lower court and is compelled to respond when the case is appealed to a higher court by an appellant.

Arraignment. The formal process of charging a person with a crime, reading that person the charge, asking whether he or she pleads guilty or not guilty, and entering the plea.

Attainder, Bill of. A legislative act pronouncing a particular individual guilty of a crime without trial or conviction and imposing a sentence.

Bail. The security, usually money, given as assurance of a prisoner's due appearance at a designated time and place (as in court) to procure in the interim the prisoner's release from jail.

Bailiff. A minor officer of a court, usually serving as an usher or a messenger.

Brief. A document prepared by counsel to serve as the basis for an argument in court, setting out the facts of and the legal arguments in support of the case.

Burden of proof. The need or duty of affirmatively providing a fact or facts that are disputed.

Case law. The law as defined by previously decided cases, distinct from statutes and other sources of law.

Cause. A case, suit, litigation, or action, civil or criminal.

Certiorari, Writ of. A writ issued from the Supreme Court, at its discretion, to order a lower court to prepare the record of a case and send it to the Supreme Court for review.

Civil law. Body of law dealing with the private rights of individuals, as distinguished from criminal law.

Class action. A lawsuit brought by one person or group on behalf of all persons similarly situated.

Code. A collection of laws, arranged systematically.

Comity. Courtesy, respect; usually used in the legal sense to refer to the proper relationship between state and federal courts.

Common law. Collection of principles and rules of action, particularly from unwritten English law, that derive their authority from longstanding usage and custom or from courts recognizing and enforcing these customs. Sometimes used synonymously with case law.

Consent decree. A court-sanctioned agreement settling a legal dispute and entered into by the consent of the parties.

Contempt (civil and criminal). Civil contempt arises from a failure to follow a court order for the benefit of another party. Criminal contempt occurs when a person willfully exhibits disrespect for the court or obstructs the administration of justice.

Conviction. Final judgment or sentence that the defendant is guilty as charged.

Criminal law. The branch of law that deals with the enforcement of laws and the punishment of persons who, by breaking laws, commit crimes.

Declaratory judgment. A court pronouncement declaring a legal right or interpretation but not ordering a specific action.

De facto. In fact, in reality.

Defendant. In a civil action, the party denying or defending itself against charges brought by a plaintiff. In a criminal action, the person indicted for commission of an offense.

De jure. As a result of law or official action.

De novo. Anew; afresh; a second time.

Deposition. Oral testimony from a witness taken out of court in response to written or oral questions, committed to writing, and intended to be used in the preparation of a case.

Dicta. *See* Obiter dictum.

Dismissal. Order disposing of a case without a trial.

Docket. A calendar prepared by the clerks of the court listing the cases set to be tried.

Due process. Fair and regular procedure. The Fifth and Fourteenth amendments guarantee persons that they will not be deprived of life, liberty, or property by the government until fair and usual procedures have been followed.

Error, Writ of. A writ issued from an appeals court to a lower court requiring it to send to the appeals court the record of a case in which it has entered a final judgment and which the appeals court will review for error.

Ex parte. Only from, or on, one side. Application to a court for some ruling or action on behalf of only one party.

Ex post facto. After the fact; an ex post facto law makes an action a crime after it already has been committed, or otherwise changes the legal consequences of some past action.

Ex rel. Upon information from; the term is usually used to describe legal proceedings begun by an official in the name of the state but at the instigation of, and with information from, a private individual interested in the matter.

Grand jury. Group of twelve to twenty-three persons impanelled to hear, in private, evidence presented by the state against an individual or persons accused of a criminal act and to issue indictments when a majority of the jurors find probable cause to believe that the accused has committed a crime. Called a "grand" jury because it comprises a greater number of persons than a "petit" jury.

Grand jury report. A public report, often called "presentments," released by a grand jury after an investigation into activities of public officials that fall short of criminal actions.

Guilty. A word used by a defendant in entering a plea or by a jury in returning a verdict, indicating that the defendant is legally responsible as charged for a crime or other wrongdoing.

Habeas corpus. Literally, "you have the body"; a writ issued to inquire whether a person is lawfully imprisoned or detained. The writ demands that the persons holding the prisoner justify the detention or release the prisoner.

Immunity. A grant of exemption from prosecution in return for evidence or testimony.

In camera. In chambers. Refers to court hearings in private without spectators.

In forma pauperis. In the manner of a pauper, without liability for court costs.

In personam. Done or directed against a particular person.

In re. In the affair of, concerning. Frequent title of judicial proceedings in which there are no adversaries but instead where the matter itself—such as a bankrupt's estate—requires judicial action.

In rem. Done or directed against the thing, not the person.

Indictment. A formal written statement, based on evidence presented by the prosecutor, from a grand jury. Decided by a majority vote, an indictment charges one or more persons with specified offenses.

Information. A written set of accusations, similar to an indictment, but filed directly by a prosecutor.

Injunction. A court order prohibiting the person to whom it is directed from performing a particular act.

Interlocutory decree. A provisional decision of the court before completion of a legal action that temporarily settles an intervening matter.

Judgment. Official decision of a court based on the rights and claims of the parties to a case that was submitted for determination.

Juries. *See* Grand jury; Petit jury.

Jurisdiction. The power of a court to hear a case in question, which exists when the proper parties are present and when the point to be decided is within the issues authorized to be handled by the particular court.

Magistrate. A judicial officer having jurisdiction to try minor criminal cases and conduct preliminary examinations of persons charged with serious crimes.

Majority opinion. An opinion joined by a majority of the justices explaining the legal basis for the Court's decision and regarded as binding precedent for future cases.

Mandamus. "We command." An order issued from a superior court directing a lower court or other authority to perform a particular act.

Moot. Unsettled, undecided. A moot question also is one that no longer is material; a moot case is one that has become hypothetical.

Motion. Written or oral application to a court or a judge to obtain a rule or an order.

Nolo contendere. "I will not contest it." A plea entered by a defendant at the discretion of the judge with the same legal effect as a plea of guilty, but it may not be cited in other proceedings as an admission of guilt.

Obiter dictum. Statements by a judge or justice expressing an opinion and included with, but not essential to, an opinion resolving a case before the court. Dicta are not necessarily binding in future cases.

Parole. A conditional release from imprisonment under conditions that, if the prisoner abides by the law and other restrictions that may be imposed, the prisoner will not have to serve the remainder of the sentence.

Per curiam. "By the court." An unsigned opinion of the court, or an opinion written by the whole court.

Petit jury. A trial jury, originally a panel of twelve persons who tried to reach a unanimous verdict on questions of fact in criminal and civil proceedings. Since 1970 the Supreme Court has upheld the legality of state juries with fewer than twelve persons. Fewer persons serve on a "petit" jury than on a "grand" jury.

Petitioner. One who files a petition with a court seeking action or relief, including a plaintiff or an appellant. But a petitioner also is a person who files for other court action where charges are not necessarily made; for example, a party may petition the court for an order requiring another person or party to produce documents. The opposite party is called the respondent.

When a writ of certiorari is granted by the Supreme Court, the parties to the case are called petitioner and respondent in contrast to the appellant and appellee terms used in an appeal.

Plaintiff. A party who brings a civil action or sues to obtain a remedy for injury to his or her rights. The party against whom action is brought is termed the defendant.

Plea bargaining. Negotiations between a prosecutor and the defendant aimed at exchanging a plea of guilty from the defendant for concessions by the prosecutor, such as reduction of the charges or a request for leniency.

Pleas. *See* Guilty; Nolo contendere.

Plurality opinion. An opinion supported by the largest number of justices but less than a majority. A plurality opinion typically is not regarded as establishing a binding precedent for future cases.

Precedent. A judicial decision that may be used as a basis for ruling on subsequent similar cases.

Presentment. *See* Grand jury report.

Prima facie. At first sight; referring to a fact or other evidence presumably sufficient to establish a defense or a claim unless otherwise contradicted.

Probation. Process under which a person convicted of an offense, usually a first offense, receives a suspended sentence and is given freedom, usually under the guardianship of a probation officer.

Quash. To overthrow, annul, or vacate; as to quash a subpoena.

Recognizance. An obligation entered into before a court or magistrate requiring the performance of a specified act—usually to appear in court at a later date. It is an alternative to bail for pretrial release.

Remand. To send back. When a decision is remanded, it is sent back by a higher court to the court from which it came for further action.

Respondent. One who is compelled to answer the claims or questions posed in court by a petitioner. A defendant and an appellee may be called respondents, but the term also includes those parties who answer in court during actions where charges are not necessarily brought or where the Supreme Court has granted a writ of certiorari.

Seriatim. Separately, individually, one by one.

Stare decisis. "Let the decision stand." The principle of adherence to settled cases, the doctrine that principles of law established in earlier judicial decisions should be accepted as authoritative in similar subsequent cases.

Statute. A written law enacted by a legislature. A collection of statutes for a particular governmental division is called a code.

Stay. To halt or suspend further judicial proceedings.

Subpoena. An order to present oneself before a grand jury, court, or legislative hearing.

Subpoena duces tecum. An order to produce specified documents or papers.

Tort. An injury or wrong to the person or property of another.

Transactional immunity. Protects a witness from prosecution for any offense mentioned in or related to his or her testimony, regardless of independent evidence against the witness.

Use immunity. Protects a witness from the use of his or her testimony against the witness in prosecution.

Vacate. To make void, annul, or rescind.

Writ. A written court order commanding the designated recipient to perform or not perform specified acts.

United States Constitution

We the People of the United States, in Order to form a more perfect Union, establish Justice, insure domestic Tranquility, provide for the common defence, promote the general Welfare, and secure the Blessings of Liberty to ourselves and our Posterity, do ordain and establish this Constitution for the United States of America.

Article I

Section 1. All legislative Powers herein granted shall be vested in a Congress of the United States, which shall consist of a Senate and House of Representatives.

Section 2. The House of Representatives shall be composed of Members chosen every second Year by the People of the several States, and the Electors in each State shall have the Qualifications requisite for Electors of the most numerous Branch of the State Legislature.

No Person shall be a Representative who shall not have attained to the age of twenty five Years, and been seven Years a Citizen of the United States, and who shall not, when elected, be an Inhabitant of that State in which he shall be chosen.

[Representatives and direct Taxes shall be apportioned among the several States which may be included within this Union, according to their respective Numbers, which shall be determined by adding to the whole Number of free Persons, including those bound to Service for a Term of Years, and excluding Indians not taxed, three fifths of all other Persons.][1] The actual Enumeration shall be made within three Years after the first Meeting of the Congress of the United States, and within every subsequent Term of ten Years, in such Manner as they shall by Law direct. The Number of Representatives shall not exceed one for every thirty Thousand, but each State shall have at Least one Representative; and until such enumeration shall be made, the State of New Hampshire shall be entitled to chuse three, Massachusetts eight, Rhode-Island and Providence Plantations one, Connecticut five, New-York six, New Jersey four, Pennsylvania eight, Delaware one, Maryland six, Virginia ten, North Carolina five, South Carolina five, and Georgia three.

When vacancies happen in the Representation from any State, the Executive Authority thereof shall issue Writs of Election to fill such Vacancies.

The House of Representatives shall chuse their Speaker and other Officers; and shall have the sole Power of Impeachment.

Section 3. The Senate of the United States shall be composed of two Senators from each State, [chosen by the Legislature thereof,][2] for six Years; and each Senator shall have one Vote.

Immediately after they shall be assembled in Consequence of the first Election, they shall be divided as equally as may be into three Classes. The Seats of the Senators of the first Class shall be vacated at the Expiration of the second Year, of the second Class at the Expiration of the fourth Year, and of the third Class at the Expiration of the sixth Year, so that one third may be chosen every second Year; [and if Vacancies happen by Resignation, or otherwise, during the Recess of the Legislature of any State, the Executive thereof may make temporary Appointments until the next Meeting of the Legislature, which shall then fill such Vacancies.][3]

No Person shall be a Senator who shall not have attained to the Age of thirty Years, and been nine Years a Citizen of the United States, and who shall not, when elected, be an Inhabitant of that State for which he shall be chosen.

The Vice President of the United States shall be President of the Senate, but shall have no Vote, unless they be equally divided.

The Senate shall chuse their other Officers, and also a President pro tempore, in the Absence of the Vice President, or when he shall exercise the Office of President of the United States.

The Senate shall have the sole Power to try all Impeachments. When sitting for that Purpose, they shall be on Oath or Affirmation. When the President of the United States is tried, the Chief Justice shall preside: And no Person shall be convicted without the Concurrence of two thirds of the Members present.

Judgment in Cases of Impeachment shall not extend further than to removal from Office, and disqualification to hold and enjoy any Office of honor, Trust or Profit under the United States: but the Party convicted shall nevertheless be liable and subject to Indictment, Trial, Judgment and Punishment, according to Law.

Section 4. The Times, Places and Manner of holding Elections for Senators and Representatives, shall be prescribed in each State by the Legislature thereof; but the Congress may at any time by Law make or alter such Regulations, except as to the Places of chusing Senators.

The Congress shall assemble at least once in every Year, and such Meeting shall [be on the first Monday in December],[4] unless they shall by Law appoint a different Day.

Section 5. Each House shall be the Judge of the Elections, Returns and Qualifications of its own Members, and a Majority of each shall constitute a Quorum to do Business; but a smaller Number may adjourn from day to day, and may be authorized to compel the Attendance of absent Members, in such Manner, and under such Penalties as each House may provide.

Each House may determine the Rules of its Proceedings, punish its Members for disorderly Behaviour, and, with the Concurrence of two thirds, expel a Member.

Each House shall keep a Journal of its Proceedings, and from time to time publish the same, excepting such Parts as may in their Judgment require Secrecy; and the Yeas and Nays of the Members of either House on any question shall, at the Desire of one fifth of those Present, be entered on the Journal.

Neither House, during the Session of Congress, shall, without the Consent of the other, adjourn for more than three days, nor to any other Place than that in which the two Houses shall be sitting.

Section 6. The Senators and Representatives shall receive a Compensation for their Services, to be ascertained by Law, and paid out of the Treasury of the United States. They shall in all Cases, except Treason, Felony and Breach of the Peace, be privileged from Arrest during their Attendance at the Session of their respective Houses, and in going to and returning from the same; and for any Speech or Debate in either House, they shall not be questioned in any other Place.

No Senator or Representative shall, during the Time for which he was elected, be appointed to any civil Office under the Authority of the United States, which shall have been created, or the Emoluments whereof shall have been encreased during such time; and no Person holding any Office under the United States, shall be a Member of either House during his Continuance in Office.

Section 7. All Bills for raising Revenue shall originate in the House of Representatives; but the Senate may propose or concur with Amendments as on other Bills.

Every Bill which shall have passed the House of Representatives and the Senate, shall, before it become a Law, be presented to the President of the United States; If he approve he shall sign it, but if not he shall return it, with his Objections to that House in which it shall have originated, who shall enter the Objections at large on their Journal, and proceed to reconsider it. If after such Reconsideration two thirds of that House shall agree to pass the Bill, it shall be sent, together with the Objections, to the other House, by which it shall likewise be reconsidered, and if approved by two thirds of that House, it shall become a Law. But in all such Cases the Votes of both Houses shall be determined by yeas and Nays, and the Names of the Persons voting for and against the Bill shall be entered on the Journal of each House respectively. If any Bill shall not be returned by the President within ten Days (Sundays excepted) after it shall have been presented to him, the Same shall be a Law, in like Manner as if he had signed it, unless the Congress by their Adjournment prevent its Return, in which Case it shall not be a Law.

Every Order, Resolution, or Vote to which the Concurrence of the Senate and House of Representatives may be necessary (except on a question of Adjournment) shall be presented to the President of the United States; and before the Same shall take Effect, shall be approved by him, or being disapproved by him, shall be repassed by two thirds of the Senate and House of Representatives, according to the Rules and Limitations prescribed in the Case of a Bill.

Section 8. The Congress shall have Power To lay and collect Taxes, Duties, Imposts and Excises, to pay the Debts and provide for the common Defence and general Welfare of the United States; but all Duties, Imposts and Excises shall be uniform throughout the United States;

To borrow Money on the credit of the United States;

To regulate Commerce with foreign Nations, and among the several States, and with the Indian Tribes;

To establish an uniform Rule of Naturalization, and uniform Laws on the subject of Bankruptcies throughout the United States;

To coin Money, regulate the Value thereof, and of foreign Coin, and fix the Standard of Weights and Measures;

To provide for the Punishment of counterfeiting the Securities and current Coin of the United States;

To establish Post Offices and post Roads;

To promote the Progress of Science and useful Arts, by securing for limited Times to Authors and Inventors the exclusive Right to their respective Writings and Discoveries;

To constitute Tribunals inferior to the supreme Court;

To define and punish Piracies and Felonies committed on the high Seas, and Offences against the Law of Nations;

To declare War, grant Letters of Marque and Reprisal, and make Rules concerning Captures on Land and Water;

To raise and support Armies, but no Appropriation of Money to that Use shall be for a longer Term than two Years;

To provide and maintain a Navy;

To make Rules for the Government and Regulation of the land and naval Forces;

To provide for calling forth the Militia to execute the Laws of the Union, suppress Insurrections and repel Invasions;

To provide for organizing, arming, and disciplining, the Militia, and for governing such Part of them as may be employed in the Service of the United States, reserving to the States respectively, the Appointment of the Officers, and the Authority of training the Militia according to the discipline prescribed by Congress;

To exercise exclusive Legislation in all Cases whatsoever, over such District (not exceeding ten Miles square) as may, by Cession of particular States, and the Acceptance of Congress, become the Seat of the Government of the United States, and to exercise like Authority over all Places purchased by the Consent of the Legislature of the State in which the Same shall be, for the Erection of Forts, Magazines, Arsenals, dock-Yards, and other needful Buildings;—And

To make all Laws which shall be necessary and proper for carrying into Execution the foregoing Powers, and all other Powers vested by this Constitution in the Government of the United States, or in any Department or Officer thereof.

Section 9. The Migration or Importation of such Persons as any of the States now existing shall think proper to admit, shall not be prohibited by the Congress prior to the Year one thousand eight hundred and eight, but a Tax or duty may be imposed on such Importation, not exceeding ten dollars for each Person.

The Privilege of the Writ of Habeas Corpus shall not be suspended, unless when in Cases of Rebellion or Invasion the public Safety may require it.

No Bill of Attainder or ex post facto Law shall be passed.

No Capitation, or other direct, Tax shall be laid, unless in Proportion to the Census or Enumeration herein before directed to be taken.[5]

No Tax or Duty shall be laid on Articles exported from any State.

No Preference shall be given by any Regulation of Commerce or Revenue to the Ports of one State over those of another; nor shall Vessels bound to, or from, one State, be obliged to enter, clear, or pay Duties in another.

No Money shall be drawn from the Treasury, but in Consequence of Appropriations made by Law; and a regular Statement and Account of the Receipts and Expenditures of all public Money shall be published from time to time.

No Title of Nobility shall be granted by the United States: And no Person holding any Office of Profit or Trust under them, shall, without the Consent of the Congress, accept of any present, Emolument, Office, or Title, of any kind whatever, from any King, Prince, or foreign State.

Section 10. No State shall enter into any Treaty, Alliance, or Confederation; grant Letters of Marque and Reprisal; coin Money; emit Bills of Credit; make any Thing but gold and silver Coin a Tender in Payment of Debts; pass any Bill of Attainder, ex post facto Law, or Law impairing the Obligation of Contracts, or grant any Title of Nobility.

No State shall, without the Consent of the Congress, lay any Imposts or Duties on Imports or Exports, except what may be absolutely necessary for executing it's inspection Laws: and the net Produce of all Duties and Imposts, laid by any State on Imports or Exports, shall be for the Use of the Treasury of the United States; and all such Laws shall be subject to the Revision and Controul of the Congress.

No State shall, without the Consent of Congress, lay any Duty of Tonnage, keep Troops, or Ships of War in time of Peace, enter into any Agreement or Compact with another State, or with a foreign Power, or engage in War, unless actually invaded, or in such imminent Danger as will not admit of delay.

Article II

Section 1. The executive Power shall be vested in a President of the United States of America. He shall hold his Office during the Term of four Years, and, together with the Vice President, chosen for the same Term, be elected, as follows

Each State shall appoint, in such Manner as the Legislature thereof may direct, a Number of Electors, equal to the whole Number of Senators and Representatives to which the State may be entitled in the Congress: but no Senator or Representative, or Person holding an Office of Trust or Profit under the United States, shall be appointed an Elector.

[The Electors shall meet in their respective States, and vote by Ballot for two Persons, of whom one at least shall not be an Inhabitant of the same State with themselves. And they shall make a List of all the Persons voted for, and of the Number of Votes for each; which List they shall sign and certify, and transmit sealed to the Seat of the Government of the United States, directed to the President of the Senate. The President of the Senate shall, in the Presence of the Senate and House of Representatives, open all the Certificates, and the Votes shall then be counted. The Person having the greatest Number of Votes shall be the President, if such Number be a Majority of the whole Number of Electors appointed; and if there be more than one who have such Majority, and have an equal Number of Votes, then the House of Representatives shall immediately chuse by Ballot one of them for President; and if no Person have a Majority, then from the five highest on the list the said House shall in like Manner chuse the President. But in chusing the President, the Votes shall be taken by States, the Representation from each State having one Vote; A quorum for this Purpose shall consist of a Member or Members from two thirds of the States, and a Majority of all the States shall be necessary to a Choice. In every Case, after the Choice of the President, the Person having the greatest Number of Votes of the Electors shall be the Vice President. But if there should remain two or more who have equal Votes, the Senate shall chuse from them by Ballot the Vice President.][6]

The Congress may determine the Time of chusing the Electors, and the Day on which they shall give their Votes; which Day shall be the same throughout the United States.

No Person except a natural born Citizen, or a Citizen of the United States, at the time of the Adoption of this Constitution, shall be eligible to the Office of President; neither shall any Person be eligible to that Office who shall not have attained to the Age of thirty five Years, and been fourteen Years a Resident within the United States.

In Case of the Removal of the President from Office, or of his Death, Resignation, or Inability to discharge the Powers and Duties of the said Office,[7] the Same shall devolve on the Vice President, and the Congress may by Law provide for the Case of Removal, Death, Resignation or Inability, both of the President and Vice President, declaring what Officer shall then act as President, and such Officer shall act accordingly, until the Disability be removed, or a President shall be elected.

The President shall, at stated Times, receive for his Services, a Compensation, which shall neither be encreased nor diminished during the Period for which he shall have been elected, and he shall not receive within that Period any other Emolument from the United States, or any of them.

Before he enter on the Execution of his Office, he shall take the following Oath or Affirmation:—"I do solemnly swear (or affirm) that I will faithfully execute the Office of President of the United States, and will to the best of my Ability, preserve, protect and defend the Constitution of the United States."

Section 2. The President shall be Commander in Chief of the Army and Navy of the United States, and of the Militia of the several States, when called into the actual Service of the United States; he may require the Opinion, in writing, of the principal Officer in each of the executive Departments, upon any Subject relating to the Duties of their respective Offices, and he shall have Power to grant Reprieves and Pardons for Offences against the United States, except in Cases of Impeachment.

He shall have Power, by and with the Advice and Consent of the Senate, to make Treaties, provided two thirds of the Senators present concur; and he shall nominate, and by and with the Advice and Consent of the Senate, shall appoint Ambassadors, other public Ministers and Consuls, Judges of the supreme Court, and all other Officers of the United States, whose Appointments are not herein otherwise provided for, and which shall be established by Law: but the Congress may by Law vest the Appointment of such inferior Officers, as they think proper, in the President alone, in the Courts of Law, or in the Heads of Departments.

The President shall have Power to fill up all Vacancies that may happen during the Recess of the Senate, by granting Commissions which shall expire at the End of their next Session.

Section 3. He shall from time to time give to the Congress Information of the State of the Union, and recommend to their Consideration such Measures as he shall judge necessary and expedient; he may, on extraordinary Occasions, convene both Houses, or either of them, and in Case of Disagreement between them, with Respect to the Time of Adjournment, he may adjourn them to such Time as he shall think proper; he shall receive Ambassadors and other public Ministers; he shall take Care that the Laws be faithfully executed, and shall Commission all the Officers of the United States.

Section 4. The President, Vice President and all civil Officers of the United States, shall be removed from Office on Impeachment for, and Conviction of, Treason, Bribery, or other high Crimes and Misdemeanors.

Article III

Section 1. The judicial Power of the United States, shall be vested in one supreme Court, and in such inferior Courts as the Congress may from time to time ordain and establish. The Judges, both of the supreme and inferior Courts, shall hold their Offices during good Behaviour, and shall, at stated Times, receive for their Services, a Compensation, which shall not be diminished during their Continuance in Office.

Section 2. The judicial Power shall extend to all Cases, in Law and Equity, arising under this Constitution, the Laws of the United States, and Treaties made, or which shall be made, under their Authority;—to all Cases affecting Ambassadors, other public Ministers and Consuls;—to all Cases of admiralty and maritime Jurisdiction;—to Controversies to which the United States shall be a Party;—to Controversies between two or more States;—between a State and Citizens of another State;8—between Citizens of different States;—between Citizens of the same State claiming Lands under Grants of different States, and between a State, or the Citizens thereof, and foreign States, Citizens or Subjects.[8]

In all Cases affecting Ambassadors, other public Ministers and Consuls, and those in which a State shall be Party, the supreme Court shall have original Jurisdiction. In all the other Cases before mentioned, the supreme Court shall have appellate Jurisdiction, both as to Law and Fact, with such Exceptions, and under such Regulations as the Congress shall make.

The Trial of all Crimes, except in Cases of Impeachment, shall be by Jury; and such Trial shall be held in the State where the said Crimes shall have been committed; but when not committed within any State, the Trial shall be at such Place or Places as the Congress may by Law have directed.

Section 3. Treason against the United States, shall consist only in levying War against them, or in adhering to their Enemies, giving them Aid and Comfort. No Person shall be convicted of Treason unless on the Testimony of two Witnesses to the same overt Act, or on Confession in open Court.

The Congress shall have Power to declare the Punishment of Treason, but no Attainder of Treason shall work Corruption of Blood, or Forfeiture except during the Life of the Person attainted.

Article IV

Section 1. Full Faith and Credit shall be given in each State to the public Acts, Records, and judicial Proceedings of every other State. And the Congress may by general Laws prescribe the Manner in which such Acts, Records and Proceedings shall be proved, and the Effect thereof.

Section 2. The Citizens of each State shall be entitled to all Privileges and Immunities of Citizens in the several States.

A Person charged in any State with Treason, Felony, or other Crime, who shall flee from Justice, and be found in another State, shall on Demand of the executive Authority of the State from which he fled, be delivered up, to be removed to the State having Jurisdiction of the Crime.

[No Person held to Service or Labour in one State, under the Laws thereof, escaping into another, shall, in Consequence of any Law or Regulation therein, be discharged from such Service or Labour, but shall be delivered up on Claim of the Party to whom such Service or Labour may be due.][9]

Section 3. New States may be admitted by the Congress into this Union; but no new State shall be formed or erected within the Jurisdiction of any other State; nor any State be formed by the Junction of two or more States, or Parts of States, without the Consent of the Legislatures of the States concerned as well as of the Congress.

The Congress shall have Power to dispose of and make all needful Rules and Regulations respecting the Territory or other Property belonging to the United States; and nothing in this Constitution shall be so construed as to Prejudice any Claims of the United States, or of any particular State.

Section 4. The United States shall guarantee to every State in this Union a Republican Form of Government, and shall protect each of them against Invasion; and on Application of the Legislature, or of the Executive (when the Legislature cannot be convened) against domestic Violence.

Article V

The Congress, whenever two thirds of both Houses shall deem it necessary, shall propose Amendments to this Constitution, or, on the Application of the Legislatures of two thirds of the several States, shall call a Convention for proposing Amendments, which, in either Case, shall be valid to all Intents and Purposes, as Part of this Constitution, when ratified by the Legislatures of three fourths of the several States, or by Conventions in three fourths thereof, as the one or the other Mode of Ratification may be proposed by the Congress; Provided [that no Amendment which may be made prior to the Year One thousand eight hundred and eight shall in any Manner affect the first and fourth Clauses in the Ninth Section of the first Article; and][10] that no State, without its Consent, shall be deprived of its equal Suffrage in the Senate.

Article VI

All Debts contracted and Engagements entered into, before the Adoption of this Constitution, shall be as valid against the United States under this Constitution, as under the Confederation.

This Constitution, and the Laws of the United States which shall be made in Pursuance thereof; and all Treaties made, or which shall be made, under the Authority of the United States, shall be the supreme Law of the Land; and the Judges in every State shall be bound thereby, any Thing in the Constitution or Laws of any State to the Contrary notwithstanding.

The Senators and Representatives before mentioned, and the Members of the several State Legislatures, and all executive and judicial Officers, both of the United States and of the several States, shall be bound by Oath or Affirmation, to support this Constitution; but no religious Test shall ever be required as a Qualification to any Office or public Trust under the United States.

Article VII

The Ratification of the Conventions of nine States, shall be sufficient for the Establishment of this Constitution between the States so ratifying the Same.

Done in Convention by the Unanimous Consent of the States present the Seventeenth Day of September in the Year of our Lord one thousand seven hundred and Eighty seven and of the Independence of the United States of America the Twelfth. IN WITNESS whereof We have hereunto subscribed our Names,

George Washington,
President and
deputy from Virginia.

New Hampshire: John Langdon,
                           Nicholas Gilman.

Massachusetts: Nathaniel Gorham,
                           Rufus King.

Connecticut: William Samuel Johnson,
                           Roger Sherman.

New York: Alexander Hamilton.

New Jersey:

William Livingston,
David Brearley,
William Paterson,
Jonathan Dayton.

Pennsylvania:

Benjamin Franklin,
Thomas Mifflin,
Robert Morris,
George Clymer,
Thomas FitzSimons,
Jared Ingersoll,
James Wilson,
Gouverneur Morris.

Delaware:

George Read,
Gunning Bedford Jr.,
John Dickinson,
Richard Bassett,
Jacob Broom.

Maryland:

James McHenry,
Daniel of St. Thomas Jenifer,
Daniel Carroll.

Virginia:

John Blair,
James Madison Jr.

North Carolina:

William Blount,
Richard Dobbs Spaight,
Hugh Williamson.

South Carolina:

John Rutledge,
Charles Cotesworth Pinckney,
Charles Pinckney,
Pierce Butler.

Georgia:

William Few,
Abraham Baldwin.

[The language of the original Constitution, not including the Amendments, was adopted by a convention of the states on September 17, 1787, and was subsequently ratified by the states on the following dates: Delaware, December 7, 1787; Pennsylvania, December 12, 1787; New Jersey, December 18, 1787; Georgia, January 2, 1788; Connecticut, January 9, 1788; Massachusetts, February 6, 1788; Maryland, April 28, 1788; South Carolina, May 23, 1788; New Hampshire, June 21, 1788.

Ratification was completed on June 21, 1788.

The Constitution subsequently was ratified by Virginia, June 25, 1788; New York, July 26, 1788; North Carolina, November 21, 1789; Rhode Island, May 29, 1790; and Vermont, January 10, 1791.]

Amendments

Amendment I

(First ten amendments ratified December 15, 1791.)

Congress shall make no law respecting an establishment of religion, or prohibiting the free exercise thereof; or abridging the freedom of speech, or of the press; or the right of the people peaceably to assemble, and to petition the Government for a redress of grievances.

Amendment II

A well regulated Militia, being necessary to the security of a free State, the right of the people to keep and bear Arms, shall not be infringed.

Amendment III

No Soldier shall, in time of peace be quartered in any house, without the consent of the Owner, nor in time of war, but in a manner to be prescribed by law.

Amendment IV

The right of the people to be secure in their persons, houses, papers, and effects, against unreasonable searches and seizures, shall not be violated, and no Warrants shall issue, but upon probable cause, supported by Oath or affirmation, and particularly describing the place to be searched, and the persons or things to be seized.

Amendment V

No person shall be held to answer for a capital, or otherwise infamous crime, unless on a presentment or indictment of a Grand Jury, except in cases arising in the land or naval forces, or in the Militia, when in actual service in time of War or public danger; nor shall any person be subject for the same offence to be twice put in jeopardy of life or limb; nor shall be compelled in any criminal case to be a witness against himself, nor be deprived of life, liberty, or property, without due process of law; nor shall private property be taken for public use, without just compensation.

Amendment VI

In all criminal prosecutions, the accused shall enjoy the right to a speedy and public trial, by an impartial jury of the State and district wherein the crime shall have been committed, which district shall have been previously ascertained by law, and to be informed of the nature and cause of the accusation; to be confronted with the witnesses against him; to have compulsory process for obtaining witnesses in his favor, and to have the Assistance of Counsel for his defence.

Amendment VII

In Suits at common law, where the value in controversy shall exceed twenty dollars, the right of trial by jury shall be preserved, and no fact tried by a jury, shall be otherwise re-examined in any Court of the United States, than according to the rules of the common law.

Amendment VIII

Excessive bail shall not be required, nor excessive fines imposed, nor cruel and unusual punishments inflicted.

Amendment IX

The enumeration in the Constitution, of certain rights, shall not be construed to deny or disparage others retained by the people.

Amendment X

The powers not delegated to the United States by the Constitution, nor prohibited by it to the States, are reserved to the States respectively, or to the people.

Amendment XI

(Ratified February 7, 1795)

The Judicial power of the United States shall not be construed to extend to any suit in law or equity, commenced or prosecuted against one of the United States by Citizens of another State, or by Citizens or Subjects of any Foreign State.

Amendment XII

(Ratified June 15, 1804)

The Electors shall meet in their respective states and vote by ballot for President and Vice-President, one of whom, at least, shall not be an inhabitant of the same state with themselves; they shall name in their ballots the person voted for as President, and in distinct ballots the person voted for as Vice-President, and they shall make distinct lists of all persons voted for as President, and of all persons voted for as Vice-President, and of the number of votes for each, which lists they shall sign and certify, and transmit sealed to the seat of the government of the United States, directed to the President of the Senate;—The President of the Senate shall, in the presence of the Senate and House of Representatives, open all the certificates and the votes shall then be counted;—The person having the greatest number of votes for President, shall be the President, if such number be a majority of the whole number of Electors appointed; and if no person have such majority, then from the persons having the highest numbers not exceeding three on the list of those voted for as President, the House of Representatives shall choose immediately, by ballot, the President. But in choosing the President, the votes shall be taken by states, the representation from each state having one vote; a quorum for this purpose shall consist of a member or members from two-thirds of the states, and a majority of all the states shall be necessary to a choice. [And if the House of Representatives shall not choose a President whenever the right of choice shall devolve upon them, before the fourth day of March next following, then the Vice-President shall act as President, as in the case of the death or other constitutional disability of the President.—][11] The person having the greatest number of votes as Vice-President, shall be the Vice-President, if such number be a majority of the whole number of Electors appointed, and if no person have a majority, then from the two highest numbers on the list, the Senate shall choose the Vice-President; a quorum for the purpose shall consist of two-thirds of the whole number of Senators, and a majority of the whole number shall be necessary to a choice. But no person constitutionally ineligible to the office of President shall be eligible to that of Vice-President of the United States.

Amendment XIII

(Ratified December 6, 1865)

Section 1. Neither slavery nor involuntary servitude, except as a punishment for crime whereof the party shall have been duly convicted, shall exist within the United States, or any place subject to their jurisdiction.

Section 2. Congress shall have power to enforce this article by appropriate legislation.

Amendment XIV

(Ratified July 9, 1868)

Section 1. All persons born or naturalized in the United States, and subject to the jurisdiction thereof, are citizens of the United States and of the State wherein they reside. No State shall make or enforce any law which shall abridge the privileges or immunities of citizens of the United States; nor shall any State deprive any person of life, liberty, or property, without due process of law; nor deny to any person within its jurisdiction the equal protection of the laws.

Section 2. Representatives shall be apportioned among the several States according to their respective numbers, counting the whole number of persons in each State, excluding Indians not taxed. But when the right to vote at any election for the choice of electors for President and Vice President of the United States, Representatives in Congress, the Executive and Judicial officers of a State, or the members of the Legislature thereof, is denied to any of the male inhabitants of such State, being twenty-one years of age,[12] and citizens of the United States, or in any way abridged, except for participation in rebellion, or other crime, the basis of representation therein shall be reduced in the proportion which the number of such male citizens shall bear to the whole number of male citizens twenty-one years of age in such State.

Section 3. No person shall be a Senator or Representative in Congress, or elector of President and Vice President, or hold any office, civil or military, under the United States, or under any State, who, having previously taken an oath, as a member of Congress, or as an officer of the United States, or as a member of any State legislature, or as an executive or judicial officer of any State, to support the Constitution of the United States, shall have engaged in insurrection or rebellion against the same, or given aid or comfort to the enemies thereof. But Congress may by a vote of two-thirds of each House, remove such disability.

Section 4. The validity of the public debt of the United States, authorized by law, including debts incurred for payment of pensions and bounties for services in suppressing insurrection or rebellion, shall not be questioned. But neither the United States nor any State shall assume or pay any debt or obligation incurred in aid of insurrection or rebellion against the United States, or any claim for the loss or emancipation of any slave; but all such debts, obligations and claims shall be held illegal and void.

Section 5. The Congress shall have power to enforce, by appropriate legislation, the provisions of this article.

Amendment XV

(Ratified February 3, 1870)

Section 1. The right of citizens of the United States to vote shall not be denied or abridged by the United States or by any State on account of race, color, or previous condition of servitude.

Section 2. The Congress shall have power to enforce this article by appropriate legislation.

Amendment XVI

(Ratified February 3, 1913)

The Congress shall have power to lay and collect taxes on incomes, from whatever source derived, without apportionment among the several States, and without regard to any census or enumeration.

Amendment XVII

(Ratified April 8, 1913)

The Senate of the United States shall be composed of two Senators from each State, elected by the people thereof, for six years; and each Senator shall have one vote. The electors in each State shall have the qualifications requisite for electors of the most numerous branch of the State legislatures.

When vacancies happen in the representation of any State in the Senate, the executive authority of such State shall issue writs of election to fill such vacancies: *Provided*, That the legislature of any State may empower the executive thereof to make temporary appointments until the people fill the vacancies by election as the legislature may direct.

This amendment shall not be so construed as to affect the election or term of any Senator chosen before it becomes valid as part of the Constitution.

Amendment XVIII

(Ratified January 16, 1919)[13]

Section 1. After one year from the ratification of this article the manufacture, sale, or transportation of intoxicating liquors within, the importation thereof into, or the exportation thereof from the United States and all territory subject to the jurisdiction thereof for beverage purposes is hereby prohibited.

Section 2. The Congress and the several States shall have concurrent power to enforce this article by appropriate legislation.

Section 3. This article shall be inoperative unless it shall have been ratified as an amendment to the Constitution by the legislatures of the several States, as provided in the Constitution, within seven years from the date of the submission hereof to the States by the Congress.

Amendment XIX

(Ratified August 18, 1920)

The right of citizens of the United States to vote shall not be denied or abridged by the United States or by any State on account of sex.

Congress shall have power to enforce this article by appropriate legislation.

Amendment XX

(Ratified January 23, 1933)

Section 1. The terms of the President and Vice President shall end at noon on the 20th day of January, and the terms of Senators and Representatives at noon on the 3d day of January, of the years in which such terms would have ended if this arti cle had not been ratified; and the terms of their successors shall then begin.

Section 2. The Congress shall assemble at least once in every year, and such meeting shall begin at noon on the 3d day of January, unless they shall by law appoint a different day.

Section 3.[14] If, at the time fixed for the beginning of the term of the President, the President elect shall have died, the Vice President elect shall become President. If a President shall not have been chosen before the time fixed for the beginning of his term, or if the President elect shall have failed to qualify, then the Vice President elect shall act as President until a President shall have qualified; and the Congress may by law provide for the case wherein neither a President elect nor a Vice President elect shall have qualified, declaring who shall then act as President, or the manner in which one who is to act shall be selected, and such person shall act accordingly until a President or Vice President shall have qualified.

Section 4. The Congress may by law provide for the case of the death of any of the persons from whom the House of Representatives may choose a President whenever the right of choice shall have devolved upon them, and for the case of the death of any of the persons from whom the Senate may choose a Vice President whenever the right of choice shall have devolved upon them.

Section 5. Sections 1 and 2 shall take effect on the 15th day of October following the ratification of this article.

Section 6. This article shall be inoperative unless it shall have been ratified as an amendment to the Constitution by the legislatures of three-fourths of the several States within seven years from the date of its submission.

Amendment XXI

(Ratified December 5, 1933)

Section 1. The eighteenth article of amendment to the Constitution of the United States is hereby repealed.

Section 2. The transportation or importation into any State, Territory, or possession of the United States for delivery or use therein of intoxicating liquors, in violation of the laws thereof, is hereby prohibited.

Section 3. This article shall be inoperative unless it shall have been ratified as an amendment to the Constitution by conventions in the several States, as provided in the Constitution, within seven years from the date of the submission hereof to the States by the Congress.

Amendment XXII

(Ratified February 27, 1951)

Section 1. No person shall be elected to the office of the President more than twice, and no person who has held the office of President, or acted as President, for more than two years of a term to which some other person was elected President shall be elected to the office of the President more than once. But this Article shall not apply to any person holding the office of President when this Article was proposed by the Congress, and shall not prevent any person who may be holding the office of President, or acting as President, during the term within which this Article become operative from holding the office of President or acting as President during the remainder of such term.

Section 2. This article shall be inoperative unless it shall have been ratified as an amendment to the Constitution by the legislatures of three-fourths of the several States within seven years from the date of its submission to the States by the Congress.

Amendment XXIII

(Ratified March 29, 1961)

Section 1. The District constituting the seat of Government of the United States shall appoint in such manner as the Congress may direct:

A number of electors of President and Vice President equal to the whole number of Senators and Representatives in Congress to which the District would be entitled if it were a State, but in no event more than the least populous State; they shall be in addition to those appointed by the States, but they shall be considered, for the purposes of the election of President and Vice President, to be electors appointed by a State; and they shall meet in the District and perform such duties as provided by the twelfth article of amendment.

Section 2. The Congress shall have power to enforce this article by appropriate legislation.

Amendment XXIV

(Ratified January 23, 1964)

Section 1. The right of citizens of the United States to vote in any primary or other election for President or Vice President, for electors for President or Vice President, or for Senator or Representative in Congress, shall not be denied or abridged by the United States or any State by reason of failure to pay any poll tax or other tax.

Section 2. The Congress shall have power to enforce this article by appropriate legislation.

Amendment XXV

(Ratified February 10, 1967)

Section 1. In case of the removal of the President from office or of his death or resignation, the Vice President shall become President.

Section 2. Whenever there is a vacancy in the office of the Vice President, the President shall nominate a Vice President who shall take office upon confirmation by a majority vote of both Houses of Congress.

Section 3. Whenever the President transmits to the President pro tempore of the Senate and the Speaker of the House of Representatives his written declaration that he is unable to discharge the powers and duties of his office, and until he transmits to them a written declaration to the contrary, such powers and duties shall be discharged by the Vice President as Acting President.

Section 4. Whenever the Vice President and a majority of either the principal officers of the executive departments or of such other body as Congress may by law provide, transmit to the President pro tempore of the Senate and the Speaker of the House of Representatives their written declaration that the President is unable to discharge the powers and duties of his office, the Vice President shall immediately assume the powers and duties of the office as Acting President.

Thereafter, when the President transmits to the President pro tempore of the Senate and the Speaker of the House of Representatives his written declaration that no inability exists, he shall resume the powers and duties of his office unless the Vice President and a majority of either the principal officers of the executive department or of such other body as Congress may by law provide, transmit within four days to the President pro tempore of the Senate and the Speaker of the House of Representatives their written declaration that the President is unable to discharge the powers and duties of his office. Thereupon Congress shall decide the issue, assembling within forty-eight hours for that purpose if not in session. If the Congress, within twenty-one days after receipt of the latter written declaration, or, if Congress is not in session, within twenty-one days after Congress is required to assemble, determines by two-thirds vote of both Houses that the President is unable to discharge the powers and duties of his office, the Vice President shall continue to discharge the same as Acting President; otherwise, the President shall resume the powers and duties of his office.

Amendment XXVI

(Ratified July 1, 1971)

Section 1. The right of citizens of the United States, who are eighteen years of age or older, to vote shall not be denied or abridged by the United States or by any State on account of age.

Section 2. The Congress shall have power to enforce this article by appropriate legislation.

Amendment XXVII

(Ratified May 7, 1992)

No law varying the compensation for the services of the Senators and Representatives shall take effect, until an election of Representatives shall have intervened.

Notes

1. The part in brackets was by section 2 of the Fourteenth Amendment.
2. The part in brackets was changed by the first paragraph of the Seventeenth Amendment.
3. The part in brackets was changed by the second paragraph of the Seventeenth Amendment.
4. The part in brackets was changed by section 2 of the Twentieth Amendment.
5. The Sixteenth Amendment gave Congress the power to tax incomes.
6. The material in brackets has been superseded by the Twelfth Amendment.
7. This provision has been affected by the Twenty-fifth Amendment.
8. These clauses were affected by the Eleventh Amendment.
9. This paragraph has been superseded by the Thirteenth Amendment.
10. Obsolete.
11. The part in brackets has been superseded by section 3 of the Twentieth Amendment.
12. See the Nineteenth and Twenty-sixth Amendments.
13. This Amendment was repealed by section 1 of the Twenty-first Amendment.
14. See the Twenty-fifth Amendment.

Source: U.S. Congress, House, Committee on the Judiciary, *The Constitution of the United States of America, as Amended*, 100th Cong., 1st sess., 1987, H Doc 100-94.

Index